D0951933

EZRA POUND

By *CHARLES NORMAN:*

THE CASE OF EZRA POUND

E. E. CUMMINGS: A Biography

POETS ON POETRY

SELECTED POEMS

Ezra Pound, October 22, 1913

EZRA POUND

by

CHARLES NORMAN

REVISED EDITION

FUNK & WAGNALLS / New York

© CHARLES NORMAN 1960, 1969

Library of Congress Catalog Card Number: 69-18876

Quotations from *The Cantos of Ezra Pound,* copyright 1934, 1937, 1940, 1948 by Ezra Pound, reprinted by permission of New Directions and Ezra Pound.

Quotations from *Personae: the Collected Poems of Ezra Pound,* copyright 1926 by Ezra Pound (copyright renewed 1954), reprinted by permission of New Directions and Ezra Pound.

Quotations from *The Letters of Ezra Pound 1907-1941* edited by D. D. Paige, copyright, 1950, by Harcourt, Brace and Company, Inc.

"In Neglect" from *Complete Poems of Robert Frost,* copyright, 1930, 1949, by Henry Holt and Company, Inc. By permission of the publishers.

Letter No. 4 from *The Selected Letters of William Carlos Williams,* copyright 1957 by William Carlos Williams, reprinted by permission of McDowell, Obolensky Inc.

Passage from *Life and the Dream* by Mary Colum, copyright 1947 by Mary Colum, used by permission of Doubleday & Company, Inc.

Funk & Wagnalls, *A Division of* Reader's Digest Books, Inc.

Printed in the United States of America

To
R. L. DE WILTON

With the real artist there is always a residue, there is always something in the man which does not get into his work. There is always some reason why the man is always more worth knowing than his books are. In the long run nothing else counts.

—Ezra Pound, *Patria Mia*

. . . there is, in all great poetry, something which must remain unaccountable however complete might be our knowledge of the poet, and that is what matters most. When the poem has been made, something new has happened, something that cannot be wholly explained by *anything that went before.*

—T. S. Eliot, *The Frontiers of Criticism*

So long as you are alive, your case is doubtful.
—Albert Camus, *The Fall*

We are all exceptional cases.
Ibid.

INTRODUCTION

I heard Ezra Pound's name for the first time in 1920, when a lady showed me two lines of his—

> I wrapped my tears in an ellum leaf
> And left them under a stone. . . .

I did not know then what an ellum tree was, nor did I ever find out; but now a friend tells me that that is the standard New England pronunciation of *elm*. The lines stayed with me; so did the name, which I thought odd but somehow stirring. I must have felt about it very much as George Moore did when, likewise young, he came across the name of Kirke White, for he has told about it in much the same way. Pound has lasted better than that English poet, and seems likely to last better still. His best work wears a perennial brightness—

> In the gloom, the gold gathers the light against it—

and there is good reason to believe that what time has not dulled will not be dulled by time.

There will be—there already are—many books about him. To judge by those already in print, chiefly critical or interpretive, there is room for another which mirrors the man, and the pleasure and profit to be found in his work. He is not a "difficult" poet. That is to say, the impact of his lines creates a response; afterwards it may be useful to know, with mention of this name in one of them, that Capaneus was one of The Seven Against Thebes, whom Jove destroyed for his pride. The dissection of poetry is one of the more gruesome aspects of the twentieth century. Perhaps, however, the dissectors are right; these are, after all, the decades of the destruction of everything.

But Pound is not merely a poet—he has been for half a century the teacher and protector of other poets, and not merely other poets, but the greatest poets of this age. And he has performed comparable services for writers of prose and practitioners in some of the other arts. For the rest, let the reader ask himself, as I have had to do: which is the real Pound—the poet and teacher, or the man who broadcast from Rome, as the reader may likewise ask himself which was the real Yeats, the man who barred the door to Maud Gonne in her peril, or the poet who addressed her in poems that endure? The broadcasts, however, are part of the story.

Pound chose all art for his province. He has written verse and prose; he has painted, he has been a sculptor; and he has composed a considerable amount of music. I have dealt with all of these aspects of his creative life. I have also tried to do justice to his ideas, political and economic. And he was gregarious. He knew so many people, some of them the most important creative personalities of our time. Yet it is unlikely that I have done more than characterize the man, recount some of his exploits, and credit him, anew, with teaching and influencing several generations of poets. It is also unlikely that anyone else will be able to do much more for some time to come, and then it will have to be in the German mode: several volumes of text, and half a dozen of exegesis. To take the matter of his magazine connections alone—Horace Gregory and Marya Zaturenska wrote in *A History of American Poetry*:

"Pound's influence can be traced through the files of at least fifty 'little' magazines published on both sides of the Atlantic from 1916 to 1939."

It is even worse than that, for the first date should really be 1912. I have concentrated on the great and justly renowned publications with which he had editorial connections—*Poetry, The Egoist, The Little Review, The Exile* and *The Dial*—although others are, of course, mentioned. Fifty, however, proved to be beyond even my powers of endurance.

Before beginning my book I wrote Mr. Pound: "As in the case of Cummings, I will refrain from bothering you with questions, the answers to which I can get elsewhere." I mention this because the reader may wonder, here or there, why I have conjectured when I might have inquired; but the conjectures are of no real importance, and they beguiled some of the tediousness of collation and composition. In short, they gave me pleasure, which I hope some readers will share.

C. N.

NOTE TO 1969 EDITION

Shortly after publication I met another lady, of more general interest than the one mentioned in the opening sentence of my Introduction: Mrs. Mary M. Cross, the former Mary Moore, to whom Pound dedicated *Personae* in 1909. I thank her for her friendship, and for helping me to fill in an important period in Pound's life. I thank her nephew, Mr. Samuel Moore, for introducing us.

I thank Mr. Alvin Langdon Coburn for informing me of the precise date when the photograph that serves as frontispiece was taken by him. I am grateful to Mr. Conrad Aiken for his clarification of the episode concerning the original publication of T. S. Eliot's "Prufrock" through his and Pound's efforts. H. D. (Hilda Doolittle) kindly sent me several corrections, which have been made, and her diary, which she requested me to turn over to Dr. Norman Holmes Pearson of Yale, her literary executor, which has been done. Mr. Richard Aldington appears to have read my book most carefully, and continued our original correspondence with many pertinent observations, some of them having to do with Pound's role, or lack of it, in World War I; he also showed Mr. Ford Madox Ford to have been in error in ascribing the famous billiard-cloth trousers to Pound. It was not Pound who wore them, but Mr. Aldington, a fact confirmed by Pound's wife. Mrs. Pound, and Mary de Rachewiltz, Pound's daughter, sent a number of corrections and suggestions through a third party, and I have utilized most of them.

To all this, I add a single clarification of my own: Chapter XIII ("Roots and Forebears") appears where it does because at that point in his life Pound took stock of himself, even to writing a brief autobiography, and it seemed to me an excellent place to follow suit. Who would have thought that a simple literary device such as this would confuse a critic? But so it came to pass.

As for my own dedication, I am glad of this opportunity to acknowledge a cherished friendship, begun when Mr. R. L. De Wilton was my editor for this and other books.

C. N.

CONTENTS

ILLUSTRATIONS

EZRA POUND

CHAPTER I

STUDENT AND TEACHER

1.

In a dormitory room at the University of Pennsylvania a young medical student sat down to write a letter to his mother. It was not the usual perfunctory letter home of collegiate youth, and it turned into a long one, for there was friendship as well as love between this mother and her son, as readers of his work know. His name was William Carlos Williams, the date March 30, 1904. As interesting as the writer and the recipient was the subject. "Dear Mama," it began. "The reason I didn't write last Sunday was because I was out of town. My friend Pound invited me to spend Saturday and Sunday with him, so on Friday I wrote to you and then set off on my trip." The Pounds lived in Wyncote, a suburb of Philadelphia, and Williams had visited them before: "His parents are very nice people and have always been exceptionally kind to me. Mrs. Pound had prepared a fine meal." He does not tell what it was. The Pound house, at 166 Fernbrook Avenue, in the Old York Road section of Wyncote, is still standing.

At the time of the letter, Williams was twenty-one, Pound only eighteen and a half. Williams was torn between his desire to become a physician and a strong, but not yet overpowering, urge to become a writer. His friend had no such conflict. "After supper," the letter continues, "Pound and I went to his room where we had a long talk on subjects that I love yet have not time to study and which he is making a life work of. That is literature, and the drama and the classics, also a little philosophy. He, Pound, is a fine fellow; he is the essence of optimism and has a cast-iron faith that is something to admire. If he ever does get blue nobody knows it, so he is just the man for me. But not one person in a thousand likes him, and a great many people detest him and why? Because he is so darned full of conceits and affectation."

They resumed in the morning; they "talked, ate, read, sang, walked in the country, but principally rested with our feet before a big fire or rather a little one."[1] Both were tall and long-legged, Pound green-eyed with a mass of golden-reddish hair, Williams slim and "romantic-looking," as he confessed to me more than half a century later in his house in Rutherford. A pleasant vignette, as it used to be called.

Williams had entered the Dental School in 1902, but transferred the following year to the Medical School, graduating in 1906; Pound had attended the University from 1901 to 1903 and then transferred to Hamilton College for two years, returning in 1905. The date of Williams's letter suggests that Pound was home on spring vacation. Williams's recollection was that Pound's father took him out of Penn because Ezra was not doing well with his studies, and this is borne out, in part, by Pound's scholastic record. There is another story, to the effect that Pound's father considered Philadelphia "too fast" for his son, and therefore packed him off to the quieter precincts of Clinton, New York. Perhaps his choice was dictated by the fact that Loomis ancestors once lived nearby. Pound's own excursion into autobiography stops abruptly at his sixteenth year; it will be referred to again.

He was not quite sixteen when he entered the University of Pennsylvania in the fall term of 1901 after preparatory schooling at Cheltenham High School in Elkins Park, and before that, at the Cheltenham Military Academy, where he first heard the *Odyssey* declaimed, as he has related in Canto LXXX. The University catalogue list of freshman students for 1901-1902 gives his name and course—"Pound, Ezra Loomis," Course "A" (Arts and Science)—and his residence as Wyncote. In the following year, 1902–1903, under sophomores, he is listed as "Pound, Ezra Weston Loomis," again under Course "A," but this time in addition to his Wyncote residence there is a University address, "Dorm. 14 P."

His letter aside, Williams's recollections tend, as is natural, to combine Pound's two enrollments at the University. They appear to have met in 1903; as Williams recalled it for me, he was playing his violin when another student came to his dormitory room to talk, if not to listen. Williams told this student that he was interested in all the arts, but particularly painting—his mother was a painter—and confessed that he had begun to jot down things in copybooks. His visitor thereupon said: "You should be interested in a guy in my sophomore class—Ezra Pound." Williams asked: "Who's he?" In this forgotten student's room Pound and Williams were introduced to each other.

"Before meeting Pound is like B.C. and A.D.," is the way Williams afterwards phrased it. "No beard, of course, then. He had a beautifully heavy head of blond hair of which he was tremendously proud. Leonine. It was really very beautiful hair, wavy. And he held his head high. I wasn't impressed but I imagine the ladies were. He was not athletic, the opposite of all the boys I'd known. But he wasn't effeminate."[2]

God forbid. Williams told me "Pound was a physical phenomenon, although not an athlete." The truth was that Pound kept himself in excellent condition. He was sparely built, with an erect carriage. He walked a great deal, walking with a kind of swarming stride; played a good game of tennis, and was taking fencing lessons from Signor Terrone, the coach of the Pennsylvania fencing team, to which Williams belonged. Williams, however, recalled Pound as "a bum fencer," but it may be because of something that took place in the house in Wyncote. One day, as Williams arrived, Pound held out two of his father's walking sticks and suggested a friendly bout. Williams, with a few flourishes, placed himself *en garde;* but Pound "came plunging wildly in without restraint, and hit me with the point of the cane above my right eye to fairly lay me out." Williams added: "You can't trust a guy like that!" (*Autobiography,* p. 65.) Another student with whom Pound fenced was Eugene McCartney, of Boothwyn, who died young. A memorial poem in *Personae,* "For E. McC," bears the subtitle: "That was my counter-blade under Leonardo Terrone, Master of Fence." Pound was also interested in football, and served as a voluntary usher in order to see the games on Franklin Field. Here he met another volunteer usher, Henry Slonimsky, a future dean of the Hebrew Union College–Jewish Institute of Religion, who recalls "a half hour acquaintance on the field." They were to meet again in London. Pound, he told me, was "an affable fellow at college; all the other things are over-compensation."

"He was always far more precocious than I," Williams wrote in his *Autobiography,* "and had gone madly on, even to Yeats—who passed through Philadelphia and read to the Penn students in 1903. I did not hear him." If Pound heard him, it must have been in December, when he journeyed down for the Christmas vacation. Yeats wore pince-nez; shortly after, Pound substituted pince-nez for plain American spectacles.

As for the "ladies" of Williams's memoirs, although he names some and alludes to others—they tried one day to pick up "a particularly lovely thing in her early teens" on Chestnut Street, who "just managed to say in a husky voice, 'Go away! Please go away! Please! Please!' " and "I remember, also, one moonlight adventure to meet two girls outside the grounds near some school at Chestnut Hill. Equally futile"—my readers will have to be content with just three. Pound was engaged to two of them.

I have been looking at a photograph of H. D. [Hilda Doolittle]. She is older than when Pound and Williams met her in Philadelphia and perhaps even more beautiful; Pound, says Williams, used to "exaggerate her beauty ridiculously." Her blond hair is worn Greek style; there are bangs over her brow; and the "gay blue eyes" of Williams's recollection—wondrously spaced and shaped—peer thoughtfully from beneath long delicately curved eyebrows. The nose is straight yet sensuous, the mouth full with a suggestion of firmness or control. Dr. Williams has observed, clinically, that she had "a long jaw." It is a beautiful head. Like her two admirers, she was tall. And there was about her, says Williams, "that which is found in wild animals at times, a breathless impatience." But she "giggled," she "dressed indifferently," she was "irritating, with a smile."

Pound saw her otherwise. Her brother was a fellow student at Penn, her father, Professor Charles Doolittle, taught astronomy there, and was the director of the Flower Astronomical Observatory. Pound was taken to the Doolittle home in Philadelphia, and also to the observatory in Upper Darby. One of the occasions was a fancy-dress Hallowe'en party, to which he wore a bright green robe. (In 1898, aged thirteen, Pound had been taken by his great-aunt-in-law to the Continent and Tunis, where he had purchased the robe.) It created a sensation, for it set off not only his green eyes but his gold-red hair. "I make five friends for my hair," he complained to Miss Doolittle, "for one for myself." He danced badly. "One would dance with him for what he might say," she recalled. His friend once took her to a Mask and Wig tryout and dance. " 'For God's sake,' I told him," Williams relates in his *Autobiography*, "I'm not in love with Hilda nor she with me. She's your girl and I know it. Don't be an ass." But it appears that he was in love, at least when he first met her, to judge by a letter he sent his brother at the time. This was during her freshman year at Bryn Mawr, which places it in 1905. She had a classmate who was to become famous, too: Marianne Moore.

A trolley ride from the campus brought the two friends to the observatory in Upper Darby and, as Williams reports, "it certainly wasn't to look through a telescope." There were woodland walks with a whole series of girls, he told me; "but Pound always went with H. D." The girls wore sweaters and "short" skirts which came "only" to their ankles.

"You cannot imagine at this late day how it was," Williams told me. "There were miles of woods and fields. You must bear in mind there were no cars—it was a different world."

It has been improved.

In addition to the rambles in Upper Darby there were parties in the Pound home in Wyncote, at which everyone—Pound, Williams, H. D. and other young men and women—sang while Mrs. Pound played the piano, an upright. Williams has described her as "erect and rather beautiful in an indifferent middle-aged way." Sometimes Williams brought his violin. Ezra, he relates, "couldn't even carry a tune."

One day, Pound gave Miss Doolittle a ring to wear to mark their engagement, an unannounced event which pleased his family but not hers, particularly the head of it when it came to his knowledge. For Pound went one day to the observatory to ask for her hand, and Professor Doolittle, a tall, gaunt man who spoke with deliberate slowness, said in his slow, deliberate voice: "Why, you're nothing but a nomad!" Now, this may have been uttered by a Penn professor aware—and indignant—that his daughter's suitor had left Penn for

Hamilton only to return; but more probably the scene took place when Pound came back from his first trip abroad after graduation. When he went abroad permanently, any semblance of an engagement was over, H. D. said. (Margaret Widdemer recalled that Pound was also engaged to a friend of Miss Doolittle's, Frances Gregg; she wrote poetry, too. "Getting engaged was a frequent pastime of youth then," Miss Widdemer told me.)

H. D.'s diary reveals a lifelong emotional attachment to Pound. But the engagement that counted for him is another matter.

From 1909 to the present day, although its contents have changed over and over and it has grown from a slim volume of 59 pages to one of 273 of his "collected poems," Pound's *Personae* has borne the same title and the same dedication:

> This Book Is For
> MARY MOORE
> Of Trenton, If She
> Wants It

Williams conjectured she may have been one of the two young women he and Pound went to meet outside the school at Chestnut Hill; but apart from having heard that Pound always entered the Moore house in Trenton, New Jersey, through a French window, because he had done so on his first visit, it is all he knows of this other "queen of the man's youth"—his phrase.

"One trait I always held against Ezra," he told me, "was that he'd never let you in on his personal affairs; close as we were for several years when we were kids I just never knew what he was up to. It didn't make really much difference but in a pal it was annoying. Never explain anything, was his motto. He carried it off well—and in his verse too, later."

"This was the time, apart from other things," Williams relates in his *Autobiography,* "when Ezra Pound was writing a daily sonnet. He destroyed them all at the end of the year; I never saw any of them. I too was writing, a monumental work, a four-book romantic poem. I have even forgotten the name of it." Williams also was filling his ten-cent copybooks with "Whitmanesque 'thoughts,' a sort of purgation and confessional, to clear my head and my heart from turgid obsessions. Ezra, even then, used to assault me (as he still does) for my lack of education and reading."

Williams told me: "He was always in Provence, and telling me about it. I didn't know a damn thing about it. I was very much impressed—he was a poet. He used to read me his poetry, which I couldn't even hear. He was an affected reader, speaking in a whisper, with gestures. He lived then in the tower room, up in the tower above the dormitory; it was there that he used to read to me. I appreciated his romantic and scholarly achievements—I had none."

This, I think, was during Pound's second attendance at the University. Between Hamilton and Pennsylvania II he met the older woman every young man meets, but this time their roles were reversed: he helped her. She was Katherine Ruth Heyman, a concert pianist, thirty-four, who gave him an heirloom diamond ring to keep until they were both "very old." He put it to a curious use.

Mary Moore was still in the future.

2.

How did other students in that far-off day see Pound? Fifty-five years after Williams's letter to his mother I wrote to Pound's surviving schoolfellows at Penn to inquire. Professor Stanley S. Swartley, now head of the Department of English at Allegheny College, replied: "I remember him, of course; he is not the kind of person you easily forget; but I barely knew him. We sat opposite each other at a long table in a course in American diplomatic history. My recollection of him is of a person aloof from his classmates and indifferent to them." This impression was confirmed by Samuel Wanamaker Fales: "In class, Ezra was very shy—a dreamer, 'lone wolf,' and didn't appear to have or care to have any particular friends." Mr. Fales remembered him as "about six feet tall—thin—pink and white complexion— light hair which stood out from the sides of his head," and "quite a chess-player."

Walter M. Johnson wrote, "Ezra Pound, a member of my section of the Class of 1905 College, University of Pennsylvania, was regarded by his contemporaries as a sort of screwball very easily duped and the basis of many practical jokes," and referred me to another classmate for examples. He was F. Granville Munson, Colonel, U.S. Army, Retired, now an attorney in Washington. He wrote me: "I sat down, last night, at home and dashed off the enclosed, all of which sounds rather foolish, fifty-five years later." On legal-size sheets he had written:

"In my Senior year (1902–1903) at Pennsylvania I moved in on the first floor of a University dormitory so new as not yet to have received a name but known simply as 'House P.' We on that floor were a mixed lot." After naming some of the lot, he came to Pound, "then a slight, light-haired chap, a sophomore."

"It soon became evident," he recounted, "that Ezra was of a naive disposition, so guileless as to be the butt of numerous college pranks, usually harmless but sometimes cruel and thoughtless, so characteristic of unthinking youngsters. There was the night, for example, we were assembled in his room, eating his sweets and crackers which he always brought back with him at weekends. By prearrangement with Brooke [one of the mixed lot] I was to crawl into Pound's bed in my 'nightie' —I wore the old-fashioned kind—and Brooke would then unexpectedly douse me with the contents of Pound's water-pitcher. This he did, to Pound's delight, especially as in my righteous indignation I appeared ready to fight Brooke (who could have tossed me over his shoulder with one hand). A towel and a dry 'nightie' of course restored me to status quo but Pound's bed was wet through and through. Ezra never 'caught on.' The next morning, I asked him how he managed to sleep in that wet bed. 'Oh,' said he, "I didn't sleep in the bed, I slept on the floor.' And then with a laugh—'But I will never forget the look on your face when Brooke threw that water on you.'"

"One night," Colonel Munson continued, "I came back very late from downtown Philadelphia, to find Moulton [another of the lot] groaning in agony and Brooke, his room-mate, bending over him in the deepest concern, while the rest of the floor, except Pound, who had gone to bed, gathered about in the deepest anxiety. 'Munson, will you go for a doctor' was my greeting. I took one look, grabbed my hat and would have been on my way, had not a loud guffaw stopped me. Then I realized it was a carefully worked up hoax."

But since Munson—a senior—had "fallen for it," it was decided to try it "on that gullible sophomore, Pound." It was one in the morning, with freezing temperature and deep snow. Brooke woke

Pound, exclaiming: "For God's sake, run for a doctor. Moulton is dying." Pound took one look and began to dress hastily. Brooke, says Munson, "would not give him time even to put on his socks and sent him scurrying out into the snow with a direction to go to '3990 Walnut Street'—a nonexistent address. After he had gone, we sat around waiting to see a disgruntled Ezra coming back to face our jibes and ridicule. But an hour went by and no Ezra, and someone suggested that probably the poor chap realized he had been duped and was waiting out in the snow until he could return unnoticed. We agreed and all went to bed. About an hour later there was a knock on my door and there stood Pound and a man with a black bag. 'I can't wake up Brooke,' said he; 'I have the doctor for Moulton.' We went to their door and another knock brought Brooke—thank Fortune, not Moulton—who took in the situation at a glance. 'Oh, he felt much better, Doctor, and I believe he has been able to get to sleep.' We went into the room and there was Moulton, sound asleep and snoring. When he awoke and saw the doctor he, too, took in the situation instantly, and being a medical student had the wit to describe the symptoms of acute indigestion. The doctor promptly confirmed his diagnosis, left some pills and departed.

"Hardly was he out of the door when we pounced on Pound. 'What did you do when you left here?' 'Why,' said Ezra, 'you gave me a wrong address. I had to wake up three doctors before I could get one to come and he only came because he was an instructor in the University.'"

Colonel Munson commented: "Perhaps the joke was on us, after all, for the doctor sent a bill for five dollars—big money in the early days of the century."

Another incident shows Pound suffering the usual fate of an undergraduate at a senior ritual: "The seniors had a ceremony, following their last chapel service, which consisted of invading class rooms of lower classes, insisting on a speech from the instructor, and then a march up the street to the lily pond in the botanical garden. No lower classman could join this march, under pain of seizure and immersion in the pond. I was marching along when I chanced to glance at the student beside me and, to my horror, I saw it was Pound. I whispered, 'Get away before someone recognizes you.' Too late!

He was forthwith seized and dragged up to the pond and all I could do was to save his glasses and his coat. And then in he went, coming out wet to the skin with a plentiful coating of mud." Munson added: "Looking back, these fifty-five years, these pranks seem childish and almost inexcusable. I can recall no conversation with Pound rising to collegiate level nor do I recall any signs of latent genius. None of our group, I am sure, could foresee an international reputation for this young good-natured sophomore nor imagine him developing into one so vindictive against the country of his birth. I never saw Pound after our college days although tempted to visit him at St. Elizabeths Hospital here after T. S. Eliot told me he thought Pound would appreciate such a visit. But Pound was under indictment for treason and I rather thought the Army would not look with favor upon social calls by retired officers."

3.

Hamilton, in its ivied quadrangle above the Oriskany River, has been described by Alexander Woollcott, '09:

"It stands on a lovely hilltop near Clinton in the State of New York; stands in a noble park still marked out with the treaty stones of the Indians, placed there as a pledge of sanctuary when first the school was built. Men whose business takes them to all the universities, both of this country and Europe, have told me that, except for the University of Upsala, in Sweden, the Hamilton campus is the most beautiful in the world."

Although Pound returned to the University of Pennsylvania, Hamilton was infinitely more important in shaping his life. It was there that Professor Shepard revealed to him the splendors of Provençal poetry, whose themes and images he made his own. Here it might be useful to pay homage to the type of teacher of which every good school appears to have at least one example; "and by 'teacher' [I am quoting Mr. Eliot on Irving Babbitt] I do not mean merely a tutor, or a man whose lectures I attended, but a man who directed my interests, at a particular moment, in such a way that the marks of that direction are still evident."

Pound's fellow students at Hamilton, Class of 1905. Robert U. Hayes, president of the Hayes National Bank, at Clinton, replied: "I knew him quite well although not rooming with him. He was a peculiar fellow, both in personality and dress. He was almost pledged to my fraternity when he came to Clinton as a sophomore from the University of Pennsylvania. My fraternity received a telegram from the U. of P. chapter saying 'Under no considerations pledge Ezra Pound.' I have forgotten what facts this wire was followed by. In college he was not popular but was interesting. I don't think he took any part in athletics. In walking he rushed along with a long stride, constantly talking."

Charles A. Springstead wrote from Elmira: "He kept strictly to himself, except as I understand it, he became quite friendly with Claude Hand, now deceased. I personally remember him as a fine-looking young man with sandy curly hair and invariably wearing a scarlet turtleneck sweater."

Claudius Alonzo Hand, afterwards general counsel for the Corporation Trust Company of New York, who roomed with Pound, recalled that Pound used to wake him in the middle of the night to read poems to him. Then, said Mr. Hand, he would tear up the manuscripts and throw them into the wastebasket.

W. E. Rogers wrote: "About all I can say is that he seemed to me to be characteristically individualistic—if there are such words; an ardent student; smoked a pipe when many of us did not indulge, and was sort of a 'lone wolf' but not in the sense of today's interpretation."

Frank E. Beach wrote from a Veterans' Hospital in Wisconsin: "My recollection is that Pound had no friends other than Professor Shepard. Pound lived his own life, and it had very little connection with the College. Dr. Shepard was the most able member of the faculty, a man of prodigious learning. He was extremely generous, if he had a student who wanted to work. If Pound had gone to the finest university he could not have had a better tutor than Shepard.

"So far as I know, there is nothing interesting about Pound, aside from his literary product. And yet there must be something. For Pound's wife stood with him through all his troubles."

The President of Hamilton College during Pound's sojourn was Melancthon Woolsey Stryker. Many alumni believe that Pound modeled himself on this vigorous, red-faced clergyman; one of them told me "President Stryker certainly explains some of Pound's eccentricities."[3]

Stryker had a talent for insulting people. He was scornful of Theodore Roosevelt, whom he called "the Idol of Mediocrity," and of President Eliot of Harvard, because of the elective system in the learnery on the Charles. He loved languages, especially Latin, and said once that while he pronounced German badly, when he went to Europe he could "always use Latin with anyone to whom he wished to talk." He was a hearty eater, especially of steaks, and a hearty singer, singing with a kind of "roar." He edited several hymnals, for which he wrote many of the texts, and selected their chorale tunes, chiefly from Bach. He was President of Hamilton for twenty-five years, and is thought by most alumni to have been the greatest—"not," my informant added, "merely because he was the most entertaining." His son, whom Pound afterwards recalled as one of the two chief headaches of President Stryker—the other being himself—was Lloyd Paul Stryker, who became an eminent attorney and was considered for the role of Pound's defense counsel.

4.

After two years at Hamilton Pound returned to the University of Pennsylvania. He is listed under regular students for 1905–1906 as "Pound, Ezra Winton" [*sic*], residence again Wyncote, "Ph.B. (Hamilton College, 1905). Romanics; first year." For 1906–1907 he is listed under "Graduate School Fellows and Scholars" as the holder of a George Lieb Harrison Foundation fellowship—"In Romanics: Ezra Weston Pound, Wyncote, Ph.B., A.M. (Hamilton College, 1905; Pennsylvania, 1906). Romanics, English literature; second year." He had received a Master of Arts degree on June 13, 1906.

Pound's father has described the scene in the house in Wyncote when Ezra arrived with his diploma: "I remember he flung the diploma into a corner and shouted, 'Well, Dad! Educated!' And I said, 'What are your plans now, Son? You've got to get busy and do something now, you know.' And with that he went off upstairs to his room, and came down a few minutes later with this poem. It's never been published except in a small-town paper out in Idaho, and as I said

Ezra Pound's birthplace: the first plastered house in Hailey, Idaho

The house where he grew up: Wyncote, Pennsylvania

Ezra Pound at Hamilton College, 1905

"Hermione": Isabel Weston Pound,
poet's mother

Homer Loomis Pound, father

before, Ezra would just about kill me if he knew I was showing it to anybody. But it's sort of nice, I think." It was called "The Mourn of Life," and began:

> There comes a time in the lives of men
> That makes their blood turn cold
> When their fathers say
> In a gentle way
> "Thou canst not stay
> Any more in the dear home fold."
>
> Twill come some time to you,
> When your noble Dad
> Your loving Dad
> Your dear Dad kind and true,
> Will no more pay
> In that generous way
> Your bills as he used to do. . . .

"Sort of human, isn't it?" said Mr. Pound. "That's just the way Ezra always was, and still is, even if he does write Cantos now that I don't catch onto exactly."

The reporter described Pound's father as "a tall, courtly, elderly gentleman with white hair and a kindly manner." Mr. Pound told her: "I've kept everything he's ever written, I guess. Ezra gets mad about it. 'For heaven's sake, Dad,' he writes now and then, 'won't you get busy and burn up all that truck of mine you've got littering up your house? I'm afraid some of it will get into print some day if you don't.' " Mr. Pound laughed. "Maybe it will, and between you and me, I wouldn't mind, because I think some of the best stuff Ezra ever wrote was written when he was a young man. Anyhow, I can understand those writings of his better than some of his later ones. Have you ever read any of his Cantos? Well, I must admit I can't make much out of some of them. Ezra told me unless I read Browning's 'Sordello' I couldn't expect to understand the Cantos. So I waded through that. Ever read it? Well, I don't advise you to. I found it didn't help me much with Ezra's Cantos anyway."[4]

John Cournos, who knew Pound in London, tells of a 1914 visit to the Fernbrook Avenue house, where he saw some of this material. Pound's parents, he wrote, were "glad to hear about their son and kept me for the night. They showed me a voluminous scrapbook of things Ezra wrote in his childhood, including a large number of letters to Santa Claus, which showed at least that Ezra's early writing career differed in no way from that of other boys."[5]

5.

Then, and later, Pound had praise for Dr. Walton Brooks Mc-Daniel, under whom he studied Latin, and Dr. Clarence Child, with whom he studied English. Dr. McDaniel remembered him sitting in a back row, "to be independent of *ex-cathedra* observation." His teacher in Romanics was Felix E. Schelling, of the Class of '81, a noted scholar. Pound also took "an odd sort of post-graduate course" under Professor Cornelius Weygandt, some of whose more recent students have told me that he never lost an opportunity to bring Pound's name into classroom discussions. But Pound himself complained (in a letter to Harriet Monroe) that Weygandt "wrote for free copies of my books just after he had come into a fortune." He added: "For sheer lack of consideration or realization give me a compatriot every time."

For this period of his studies it may well be that Dr. Hugo Rennert, Professor in Romance Languages and author of a life of Lope de Vega, was the most important single influence on Pound at Pennsylvania, as was the case with Professor Shepard at Hamilton.

"I can still see Dr. Rennert manicuring his finger nails in seminar," Pound afterwards wrote, "pausing in that operation, looking over his spectacles and in his plaintive falsetto, apropos someone who had attempted to reprint the *Cid* with ten syllables in *every* line: 'Naow eff a man had sense enough to write a beautiful poem like this is, wudn't yeow think he wudda had sense enough to be able to keount ep to ten on his fingers *ef he'da wanted tew?*' "[6]

Pound's ability to reproduce speech which characterizes the speaker, as in the example just quoted, is probably unsurpassed by any American writer except Hemingway, who may have learned something from him. Had he not become a consummate poet he could have been a playwright, and plays, it may be thought, would have been an excellent vehicle for the expression of some of his ideas.

By the terms of his fellowship Pound was to "devote his undivided time to the prosecution of his studies"; neither teaching nor other "outside work" was permitted. To be eligible, he had been "required to hold a baccalaureate degree, and to have had one year of graduate work, both of which must be satisfactory to the Executive Committee. He must possess a good reading knowledge of French and German." Harrison Fellows were exempt from the payment of tuition fees, and there was a stipend of five hundred dollars per annum, but no individual could hold a Fellowship for more than two years. Pound held it for one, and was the only Fellow in Romanics.

With the Fellowship money Pound went abroad and saw the Old World with a young man's eyes. In Madrid, pursuing his studies of Lope de Vega, he received permission—with the assistance of the American consul—to use the royal library, and was in the crowd of spectators outside the palace who witnessed the attempt to assassinate young King Alfonso and his bride. In an article which he sent back from Spain, and which appeared in the October, 1906, issue of *The Book News Monthly,* a publication of the John Wanamaker Store in Philadelphia, he wrote:

"I left Madrid about the time the anarchist suspects and uncatalogued foreigners began to be confused in the eyes of the law."

The article, entitled "Burgos: A Dream City of Old Castile," relates his wanderings through the city of the Cid, and contains the first of at least three accounts by him of that redoubtable hero—the other two being in *The Spirit of Romance* and the *Cantos.* In the article he wrote:

"Although of the Cid's house there remains nothing but a 'Solar,' with a few emblazoned pillars to mark the place where it lay, there are still many doorways in Burgos to which he might have come, as in the old 'Poema,' battering with his lance butt at the door closed *por miedo del Rey Alfonso*—for fear of the king Alfonso, who had sent letters saying that 'none should open to Ruy Diaz, and that whoso open to Ruy Diaz would lose his possessions, and the eyes of his head to boot.' The only one of all Burgos that dared tell these tidings to the Cid was a little maid of nine; and there are yet in Burgos window and balcony from which she might have leaned, with her black eyes wonder wide, and held parlance with the stern-bearded Campeador, saying:

> Aie Campeador, in good hour girt ye on your sword.
> The King hath forbidden it; last night came his letter
> With great escort, strongly sealed.
> We dare not open to you nor in any wise give ye aid,
> For we would lose our havings and our homes
> And the eyes of our faces to boot.
> Cid, in our ill you will gain nothing;
> But the Criador (creator) avail you and all his holy virtues.

"So the Cid smiled and rode out of Burgos.

"The little girl is still in the capital of 'Castilla.' I saw her, but she does not remember the Campeador."

He saw her on the hill above the city, whither he had gone to look at the ruins and the view:

"The hill crest itself is covered with fallen fortifications of various times. At the gate of these we were met by a very small and noisy dog. My guide, a boy of eleven, called: 'Open! Open! for I come, and with me a Franthes'—spelled frances, and meaning French. I explained that I was not 'Frances' but 'Americano'; to which the boy replied: 'It is all one. Here we know no other name for strangers save "franthes." '

"And then there came a pair of very big black eyes, and a very small girl tugging at the gate latch; and I knew of a surety that she had sent away the Campeador at the king's bidding."

Of the view itself, he wrote:

"Old Castile, as it lies spread before one from the castle of Burgos, is for the painter. I was indeed taken up into a very high mountain, and tempted to forget there were such prosaic things as doctors' theses to be writ."

Either on this trip, or possibly on the one two years later, he had the experiences recounted in Canto XXII. The scene is Gibraltar; Yusuf is a guide. Pound says he went off to Granada, came back,

> And another day on the pier
> Was a fat fellah from Rhode Island, a-sayin'

"Bi Hek! I been all thru Italy
   An' ain't never been stuck!"
"But this place is plumb full er scoundrels."
And Yusuf said: Yais? an' the reech man
In youah countree, haowa they get their money;
They no go rob some poor pairsons?
And the fat fellah shut up, and went off.
And Yusuf said: Waot, he iss all thru Eeetaly
An' ee is nevair been stuck, ee ees a liar.
W'en I goa to some forain's country
I am stuck.
    W'en yeou goa to some forain's country
You moss be stuck; w'en they come 'ere I steek thaim.

Pound mentions a trial, then describes one found in a book—the
"studied discontinuity" of Hugh Kenner's perceptive phrase:

And the judge says: That veil is too long.
And the girl takes off the veil
That she has stuck onto her hat with a pin,
"Not a veil," she says, " 'at's a scarf."
And the judge says:
    Don't you know you aren't allowed all those buttons?
And she says: Those ain't buttons, them's bobbles.
Can't you see there ain't any button-holes?
And the Judge says: Well, anyway, you're not allowed ermine.
"Ermine?" the girl says, "Not ermine, that ain't,
" 'At's lattittzo."
And the judge says: And just what is a lattittzo?
And the girl says:
    "It'z a animal."

It'z a skin of a suckling animal; see, also, p. 460.
And one day, in the company of Yusuf, he entered the synagogue,

All full of silver lamps
And the top gallery stacked with old benches;

And in came the levite and six little choir kids
And began yowling the ritual
As if it was crammed full of jokes,
And they went through a whole book of it;
And in came the elders and the scribes
About five or six and the rabbi
And he sat down, and grinned, and pulled out his snuff-box,
And sniffed up a thumb-full, and grinned,
And called over a kid from the choir, and whispered,
And nodded toward one old buffer,
And the kid took him the snuff-box and he grinned,
And bowed his head, and sniffed up a thumb-full,
And the kid took the box back to the rabbi,
And he grinned, e faceva bisbiglio,
And the kid toted off the box to
         another old bunch of whiskers,
And he sniffed up his thumb-full,
And so on till they'd each had his sniff;
And then the rabbi looked at the stranger, and they
All grinned half a yard wider, and the rabbi
Whispered for about two minutes longer,
An' the kid brought the box over to me,
And I grinned and sniffed up my thumb-full.
And then they got the scrolls of the law
And had their little procession
And kissed the ends of the markers.

He also went to France, Italy and Germany. He wrote in Canto **XX**:

And that year I went up to Freiburg,
And Rennert had said: Nobody, no, nobody
Knows anything about Provençal, or if there is anybody,
It's old Lévy."
And so I went up to Freiburg. . . .
Freiburg im Breisgau,
And everything clean, seeming clean, after Italy.

They discussed Arnaut Daniel. Pound afterwards wrote in *Instigations:* "Any man who would read Arnaut and the troubadours owes great thanks to Emil Lévy of Freiburg for his long work and his little dictionary (*Petit Dictionnaire Provençal-Français*)." The long work is *Provenzalisches Supplement-Wörterbuch, Berichtigungen und Ergänzungen zu Raynouards Lexique Roman,* in eight volumes.

6.

He was home again in January, 1907. He was full of ambition. He told his parents: "I want to write before I die the greatest poems that have ever been written." He was full of good will for all. In an unpublished poem, "Dawn Song," one of many that he discarded but which his father saved, he wrote:

> God hath put me here
> In earth's goodly sphere
>   To sing the song of the day,
> A strong, glad song,
> If the road be long,
>   To my fellows in the way.

He wrote to Professor Schelling: "I have already begun work on 'Il Candelaio' which is eminently germane to my other romance work."

He relaxed at the Doolittle house. Finally, Professor Doolittle said to him: "I do not forbid you the house, but come less often."

He met Mary Moore.

It happened, not in Trenton, but at Scudder's Falls, Pennsylvania. John Scudder, a young man she knew, took her there in a buggy. She was wearing a light summer dress, perhaps one of those middy dresses in which young women "practically lived" in those days, she recalled. Her brown hair was "heaped" on top of her head. Her eyes were "greeny-gray." When she got up on the porch of the Scudder house, she told me, "there was this mop of Lancaster County *stroobly,* and I said: 'What have you got in the hammock?' " It was Ezra Pound, who was tutoring Scudder. (*Stroobly* or *shtroobly*: Pennsylvania Dutch for uncombed, tangled.)

The next time Scudder went to call on Miss Moore he took Pound along; then Pound began to call by himself, entering the Moore house by the French window. Soon, she was meeting his other friends, including Miss Doolittle, and was a visitor at the Pound house in Wyncote. She thought Pound "pixyish—like his mother."

They took long walks in the country around the Delaware Bridge. There was "a big rock," she recalled, where they ate for hours and talked. They went canoeing. She tipped the canoe over—so he always thought—and found herself in the water. She looked back. "There he was, paddling with his hands—the paddles were gone." From time to time he gave her books. He gave her his photograph. They were "engaged." Had he married her at once, she would have saved him from his first fiasco.

That year, Pound accepted a teaching offer from Wabash College in Crawfordsville, Indiana. When he arrived for the Fall term literary talk centered around General Lew Wallace, who had lived there; by the time he left, four months later, the author of *Ben-Hur* was almost forgotten. The new instructor in French and Spanish found himself "stranded in a most Godforsakenest area of the Middle West."[7] But perhaps he could find consolation in books, a whole college library being at his disposal. "The college library was utterly useless."[8] Nothing was right: "this Godforsaken state has a law against the sale of cigarettes," he complained to Miss Moore. Indiana was the "sixth circle of desolation," he told L. Bertram Hessler, a college friend.

He liked a "Tennesseean" who was professor of math, and another, professor of Greek. "But the faculty wives!! Herr Gott." A fellow teacher, Rollo Walter Brown, recalled him as follows in 1944 (wartime): "The trace of the showman and charlatan in him was very strong at the time. He was half a brilliant—at least superficially brilliant—and interesting man. . . . But by the time he had stayed from four on Sunday afternoon till twelve or one at night, and had crawled all over the sofa and stuck his feet up against the wall. . . . I was' at least glad to see him go" (from an unsigned letter in the University of Kansas City *Review*.)[9]

Pound had fifty-seven students "to begin French," thirty in Spanish. He taught French literature to another dozen or so. One of the students at Wabash, though not in his classes, was Thurman Arnold, who, half a century later, brought about the dismissal of the indictment for treason against Pound.

He stayed first at a hotel, The Crawford, and then found lodgings in a house on Milligan Terrace. The house was on a lane which led to the campus. It had Gothic windows and a garden, "the tree-yest place here." He had the use of the parlor, where there was a piano. The rooms that were let were on the ground floor, with a private entrance. He was making it sound cozy enough, if temporary, for his bride-to-be.

He reported a coincidence: he had become friends with a Mrs. Young, a widow, whose maiden name was Mary Moore Shipman.

The question of a ring was on his mind. He did not think anything he could find in Crawfordsville would satisfy either of them "Perhaps you had better take this one—for now." He sent Miss Moore the diamond ring Katherine Ruth Heyman had given him to keep until they were "very old."

His letters were numerous and endearing. Some are more than a thousand words long. Suddenly, a disquieting note appears: she had told him about a new suitor. Yet she loved Pound "desperately." He asked her where he stood. "You see, oh delightful upsetter of canoes, you are 'indefini.' " He appears at first to have taken the new turn of events lightly, but not for long: "Surely if you call me I come."

Miss Moore did not call him. She did not marry that particular suitor, either. Whether she would have married Pound, after all, is problematical. The engagement "just faded away," she told me. Perhaps what helped the dissolution was the event that stirred Wabash College in particular, and Crawfordsville in general. He was found with a woman in his room; and not just a woman, but an actress! He told Miss Moore that her namesake was being very kind, "but she reproves me when I share my frugal meal with the stranded variety actress who rooms across the hall, and get caught in the act by two stewdents." The town-and-gown consensus was—he would have to get married if he wanted to stay.

Miss Moore remained in Trenton, and Pound was dismissed from his post. Of this dismissal he later noted that all accusations—that he was too European, too unconventional—were "ultimately refuted save that of being 'the Latin Quarter type.' " Mrs. Young defended him loyally, hence the diminished charge.

The event—Pound's dismissal—was decisive in his life and career. Despite his already strong predilection for Europe and things European, he might yet have stayed on in the United States for many years, and so become—what he was eminently equipped to become—a great teacher as well as a great poet. In his first letter to Williams from London the following year he commented on the event itself and his withdrawal from American life:

"As to the unconstrained vagabondism. If anybody ever shuts *you* in Indiana for four months and you don't at least *write* some unconstrained something or other, I'd give up hope for your salvation. Again, if you ever get degraded, branded with infamy, etc., for feeding a person who needs food, you will probably rise up and bless the present and sacred name of Madame Grundy for all her holy hypocrisy. I am not getting bitter. I have been more than blessed for my kindness and the few shekels cast on the water have come back ten fold and I have no fight with anybody."

And yet, the incident must have rankled, coupled with the fact that his own Alma Mater—the real one—the one to which he had returned to achieve his M.A. and at whose Graduate School he had embarked on important studies—had not thought enough of him and his gifts to offer him a job. Twenty-one years later it poured over. He wrote the alumni secretary of Penn, who was soliciting funds:

"Sir: Your circular letter of April 8 is probably excusable as a circular letter. If it were a personal letter I shd. be obliged to correct it.

"Any news that the grad. school or any other 'arts' segment of the U. of P. had started to take an interest in civilization or 'the advancement of knowledge' or any other matter of interest wd. be of interest.

"The matter of keeping up one more otiose institution in a retrograde country seems to me to be the affair of those still bamboozled by mendicancy, rhetoric, and circular letters.

"In other words what the HELL is the grad. school doing and what the HELL does it think it is there for and when the hell did it do anything but try to perpetuate the routine and stupidity that it was already perpetuating in 1873?

"P.S. All the U. of P. or your damn college or any other god damn American college does or will do for a man of letters is to ask him to go away without breaking the silence."

7.

It may have been after his return from Crawfordsville and on the eve of sailing to Europe again that Pound met Witter Bynner, with important results. Bynner was poetry editor of *McClure's Magazine;* as such, he had introduced some of the poems in *A Shropshire Lad* to American readers. He had also published a quatrain of his own or, rather, half his own, for he realized after its publication that two of the lines were by Dante Gabriel Rossetti. This is how he recounted the exploit in 1956:[10]

"This quatrain, half of it very good, may have been the principal poem of mine which several years later had sufficiently recommended itself to a citizen of, I think, Pennsylvania that he sent his son to me with poems. Since all of it happened forty or fifty years ago, details blur; but I vividly remember the youth who came to me in New York with either a written message from his father or a verbal message conveyed by the son, who was not on that occasion 'soft-spoken' as he has been remembered by others, but firm-spoken and confident.

" 'Would I look at these poems by young Ezra and see if I thought they warranted his being sent abroad for stimulus and study.'

"Not only was my ready answer 'Yes, if that was what the son greatly wished,' but it developed later into arrangement that Small, Maynard & Company of Boston, who had published my own first book in 1907, should publish two books by Pound. I cannot give the date or dates, but I should say that the titles were *Personae* and *Exultations*."

Small, Maynard published, in December, 1910, a volume entitled *Provença,* "poems selected from *Personae, Exultations,* and *Canzoniere* of Ezra Pound." The first two had appeared the previous year in London; the following year—1911—Pound had second thoughts about the title of the third, and it was changed to *Canzoni.* He was also to have second thoughts about its contents. A fellow graduate student of Pound's in 1906, now Professor William S. Dye of the Department of English at Pennsylvania State University, reviewed *Provença.* "Ezra did not like my criticism and told me so in a letter."

It may be that Bynner, like Williams, is merging two separate periods—a first visit when Pound brought some poems in manuscript, and a second one, two or three years later, when Pound came to him with the volumes already published, which Bynner's secretary recently unearthed for him and which were, he wrote me, "probably the very copies I took to Small, Maynard." His description of Pound seems to fit the later time, though he terms it earlier:

"My memory of Pound, at that first meeting when he read his

poems to me, is the eager face, voice and insistent spirit behind them
and then a sense of his being an even more happily cuckoo troubadour
than the young Vachel Lindsay. But never have I seen Lindsay attired
for it as Pound was. I should say that his jacket, trousers and vest had
each a brave color, with a main effect of purple and yellow, that one
shoe was tan, the other blue, and that on a shiny straw hat the ribbon
was white with red polka dots."

8.

Pound went abroad again in 1908, bound for Venice—"an excellent
place to come to from Crawfordsville, Indiana."[11] But Crawfordsville
had made the trip possible, for Wabash College paid up on its contract. On a stopover in Paris, either before or after the Venice sojourn,
he found himself one day at a bookstall on the quais. (He is himself
quite vague about the time, saying merely it was "in the year of grace
1906, 1908, or 1910.") And he held in his hands a Latin version of
the *Odyssey* by Andreas Divus Justinopolitanus, printed in 1538,
price unspecified. He bought it. There was also a companion volume,
a Latin *Iliads*, price four francs, which he could not afford, "these
coins being at that time scarcer with me than they ever should be
with any man of my tastes and abilities." This suggests that it was
after the sojourn in Venice, where he spent some of the eighty dollars
he brought over with him. The Paris purchase was important, for
Divus's version afterwards provided the material for the opening
poem of the *Cantos*.[12]

It is believed that, to conserve his limited funds, Pound worked his
way over on a cattle boat. Ford Madox Ford, in commenting on the
Westernness of the American writers he met in Paris—every one
of them seemed, to him, to have been a cowboy, more or less—concludes with the statement: "And Mr. Pound had come over to Europe
as a cattle-hand!"[13] If he had, it was probably when he went abroad
on his Fellowship, this type of passage having been not unusual for
collegiate youth.

Pound's destination—Venice—at this particular juncture is significant, it being the first of his many visits there in times of indecision

or trouble. But London was already in his thoughts, for he wanted to meet Yeats, whom he considered the greatest living poet.

In 1908, Pound was in his twenty-third year. He had a batch of poems, old and new. One of the new ones was entitled "Scriptor Ignotus," and is dedicated to "K. R. H." The initials stand for Katherine Ruth Heyman, the pianist, whom he had met before, perhaps in Philadelphia; among her papers there is a note reading merely, "Pound 1904." Miss Heyman had made her debut with the Boston Symphony Orchestra, and was to become the foremost exponent of Scriabin in the world. Although she was at least fifteen years older than Pound, he fell completely under her spell, a not uncommon experience where she was concerned, for hers was a forceful, dynamic and imperious personality. Now they were together again in Venice. She encouraged him. He was grateful. He wrote a poem to her. The third stanza reads:

> Dear, an' this dream come true,
> Then shall all men say of thee
> "She 'twas that played him power at life's morn,
> And at the twilight Evensong,
> And God's peace dwelt in the mingled chords
> She drew from out the shadows of the past,
> And old world melodies that else
> He had known only in his dreams
> Of Iseult and of Beatrice. . . ."

The poem appears in *A Lume Spento* and the original *Personae;* later, it was dropped. He must have wanted to impress her a great deal in Venice. One night, he shaved off one of his luxuriant red sideburns, then burst into her room to show what he had done "to fight vanity." He explained that the other would have to follow. It followed. Later, he grew both back. He told Iris Barry:

"My first friend was a painter, male, now dead [*A Lume Spento* is inscribed to him]. 2nd a Pyanist, naturally 15 years plus agée que moi. That was in 'The States.' I entered London more or less under her wing; I was even an impresario, I borrowed the Lyceo Benedetto Marcello in Venice for a press recitation, in the absence of Wolf-Ferrari, author of *Das Neues Leben* and other operas, etc."

It is a fact that on June 14, 1908, he wrote to Hessler, now at

the University of Michigan, that he had given up lyric poetry and
scholarship to manage Miss Heyman's concert tours. He asked Hessler,
holding out the lure of a commission, to arrange a recital for her at
Ann Arbor. His letter concludes:

"Don't write my family or they will think I've gone clean crazy
instead of part way."

The next day, June 15th, he sent the following note to the New
York *Herald,* Paris edition, and it duly appeared in the letters
column:

"Katharine Ruth Heyman, whose American tournée is predicted
as the event of the coming piano season there, may give certain concerts in Paris on her way West.

"Her playing in London before sailing is also to be announced.
                                                          "E. P.
"Venice."

She also went into the *Cantos:*

> Does D'Annunzio live here?
> said the american lady, K.H.
> "I do not know" said the aged Veneziana,
> "this lamp is for the virgin."

> (Canto LXXVI)

Pound had second thoughts. That same June in Venice, at the press
of A. Antonini, Cannaregio, 923, he spent some of his meager funds
printing *A Lume Spento,* the first collection of his work. It has a
curious title page:

This Book was

LA FRAISNE
(THE ASH TREE)

dedicated

> *to such as love this same
> beauty that I love, somewhat
> after mine own fashion.*

But sith one of them has gone out very quickly from amongst us it [is] given

A LUME SPENTO
(With Tapers Quenched)

in memoriam eius mihi caritate primus

William Brooke Smith
Painter, Dreamer of dreams.

Smith was a young man he had known in his University days in Philadelphia. "A lume spento" is a phrase from Dante's *Purgatorio*. In a letter to William Carlos Williams in 1921 Pound wrote, replying to a query:

"Any studio I was ever in was probably that of some friend or relative of Will Smith, who avoided a very unpleasant era of American life by dying of consumption to the intimate grief of his friends. How in Christ's name he came to be in Phila.—and to know what he did know at the age of 17-25—I don't know. At any rate, thirteen years are gone; I haven't replaced him and shan't and no longer hope to."

9.

A Lume Spento, in an edition of one hundred copies, consisted of 72 pages, paperbound, to be sold at five lire.[14] John Gould Fletcher may have seen it, for he was in Venice two months later. It is probable that Pound gave away more copies than were ever sold. The first of his letters to Williams from London—there were to be hundreds in the ensuing years—is dated October 21, 1908. He had, of course, sent Williams a copy of the book. Williams was not ecstatic about it, but Pound was glad to hear from him "at last," adding: "Good Lord! of course you don't have to like the stuff I write. I hope the time will never come when I get so fanatical as to let a man's like or dislike for what I happen to 'poetare' interfere with an old friendship or a new one." He had also sent the book to Hilda Doolittle, with similar results. But having got past the amenities, he proceeded to state his poetic views, particularly as they concerned his own work:

"To me the short so-called dramatic lyric—at any rate the sort of thing I do—is the poetic part of a drama the rest of which (to me the prose part) is left to the reader's imagination or implied or set in a short note. I catch the character I happen to be interested in at the moment he interests me, usually a moment of song, self-analysis, or sudden understanding or revelation. And the rest of the play would bore me and presumably the reader. I paint my man as I *conceive* him. Et voilà tout!"

It is interesting to note that an English reviewer praised precisely this aspect of Pound's work one year later: "He plunges straight into the heart of his theme, and suggests virility in action combined with fierceness, eagerness, and tenderness" (R. E. Scott-James in the London *Daily News*).

Pound's letter continues: "I wish you'd spot the bitter, personal notes and send 'em over to me for inspection. Personally I think you get 'em by reading in the wrong tone of voice. However, you may be right. Hilda seems about as pleased with the work as you are. Mosher is going to reprint."

Thomas B. Mosher—who reprinted almost everything of worth he could lay hands on, chiefly of the genus "pirated," at his fine press in Portland, Maine, in limited editions on beautiful handmade paper imported from Holland and Japan—did not reprint *A Lume Spento*. Pound had also sent a copy to Yeats: "W. B. Yeats applies the adjective 'charming.' " This is the first mention of Yeats in his correspondence. They had not yet met.

Pound's letter ends: "My days of utter privation are over for a space."

10.

He had found a job teaching at the Regent Street Polytechnic which, with its branch institutions, had been overhauled the year before, through enlarged benefactions and the addition of cultural—as opposed to merely utilitarian—courses; it may account for Pound's acceptance as a teacher. His father told a reporter in Philadelphia:

"He found funds were getting low, as usual, so he went to the Polytechnic Institute and presented his name. 'Do you want to register as a student?' he was asked. 'No,' said Ezra, 'I want to register as a teacher. I want to give a course on the Romance Literature of Southern Europe.' 'But we don't want a course on the Romance Literature of Southern Europe,' he was told; 'besides, who are you?' 'Let me give the course,' said Ezra, 'and you'll see.' "[15]

Pound lectured at The Polytechnic during the winter of 1908–1909 on "Developments of Literature in Southern Europe," and the winter of 1909–1910 on "Medieval Literature." No schedule exists for the earliest lectures he gave, possibly because there was no time for a formal announcement. His needs were urgent, his persuasion effective. But beginning with the second series the records are complete. The "synopsis of lectures" issued by The Polytechnic reveals Pound's interests and erudition, only partially set forth in *The Spirit of Romance*. (I have corrected some spellings, probably Pound's own.) The announcement read:

> A Short Introductory Course of Lectures on The Development of Literature in Southern Europe will be given by Ezra Pound, M.A. (sometime Fellow in the University of Pennsylvania) author of "A Lume Spento," "A Quinzaine for this Yule," etc., on Thursday afternoons at 5 o'clock. Commencing January 21st, 1909, in the Marlborough Room.
>
> Fee for the course 7s. 6d.
> " for single lecture 1s. 6d.

This was followed by a synopsis of the six lectures. A note stated: "At the introductory Lecture (which is free) the Lecturer will explain fully the whole scheme."

Jan. 21st. Introductory Lecture.

I   The search for the essential qualities of Literature. Dicta of the great critics:—Plato, Aristotle, Longinus, Dante, Coleridge, De Quincey, Pater and Yeats.

Jan. 28th. The Rise of Song in Provence. The Troubadours.

II   The Belangal Alba, Bernard of Ventadorn, Bertrand of Born, Giraut of Borneilh, Jaufre Rudel, Arnaut Daniel,

Pere Bremon Lo Tort, Peire Cardinal, Sordello and King Richard Coeur de Leon.

Feb. 4th. Mediaeval Religious Feeling. The Childrens Crusade.

III   The Fioretti of St. Francis of Assisi.

Feb. 11th. Trade with the East. Portuguese and Dutch Literature.

IV   Camoens "Os Lusiadas." Vondel, "Lucifer."

Feb. 18th. Latin Lyrists of the Renaissance.

V   Period of Bembo, Sanazzaro, and Politian; Castiglione, Flamininus, Amalthei, Navagaro and the Capiloupi.

Feb. 25th. Books and their makers during the Middle Ages.

VI   Papyrus, Parchment, Illumination, The Copyists, Books in the Monasteries, in the Universities. The Trade, the early Printers, Aldus, Caxton and Elzevir.

A Quinzaine for this Yule, Being selected from a Venetian sketch-book 'San Trovaso', 27 pages, in an edition of one hundred copies was, according to the English *Bookman,* "for private circulation." But he was becoming known.

"The smallness of his output," said *The Bookman,* "does not indicate barrenness or indolence, but that he has a faculty of self-criticism; he has written and burned two novels and three hundred sonnets."

The sonnets are probably those that Williams has told about. Nothing is known of the novels, but in a letter to Iris Barry he reveals his method of composition. He was writing other prose. On a day in February he sat down to write what he felt about Whitman. February in London—perhaps he had on the fur-lined overcoat which Williams was to remember after half a century. "What I feel about Walt Whitman by Ezra Pound," he wrote on a sheet of paper and put it aside and started on another headed merely "Whitman," which he underlined, to begin his little essay. There are seven sheets in all, counting the title; they are before me in photostat—clearly written, only a single word and an ampersand crossed out, a preposition omitted; but full of odd spellings of simple words: "conventionaly," "echos," "classicaly," "rythms," "maramis" [?marasmus], "mentaly," "colar," "personaly," "temporarialy," "realy." No matter; it is one of the most revealing of his prose compositions, an estimate of himself as well as of Whitman, and it joins the past with the future. Aside from its effectiveness, it is also utterly charming—the writer, after all, was only twenty-three. He wrote:

"From this side of the Atlantic I am for the first time able to read Whitman, and from the vantage of my education and—if it be permitted a man of my scant years—my world-citizenship: I see him America's poet. The only Poet before the artists of the Carmen-Hovey period, or better, the only one of the conventionaly recognized "American Poets' who is worth reading.

"He *is* America. His crudity is an exceeding great stench, but it *is* America. He is the hollow place in the rock that echos with his time. He *does* 'chant the crucial stage' and he is the 'voice triumphant.' He is disgusting. He is an exceedingly nauseating pill, but he accomplishes his mission. Entirely free from the renaissance humanist ideal of the complete man or from the Greek idealism, he is content to be what he is, and he is his time and his people. He is a genius because he has vision of what he is and of his function. He knows that he is a beginning and not a classicaly finished work.

"I honor him for he prophesied me while I can only recognize him as a forebear of whom I ought to be proud.

"In America there is much for the healing of the nations, but woe unto him of the cultured palate who attempts the dose."

He concluded:

"It is a great thing, reading a man to know, not 'His tricks are not as yet my tricks; but I can easily make them mine' but 'His message is my message. We will see that men hear it.' "

He had come almost to the bottom of the last sheet, and there, at the bottom, he wrote his name again, and the date: "Feb. 1. 09."[16]

He was not yet through with his subject. For in time to come, in moments of doubt or despair, the achievement of Whitman sustained him; and along with Whitman, the other renowned American, Whistler.

11.

By the fall of 1909 *Personae* had appeared, and it was duly noted in The Polytechnic's printed announcement:

"A COURSE OF LECTURES ON MEDIAEVAL LITERATURE will be given by EZRA POUND, M.A. (Sometime Fellow in the University of Pennsylvania) Author of 'Personae.' On Monday evenings at 8:30 o'clock, commencing October 11th, 1909."

The synopsis of Part I included Pound's Introduction, the "Pervigilium Veneris," the beginnings of "Romance," Provence and the Troubadours, the Albigenses, the Mediaeval Epic in France and Spain, "Chançon de Roland," "Poema del Cid," Marie de France, Chretien de Troyes, the "Tristram and Ysolt," the "Aucassin and Nicolette," Tuscan Literature, Guido Guinicelli, St. Francis, Dante's "Life," and Dante's "Vita Nuova." Part II was scheduled to start on January 17th. The fee for Part I was 15 shillings, for the full course, 25; single lecture, 2. Part II dealt with Dante's "Inferno," "Purgatorio" and "Paradiso," and with Villon, Lope de Vega and his contemporaries, Latin writers in Italy, and concluded with a "survey" about books and their makers. The records at The Polytechnic do not include information as to payments made to teachers at that time.

"Well, they let him give it, heaven knows why," Homer Pound told the reporter; but perhaps his son's prospectus had something to do with it. He added: "And among the students who registered for the course was a Miss Dorothy Shakespear and her mother. Ezra promptly fell in love with his pupil, and she with him, and they were married and have lived happily ever after."

Dorothy Shakespear was twenty-one or twenty-two, depending on which year she enrolled. She was twenty-seven, a year younger than Pound, when she married him in 1914. Her mother, Mrs. Olivia Shakespear, was a prominent London hostess and the friend of many literary men, in particular, of William Butler Yeats, who had been introduced to her by her cousin, Lionel Johnson. Hers is the "lovely face" of the first line of Yeats's poem, "Memory."

12.

Pound had been living in a succession of furnished rooms, from at least one of which he had been evicted; now he found permanent quarters at 10 Church Walk, Kensington, hard by St. Mary Abbot's. It was the last in a cul-de-sac of two-story houses, reached by a narrow passageway beside the church and a graveyard thronged by blackened gravestones. His flat—a single room—was on the top floor, rent eight shillings a week. There were two windows, under one an iron wash-stand, under the other a long oak table, littered with manuscripts and letters, on which stood a battered typewriter. Between the windows was a fireplace. A white enameled bedstead was next to the door, and opposite a tall wardrobe. A smaller table was in the center of the room. Books were everywhere; folios underneath appeared to be holding up a sagging sofa. Here he lived until his marriage. He began the day with a coffee-making ritual. From a tightly-closed jar of pow-dered Dutch coffee he took a teaspoonful and placed it on a piece of cloth which had been stretched over his cup. Through the coffee and the cloth he poured boiling water, a drop at a time.

Only one thing marred his happiness. The bells of St. Mary Abbot's strode through his room with an insistent clangor, and the layers of sound gradually built up layers of resentment.

CHAPTER II

POUND IN LONDON

1.

*" 'Tis the white stag, Fame, we're a-hunting,
Bid the world's hounds come to horn!"*
—"The White Stag," *Personae,* 1909

Fame came suddenly and spectacularly to Ezra Pound with the appearance, on April 16, 1909, of a slender little book measuring $4\frac{1}{2}$ by 7 inches, in brown boards stamped with gold lettering, with a sentimental epigraph on the dedication page—"Make-strong old dreams lest this our world lose heart"—and with the famous and durable dedication. It numbered 59 pages, three—at the end—consisting of notes, and it sold for six shillings, sixpence. Its title was *Personae of Ezra Pound.*

Pound's father is the source of a charming story about the negotiation which led to its appearance.

"When he'd spent every cent he'd saved out of his allowance," Homer Loomis Pound told a reporter in Philadelphia, "he walked into a little bookshop in London and handed the manuscript of a book of poems, *Personae,* to the owner, Elkin Mathews, who had 'discovered' Yeats.

" 'If you can make an advance payment on this manuscript,' said Mr. Mathews, after he'd read it, 'I might consider bringing it out.' 'Well,' said Ezra, 'I've only got a shilling, but you're welcome to that if you want it.' 'No, never mind,' said Mr. Mathews, 'I want to bring the book out anyway.' "[1]

Mr. Mathews was not only a publisher but a bookseller, with a shop on Vigo Street, off Regent. He brought the book out, and the response was immediate and gratifying. The reviews could not have been more laudatory. I give those excerpts which Pound or Mathews —or both together—garnered for reproduction in a leaflet, of which more later.

The Observer: "It is something, after all, intangible and indescribable that makes the real poetry. Criticism and praise alike give no idea of it. Everyone who pretends to know it when he sees it, should read and keep this little book."

The Bookman: "No new book of poems for years past has had such a freshness of inspiration, such a strongly individual note, or been more alive with undoubtable promise."

The Daily Chronicle: "All his poems are like this, from beginning to end, and in every way, his own, and in a world of his own. For brusque intensity of effect, we can hardly compare them to any other work. It is the old miracle that cannot be defined, nothing more than a subtle entaglement of words, so that they rise out of their graves and sing."

The last item in the Mathews leaflet has for prelude "from a $3\frac{1}{2}$ page detailed critique, by Mr. Edward Thomas, in the *English Review*: He has . . . hardly any of the superficial good qualities of modern versifiers; . . . He has not the current melancholy or resignation or unwillingness to live; nor the kind of feeling for nature that runs to minute descriptions and decorative metaphor. He cannot be usefully compared with any living writers; . . . full of personality and with such power to express it, that from the first to the last lines of most of his poems he holds us steadily in his own pure, grave, passionate world. . . . The beauty of it ('In praise of Ysolt') is the beauty of passion, sincerity and intensity, not of beautiful words and images and suggestions; . . . the thought dominates the words and is greater than they are. Here ('Idyl for Glaucus') the effect is full of human passion and natural magic, without any of the phrases which a reader of modern verse would expect in the treatment of such a subject. This admirable poet. . . ."

Edward Thomas was the poet friend of Robert Frost. He died, with a golden host, in World War I. Rupert Brooke reviewed *Personae*—favorably—in the *Cambridge Review*, December 2, 1910. *Punch*, too, was to add its prestige to the chorus. To judge by the pun it made—"Mr. Ezekiel Ton, by far the newest poet going, whatever other advertisements may say"—it may have started out to kid, but left off to praise: "He has succeeded where all others have failed in evolving a blend of the imagery of the unfettered West, the vocabulary of Wardour Street, and the sinister abandon of Borgiac Italy. His verse is the most remarkable thing in poetry since Robert Browning." But now it is necessary to return to Edward Thomas, whose review had surprised older members of the Square Club, of which he was a member.

The quotations in the Mathews leaflet were necessarily incomplete, in part to fit the available space. But Thomas had important things to say, and though a phrase or two from his review will, perforce, be repetitions, I give a verbatim passage; and I do it so that my reader will perceive that, felicities and subject matter aside, Pound had broken with the past so far as his metrics were concerned—that is, he had ushered in a revolution which is still going on. Thomas wrote:

"To say what this poet has not is not difficult; it will help to define him. He has no obvious grace, no sweetness, hardly any of the superficial good qualities of modern versifiers; not the smooth regularity of the Tennysonian tradition, nor the wavering, uncertain languor of the new, though there is more in his rhythms than is apparent at first through his carelessness of ordinary effects. He has not the current melancholy or resignation or unwillingness to live; nor the kind of feeling for nature that runs to minute description and decorative metaphor. He can not be usefully compared with any living writers, though he has read Yeats."

Although Yeats is mentioned on the first page of Pound's notes, it was not till later that any really perceptible influence is apparent. The enlarged *Personae* no longer opens with the opening poem of the 1909 volume, "Grace Before Song," but with "The Tree" which, though individual as it can be, reveals that Pound had indeed read Yeats; but I give it here more for the pleasure of it than for the sake of any comparison:

> I stood still and was a tree amid the wood,
> Knowing the truth of things unseen before;

Of Daphne and the laurel bow
And that god-feasting couple old
That grew elm-oak amid the wold.
'Twas not until the god had been
Kindly entreated, and been brought within
Unto the hearth of their heart's home
That they might do this wonder thing;
Nathless I have been a tree amid the wood
And many a new thing understood
That was rank folly to my head before.

Yeats had written, in *The Wind Among the Reeds,* published by Mathews in 1899 and reissued in 1911:

I have drunk ale from the Country of the Young
And weep because I know all things now:
I have been a hazel-tree. . . .

The Square Club had been founded by G. K. Chesterton and Conal O'Riordan to do honor to Fielding and, according to Edgar Jepson, afterwards Pound's friend, was "the literary club of the Edwardian revival." Often to be seen at its monthly dinners were John Masefield, John Galsworthy, Walter da la Mare, E. C. Bentley, of *Trent's Last Case* and Clerihew fame, Ford Madox Hueffer and latterly Pound. There were also critics. Mr. Jepson wrote: "The critics' eyes would shine. We knew what had happened: they had discovered a poet and were making him." But when Thomas wrote his review about Pound it came as a surprise to the members. "How *could* he have liked the verse of a man whom none of them had discovered much less made? Why, none of them even knew him!" wrote Mr. Jepson. He added, however, that it was at the Square Club that he met him, and as he has described Pound's appearance at this time I give it here:

"In his black velvet jacket and abundant hair, he looked very much more of a poet than either Walter de la Mare or our Laureate. In those days he was not bearded; indeed, as I remember, his beard was recurrent; also he had not gotten into his stride, for I sat next to him, and he did not hand the fiery cross to me as he did at so many of our

later meetings. He was, I take it, feeling his way and not letting these
hostile critics see the fighter he afterwards became."[2]

2.

Pound wrote in *The Spirit of Romance*: "The single line is, it is true,
an insufficient test of a man's art, but it is a perfect test of his natural
vigor, and of his poetic nature."

Pound's poetic nature is revealed by his choice and treatment of
subject matter. He had, of course, read widely; he incorporated his
reading wholesale in what he wrote, and his eclecticism—like Eliot's—
was to dazzle a later generation which had never read much of anything. But while Eliot sprang, as it were, a full-fledged modern from
the halls of Harvard, Pound remained for many years in a dim pre-
Raphaelite realm, an American recruit to the brotherhood whose
medieval yearnings are reflected in their portraits as well as in their
work. He had also a marked affinity with the men of the Nineties,
particularly Lionel Johnson and Ernest Dowson, as had Yeats who had
known them. "I think I first heard of Johnson in an odd sort of post-
graduate course conducted by Dr. Weygandt," Pound afterwards
wrote. "One was drunk with 'Celticism,' and with Dowson's
'Cynara.' "[3]

Pound had read widely; he had also read what was best for him—
Browning, in particular; the troubadour poets; Whitman. He had
also sustained admiration for FitzGerald's *Rubáiyát*, whose stanza he
was often to imitate with great felicity. Among the earlier English
poets, Waller made a profound impression. Waller had not only
written excellent poems—he had reformed English versification.

There have been first books—for *Personae* must be considered as
such since it was the first of Pound's to be made generally available
to the public—that have struck a more consistent or a more personal
note. From the vantage point of half a century exceptions might be
taken to a pervasive pre-Raphaelite tone, to its bookishness, to the
reliance on translation and paraphrase; but when it is considered what
poetry was, who the pallid poets were, in 1909, and Pound's age that
year, it is a remarkable book. It contains, in addition to tags and titles
from Dante and the troubadours, portraits and paintings of the lost

bright world of Provence, and charming fragments still able to charm, with their foretaste of the personal language to come:

> Your songs?
>> Oh! The little mothers
> Will sing them in the twilight,

and:

> In vain have I striven
>> to teach my heart to bow;
> In vain have I said to him
> "There be many singers greater than thou."

> But his answer cometh, as winds and as lutany,
> As a vague crying upon the night
> That leaveth me no rest, saying ever,
>> "Song, a song."

He pays tribute to his hero, Browning—

>> ye old mesmerizer
> Tyin' your meanin' in seventy swadelin's,
> One must of needs be a hang'd early riser
> To catch you at worm turning. Holy Odd's bodykins!

—and twenty-three pages later announces his revolt "against the crepuscular spirit in modern poetry":

> I would shake off the lethargy of this our time,
>> and give
> For shadows—shapes of power
> For dreams—men.

"For E. McC" is preceded by another poem dealing with the imagery of sword-play, and now unaccountably missing from the collected edition. It is the famous "Ballad for Gloom," with its dramatic conclusion:

For God, our God, is a gallant foe
                that playeth behind the veil,
Whom God deigns not to overthrow
                Hath need of triple mail.

The last poem in the collection—"Piccadilly"—is "modern" in tone, but its overtones are Whitmanesque:

Beautiful, tragical faces,
Ye that were whole, and are so sunken;
And, O ye vile, ye that might have been loved,
That are so sodden and drunken,
           Who hath forgotten you?

O wistful, fragile faces, few out of many!

The gross, the coarse, the brazen,
God knows I cannot pity them, perhaps, as I should do,
But, oh, ye delicate, wistful faces.
           Who hath forgotten you?

"He wrote that," said his father, "when he was just out of college, and I remember his telling me that though he called it 'Piccadilly' he might just as well have called it 'Broad and Lombard' or 'Front and Chestnut' [streets in Philadelphia], for it pictures what is to be seen in every large city anywhere."[4]

In Trenton, Mary Moore received her copy of *Personae*. Under the printed dedication Pound had written: "In attestation whereof I do set my hand and sign." The writing is clear enough—but the sign? It was Pound's "dragonfly," she told me, a squiggly *E* and *P*.

He also wrote her: "I am without doubt the greatest poet of the age."

He believed this only in part.

3.

In Rutherford, that year, Williams put together twenty-six of his rhymed verses, gave them the title *Poems,* and took them to the local printer, who agreed to print them for fifty dollars. The resultant pamphlet sold for twenty-five cents. "About four copies were sold." He sent one to Pound. Pound had asked Williams to be frank; he could reciprocate. He wrote above his salutation: "I hope to God you have no feelings. If you have, burn this *before* reading." He asked:

"?Is it a personal private edtn. for your friends, or??

"As proof that W. C. W. has poetic instincts the book is valuable. Au contraire, if you were in London and saw the stream of current poetry, I wonder how much of it you would have printed? Do you want me to criticise it as if [it] were my own work?

"I have sinned in nearly every possible way, even the ways I most condemn. I have printed too much. I have been praised by the greatest living poet. I am, after eight years' hammering against impenetrable adamant, become suddenly somewhat of a success.

"From where do you want me to show the sharpened 'blade'? Is there anything I know about your book that you don't know?

"Individual, original it is not. Great art it is not. Poetic it is, but there are innumerable poetic volumes poured out here in Gomorrah. There is no town like London to make one feel the vanity of all art except the highest."

He advised Williams to read Aristotle's *Poetics,* and Longinus *On the Sublime;* De Quincey's and Yeats's essays; and sent him at least one of these books. When Williams came to write his *Autobiography* he found De Quincey's *Literary Criticisms* "signed on the flyleaf E. Pound." Pound may have sent the others; Williams admits he read Longinus at Pound's behest. Pound's letter ends: "Remember a man's real work is what *he is going to do,* not what is behind him."

Pound's letters to Williams mark the beginning of the criticism, advice and encouragement which were to flow from him to poets great and small, and in many lands—flow steadily, earnestly, patiently, for half a century, with hardly a break, an unparalleled record of dedication to an art. There were also letters to presidents and premiers; to legislators; to bankers and "orthodox" economists and, of course, to editors and reviewers. For Pound was not only a poet and teacher of poets—he was a crusader and reformer, with all the terrifying intensity of that ilk, and all the incomprehensible hatreds and absence of humor. The vision of a better world was his, and he fought for it like the zealots of old, and with as little command of his passions.

Letters came to him. A better summary than I can—or need to—make will be found in the Introduction to *The Letters of Ezra Pound 1907–1941* by the editor, D. D. Paige.

"In addition to letters from old friends and contemporaries there came, for the most part unsought," Mr. Paige declared, "letters from instructors of history, from diplomatic officials, from classical scholars, from politicians, from professors of economics—from those of them, that is, who wanted frank speaking along lines of unofficial thought. Above all, letters arrived from 'les jeunes'—as he never tired of calling them—from batch after batch of them. Fifteen and twenty years after those great days when he got himself, Eliot, Lewis and Joyce into the pages of a single magazine, each succeeding generation still considered him as one of them, with, perhaps, a slight edge of experience, and still sought him out. From as far off as Japan!"

Pound, he added, "very rarely writes gossip or sends news of himself."[5]

4.

Personae was followed, in the fall of the same year, by *Exultations of Ezra Pound,* also under Mathews's imprint. In addition, some individual poems appeared in an English publication, an event which proved to be of great importance to Pound because of the friendship which resulted between him and the editor.

Between 1906, when "Burgos: A Dream City of Old Castile" was published in Wanamaker's *Book News Monthly,* and 1909, nothing of Pound's had appeared in a magazine. In that memorable latter year, however, *The English Review* published four of his poems—"Sestina: Altaforte" in June, and "Ballad of the Goodly Fere," "Nils Lykke" and "Un Retrato" in October. Of the group of three, the "Ballad" is too well known for comment, while the other two have disappeared from the canon of Pound's works. "Sestina: Altaforte" is worth examining.

It is, to begin with, an example of the "so-called dramatic lyric" which he had explained to Williams—"the sort of thing I do." It has a famous first line—

> Damn it all! all this our South stinks peace.

The second line—"You Whoreson dog, Papiols, come! Let's to music!"—suggests some dabbling in the Elizabethans; Cleopatra is there. The first stanza—there are six, with an envoi of three lines—continues with great vigor:

> I have no life save when the swords clash.
> But ah! when I see the standards gold, vair, purple, opposing
> And the broad fields beneath them turn crimson,
> Then howl I my heart nigh mad with rejoicing.

The poem is not much more than an exercise in the sestina form, whose stanzas retain the same ending words in rotation. Its subject—the celebration of war—is not typical troubadour poetry. Spring, with its bright twigs and twittering of birds, woman-worship, love, were the usual themes; but then Bertran de Born was "lover of strife for strife's sake," as Dante says. It differs from what Austin Dobson and Andrew Lang and a host of minor but skillful versifiers had done with other Romance forms—the ballade and the villanelle, for example—and Kipling and Swinburne had done with the sestina, only by its dramatic setting; but, of course, Browning had paved the way for this. But the vigor of it! Pound, having said what he had to say, did not pause to lick the lines into a smooth measure, or any recognizable measure at all. I am otherwise at a loss to account for the praise that has been lavished on it,[6] for it is, after all, in its most significant part, an adaptation from Bertran de Born himself—"Quan vey pels vergier desplegar." De Born's castle was called Hautefort, in the bishopric of Périgord; de Born drove his brother out to become sole master of it. Pound also adapted de Born's elegy for Henry Plantagenet, elder brother of Richard, whom he had served with sword and pen—"Planh for the Young English King"—and de Born's most famous love poem, "Dompna pois de me no'us cal," in which the troubadour put together an "ideal beauty" or, as Pound terms it in his note to "Na Audiart," another go at the theme, "Una dompna soiseubuda." De Born died in the odor of sanctity, signing himself "monk." Nevertheless, Dante put him in Hell, where he appears carrying his severed head as punishment for having "severed father and son."

The first public reading of "Sestina: Altaforte" was an event of some importance. Ford Madox Ford has given us a glimpse of Pound plunging into traffic, "waving his cane as if he had been Bertran de Born about to horsewhip Henry II of England," but this was as nothing compared to the drama of the reading.

The group to which Pound read it, though often referred to as the Poets' Club, had in fact no such designation. But there had been a "club," founded in 1908 by Thomas Ernest Hulme, which met at the Eiffel Tower Restaurant, Percy Street, on Wednesday evenings to dine and read and discuss, chiefly members' verses, and next to their own verses art and aesthetics in general. Hulme was a Cambridge man, a poet and a philosopher with a clear vision and a sharp style. The portrait bust of him by Jacob Epstein shows a strong and forceful face in which high-browed intellectuality blends with skepticism, but it is a skepticism prepared to probe rather than to scoff. The eyes are aloof, almost disdainful, the nose large and imperious, the chin aggressive. Indeed, a first glance at this portrait gives the impression of a sneering countenance. Hulme dominated the group for the year of its existence, and when he left it, it fell apart. One night, over the spaghetti and the wine, there was a flare-up, and Hulme withdrew. Nothing more is heard of the other members, who neither then nor later set the Thames on fire.

But Hulme needed an outlet for his ideas, which he was continually jotting down—sentences, paragraphs, essays, all published posthumously since he, too, died in World War I. "Through all the ages, the conversation of ten men sitting together is what holds the world together," he noted. When he received an intelligent letter from a young poet he responded; their correspondence led to friendship, and the friendship to a new group.

Frank Stewart Flint was twenty-four years old—two years younger than Hulme—when they met. He knew a great many languages—one estimate says ten—and wrote French as fluently as English. Early in 1909 Hulme proposed to him that "a few congenial spirits" should

Mary Moore in a "Peter Thompson" dress

Mary Moore, with John Scudder, *circa* 1907

get together for weekly meetings in a Soho restaurant. This time it was to be on Thursdays.

The first meeting of the new brotherhood, which was never given a name, took place on March 25th. Hulme expounded his ideas: romanticism was dying, if not already dead. "We shall not get any new efflorescence of verse until we get a new technique, a new convention, to turn ourselves loose in." He foretold Eliot: "I prophesy that a period of dry, hard, classical verse is coming." He distinguished between vague Victorian emotions and the transference of experience from poet to reader: "Images in verse are not merely decoration, but the very essence of an intuitive language."[7]

In addition to a few minor mediocrities—I speak, of course, only of their verse—there were present, besides Hulme and Flint, the Irish poet, Joseph Campbell, and two of Flint's friends, Desmond Fitzgerald and Florence Farr, that scholarly woman and actress, whom Pound had met at a Yeats "evening." Elkin Mathews published that year *The Music of Speech* by her, with its interesting inscription: "I dedicate this book to W. B. Yeats, who suggested to me the notation of speech; also to Arnold Dolmetsch, who invented for me a musical instrument sympathetic to the speaking voice, calling it a psaltery."

Four weeks later—on April 22nd—Miss Farr introduced Pound, whose *Personae* had been published only six days before. He listened to the verses that were read; when it came his turn, he found that he had something in his pocket, something scheduled for publication in *The English Review*. "Damn it all! all this our South stinks peace," he began, not in the collegiate whisper recalled by Williams, but in organ tones—loud, full of quavers and vibrations which followed the snarl of the first line into the corners of the restaurant. Waiters stopped on their rounds, forks and spoons halted between tablecloth and chin, heads turned and astonished eyes stared. He read the whole of "Sestina: Altaforte."

He had identified himself with Bertran de Born quite thoroughly; in a later poem—"Near Perigord"—he even wonders if the troubadour had " a red straggling beard" and green eyes, like himself. It is, of course, possible—poets do have a way of resembling each other, even when they belong to different centuries.

Such was Pound's introduction to the group from which the Imagist movement sprang.

"The form of a poem is shaped by its intention," said and wrote Hulme. "Smoothness. Hate it. This is the obsession that starts all my theories."

"I want to maintain," he said and he wrote, "that after a hundred years of romanticism, we are in for a classical revival. . . . What I mean by classical in verse, then, is this. That even in the most imaginative flights there is always a holding back, a reservation. The classical poet never forgets this finiteness, this limit of man. He remembers always that he is mixed up with earth. He may jump, but he always returns back; he never flies away into the circumambient gas. . . . Hugo is always flying, flying over abysses, flying up into the eternal gases."

One of Hulme's own poems, which the Imagists were often to point to as the first example of the new mode, was entitled "Autumn" and follows in its entirety:

> A touch of cold in the Autumn night—
> I walked abroad,
> And saw the ruddy moon lean over a hedge
> Like a red-faced farmer.
> I did not stop to speak, but nodded,
> And round about were the wistful stars
> With white faces like town children.

The man who could express the thoughts above and write this poem was someone Pound could respect. But there was another side to him. John Cournos described Hulme to me as "big and overbearing." Flint termed Hulme "dangerous." Richard Aldington wrote: "Hulme had a coarse and cynical way of talking about women which repelled me." David Garnett gives chapter and verse: "Hulme would suddenly pull out his watch while a group of his acquaintances sat talking with him at a table in the Café Royal. 'I've a pressing engagement in five minutes' time,' he would say and stride out of the building. Twenty minutes later he would return, wipe his brow, and complain that the steel staircase of the emergency exit at Piccadilly Circus Tube Station was the most uncomfortable place in which he had ever copulated."[8]

His wit is more apparent in an incident related by Edward Marsh.

One day, Hulme was "making water" in Soho Square in broad daylight. A policeman approached, saying: "You can't do that here." Hulme replied: "Do you realize you're addressing a member of the middle class?" The policeman withdrew, murmuring, "Beg pardon, sir."

5.

The English Review had been dreamed up in Joseph Conrad's house in Leicestershire in 1908 by four men—Conrad himself; Arthur Marwood, who backed it, but not enough; H. G. Wells, and Joseph Leopold Ford Hermann Madox Hueffer, later Ford Madox Hueffer and —later still—Ford Madox Ford, the nominal editor, who once described himself, in Hokusai's manner, as "an Englishman a little mad about Good Letters." An office was rented at 84 Holland Park Avenue, the office being in reality a maisonette over a combination poulterer's and fishmonger's, and there the editor lived. A brown door, once the side entrance of the shop, bore now a plaque with "English Review, Ltd." in gilt letters. The plaque was over a bell, which no one used, the door being always open. Ford was nothing if not hospitable.

When Pound brought his poems there he saw, lining the stairs to the office, pre-Raphaelite portraits of Ford's aunt, Christina Rossetti; of his grandmother, Mrs. Ford Madox Brown; Rothenstein's portraits of Conrad and others; and here and there a photograph. There was a bathroom halfway up. The editorial office occupied the first floor, a long eighteenth-century drawing room, and there were a kitchen, dining room and two small bedrooms above. Ford was a good cook— some have said, a great one—and invitations to his dinners were prized as well as a godsend. He received visitors, as a rule, in a brown velvet coat that had belonged to Rossetti. He composed from time to time, and there was a large Broadwood piano in one corner, where Douglas Goldring found him one day, "humming a song and playing over the accompaniment" from a printed sheet.

"One of my few popular successes, my dear Goldring," said Ford mysteriously, getting up and shutting the piano.

There was also a Chippendale bureau on which, according to Ford, Christina Rossetti had written her poems, and a cabinet which he said had belonged to the Duke of Medina-Sidonia, and now was crammed with manuscripts.

Ford was a tall blond man with china-blue eyes set in a pink face. David Garnett speaks of "the rabbit teeth in his shark's mouth." Ford was already inclined to that stoutness and shortness of breath which were so marked in later years in Paris and New York, where I have seen him sitting on the very edge of a chair, gasping—like a frog, I could not help thinking—and emptying one tall glass after another as though they held naught but water, showing no effects, talking endlessly, tirelessly, but never boringly, everyone in the room standing around him or squatting on the floor to catch each word. He talked of his collaboration with Conrad, his friendship with James and Turgeniev, of all the giants before the flood, he being one of them, for it is as certain as anything can be that *The Good Soldier* is a masterpiece.

Mr. Marwood is not without interest for readers of this book. Violet Hunt has described him as "a dandy in London and a farmer in Kent," and Ford has projected him as Tietjens of Groby in his series of "Tietjens novels." He was also something of an expert in financial matters, and had worked out a plan, published in the first two issues of *The English Review,* "for insuring John Doe against all the vicissitudes of Life," and this plan, according to Goldring, "excited the imagination of Ezra Pound." Goldring also says that Marwood's proposals anticipated "to some extent" those of Major Douglas. In effect, the plan stipulated that every employer was to assure every employe of four hundred pounds a year "before being granted a license to start a company or build a factory." Marwood told Ford that it was "actuarially perfectly practicable."

The English Review published Hardy, whose poem, "A Sunday Morning Tragedy," leads off the first issue; Conrad, W. H. Hudson, Henry James, Galsworthy, Wells, Meredith and Arnold Bennett. And it also published "les jeunes" or "the haughty and proud generation," Ford's terms for the newcomers. One of them, in addition to Pound, was Wyndham Lewis, who came to the editorial office and found the editor in his tub between floors. Lewis improved the occasion by reading the story he had brought, and it was accepted. Thus it was that two of "the men of 1914"—Pound, Joyce, Eliot and Lewis himself—the phrase is his—were brought together through Ford, the other two being added by Pound.

As regards Ford's relations with his contributors, Goldring says that he became most intimate with Pound and Lewis. Goldring, who was assisting Ford, wrote:

"I was a bit suspicious of Ezra at first, and, though I am rather ashamed to admit it, perhaps a trifle jealous of him. He struck me as a bit of a charlatan, and I disliked the showy blue glass buttons on his coat; indeed, his whole operatic outfit of 'stage poet,' stemming from Murger and Puccini. . . . But one day I happened to see round Ezra's pince-nez, and noticed that he had curiously kind, affectionate eyes. This chance discovery altered my whole conception of him. Perhaps it reveals part of the secret of his hold over Ford. Ezra could be a friend, and not merely a fair-weather one."

Goldring has described both Pound and Lewis as they appeared at this time (he did not care for Lewis's get-up, either):

"Both Ezra (who was introduced to Ford by May Sinclair) and Wyndham Lewis, who introduced himself, made no secret of their calling, in clothes, hairdressing and manner. Ezra, with his mane of fair hair, his blond beard, his rimless pince-nez, his Philadelphia accent and his startling costume, part of which was a single turquoise ear-ring, contrived to look 'every inch a poet,' while I have never seen anyone so obviously a 'genius' as Wyndham Lewis. . . . tall, swarthy and with romantically disordered hair, wearing a long black coat buttoned up to his chin."[9]

D. H. Lawrence termed Ford "the first man I ever met who had a real and a true feeling for literature. He introduced me to Edward Garnett, who, somehow, introduced me to the world." First, however, Ford introduced Lawrence to *his* world. It was the end of November, 1909, that Lawrence and Jessie Chambers called at the flat in Holland Park and accompanied Ford to South Lodge, where they were to lunch. Pound was there when they arrived. He startled Miss Chambers "by springing to his feet and bowing from the waist with the stiff precision of a mechanical toy." The cooking, she says, was "excellent"—a joint, Brussels sprouts and plum pudding. "How the gravy ran down into the dish when Violet Hunt carved the joint, and the brussel sprouts I never had seen so perfectly cooked—each one sound and whole. Our hostess told us that the plum pudding was one from the Christmas before." There was also champagne. "The young American poet was the life of the party. He flung out observations in an abrupt way that reminded me of his poetry." One of them was in the form of a question to Miss Hunt: "Why do you give us solid stuff like roast beef and plum pudding for lunch?" He appears, from the accounts of this luncheon, to have behaved like a child to whom not enough attention is paid, for he now asked, according to Miss Chambers: "Shall I show you how an American eats an apple?" Whether or not anyone took him up, "he speared an apple with his knife, chopped it into quarters and gobbled it ostentatiously."

The ladies retired. "Presently the gentlemen came in. The American poet continued to rattle off his questions like a succession of squibs. Finally he put a question to Hueffer that electrified me.

" 'How would *you* speak to a working man?' he asked. 'Would you speak to him just the same as to any other man, or would you make a difference?' "

Miss Chambers held her breath, Hueffer hesitated, looked at her, then said: "I should speak to a working man in exactly the same way that I should speak to any other man, because I don't think there is any difference."[10]

Lawrence's revenge was a take-off. All commentators are agreed that he was a master at ludicrous imitation; David Garnett terms him "a natural copy-cat" and "the only great mimic I have ever known." "He had a genius for 'taking people off,' " Garnett wrote, "and could reproduce voice and manner exactly. He told you that he had once seen Yeats or Ezra Pound for half an hour in a drawing-room, and straightway Yeats or Pound appeared before you."[11]

There was an old and close association between the Garnett and Rossetti families, and young David—he was seventeen at the time— was sometimes invited to the parties at 84 Holland Park Avenue. He recalls one at which Pound and other poets competed for a crown of bay leaves by writing *bouts-rimés*. Dolly Radford won first prize, Hilaire Belloc the second. The winner, he recalled, "looked very much like an Italian painting in the crown of bay-leaves." Pound, uncrowned, wore a single ear-ring. Ford recalled his reading style thus: "Ah me, the darn, the darn it comes tue sune." His line combines Pound's and Swinburne's translations of the same Provençal poem.

The *Review*, under Ford's guidance, had only about a year to go when Pound submitted his work there. Sir Alfred Mond—*vide* Eliot's "A Cooking Egg"—purchased *The English Review* for political purposes; he and Ford did not see eye to eye, and Ford went.[12]

He had other difficulties. His wife would not divorce him, and he was in love with Violet Hunt, whom Henry James adored until he heard of her liaison, and then he would not let her call at Lamb House. Garnett's description is a close-up: "Violet Hunt was a thin viperish-looking beauty with a long pointed chin and deep-set, burning brown eyes under hooded lids. There was a driving force within her, which I afterwards recognized as insatiable ambition." His father did not like her, either. Miss Hunt was the daughter of the pre-Raphaelite water-colorist, Alfred Hunt. Her mother had been the friend of Browning, of the Rossettis, of Ruskin, and of Ford Madox Brown, Joseph Leopold's grandfather, who was also an intimate friend of her father's. So they had met as children. They met again at a dinner in John Galsworthy's house. She, too, was now a writer. They walked back together along the Kensington Road, "talking of pre-Raphael-itism and the price of copper." She did not see him again for a year. Then Wells sent her to the office of *The English Review*.

And so Pound met her, too. She wrote:

"We had tennis in the garden nearly every afternoon while my mother, in the white Chuddah shawl that is the uniform of old-ladyhood, looked on at a foursome, say, between Mr. Hugh Walpole and Ezra Pound and two beauties, Amber Reeves and Kitty Rome. The young American poet played like a demon or a trick pony, sitting down composedly in his square and jumping up in time to receive his adversary's ball, which he competently returned, the flaps of his polychrome shirt flying out like the petals of some flower and his red head like a flaming pistil in the middle of it."

She wrote almost two decades later, and wrote of him with un-diminished affection: "Ezra, a dear, lived near us, and was in and out all day. He was very kind to the editor, and would do any sort of job for him or me, using up his intense and feverish energy in taking down winged words at dictation, or tying up my creeper for me. He would wear my Connemara cloak or the editor's old Rossetti coat—any old covering—with serenity."[13] But what he wore, according to Ford, was "trousers made of green billiard cloth, a pink coat, a blue shirt, a tie hand-painted by a Japanese friend, an immense sombrero, a flaming beard cut to a point, and a single large blue ear-ring."[14] (But see p. 149.) As for the stick Pound always carried, Ford says Ezra would approach "with the step of a dancer, making passes with a cane at an imaginary opponent."

The garden was a part of South Lodge, on Campden Hill, where Ford had gone to live with Miss Hunt and her mother. Later, to lend an even greater air of respectability, Ford persuaded his sister-in-law, and even his mother, to live there. When Ford was afterwards "detained at his Majesty's pleasure for a week," for failure to keep up with his alimony payments, his friends, wrote Violet Hunt, "took it all as a joke. Ezra Pound, from Lago di Garda, called him the Apostle in Bonds, and perpetrated shocking parodies on the comic event in the style of 'The Ballad of Reading Gaol.'" She does not give an example; perhaps it was like the doggerel he wrote for his father after graduating from Penn. He was more comforting close at hand. The following year, when Ford went over to Germany to see if he could not regain German citizenship, in order to get a divorce there, Pound went with him, "rushing about the duchy that he [Ford] desired to adopt him, and other duchies, in cars."

Because there were several months to wait before he could enter the Imperial College, David Garnett also went to Germany. Through Ford's efforts he was accepted, as a paying guest, in the house of the widow of a Prussian major. The family consisted of the widow, her mother, and two sons, both in uniform. Their name was Heider. Garnett was asked if he wished to accompany the family to Mass or, if he was a Protestant, they would direct him to the Lutheran church. It did not occur to him to say that he was Church of England, which would have solved everything; he replied, instead, that he was neither Catholic nor Protestant. The Heiders pondered this for twenty-four hours, then asked if he were a Jew.

"Unfortunately, I did not recognize the word and was not expecting the question, and my reply: 'What is a Jew? *Was ist dann ein Jude?*' failed to convince and appeared like an admission. A rapid-fire discussion followed in which Ferdinand, with legal acumen, pointed out that David was a Jewish name and garnet a semi-precious stone.

"These points were put to me. I admitted the name David was Jewish and explained that it was that of my maternal grandfather [who was a Scotsman], but I flatly denied that Garnett was Jewish or that my name indicated that I was a Jew.

" 'But are you not a Jew?' the Heiders yelped at me in chorus. 'If you are not a Jew, why do you read Heine?' asked Lieutenant Heider."

Ford's titled great-aunt saved the day.

"His great-aunt was socially vastly superior to the Heiders and had invited me to tea. So my persecution as a Jew was called off."[15]

He was eighteen years old.

The soil was ready.

6.

From Germany, where he had taken a postgraduate course, came Dr. William Carlos Williams—April, 1910. He found his friend in the Church Walk flat and in "his most romantic period," as he was to term it. The room struck him as very small. "You could touch all the walls standing in the middle of it," he told me. It was there that he observed, with an astonishment that lingered, Pound's coffee-making ritual. It was "the only way" to make coffee, Pound told him. Williams found it "strong and good."

"He really lived the poet as few of us had the nerve to live that exalted reality in our time," Williams once wrote me; and I have, from the same communication, an earlier version of an incident related in the *Autobiography*. The two friends had set out from Pound's room, Pound garbed in a broad-brimmed hat and a fur-lined overcoat which he also wore indoors against the cold. "We were passing a church in Kensington with a high, spiked fence around it. On the pavement before us lay a very much battered bunch of violets dropped no doubt by some child or lady. After a step or two Ezra stopped, turned back, raised the flowers with a great show from their neglected position and placed them honored upon the iron fence-rail. We moved on, he insisting on being one step in advance of me as always."

In retelling this incident Williams failed to mention Pound's walking ahead, like a German husband; in the account he sent me he had added: "I remember my brother once in the same situation turned and walked off in the opposite direction." There was also a scene in a restaurant; Williams tried to help Pound on with his coat, but Pound rebuffed him and called the waiter to perform this service. There was a scene in the National Gallery, where a mild sort of flirtation took place between Pound and a young woman "of exceptional attractiveness, a tall, rather wan creature." Pound, wrote Williams, "postured, leaning back on his cane (did he have a cane? perhaps not), his legs apart, his pointed beard atilt, and stared steadily toward her. She, on her part, conscious of his position, began to move her thighs and pelvis in such a way that it became very apparent that she was thoroughly conscious of what was going on. She turned her head away, but it was plain that she was greatly moved and excited."

Nothing came of it.

The flirtation notwithstanding, Pound—Williams told me—"was very much in love with someone whose picture he kept on his dresser, with a candle perpetually lighted before it. He never explained who she was." She was probably Dorothy Shakespear, for in that same April week in 1910 Pound introduced Williams to her and her mother, and he went with them to meet Yeats at 18 Woburn Buildings.

It was a Monday evening. They were ushered into a dimly lighted room where Yeats was reading Dowson's "Cynara" to a small group of Abbey actors and actresses. He read "very impressively," Williams told me, making a face over the poem. In his *Autobiography* he explained, "it was not my dish," and added: "After a while, never even having been greeted, we got up to leave," but just as they were at the door, Yeats called out to Mrs. Shakespear: "Was that Ezra Pound? Tell him to wait—I want to talk to him."

Nothing is known of the exchange that took place between the two poets, Pound as usual being close-mouthed where his own affairs were concerned. They had already met. In a letter to Lady Gregory dated December 10, 1909, Yeats has a reference—the first in his correspondence—to "this queer creature Ezra Pound, who has become really a great authority on the troubadours [and] has I think got closer to the right sort of music for poetry than Mrs. Emery [Florence Farr]—it is more definitely music with strong marked time and yet it is effective speech. However he can't sing as he has no voice. It is like something on a very bad phonograph."

Yeats himself was tone-deaf.

Williams was lucky, although he chose to think otherwise. Many a visitor who came to Yeats's flat to hear poetry read or discussed heard, instead, spiritualism and mysticism expounded, which was not at all the same thing. Sometimes he took his friends to séances where, in eerie darkness and other spiritualistic hocus-pocus, they were exquisitely bored. Yeats recorded his disappointments as well as confirmations. The following is from his manuscript book:

"Last Monday Madame ———— said that she would die, (disappear was the word), between Dec. 2nd and Dec. 5th next. Pound and Sturge Moore present."

He left space beneath this, and awaited the event. A year later he wrote:

"NO, Madame ———— is in excellent health."

7.

It was probably through Yeats that Pound met another member— and founder—of the Rhymers' Club of the Nineties, Ernest Rhys, who was characterized by Lionel Johnson as one who was "best in Celtic things of the gentler sort and in a kind of shy and reverent love-poetry." At the Rhys house in Hermitage Lane there were often literary suppers and readings, "resuming the nights at the Old Cheshire Cheese of the Rhymers' Club." On one such night—"the most memorable," Rhys termed it—Ford Madox Ford brought D. H. Lawrence. "Ford always had the air of a man-about-town used to town occasions, while Lawrence looked shy and countrified; perhaps a little overwhelmed by the fanfaron of fellow poets heard in the room, with W. B. Yeats and Ezra Pound dominating the chorus."

Miss Farr was also there; she had come, "carrying a psaltery, for she had lately been practising a mode of intoning verse to that monotonous instrument. During the supper, Yeats, always a good monologuer, held forth at length on this new way of bringing music and poetry together, and possibly Ezra Pound, who could also be vocal on occasion, may have felt he was not getting a fair share of the fun. So, in order to pass the time perhaps, and seeing the supper table dressed with red tulips, he presently took one of the flowers and proceeded to munch it. As Yeats, absorbed in his monologue, did not observe this strange behaviour, and the rest of us were too well-bred to take any notice, Ezra, having found the tulip to his taste, did likewise with a second flower."

When Mrs. Rhys told this story to Iris Barry about five years later, "with reminiscent affection but not without a trace of the consternation natural at the time," the tulips had become roses, Pound had refused all offers of food, but snatched instead a handful of petals and carefully ate them. Then, as they were about to get up from the supper table, he emptied a carafe of water at a single draught and "flung himself full-length upon a sofa where he reclined, gurgling." The prophet Ezra also ate flowers (2 Esdras 9:26).

After supper, most of the poets present read their verses aloud. Yeats declined to read "The Lake Isle of Innisfree," and read instead the poem beginning "She lived in storm and strife." Ford read a burlesque sonnet, and Lawrence, once started, could not be made to stop. Mrs. Rhys appealed to her husband: "What am I to do?" He replied: "Tell him he must want a little rest."

"And now Ezra Pound, fortified, if anything, by the tulips, started up, asking if we minded 'having the roof taken off the house?' He went on to declaim in a resonant, histrionic voice, a little like Henry Irving with an American accent, his imaginative 'Ballad of the Goodly Fere.'"

Someone asked Pound where he had "dug up the fearsome word 'Fere.'" A discussion followed, and it was agreed that every poet had "a right to make his own dialect." The evening was topped by Miss Farr's performance on the psaltery, to Yeats's poem, "The Man Who Dreamed of Fairyland." Only Yeats was pleased.[16]

Pound was meeting everyone:

> Swinburne my only miss
> and I didn't know he'd been to see Landor
>   *and* they told me this that an' tother
> and when old Mathews went he saw the three teacups
>   two for Watts Dunton who liked to let his tea cool,
> So old Elkin had only one glory
>   He did carry Algernon's suit case *once*
> when he, Elkin, first came to Lond.

But given what I know now I'd have
got thru it somehow. . . .

(Canto LXXXII)

8.

Shortly after Williams left London for the United States, Pound
received, from the Alumni Catalogue Committee of the University
of Pennsylvania, a four-page form requesting information "as full
as would be required for a complete biographical dictionary," although
the committee did not contemplate such a volume "at the present time;
but the purpose is to preserve material collected in such permanent
form as to make it available for future use." I now make use of it,
having found it in a battered box, stuffed with odds and ends, in
the University archives.

Under "Occupation since leaving the University. Positions held
(business, professional or honorary), with dates," Pound wrote in
a clear, bold hand: "Lecturer to Regent St. Polytechnic. London,"
without dates, and beneath this, "Author." He then gave his publications, "1909 'Personae' (poems) 1909 'Exultations' (poems)," and
under these titles, which are on one line, "about to appear, 'The Spirit
of Romance.'" (*The Spirit of Romance* was published on June 20,
1910.)

His name, and the names of his parents, together with his father's
designation, "Asst. Assayer, U.S. Mint, Phila., Pa.," were already
written in on the form; Pound crossed out his middle names—
"Weston Loomis"—with broad diagonal strokes from left to right,
and with the same bold strokes—there are seven of them in this
line—crossed out his address—"10 Church Wall, Kensington W.
London England"—and wrote in the left-hand margin, after loop-
ing his name to his father's: "care of." He was homeward bound.

One additional matter seems worth calling attention to, for Pound
called it to the attention of the alumni committee. On the last page
of the four-page form, which was blank, he pasted the leaflet put
out by Elkin Mathews, which announced as "Now ready. Foolscap
8vo, 2*s*. 6*d*. net" the volume entitled *Exultations of Ezra Pound,*
"uniform with *Personae*," with the four reviews of the latter, pre-

viously given. It is not to be wondered at that Pound wished this precious leaflet to be wafted to the groves of academe, for the academicians to ponder, and he glued it on so firmly that it is still there.

That summer of 1910 Harriet Monroe passed through London on her way around the world—"from Chicago to Chicago." She did not meet Pound, who was in the United States; but May Sinclair took her to Elkin Mathews's shop on Vigo Street, where she was introduced to the proprietor. "Mathews," she wrote later, "was vividly enthusiastic about the work of a young American in London, Ezra Pound. 'That is real poetry!' he exclaimed, as he showed me the *Personae* and *Exultations*; so I bought the tiny volumes, and later beguiled the long Siberian journey with the strange and beautiful rhythms of this new poet, my self-exiled compatriot."[17]

CHAPTER III

THE POET IN NEW YORK

1.

Pound arrived in the United States famous, as was to be the case with Frost several years later, and for the same reason: publication in England accompanied by the highest praise, which was echoed in American publications. He spent several months in Wyncote with his parents, then went to New York to live. He returned Williams's call, visiting him in Rutherford with Hilda Doolittle. "Floss was not at ease with either of them, but we all got along together more or less." Williams was engaged to Floss—Florence Herman—whom he married in 1912. Pound came again, this time alone. "The Hermans had us to supper one night with wine, Rudesheimer 1905, I think. Ezra, in an excess of enthusiasm, knowing New Jersey's reputation, stood on his chair at table to kill a mosquito on the ceiling."[1] He came again, this time with a book, which he left behind. More irritation.

It appears that both young men read their latest poems, without impressing each other, and worse, incensing Williams's father. Both caught it hard, but Pound harder. "Idle nonsense," said Mr. Williams, dismissing his son's lucubrations. As for Pound and a particular poem—"What in heaven's name did you mean by 'jewels'?" he demanded. (Williams lists them as "rubies, sapphires, amethysts and what not.") Pound explained he meant the backs of books as they gleamed on the shelf. "But why in heaven's name don't you say so then?" His son terms it a "triumphant and crushing rejoinder."

It is curious to reflect that the scene here described occurs in a book Williams wrote with Pound's encouragement if not direct assistance. *Kora in Hell: Improvisations*—"I am indebted to Pound for the title"—is a collection of random jottings with interpretations beneath. "I was groping around to find a way to include the interpretations when I came upon a book Pound had left in the house, *Varie Poesie* dell' Abate Pietro Metastasio, Venice, 1795. I took the method used by the Abbot of drawing a line to separate my material."

Pound's recollection, ten years later, when *Kora in Hell* appeared, was:

"Re the dialog. with your old man, which I don't bloody remember . . . remember we did talk about 'Und Drang' but there the sapphires certainly are NOT anything but sapphires, perfectly definite visual imagination."

The seventh poem of the series entitled "Und Drang" in *Canzoni* has these lines:

> And I have seen her there within her house
> With six great sapphires hung along the wall. . . .

In *I Wanted to Write a Poem*, Williams retells this incident in somewhat terser form. "Pop said, 'If you mean that, why don't you say it?'" Pop served "goldwasser," and the dispute was forgotten. (But not the "goldwasser.")

"He liked my father very much. My mother? I suppose he was conscious of her. He allowed her to exist."

Pound not only "allowed" Mrs. Williams "to exist"—he listened to her, for he began his long essay in *The Dial* about her son by quoting her:

"There is an anecdote told me by his mother, who wished me to understand his character, as follows: The young William Carlos, aged let us say about seven, arose in the morning, dressed and put on his shoes. Both shoes buttoned on the left side. He regarded this untoward phenomenon for a few moments and then carefully removed the shoes, placed shoe *a* that had been on his left foot, on his right foot, and shoe *b*, that had been on his right foot, on his left foot; both sets of buttons again appeared on the left side of the shoes.

"This stumped him. With the shoes so buttoned he went to school, but . . . and here is the significant part of the story, he spent the day in careful consideration of the matter."[2]

The friendship between Pound and Williams is unique for its duration, its more than a half century of indestructible affection, its triumphs over disagreements which are usually fatal between creators. Williams, it may be useful to point out, is the only individual in Pound's life who ever stood up to him, and kept his friendship.

2.

In New York, Pound lived at 270 Fourth Avenue (now Park Avenue South: why?) at the northwest corner of Twenty-first Street directly across from Calvary Episcopal Church and half a block from Gramercy Park. He was greatly stirred by the city, which he explored for the first time. He was struck by the vitality of the American people. He was to write a great deal about it; in fact, almost all that is known of his New York sojourn is related by himself in the essay he wrote in London on his return, afterwards—thirty-seven years afterwards— a book, *Patria Mia.* He also paid some social calls. He saw Warren Dahler, a painter who lived on Patchin Place, mentioned in the *Cantos;* Carlton Glidden, another painter, who lived God knows where, and is not mentioned in the *Cantos*; and Katherine Ruth Heyman, who was living at the Judson Hotel on Washington Square South. Prokofiev was a frequent visitor to her studio, and Pound may have heard him play there. Miss Heyman was now interested in Buddhism, and he may have met in her company the founder of the first Buddhist church in New York.

Social calls aside, he was astonished; delighted a few times; indignant most of the time. Let us follow him as he plunges into the never-ending human stream of O. Henry's Bagdad-on-the-Subway:

"I see also a sign in the surging crowd on Seventh Avenue. A crowd pagan as ever imperial Rome was, eager, careless, with an animal vigour unlike that of any European crowd that I have ever looked at. There is none of the melancholy, the sullenness, the unhealth of the London mass, none of the worn vivacity of Paris. I do not believe it is the temper of Vienna.

"One returns from Europe and one takes note of the size and

vigour of this new strange people. They are not Anglo-Saxon; their gods are not the gods whom one was reared to reverence. And one wonders what they have to do with lyric measures and the nature of 'quantity.'

"One knows they are the dominant people and that they are against all delicate things. They will never imagine beautiful plaisaunces. They will never 'sit on a middan and dream stars,' as the Irish peasant said to Joseph Campbell.

"This new metropolitan has his desire sated before it is aroused. Electricity has for him made the seeing of visions superfluous. There is the sham fairyland at Coney Island, and, however sordid it is when one is in it, it is marvelous against the night as one approaches or leaves it. And the city itself about him, Manhattan! Has it not buildings that are Egyptian in their contempt of the unit?"

He liked Pennsylvania Station and the Metropolitan Life Tower, even though "the 'campanile' form has been obsolete for some centuries," watchtowers being no longer needed. A building nearer home he admired only partly: "There is on Gramercy Park, and in sight of what were my windows, a candid and new building. Its ground plan is the shape you would have if you took three rows of three squares each, on a checkerboard and then removed the middle square of the front row. And as the indenture is in shadow, one seems, in looking down Twenty-first Street and across the square, to see two twin towers. And this also is a delightful use of the campanile motif. But the ass who built it has set a round water-tank just where it spoils the sky line. And for the next three decades nothing will prevent this sort of imbecility."

Nothing has, for five.

He was critical of the New York Public Library. With him, to be critical was to act. He went to the office of the architect. "I found it impossible to make a younger member of the architect's firm understand any of this"—the "hideous" shape of the roof, the violation of "the basic principle of art which demands that the artist consider from what angle and elevation his work is to be seen," in this case from above, the library being surrounded by tall buildings.

He went down to the harbor and looked back at the city. Next to him stood a huge Irishman. "He tried vainly to express himself by repeating, 'It uccedes Lundun, It uccedes Lundun.' I have seen Cadiz from the water. The thin, white lotus beyond a dazzle of blue. I know somewhat of cities. The Irishman thought of size alone. I thought of the beauty, and beside it Venice seems like a tawdry scene in a playhouse. New York is out of doors.

"And as for Venice: when Mr. Marinetti and his friends shall have succeeded in destroying that ancient city, we will rebuild Venice on the Jersey mud flats and use the same for a tea-shop."

He wondered if New York were not the most beautiful city in the world. "It is not far from it. No urban nights are like the nights there. I have looked across the city from high windows. It is then that the great buildings lose reality and take on their magical powers. They are immaterial; that is to say one sees but the lighted windows."[3]

He wrote a poem:

> My City, my beloved,
> Thou art a maid with no breasts,
> Thou art slender as a silver reed.
> Listen to me, attend me!
> And I will breathe into thee a soul,
> And thou shalt live for ever.

All the same, he left her.

As for Coney Island, he went there with John Butler Yeats, father of the poet, who had settled permanently in New York, and John Quinn, lawyer and art patron, who entertained both in his apartment on Central Park West. Yeats's portrait by his father hung on the wall, as did pictures by the Irish poet and painter George Russell (AE). Soon the apartment was to be crowded with the books, manuscripts, drawings, paintings and sculpture of Pound's friends.

Pound afterwards wrote Quinn: "I have still a very clear recollection of Yeats père on an elephant (at Coney Island), smiling like Elijah in the beatific vision, and of you plugging away in the shooting gallery. And a very good day it was." J. B. Yeats wrote his son, February 11, 1911, from New York:

"Have you met Ezra Pound? Carlton Glidden, an artist of talent who has a lot to learn, but who is a very nice fellow indeed, told me to-day that Ezra Pound was at his studio a few days ago and talked a lot about you, quoting quantities of your verse, which he

had by heart, placing you very high, and as the best poet for the
last century and more. I tell you this as he is going in a few days to
Europe to stay in Paris, etc. Quinn met him and liked him very
much. The Americans, young literary men, whom I know found him
surly, supercilious and grumpy. I liked him myself very much, that
is, I liked his look and air, and the few things he said, for tho' I was
a good while in his company he said very little."[4]

                                3.

Pound's favorite haunt while living on Fourth Avenue was the Little
Book Shop Around the Corner, across the street from the church
with the similar name near Fifth Avenue on Twenty-Ninth Street.
Laurence J. Gomme, the English proprietor, remembers Pound
dropping in—"walking in with gusto," as he put it—"and spreading
himself over a chair. He was very informally dressed, dark shirt, loose
tie, definitely bohemian, with very heavy sideburns." Pound told
Gomme about his teaching in England, but did not talk about his
own work. The shop drew other writers, and one day—Pound usually
came in around noon—Gomme heard him holding forth on early
French forms, and in the discussion that followed "being sharply
critical of others' remarks." He was a leisurely talker, Gomme said.
Among the writers whom Pound met there were Orrick Johns, Joyce
Kilmer and Harry Kemp. (One day, about two years later, Kemp
came into the bookshop and told Gomme he was sailing to England
"that very day." He had under his arm a newspaper-wrapped parcel
—his luggage. He was stowing away.)

In addition to his exploration of the city Pound examined the
publications that appeared in it. He concluded that "all editors who
are not by nature and inclination essentially base, do, by any continuing practice of their trade become so." The conclusion may have
been based on personal experience. He mentions names: "It is well
known that in the year of grace 1870 Jehovah appeared to Messrs.
Harper and Co. and to the editors of 'The Century,' 'The Atlantic,'
and certain others, and spake thus: 'The style of 1870 is the final
and divine revelation. Keep things always as they are now.'" He
paraphrases a letter of rejection: " 'Dear Mr. ———, Your work,

etc., is very interesting, etc. etc., but you will have to pay more attention to conventional form if you want to make a commercial success of it.' " He admits that "at twenty I should have counted it some honour to have been printed in the 'Atlantic.' There are any number of young people in America who know no better." He warns such, though "young, unknown and in poverty," that they "can not interrupt, afford to interrupt a life-work to earn doles of 25 dollars."

He returned to the attack: "There is no interest whatever in the art of poetry, as a living art, an art changing and developing, always the same at root, never the same in appearance for two decades in succession."

He found something to praise: "in the composition of advertisements there is some attention paid to a living and effective style. Wherever there is an immediate ratio between action and profit the American will at once develop his faculties." He summed up: "Yet it is the glory of a nation to achieve art which can be exported without bringing dishonour on its origin. Letters are a nation's foreign office. By the arts, and by them alone do nations gain for each other any understanding and immediate respect. It is the patriotism of the artist, and it is almost the only civic duty allowed him."[5]

He brought back with him a plan for a college of the arts. He wrote in *Patria Mia*: "I respect the founders of our academy in Rome, who subsidise ten artists, to stay there and study and work together. But there should be a respectable college of the arts in New York (or Chicago, or San Francisco, or in all three), a college of one hundred members, chosen from all the arts, sculptors, painters, dramatists, musical composers, architects, scholars of the art of verse, engravers, etc., and they should be fed there during the impossible years of the artist's life—i.e., the beginning of the creative period.

"As it is you can, in the United States, get subsidised for 'research,' you can make a commentary on Quinet and draw pay for three years doing it, or you can write learnedly on 'ablauts' with similar result."

He visualized his college as not unlike a graduate school, but its cost "a trifle in comparison to the funds used in endowment of universities in which the system of instruction is already obsolescent, whenever it has concern with anything save utilitarian knowledge." He actually drew up the "constitution" of such a college.

"I tried vainly to get it printed when I was last in New York."

He was to return to the subject. The direction that his life took is inextricably bound up with this "passion to teach"—Eliot's phrase.

4.

There is a final glimpse of him in New York.

The scene is the National Arts Club on Gramercy Park, the occasion one of the first public meetings of the newly formed Poetry Society of America. It is possible that Witter Bynner brought Pound there, although the invitation may have come from the Society whose printed records, unfortunately, start later. Jessie B. Rittenhouse, who was present, recalled that Bynner was the reader of the evening— that is, he read the poems which members had submitted—anonymously—for open discussion; in this, Pound took part. Among those read was "Helen of Troy" by Sara Teasdale.

"Just back of her sat Ezra Pound, on his one and only visit to the Society, as he was about to sail for England, being unable longer to 'bear the brunt of America.' I fancy this was the last public gathering at which Ezra was seen in New York, as he left so soon after for what proved to be his continuous expatriation.

"Surely no one could have been more charming, more boyish, more delightfully provocative than Ezra that night. Young and handsome, with his mass of golden-brown hair, his keen, merry eyes, his careless ease of dress—I can see him now sitting near the front, in the end of the seat by the wall, where he could, by turning, face both sections of the audience."[6]

Miss Rittenhouse does not give the year, and Mr. Bynner wrote me "that dates are mounts which jump out from under me and I usually have to clear fences without them." Bynner met Pound in the summer of 1910—that straw hat! and the arrangements for the publication of *Provença*; and the Poetry Society began to meet in 1911. Pound was back in London in the spring or summer of that year; but first he went to Venice. In London he resumed where he had left off—friends, writing, correspondence, and the flat at 10 Church Walk. Hilda Doolittle came to London that fall, and early in 1912 Pound met Richard Aldington at the home of Mrs. Deighton Patmore.[7] A new circle was in the making, and his attractive personality and single-mindedness of purpose made Pound the natural leader of it.

5.

With his resettlement in England the long period of expatriation began. He was not to see the United States again for twenty-eight years—in 1939—and then only on a brief visit. He lost touch. But, unlike James and Eliot, who became British subjects, Pound remained unreconstructedly, disconcertingly American. Even his speech did not undergo that transmogrification which has invariably affected other long-term residents and Rhodes Scholars from the States. It never changed; the English always saw Pound as an American. Wyndham Lewis, who knew him early, has recalled him when they first met as an "uncomfortably tensed, nervously straining, jerky, reddish-brown young American," and stresses the American side of him, it being, he wrote, "of primary significance where his personality is concerned."[8]

But to another early friend, the fact that Pound left his native country and stayed abroad outweighs the very obvious fact that he remained an American. Williams wrote me:

"Ezra is one of a well recognized group of Americans who can't take the democratic virus and stand up under it, very distinguished men most of them who owe their distinction largely to their American origins. They owe their overall genius, of course, to their immediate ancestry, such traits as appeared both in William and Henry James. But with the artist, and we are speaking of the artist in this case, the distinguishing genus of their characteristics has been definitely the environment, the fact of their new world origins—from which they recoil.

"Pitiful to relate, revulsion is invariably the type of reaction they suffer. No use to go into further detail, it is common. And I for one believe that had they remained nearer to the fountain which gave them originally their power to go abroad and develop their traits, even in the case of Henry James—their work would have assumed more impressive proportions. Nor am I blind to the knowledge that had they not gone abroad, they might have perished. I think they could have lived it out here somehow without perishing."

Dr. Williams is, as usual, forceful and persuasive. But is he right? Each man does what he must do, and whatever happens, he becomes himself in the process—not someone else. James's justification is the body of his work; it will be so with Pound. Pound did not benefit himself alone by remaining an expatriate. His services to American —and English—letters will shortly receive the exposition they deserve. A lasting consciousness of America's destiny, a deep concern for its place in the world as a new seat of culture, nevertheless make Pound's exile a paradox. America was constantly in his thoughts. In *Patria Mia* he declared:

"I believe in the immanence of an American Renaissance."

" 'Renaissance' is not *le mot juste*, but it has come by usage to mean almost any sort of awakening. 'Risvegliamento' would be the better term if one must stick to Italian."

He returned to Whitman:

"Whitman established the national *timbre*. One may not need him at home. It is in the air, this tonic of his. But if one is abroad; if one is ever likely to forget one's birthright, to lose faith, being surrounded by disparagers, one can find, in Whitman, the reassurance. Whitman goes bail for the nation."[9]

He also paid homage to James and Whistler:

"I have taken deep delight in the novels of Mr. Henry James, I have gathered from the loan exhibit of Whistler's paintings now at the Tate (September, 1912), more courage for living than I have gathered from the Canal Bill or from any other manifest American energy whatsoever.

"And thereanent I have written some bad poetry and burst into several incoherent conversations, endeavoring to explain what that exhibit means to the American artist."[10]

TO WHISTLER, AMERICAN

On the loan exhibit of his paintings at the Tate Gallery

You also, our first great,
Had tried all ways;
Tested and pried and worked in many fashions,
And this much gives me heart to play the game.

Here is a part that's slight, and part gone wrong,
And much of little moment, and some few
Perfect as Dürer!
"In the Studio" and these two portraits,* if I had my choice!
And then these sketches in the mood of Greece?

You had your searches, your uncertainties,
And this is good to know—for us, I mean,
Who bear the brunt of our America
And try to wrench her impulse into art.

You were not always sure, not always set
To hiding night or tuning "symphonies";
Had not one style from birth, but tried and pried
And stretched and tampered with the media.

You and Abe Lincoln from that mass of dolts
Show us there's chance at least of winning through.

Although he depreciated the poem he sent it to Harriet Monroe,
and it appeared in the first number of *Poetry: A Magazine of Verse.*
The two final lines were widely resented. The poem was not included
in any of his books until 1949, when it was added to *Personae* under
"early poems."

He was right to depreciate it—it is not a good poem. Is it a poem
at all? But as personal history, as a rather large footnote on the text
of his life at this time, it is valuable. Whistler, who died in 1903,
who had more than held his own against Wilde and Ruskin, was
more than merely a symbol of the artist in exile: he was a living presence, still spoken of by men and women who had known him, an
American who was an acknowledged master. Perhaps Pound saw himself as another Whistler, in another medium. He was photographed
in a profile pose, seated, with draped cloak falling away from his
shoulders, like Whistler's portrait of Carlyle.

* "Brown and Gold—de Race." "Grenat et Or—Le Petit Cardinal." (Pound's
footnote.)

CHAPTER IV

THE POET AND HIS BOOKS

1.

Between 1910 and 1912 Pound published four books. One has been mentioned: *The Spirit of Romance*. Two were books of verse, and the fourth *The Sonnets and Ballate of Guido Cavalcanti*.

The title page of *The Spirit of Romance* describes the book as "an attempt to define somewhat the charm of the pre-Renaissance literature of Latin Europe by Ezra Pound, M.A." He had already attempted this, of course, in his lectures at the Regent Street Polytechnic. He had also lectured privately; Aldington has an account of a talk Pound gave on Provençal poetry in Lady Glenconner's drawing room. Housman's friend, Professor W. P. Ker, was present. "His wrinkled and slightly acid face seemed petrified with incredulous astonishment."[1] Pound was not crazy about Ker, either.[2] But whatever his lectures may have been like with their—if Aldington is to be believed—"I mean to say" and "what I mean is, er-er"—the book is prime scholarship. Nor has half a century dimmed the charm of his homage to Lope de Vega, Villon, the troubadors cited by Dante, including Bertran de Born; Dante himself, and Arnault Daniel, whom Dante had praised as "il miglior fabbro"—"the better craftsman"— a term Eliot was later to apply to Pound.

Pound wrote in the preface: "The aim of the present work is to instruct. Its ambition is to instruct painlessly." He remembered his own instructor: "My thanks are due to Dr. William Pierce Shepard

72

of Hamilton College, whose refined and sympathetic scholarship first led me to some knowledge of French, Italian, Spanish and Provençal." He acknowledged the encouragement received from his editor: "Some stigma will doubtless attach to Mr. Ernest Rhys, at whose instigation the present volume was undertaken. Guilty of collusion, he is in no way responsible for its faults." Most important: "Certain portions of the book are in the strictest sense original research. Throughout the book all critical statements are based on a direct study of the texts themselves and not upon commentaries."

In a postscript added in 1929 he declared: "I have no doubt that the work could be greatly improved, but one kind of improvement would falsify at least one of the measurements, the main difference of outlook being simply that I then knew less and had more patience." It is a "young" book, of gathered knowledge which intuition illuminates; a true marriage, like a spring wind that cannot move except the light move with it.[3]

It is interesting to note that he everywhere writes "Shakespear" without the terminal "e": "Shakespear alone of the English poets endures sustained comparison with the Florentine. Here are we with the masters; of neither can we say, 'He is the greater'; of each we must say, 'He is unexcelled.'" But it is Dante who pervades this book. "Villon's poetry seems, when one comes directly from the *Paradiso,* more vital, more vivid; but if Dante restrains himself, putting the laments in the mouths of tortured spirits, they are not the less poignant. He stands behind his characters, of whom Villon might have made one." Again: "Dante is many men, and suffers as many. Villon cries out as one. He is a lurid canto of the *Inferno,* written too late to be included in the original text."

The Spirit of Romance was published by J. M. Dent and Company in an edition of 1,250 copies, bound in cloth, price six shillings. Three hundred copies were imported by E. P. Dutton and Company and sold in New York at $2.50, a price which rather appalled Pound when he was there. He wrote John Quinn from London:

"Henry IV took off the octroi from books coming into Paris some centuries since, because they made for the increase of learning, and it is high time America followed suit. The absurd tariff (25% it was) *and* the egregious price the American booksellers stick on a foreign book, unnecessarily, 'because of the tariff,' are just enough to prevent

sales. Example, I caught a publisher selling my *Spirit of Romance* at
2 ½ dollars. No fool would pay that for a six shilling book. Besides,
that damn swindler had bought the book at 3 shillings by special
arrangement so as to be able to sell it at the English price (I being
paid at 3/)."

He had also written to President Wilson to protest the duty on
books, this being the first instance on record of a letter by him to the
head of a state.

2.

Guido Cavalcanti is another of the poets praised by his fellow Florentine who was his "first friend," later his enemy, and who alone of
the Italian poets surpassed him. Both belonged to the group of poets
known as the *stilnovisti*, from *dolce stil novo*, the "sweet new style,"
which was metaphysical. In *The Spirit of Romance* Pound said:
"Dante himself never wrote more poignantly, or with greater intensity
than Cavalcanti." In *The Sonnets and Ballate*[4] he enlarged upon this:
"Than Guido Cavalcanti no psychologist of the emotions is more
keen in his understanding, more precise in his expression; we have
in him no rhetoric, but always a true description, whether it be of
pain itself, or of the apathy that comes when the emotions and possibilities of emotion are exhausted." He thought Dino Compagni's
description of Cavalcanti apt: " 'cortes e ardito, ma sdegnoso e
solitario,' at least I would so think of him, 'courteous, bold, haughty
and given to being alone.' "

Horace Gregory has forestalled me—in his *A History of American
Poetry 1900–1940*[5]—by turning to the first edition of Pound's book
and comparing it with Rossetti's *The Early Italian Poets,* which appeared in 1861. Pound, to be sure, would not have translated Cavalcanti had he thought Rossetti's versions adequate, and indeed he
criticizes certain lines "of which Rossetti completely loses the significance." But he pays great homage to his predecessor: "In the matter
of these translations and of my knowledge of Tuscan poetry, Rossetti
is my father and my mother," adding: "but no man can see everything
at once." Gregory's examination of the two books brought one
obvious discovery, one not so obvious. He found that Rossetti had
dedicated his as follows, "Whatever is mine in this book is inscribed

to my wife," and that Pound wrote in his: "As much of this book as is mine I send to my friends Violet and Ford Madox Hueffer." And then Gregory made a discovery of which he fully availed himself. He found, after the dedication page of *The Sonnets and Ballate,* on a leaf where a half-title usually appears, the following two lines:

> I have owed service to the deathless dead
> Grudge not the gold I bear in livery.

"Whatever their origin may have been, the speech was not Rossetti's," Gregory commented, meaning it was not pre-Raphaelite. I think it is possible to go even further—to say that these two lines are like milestones; the writer of them had passed over the pre-Raphaelite boundary and was standing alone in the country of the future. Although the lines no longer appear anywhere in Pound's work, and the mode of speech they embody does not recur in the translations from Cavalcanti, Pound had found his voice. All that is true in his work, all that is lasting, is foreshadowed in this couplet which, for all its freightage from the archaic past, was living speech.

3.

Canzoni of Ezra Pound, published in July, 1911, was dedicated to Olivia and Dorothy Shakespear. A poem entitled "Canzoni—To Be Sung Beneath a Window" shows the poet in love, but does not show much else:

> Man's love follows many faces.
> My love only one face groweth. . . .

There are several stanzas, which need not detain us. The attempts at something "modern" are hardly more successful—

> I suppose, when poetry comes down to facts. . . .

The book need not detain us. In an authorized account of Pound's poetry the following sentence is all that is offered on its text of 51 pages: "Contains many false starts never reprinted."[6]

But every real poet is a phoenix.

Between *Canzoni* and *Ripostes of Ezra Pound* there is an interval of only a year. "The proofs of *Ripostes* are on my desk," he wrote Harriet Monroe on August 18, 1912, "and I've been working for three months on a prose book. Even the *Ripostes* is scarcely more than a notice that my translations and experiments have not entirely interrupted my compositions." His industry aside, the new volume was like one of those automobiles everywhere appearing; it bore him, and modern poetry as well, swiftly out of a crepuscular world into the future. *Ripostes* established Pound as a poet of durability, for some of its poems have withstood fifty years of changing fashions in verse, and have had, in addition, a profound influence on the practitioners who count. One or two may be worth reexamination.

It is a curious fact of literature that the three most eminent of modern American expatriates should all have tried their hands at a portrait of a lady. James never married, Pound and Eliot comparatively late. The drawing room knew them: "In the room, the women come and go," but the hostess remains, a type: "Great minds have sought you—lacking someone else." Pound's portrait precedes Eliot's, as James's preceded Pound's and may have suggested it. Pound called his, "Portrait d'une Femme." I lift four lines from their context, their movement being something new:

> You have been second always. Tragical?
> No. You preferred it to the usual thing:
> One dull man, dulling and uxorious,
> One average mind—with one thought less, each year.

It is blank verse from which all sonority has been excluded. It is closer to Browning and Shakespeare than to Marlowe or Milton, without being like either. Unlike Browning, everything theatrical has been excluded. There is no prompter in the wings. The drama is implicit. The speech is quiet as the room in which the lady sits. The accents are modern.

The whole poem consists of thirty lines, which would have been twenty-nine had Pound not prodded the last line apart to make two, a vivid touch which gives the poem a typographical ornament and the reader a summation in four words. There is one other short line, the fifteenth—"And takes strange gain away"—but the fourteenth carries two extra iambs, and it carries them because Pound saw that if he left this line alone—that is, left it as a line of iambic pentameter—it would be banal:

> You are a person of some interest.

He therefore took the first two feet from the following line, which not only heightened the interest of the fourteenth line, but enriched the movement of both:

> You are a person of some interest, one comes to you
> And takes strange gain away. . . .

Finally, even the rhymes—there are six rhyming words—are placed or left with exceptional care for effect, for wherever they occur they are like a brush stroke which completes a portion of the portrait.

PORTRAIT D'UNE FEMME

> Your mind and you are our Sargasso Sea,
> London has swept about you this score years
> And bright ships left you this or that in fee:
> Ideas, old gossip, oddments of all things,
> Strange spars of knowledge and dimmed wares of price.
> Great minds have sought you—lacking someone else.
> You have been second always. Tragical?
> No. You preferred it to the usual thing:
> One dull man, dulling and uxorious,
> One average mind—with one thought less, each year.
> Oh, you are patient, I have seen you sit
> Hours, where something might have floated up.
> And now you pay one. Yes, you richly pay.
> You are a person of some interest, one comes to you
> And takes strange gain away:
> Trophies fished up; some curious suggestion;
> Fact that leads nowhere; and a tale or two,

Pregnant with mandrakes, or with something else
That might prove useful and yet never proves,
That never fits a corner or shows use,
Or finds its hour upon the loom of days:
The tarnished, gaudy, wonderful old work;
Idols and ambergris and rare inlays,
These are your riches, your great store; and yet
For all this sea-hoard of deciduous things,
Strange woods half sodden, and new brighter stuff:
In the slow float of differing light and deep,
No! there is nothing! In the whole and all,
Nothing that's quite your own.
              Yet this is you.

Such is one of the poems in *Ripostes,* musical and mature, which gave to the world what it has so seldom received from poets, even good ones—a personal idiom, in which structure and rhythms are inherent, not imposed. Pound offered it to a magazine; "and they wrote back that I used the letter 'r' three times in the first line, and that it was very difficult to pronounce, and that I might not remember that Tennyson had once condemned the use of four 's's' in a certain line of a different metre."[7] It finally appeared in *Smart Set,* where there was no "poetry editor," only a man with an open and inquiring mind.[8]

Ripostes was also a book with an enormous range. "The Return" is too well known for inclusion or comment. It pleased Yeats, and I have related elsewhere its effect on E. E. Cummings when he read it while still an undergraduate.[9] Its sculptured lines seem as enduring as a monument.

4.

Pound's range in *Ripostes* is part of his personal biography, for some of the poems reveal his activities as well as his thoughts.

The eyes of this dead lady speak to me

was written after seeing "Venus Reclining" by Jacopo del Sellaio, probably in the National Gallery but possibly in the Louvre—del

Mrs. Mary Moore Cross, at the author's house,
March 1, 1966. *Crayon sketch by Diana Norman.*

A pride of poets, January 18, 1914. Place: "Newbuildings," home of Wilfred Scawen Blunt. Occasion: a dinner. Main course: roasted peacock. Left to right: Victor Plarr, Sturge Moore,

Sellaio painted two of her, very similar, except for background; in any case, Pound went often to Paris, as often as his finances permitted.

He listened to music, God knows where—"From a Thing by Schumann" is the title; perhaps at that Mrs. Fowler's, mentioned in one of his letters, where Walter Morse Rummel played before one of his public concerts. The two men had worked together on a fragment of Provençal melody, which they tried to fit to a fragment of Provençal song, without much success. They were associated in yet another way. In 1912, Rummel published a book of musical settings entitled *Neuf Chansons de Troubadours des XIIième et XIIIième Siècles pour une voix avec accompagnement de Piano*. The title page states that the "adaptation anglaise" was by Ezra Pound, while in the preface Rummel wrote: "The two Daniel melodies are here published for the first time to the writer's knowledge, and he is indebted to Mr. Ezra Pound, M.A., for communicating them from the Milan Library."

Music or no music, the city was too much with him—

> Love, you the much, the more desired!
> Do I not loathe all walls, streets, stones,
> All mire, mist, all fog,
> All ways of traffic?
> You, I would have flow over me like water,
> Oh, but far out of this!
> Grass, and low fields, and hills,
> And sun,
> Oh, sun enough!
> Out and alone, among some
> Alien people!

He was not so crazy about the country as all that.

There is now, also, a love poem—a sonnet—whose texture flashes its many facets through the difficulties of form and obscurities of language—a great feat of virtuosity. It is called "A Virginal":

> No, no! Go from me. I have left her lately.
> I will not spoil my sheathe with lesser brightness,
> For my surrounding air hath a new lightness;

Slight are her arms, yet they have bound me straitly
And left me cloaked as with a gauze of aether;
As with sweet leaves; as with subtle clearness.
Oh, I have picked up magic in her nearness
To sheathe me half in half the things that sheathe her.
No, no! Go from me. I have still the flavour,
Soft as spring wind that's come from birchen bowers.
Green come the shoots, aye April in the branches,
As winter's wound with her sleight hand she staunches,
Hath of the trees a likeness of the savour:
As white their bark, so white this lady's hours.

It was not for *Harper's*. . . .

There is a love poem which is better still, cast in a new mould—Pound's own. It has a Greek title—"Δώρια"—"Doria," perhaps for Dorothy:

> Be in me as the eternal moods
>   of the bleak wind, and not
> As transient things are—
>   gaiety of flowers.
> Have me in the strong loneliness
>   of sunless cliffs
> And of grey waters.
>   Let the gods speak softly of us
> In days hereafter,
>   The shadowy flowers of Orcus
> Remember thee.

The book also contains "The Seafarer," a 111-line translation from the Anglo-Saxon; a brace of "Echoes," from Guido Orlando and Asclepiades (Julianus Aegyptus); and "Dieu! Qu'il La Fait," from Charles d'Orléans—"for music." There is a paean to Swinburne, termed "High Priest of Iacchus," five and a half pages of it, saved from a past time—a note at the end reads: "This apostrophe was written three years before Swinburne's death." The writer of it was then very much younger. It has been suppressed. But why is "An Immorality" missing from the enlarged *Personae* and *Selected Poems?*

Sing we for love and idleness,
Naught else is worth the having.

Though I have been in many a land,
There is naught else in living.

And I would rather have my sweet,
Though rose-leaves die of grieving,

Than do high deeds in Hungary
To pass all men's believing.

This poem, a favorite of many, was the favorite of Pound's mother.[10] It was set to music by Aaron Copland.

5.

In the fall of 1912, Pound was at King's College, Cambridge, where he read a paper, presumably on the troubadours. Hulme came to hear him, bringing Edward Marsh, editor of the *Georgian Poets* and friend of Winston Churchill. Marsh also attended Hulme's "discussion evenings" in Mrs. Kibblewhite's house in Frith Street; on one occasion, he relates, he sat on the floor between Pound and Rupert Brooke.

It was Marsh's friendship with Brooke, and enthusiasm for his poetry, that led him to undertake the Georgian collections, the success of which was to give Pound the idea for an anthology of his own. Marsh took his plan to Harold Monro, editor of the *Poetry Review,* whose bookshop was to become famous in its new premises in Devonshire Street, near Gray's Inn. The shop was in a small eighteenth century building. Above it was the lecture or reading room, where poets held forth; they were called "squashes," with good reason. At the top were spare rooms where poets stayed on town visits; Hulme and Wilfrid Gibson were early tenants. Monro was willing, but could not finance the project, and Marsh assumed the responsibility.

Marsh, having already written to his favorite English contemporaries, asked Pound for two of his poems—"The Goodly Fere" and "Portrait d'une Femme." Pound wrote back:

"I'm sorry I can't let you have *that* poem as I'm just bringing it out in a volume of my own. Is there anything in the earlier books that you like? (not *The Goodly Fere* as it doesn't illustrate any *modern* tendency). Also I'd like to know more or less what gallery you propose to put me into. *Canzoni* is the only one that comes within your two years radius. I'm usually in on Tuesday evenings if you care to talk over the matter."

When Marsh called he told Pound "there was nothing in *Canzoni* which he thought suitable." (It took Pound a little longer to agree.) By the time the second Georgian collection was under way, Marsh had decided to exclude anyone not British, with the result that neither Pound nor Frost, recommended by Gibson, was ever represented.

Marsh relates a curious conversation that he had with Pound. "Georgians" who lived in London, or came to town, gathered for lunch or dinner in little Soho restaurants, Harold Monro presiding. On one such ocasion—it was a dinner at the Chantecler in September, 1912—the main table being full, he sat "*tête-à-tête* at a Katzentisch" with Pound. In the middle of dinner Pound asked him if he was familiar with the new system of quantitative verse, to which Marsh replied that he was, that he "had studied William Stone's paper on the subject and been further indoctrinated by Robert Bridges." Pound, he says, took from his pocket a version of Sappho's "Ode to Aphrodite" and asked if he had made any mistakes in versification. "He had; and when I pointed them out, he put the paper back in his pocket, blushing murkily, and muttering that it was only a first attempt." When Pound published the poem "without a single amendment," Marsh wrote, it "implanted in me a lasting suspicion of his artistic seriousness,"[11] and, his biographer adds, "they never met again."[12]

6.

I have saved, for final comment, the legend which appears on the title page of *Ripostes*—"Whereto are appended the complete poetical works of T. E. Hulme, with prefatory note." They consisted at that time of "Autumn" and four other poems; a sixth was found among

Hulme's papers by his editor. The longest is nine lines. The "Prefatory Note" said:

"In publishing his *Complete Poetical Works* at thirty [here a footnote protests: "Mr. Pound has grossly exaggerated my age.—T.E.H." Actually, Hulme was 29], Mr. Hulme has set an enviable example to many of his contemporaries who have had less to say.

"They are reprinted here for good fellowship; for good custom, a custom out of Tuscany and of Provence; and thirdly, for convenience, seeing their smallness of bulk; and for good memory, seeing that they recall certain evenings and meetings of two years gone, dull enough at the time, but rather pleasant to look back upon."

Other evenings and meetings were not forgotten. *Ripostes* is dedicated to William Carlos Williams.

"Two years gone"—1910. The second group conjured up by Hulme to discuss rare things had, like the first, fallen apart; and, like its predecessor, in about a year. Soho soup, Soho spaghetti for even a fifth part of a lustrum might sufficiently account for the end, bearing in mind those inexorable Thursdays. But possibly it was boredom, as Pound seems to suggest.

Pound gave the group a local habitation and a name. The second half of the "Prefatory Note" reads:

"As for the 'School of Images,' which may or may not have existed, its principles were not so interesting as those of the 'inherent dynamists' or of *Les Unanimistes,* yet they were probably sounder than those of a certain French school which attempted to dispense with verbs altogether; or of the Impressionists who brought forth:

'Pink pigs blossoming upon the hillside';

or of the Post-Impressionists who beseech their ladies to let down slate-blue hair over their raspberry-coloured flanks.

"*Ardoise* rimed richly—ah, richly and rarely rimed!—with *framboise.*

"As for the future, Les Imagistes, the descendents of the forgotten school of 1909, have that in their keeping."

They had it for almost a decade, even after the classicist Eliot came along. The real future—the future that was to count—was to belong to Eliot and his followers. It was, of course, an Eliot profoundly influenced by Pound, who also helped him on the way.

CHAPTER V

POETRY'S
FOREIGN CORRESPONDENT

1.

"Mr. Ezra Pound, the young Philadelphia poet whose recent distinguished success in London led to wide recognition in his own country, authorizes the statement that at present such of his poetic work as receives magazine publication in America will appear exclusively in *Poetry*."

This note, by Harriet Monroe, appeared in the first number—October, 1912—of *Poetry: A Magazine of Verse*. It is a paraphrase of the reply she received when she invited Pound to become a contributor, and it marks the beginning of an association of significance to the literary, hence cultural, development of the United States in the decades which preceded and followed World War I.

The previous August in Chicago, Miss Monroe, after truly heroic labors—of reading in the public library, "not only recent books by the better poets, but also all the verse in American and English magazines of the previous five years," and of mustering a hundred subscribers to put up fifty dollars a year for five years—was ready to launch her magazine. She wrote to the poets she deemed "interesting" to ask for their work. With her letters went a "poets' circular." It explained the financial basis of the new publication and the opportunity it offered to poets to appear "in their own place, without the

limitations imposed by the popular magazine." Within space limitations, "we hope," she declared, "to print poems of greater length
and of more intimate and serious character than the other magazines
can afford to use." Finally, poets were to be paid for their contributions, and there would also be prizes.

The poets responded. A sampling of their replies may be seen in
Miss Monroe's autobiography;[1] Ernest Rhys wished her venture "all
good luck," and Edwin Arlington Robinson asked querulously or
jokingly "why you have concentrated so much deadly emphasis into
the sub-title of your magazine." Twenty-five years had passed when
Miss Monroe sat down to write *A Poet's Life,* and there had been
many quarrels between them; yet the excitement which attended the
arrival of Pound's first letter to her was still vivid in her mind; it
"made the first of September an exciting day." The letter was dated
August 18th.

"Dear Madam [he wrote]: I *am* interested, and your scheme as
far as I understand it, seems not only sound, but the only possible
method. There is no other magazine in America which is not an insult
to the serious artist and to the dignity of his art.

"But? Can you teach the American poet that poetry *is* an *art,* an
art with a technique, with media—an art that must be in constant
flux, a constant change of manner, if it is to live? Can you teach
him that it is not a pentametric echo of the sociological dogma printed
in last year's magazines? Maybe. Anyhow you have work before you.

"I may be myopic, but during my last tortured visit to America I
found no writer and but one reviewer who had any worthy conception
of poetry, The Art. However I need not bore you with jeremiads.

"At least you are not the usual 'esthetic magazine,' which is if anything worse than the popular; for the esthetic magazine expects the
artist to do all the work, pays nothing, and then undermines his credit
by making his convictions appear ridiculous.

"*Quant a moi:* If you conceive verse as a living medium, on a par
with paint, marble, and music, you may announce, if it's any good to
you, that for the present such of my work as appears in America
(barring my own books) will appear exclusively in your magazine.
I think you might easily get all the serious artists to boycott the rest
of the press entirely. I can't send you much at the moment, for my

Arnaut Daniel has gone to the publisher, and the proofs of *Ripostes* are on my desk, and I've been working for three months on a prose book. Even the *Ripostes* is scarcely more than a notice that my translations and experiments have not entirely interrupted my compositions.

"I sincerely hope, by the way, that you mean what you say in your letter—that it isn't the usual editorial suavity of which I've seen enough—for I am writing to you very freely and taking you at your word.

"Are you for American poetry or for poetry? The latter is more important, but it is important that America should boost the former, provided it don't mean a blindness to the art. The glory of any nation is to produce art that can be exported without disgrace to its origin.

"I ask because if you do want poetry from other sources than America I may be able to be of use. I don't think it's any of the artist's business to see whether or no he circulates, but I was nevertheless tempted, on the verge of starting a quarterly, and it's a great relief to know that your paper may manage what I had, without financial strength, been about to attempt rather forlornly.

"I don't think we need go to the French extreme of having four prefaces to each poem and eight schools for every dozen of poets, but you must keep an eye on Paris. Anyhow I hope your ensign is not 'more poetry!' but more interesting poetry, and *maestria!*

"If I can be of any use in keeping you or the magazine in touch with whatever is most dynamic in artistic thought, either here or in Paris—as much of it comes to me, and I *do* see nearly everyone that matters—I shall be glad to do so.

"I send you all that I have on my desk—an over-elaborate post-Browning 'Imagiste' affair and a note on the Whistler exhibit. I count him our only artist, and even this informal salute, drastic as it is, may not be out of place at the threshold of what I hope is an endeavor to carry into our American poetry the same sort of life and intensity which he infused into modern painting.

"Sincerely yours,

"Ezra Pound

"P.S. Any agonizing that tends to hurry what I believe in the end to be inevitable, our American Risorgimento, is dear to me. That awakening will make the Italian Renaissance look like a tempest in a teapot! The force we have, and the impulse, but the guiding sense, the discrimination in applying the force, we must wait and strive for."

When Pound wrote the "post-Browning 'Imagiste' affair," entitled "Middle-Aged," probably he and God knew what it meant. It was not included in any of his books until 1949, when it was added to *Personae,* together with "To Whistler, American."

2.

Pound's first letter to Harriet Monroe was one to please a woman who had been a schoolteacher: a prize pupil's paper. Miss Monroe, twenty-five years older than her correspondent, was that American phenomenon, the spinster citizen devoted to a cause, with alive eyes behind pince-nez flashing zeal and strength. She sent an "enthusiastic answer," asking him to represent *Poetry* abroad as "Foreign Correspondent." On September 21st he wrote back accepting the unsalaried job:

"All right, you can put me down as 'foreign correspondent' or foreign editor if you like, and pay me whatever or whenever is convenient. If I were in the trade for the cash to be gotten from it, I should have quit some time ago. There is rather a fine saying of Browning's which is not so well known as it might be: 'Money! If I'd made matches with my hands I'd have made more out of it.'"

He promised to send "some of young Aldington's stuff," adding: "As touching Boston and New York—if their press is too much amused by Chicago's having a poetry magazine, you might send me some of the clippings and perhaps I can riposte on them from a less expected quarter."

He gave some news about himself:

"I'm doing a series of articles on America for the *New Age* beginning Sept. 5th—rather badly and in a paper that I don't unreservedly approve, but still I might be able to check their unruly mirth, if it is worth paying so much attention to, which I partly doubt."

The reference was to *Patria Mia,* from which I have already quoted. It ran as a weekly series in the *New Age* from September 5th to November 14th. Despite his doubt, he became a frequent contributor, and at length art critic under the pseudonym "B. H. Dias," and music critic as "William Atheling." The editor of the *New Age* was Alfred Richard Orage, a Guild Socialist, who had many plans for a better world, some of them pungent with anti-semitism.

Pound's third letter to Miss Monroe was dated September 24th; she was understandably "elated":

"I've just written to Yeats. It's rather hard to get anything out of him by mail and he won't be back in London until November. Still I've done what I can, and as it's the first favor or about the first that I've asked for three years I may get something—'to set the tone.'

"Also I'll try to get some of the poems of the very great Bengali poet Rabindranath Tagore. They are going to be *the* sensation of the winter."

He dined with Yeats, who told him Tagore was "greater than any of us—I read these things and wonder why one should go on trying to write."

Pound to Miss Monroe: "This is *The Scoop*. Reserve space in the next number for Tagore. . . . He has sung Bengal into a nation."

He sent Tagore; he sent Aldington; he sent five poems by Yeats. He sent advice:

"We must be severe if we are to count, and if our voice is going to be, as it should and must be, *the* authority.

"If we print the slight verse, or young verse, let us do so saying, 'this is slight, or young, or this is a sketch, an experiment.' And let us for God's sake stick to the sketches and experiments of those who really mean to go on, and whose sketches and experiments are made in the serious determination that their own later work and that of their successors is to be better and is to profit by their present labor. I don't think it will do *les jeunes* any harm to know what they look like from this side of the water."

He offered to help them: "If your younger writers think my criticism would be of use to them, I shall be glad to give it. I remember how I used to starve for someone with whom I could talk about poetry." Again: "If a man writes six good lines he is immortal—isn't that worth trying for?"

He sent poems by H. D.

"I've had luck again, and am sending you some *modern* stuff by an American, I say modern, for it is in the laconic speech of the Imagistes, even if the subject is classic."

H. D. went abroad in the summer of 1911, going first to Italy. In the fall, instead of returning to Philadelphia, she went to London; Pound sent Bridget Patmore to meet her. It was at Mrs. Patmore's that she met Aldington. Pound, Mrs. Patmore, Aldington, and H. D. met almost every afternoon for tea at the Grosvenor Gallery in Regent Street. These teas, Pound wrote H. D. in 1960, were among his happiest memories. Aldington wrote me the same year: "It seems odd Dorothy wasn't there, but in those days even grown-up girls were very closely supervised."

Mary Moore arrived in the spring of 1912. This time, Pound met the boat train himself. He introduced her to the Shakespears, to Yeats, Ford, and May Sinclair. She was back in Trenton in June; in July she married James Frederick Cross, an advertising executive. Pound's letter to her in August about this event reveals that he was greatly distressed.

3.

Richard Aldington was a bare nineteen when he met Pound. He had attended University College in London, where he had seen Housman "cruising gloomily about the corridors, probably depressed by the sins of German commentators on Manilius," and had had a "little contact" with W. P. Ker. When he left the College for the last time he walked down Gower Street in the direction of Bloomsbury and Soho. He confesses that there was, in this, "an accidental symbolism which is rather pleasing."[2] He had with him several poems of great beauty and in a novel form. He told Pound over a beefsteak in Kensington, and later Amy Lowell in a letter:

"I began to write vers libre about the early part of 1911, partly because I was fatigued with rhyme and partly because of the interest I had in poetic experiment. I didn't know Heine or Patmore's 'Unknown Eros,' and never suspected the existence of the French vers librists. I got the idea from a chorus in the Hippolytus of Euripides."[3]

This referred to "Choricos," which was to become a prize exhibit of the Imagists; but obviously its composition had nothing to do with their tenets. Pound, Aldington related, looked at his poems, and said: "Well, I don't think you need any help from me."

Pound, of course, introduced him around. Of the many luminaries

he met, the one who impressed him most—after H. D.—was a Polish-
American philosopher, author of *Heraklit und Parmenides* (1912),
whom Pound had met as a student at the University of Pennsylvania.
His name was Henry Slonimsky. "As a personality he stands for me
alongside Yeats and Lawrence," Aldington was to write. He was
particularly impressed by Slonimsky's "skill and eloquence in refuting
the arguments of the English Bergsonian, T. E. Hulme." He added:
"Ezra never appreciated Slonimsky, because Ezra never listened to
him."[4]

Aldington, understandably, had already paid his respects to the
Poetry Book Shop and had become acquainted with its owner. They
parted over Pound:

"At a 'Dutch' Soho dinner collected by Harold Monro, everyone
was deploring Ezra and running him down. Finally I could stand it
no longer. I stood up and said: 'Ezra Pound has more vitality in his
little finger than the whole lot of you put together,' and walked out.
That queered my pitch with a large and powerful clique, but I have
never regretted it."[5]

He has a vivid characterization of Pound at this time:

"The Georgians were regional in their outlook and in love with
littleness. They took a little trip for a little week-end to a little cottage
where they wrote a little poem on a little theme. Ezra was a citizen
of the world, both mentally and in fact. He went off to Paris or
Venice with vastly less fuss than a Georgian affronting the perils of
the Cotswolds."[6]

In the spring of 1912 Aldington went to Paris. Like everyone else,
he "fell in love with Paris at first sight." He wrote poems, made
translations, but most of the time he spent "seeing the city." He had
good company—Pound and H. D. One day, Pound took Aldington
to call on Walter Morse Rummel, now famous as the interpreter of
Debussy. Rummel was in his "working clothes" when they arrived,
and he retired to change. There was an open grand piano in the
room, and Pound went over to it and began to play Debussy with one
finger. Out rushed Rummel in his underclothes, shouting: "Ezra!
Ezra! If you touch that piano once more I'll throw you out the
window!"

"I expected an explosion," Aldington wrote, "but Ezra merely
blinked and desisted."

What Aldington terms "the greatest piece of luck on this trip" was his encounter, outside the Luxembourg Gardens, with Slonimsky. "H. D., with her swift unerring response to whatever is beautiful and lofty, at once comprehended his greatness and his charm. What evenings we spent listening to him in Paris! *Noctes Atticae*. On a bench under the trees in the Petit Luxembourg, away from the noise and glare of the cafés, we would sit for hours while he talked to us of Hellas and Hellenism, of Pythagoras and Plato—'a kindly man'— of Empedocles and Heraclitus, of Homer and Thucydides, of Aeschylus and Theocritus. We knew just enough to understand, to be moved by the beauty and grandeur of what he set before us."[7]

But all Pound remembered of him was his supposed accent—

"Haff you gno bolidigal basshunts? . . .
Demokritoos, Heragleitos" exclaimed Doktor Slonimsky 1912—

as memorialized in Canto LXXVII. When I saw him he remarked: "My English is exactly like his—Philadelphia English." There was no accent. A tall, white-haired man with clear blue eyes, he had been a teacher of philosophy at Columbia and Johns Hopkins, and in recent years dean of the Hebrew Union College-Jewish Institute of Religion in New York City.

It was from him that the poets first heard of the possibility of a European war. "I listened incredulously," Aldington recalled.

4.

Pound sent Harriet Monroe twelve of his own poems, saying: "You must use your own discretion about printing this batch of verses. At any rate, don't use them until you've used 'H. D.' and Aldington, s.v.p."

"Choricos" appeared in the second number, which announced Pound as foreign correspondent and described Aldington as "one of the *'Imagistes,'* a group of ardent Hellenists who are pursuing interesting experiments in *vers libre;* trying to attain in English certain subtleties of cadence of the kind which Mallarmé and his followers have studied in France." Miss Doolittle's group of poems appeared in the January, 1913, number with the signature, "H. D., *Imagiste*."

The March number carried an article entitled *"Imagisme"* signed by F. S. Flint but written with the assistance of Pound, and Pound's "A Few Don'ts by an *Imagiste*."

Flint's article began:

"Some curiosity has been aroused concerning *Imagisme,* and as I was unable to find anything definite about it in print, I sought out an imagiste [i.e., Pound], with intent to discover whether the group itself knew anything about the 'movement.' I gleaned these facts.

"The *imagistes* admitted that they were contemporaries of the Post-impressionists and the futurists; but they had nothing in common with these schools. They had not published a manifesto. They were not a revolutionary school; their only endeavor was to write in accordance with the best tradition, as they found it in the best writers of all time—in Sappho, Catullus, Villon. They seemed to be absolutely intolerant of all poetry that was not written in such endeavor, ignorance of the best tradition forming no excuse. They had a few rules, drawn up for their own satisfaction only, and they had not published them. They were:

"1. Direct treatment of the 'thing,' whether subjective or objective.

"2. To use absolutely no word that did not contribute to the presentation.

"3. As regarding rhythm: to compose in sequence of the musical phrase, not in sequence of a metronome.

"By these standards they judged all poetry, and found most of it wanting."

Pound's began with explanation for the general reader:

"An 'Image' is that which presents an intellectual and emotional complex in an instant of time. . . . It is the presentation of such a 'complex' instantaneously which gives that sense of sudden liberation; that sense of freedom from time limits and space limits; that sense of sudden growth, which we experience in the presence of the greatest works of art."

He proffered advice to poets:

"Go in fear of abstractions. Don't retell in mediocre verse what has already been done in good prose."

He referred back to Flint:

"The first three simple proscriptions will throw out nine-tenths of all the bad poetry now accepted as standard and classic; and will prevent you from many a crime of production."

He could not resist a gibe:

". . . '*Mais d'abord il faut être un poète,*' as MM. Duhamel and Vildrac have said at the end of their little book, *Notes sur la Technique Poétique;* but in an American one takes that at least for granted, otherwise why does one get born upon that august continent!"

In "Sevenels," her home, a stout, sensitive American lady of Brookline, Massachusetts, read the new emanations from London, and was strangely stirred. She puffed her cigar and pondered them. Suddenly she exclaimed: "Why, I too am an *Imagiste!*"

It was like Molière.

She arose and went to England, taking with her innumerable trunks and suitcases, and a letter of introduction from Harriet Monroe to Ezra Pound.

5.

Hulme had said: "We shall not get any new efflorescence of verse until we get a new technique, a new convention, to turn ourselves loose in." Unfortunately, the "new technique" quickly turned into "a new convention." An examination of Imagist poetry today, which dominated the field on both sides of the Atlantic for so many years, can only result in disappointment, for it stretches endlessly from book to book, anthology to anthology, like a panorama of paper clouds and flowers.

Margaret Anderson, editor of the *Little Review,* was very enthusiastic about the Imagists, and composed an article consisting "entirely of their sharp pictures." A few lines from her article will save pages of exposition: "Sea orchards, and lilac on the water, and color dragged up from the sand; drenched grasses, and early roses, and wind-harps in the cedar trees; flame-flowers, and the sliding rain; frail sea-birds, and blue still rocks," and so forth. Upon seeing the article Fletcher wrote her it was "a splendid thing to have done." Witter Bynner dissented: "They build poems around phrases, usually around adjectives."

If the test of a movement is the distinguished work it produces it is not too much to say that of all those who dabbled in the new medium, only H. D. and Richard Aldington excelled; and Aldington, as previously indicated, had come armed into the Imagist camp.

The statements by Flint and Pound were all very well; something of the sort had been needed for a long time. But the three Imagist principles, or proscriptions, as Pound termed them, while they might have served to educate the reader of poetry could not, in practice, have been of more than temporary use to the writer of it, by showing him the danger of padding or, what amounts to the same thing, the danger of a too regular measure. Only H. D. lived up to the first two; as for the third, seemingly the most important, it proved—to judge by the results—the greatest stumbling block to original work. In attempting to apply it too rigorously, and too long, the Imagist poets more often than not wrote prose, and not always good prose. For, in the end, what differentiates one poet from another is the structure of his line, and as this structure comes from the very depths of his being it is unlikely that it can be taught, and if taught, followed. The poet's line reveals not only his manner of expression, hence the way he thinks; it reveals his intensity—almost, it might be said, his way of breathing. And this individual structure is all that can be called different in the poets, for they resemble each other more often than they do not. For while the schoolmen like to occupy themselves with poets who have "systems," like Dante and Milton, for example, most poets have no such "systems," not even a philosophy but that of imagination or beauty; yet they manage, century after century, to treat the same themes successfully because all have a particular way of "seeing," thinking and feeling, and of expressing themselves. Thus, no matter where the discussion starts, it is always necessary to return to the line and its structure.

The Imagists were not even radical experimenters, as Bridges and Hopkins were, and even Bridges and Hopkins, for all their experiments with "sprung rhythm," were closer to their predecessors than some like to think. For the fact is that the basic English line, evolving from the basic iambic structure of the language itself, can only be varied toward speech; it is varied best, perhaps, by the iamb's noble opposite, the trochee. But whatever be the measure, the structure of the line can come only from the poem's necessity, or the poet's, it being the most personal thing in any poem. Here, then, rules made by others can be of little use. Those who write by the metronome—te-dum, te-dum, te-dum, and so forth—have not learned the lesson of the English poets. Pound himself wrote, in a letter to Miss Monroe: "Laws do not begin with the man who puts them in print; whatever 'laws of imagisme' are good, have been good for some time."

Pound went on to other things. But first he expended a great deal of time and energy; then he had to deal with the invader from Brookline.

6.

He congratulated Miss Monroe on the March number, but flayed a few contributors: "Good god! isn't there one of them that can write natural speech without copying clichés out of every Eighteenth Century poet still in the public libraries?"

He began to wonder about the editorial office in Chicago: "I think you are probably taking the best of what comes in, but I do now and then have a twinge of curiosity about what is being cast out."

Williams had sent some poems: "I'm glad you're going to print 'Bill,' i.e. Wm. Carlos Williams."

Witter Bynner had already appeared: "Bynner is at least aware of life as apart from brochures. Yet he himself is most aptly described in just that ultimate term 'brochure.' And his tone of thought smacks of the pretty optimism of McClure and E. W. Wilcox. If America should bring forth a real pessimist—not a literary pessimist—I should almost believe."

He reviewed D. H. Lawrence—"Detestable person but needs watching. I think he learned the proper treatment of modern subjects before I did."

He was taking his job very seriously: "I've got a right to be severe. For one man I strike there are ten to strike back at me. I stand exposed. It hits me in my dinner invitations, in my week-ends, in reviews of my own work. Nevertheless it's a good fight."

He advised her to do likewise: "Mistrust any poet using the word *cosmic*." He emphasized: "Objectivity and again objectivity, and no expression, no hind-side-beforeness, no Tennysonianness of speech—

nothing, *nothing,* that you couldn't in some circumstance, in the stress of some emotion, *actually say."*

In 1937, when Miss Monroe was preparing her book for the press, Pound commented on this passage: "It should be realized that Ford Madox Ford had been hammering this point of view into me from the time I first met him (1908 or 1909) and that I owe him anything that I don't owe myself for having saved me from the academic influences then raging in London."[8]

Miss Monroe wrote in *A Poet's Life*:

"Thus began the rather violent, but on the whole salutary, discipline under the lash of which the editor of the new magazine felt herself being rapidly educated, while all incrustations of habit and prejudice were ruthlessly swept away. Ezra Pound was born to be a great teacher. The American universities which, at this time of his developing strength, failed, one and all, to install him as the head of an English department, missed a dynamic influence which would have been felt wherever English writing is taught. It is not entirely his fault if he has become somewhat embittered and has spent upon trivial quarrels and temperamental exaggerations the energy which should have gone into important progressive work. The power which would have been stimulating has become explosive." (Her book was published in 1938.)

7.

There was transatlantic wrangling over his own poems, which included the famous "In a Station of the Metro." Miss Monroe was puzzled by some of the typographical arrangements, and was shocked by certain expressions. When the poems appeared in the April, 1913 number, under the general heading of "Contemporania," they were violently attacked by "poets" as well as professors of literature. They were also parodied. I should like to give them all; I shall give two. How fresh and charming they must have been in that far-off day and place; how fresh and charming they are now! The poet speaks to us directly, and it hardly matters whether they are good poems or not. They are not bad. And the "poets" and the professors and the half-educated wrote in, in defense of the Georgians, and "tradition," and they asked what was poetry coming to, not to mention the world!

THE GARRET

Come, let us pity those who are better off than we are.
Come, my friend, and remember
      that the rich have butlers and no friends,
And we have friends and no butlers.
Come, let us pity the married and the unmarried.

Dawn enters with little feet
      like a gilded Pavlova,
And I am near my desire.
Nor has life in it aught better
Than this hour of clear coolness,
      the hour of waking together.

THE GARDEN

          En robe de parade.
          Samain

Like a skein of loose silk blown against a wall
She walks by the railing of a path in Kensington Gardens,
And she is dying piece-meal
      of a sort of emotional anaemia.

And round about there is a rabble
Of the filthy, sturdy, unkillable infants of the very poor.
They shall inherit the earth.

In her is the end of breeding.
Her boredom is exquisite and excessive.
She would like someone to speak to her,
And is almost afraid that I
      will commit that indiscretion.

Amid the general howl that went up over "Contemporania" there was one sane, if enthusiastic, note. Under the heading, "To a Poet," Floyd Dell wrote in the Chicago *Evening Post Literary Review*:

"Ezra Pound, we salute you!

"You are the most enchanting poet alive.

"Your poems in the April *Poetry* are so mockingly, so delicately, so unblushingly beautiful that you seem to have brought back into the world a grace which (probably) never existed, but which we discover by an imaginative process in Horatius and Catullus."

Pound wrote to Miss Monroe:

"Dell is very consoling. It's clever of him to detect the Latin tone."

It was as simple as that.

8.

Pound has told how he came to write "In a Station of the Metro," and of the phases it underwent before he achieved its final form:

"I got out of a 'metro' train at La Concorde, and saw suddenly a beautiful face, and then another beautiful woman, and I tried all that day to find words for what this had meant to me, and I could not find any words that seemed to me worthy, or as lovely as that sudden emotion. And that evening, as I went home along the rue Raynouard, I was still trying and I found, suddenly, the expression. I do not mean that I found words, but there came an equation . . . not in speech, but in little splotches of colour. It was just that—a 'pattern,' or hardly a pattern, if by 'pattern' you mean something with a 'repeat' in it. But it was a word, the beginning, for me, of a language in colour. . . .

"That evening in the rue Raynouard, I realized quite vividly that if I were a painter, or if I had, often, *that kind* of emotion, or even if I had the energy to get paints and brushes and keep at it, I might found a new school of painting, of 'non-representative' painting, a painting that would speak only by arrangements in colour.

"And so, when I came to read Kandinsky's chapter on the language of form and colour,[9] I found little that was new to me. I only felt that some one else understood what I understood, and had written it out very clearly. It seems quite natural to me that an artist should have just as much pleasure in an arrangement of planes or in a pattern of figures, as in painting portraits of fine ladies, or in portraying the Mother of God as the symbolists bid us. . . . That is to say, my experience in Paris should have gone into paint. If instead of colour I had perceived sound or planes in relation, I should have expressed it in music or in sculpture. Colour was, in that instance, the 'primary pigment'; I mean that it was the first adequate equation that came into consciousness. . . . All poetic language is the language of exploration. Since the beginning of bad writing, writers have used images as ornaments. The point of Imagisme is that it does not use images *as ornaments*. The image is itself the speech. The image is the word beyond formulated language. . . . "The 'one-image poem' is a form of super-position, that is to say, it is one idea set on top of another. I found it useful in getting out of the impasse in which I had been left by my metro emotion. I wrote a thirty-line poem, and destroyed it because it was what we call work 'of second intensity.' Six months later I made a poem half that length; a year later I made the following *hokku*-like sentence:

> 'The apparition of these faces in the crowd:
> Petals, on a wet, black bough.' "[10]

9.

For a number of years, Mrs. Ernest Fenollosa, the widow of the American who was Imperial Commissioner of Arts in Japan, had been on the lookout for a writer to whom she could entrust her husband's translations and notes. "Contemporania" convinced her that Pound was the man, and she sent him Fenollosa's mauscripts. Pound's excitement was immediate and sustained, perhaps comparable to the excitement Whistler felt when, several decades before, he had entered Madame Desoyes's shop in the rue de Rivoli and discovered the art of Japan.

Pound may have known something about this American scholar, who had lived in Japan from 1878 to 1890, and who had died in England five years before, in 1908. Fenollosa, born in Salem, Massachusetts, had been educated at Harvard. His life, Pound was to write, "was a romance par excellence of modern scholarship. He went to Japan as a professor of economics. He ended as Imperial Commissioner of Arts. He had unearthed treasure that no Japanese had heard of. It may be an exaggeration to say that he had saved Japanese art for Japan, but it is certain that he had done as much as any one man could have to set the native art in its rightful preeminence and to stop the apeing of Europe. He had endeared himself to the government and laid the basis for a personal tradition. When he died suddenly in England the Japanese government sent a warship for his body, and the priests buried him within the sacred enclosure at Miidera."[11]

Pound's acquisition of Fenollosa's manuscripts, from a stranger who had come upon his own poems in the pages of *Poetry,* provided a sequel to the "romance par excellence of modern scholarship." He held in his hands the deeds, as it were, to two immense and exotic provinces of literature which were as yet unknown and undreamt of in the Western world. From them were to come two notable books, and a lifelong preoccupation with things Chinese and the Chinese written character, or ideograph.

"As for *Cathay,*" Eliot was to write, "it must be pointed out that Pound is the inventor of Chinese poetry for our time." As for *Certain Noble Plays of Japan*—the Noh plays—Yeats was to find in Pound's versions of Japan's immemorial drama inspiration for a new dramatic phase of his own.

Pound's instinct was equal to Mrs. Fenollosa's intuition. "I had not the philological competence necessary for an ultimate version," he afterwards wrote Glenn Hughes, "but at the same time Mrs. F's conviction was that Fen. wanted it transd *as* literature not as philology." He sought expert advice—he mentions Professors Mori and Ariga on the title page of *Cathay*—but he approached his material less as a scientist of language, and more with a love of learning and literature, the older and true meaning of the term "philology."

CHAPTER VI

POUND AND AMY LOWELL

1.

Ensconced like a queen in a suite in the Berkeley Hotel, with a view across Piccadilly to the Green Park, Amy Lowell sent the letter of introduction Harriet Monroe had given her, and Pound came to dinner. It was served privately, as she did not like to appear in the dining room. They talked poetry into the late hours—"a most delightful evening," she termed it, and set about describing him for Miss Monroe:

"Figure to yourself a young man, arrayed as 'poet' and yet making the costume agreeable by his personal charm; a sweep of conversation and youthful enthusiasm which keeps him talking delightfully as many hours as you please; the violence of his writings giving way to show a very thin-skinned and sensitive personality opening out like a flower in a sympathetic circle, and I should imagine shutting up like a clam in an alien atmosphere; in personal conversation not in the least didactic, rather dreading the attitude, in fact. That he will outgrow some of his theories, I feel sure. His taste is too fine to confine itself within the walls of any school, even his own. He is so young that all sorts of developments may be expected. I think the chip-on-the-shoulder attitude will disappear in time."[1]

Miss Lowell was eleven years older than Pound. It seems strange that she does not mention his beard, or green eyes and gold-red crest of hair. Pound, she said, had taken one of her poems for *The New Freewoman* and "arranged for me to meet Yeats this week, and is to take me to tea at the Ford Madox Hueffers'." The poem was "In a Garden," which she termed her only "Imagiste" poem.

"What especially pleases me," she wrote, "is his evident interest in my work. Mr. Pound is no flatterer, but his reticent praise is good to hear."

There were other evenings. On one of them Pound brought John Gould Fletcher, whom he had finally met that year. Fletcher recalled that Pound did most of the talking; he also read "The Seafarer," from *Ripostes*. Miss Lowell read from her book, *A Dome of Many-Coloured Glass*.

2.

Although Fletcher had resided in London—he published five books of verse there under four different imprints at his own expense in a single year—he and Pound met in Paris. One spring night in 1913, as he was sitting with Skipwith Cannéll—another Philadelphian—on the terrace of the Closerie des Lilas near the Luxembourg Gardens, their table was approached by two men, one of whom Fletcher knew. This was John Duncan Fergusson, a painter, who explained that he and his companion had been sitting inside, and "the thought had come to him that two Americans who were also poets ought to know each other." He thereupon introduced Pound, and left. Fletcher had heard of Pound and had even read his work, "with attraction and repulsion almost equally balanced." He saw a man "of about my own age and height," in a brown velvet coat, shirt open at the neck, no necktie, and pearl-gray trousers. "His fine-chiseled, forward-jutting features were set off by a rounded mass of fiery curly red hair and a beard and mustache similarly red and curly, trimmed to a point. Gray-blue penetrating eyes, shielded by pince-nez, peered at the world behind high-projecting cheekbones; and a high-pitched, shrill, almost feminine voice provided strange contrast to the pugnacious virility of the poet's general aspect." He noted Pound's hands—"slender feminine hands, which, as he talked, he fluttered to and fro."[2]

It is probable that Fletcher's future disagreements with, and dislike of, Pound had their genesis in the discussion that night, which was about free verse and which, says Fletcher, "I supposed myself to be practicing." But other opportunities were not lacking. To the characterization above he added: "Pound immediately averred that he had been writing vers libre for years, and promptly regaled us with a long account of his own theories. This account, involved as it was, was frequently interrupted by gesticulations and by a slight cough which came between every other word. It involved reference to so many critics and theorists whose works I had not read, from Gustave Kahn down to the Italian futurists, that I decided to keep silence."

But Cannéll said: "As for me, I don't know much about all these French and Italian theories; but the best vers libre is still that of the King James version of the English Bible." Pound, says Fletcher, took off his glasses and polished them nervously.

Pound asked Cannéll to show him some of his poems, and promised Fletcher a review of his early volumes in *Poetry*. "He was as good as his word." They met several more times in Paris. Fletcher noted that Pound "perpetually wore pearl-buttoned velvet coats, fawn or pearl-gray trousers, a loose-flowing dark cape, sported a Malacca cane with silver top, and, though usually hatless, sometimes affected a sombrero." Pound, he said, "seldom or almost never discussed his own poetry, I noticed, except with an apologetic cough and a nervous twitching of his fine, leonine head. But about poetry in general he rapidly became dogmatic. His three chief hatreds were superfluity of adjectives, inversions, and rhetoric, all three being summed up in his special cause for detestation, John Milton. He disliked equally all the Georgians, with the solitary and surprising exceptions of Davies and Walter de la Mare." Wordsworth was "that stupid old ass," from whom flowed all the faults of the Georgians—i.e., "of tacking morals onto poems where they did not belong, and of lapsing from concrete statement into woolly abstractions."[3]

Although Fletcher shared some of these views, it is apparent from his tone that no great friendship between him and Pound was possible; and so it proved. Nevertheless, after his return to London the first person he sought out was Pound at 10 Church Walk. Suddenly the bells of St. Mary Abbot's rang out, thronging the room with their clangor, and the two men looked at each other, Pound visibly annoyed. He told Fletcher that the ringing of those bells was "the greatest nuisance of my life." On "the general shabbiness of the surroundings," Fletcher noted: "When I first saw Pound in Paris I had been

struck by his dandified airs, and by the general splendor of his ex-
terior. . . . Here, however, it was immediately obvious that all this
display merely concealed a state of poverty bordering upon indi-
gence."[4]

They discussed his work. He did not take kindly to Pound's strictures. In the series of poems afterwards called *Irradiations* Pound
thought the internal rhymes "too obvious," but Fletcher pointed out
that the French symbolists were using "my own devices of internal
rhyme, vowel assonance, and the like." Pound, he says, thereupon
"borrowed an armful of my French books."

"When I next saw him, he was already enthusiastic over de Gourmont, Corbière, and the early Francis Jammes."

They quarreled, and made up.

"I could not help admiring the dignity with which he bore the
affront I had chosen to administer, nor the real generosity with which
he, a poor man, was ready to help a well-to-do poet like myself to
gain a hearing."[5]

Cannéll also turned up with his good-looking wife. Kathleen Cannéll told me that Pound took them to Romano's for lunch to mark
their first day in London—"and spilled a bottle of Burgundy in my
lap; it was my best frock, too." She added that Fletcher, when he
learned of this, told her that Pound was "quite capable of having done
it on purpose to create an impression," but she said Pound was obviously embarrassed. Despite his awkwardness—"he was always dropping his cane, treading on people's toes"—he was a good dancer, she
said, as was Ford. Pound got the Cannélls lodgings below him at 10
Church Walk, and they heard the bells "all hours." They also heard
Pound singing as he bathed himself in his tin tub.

Pound, of course, introduced them to his friends.

"We played tennis at Ford's every afternoon. Ezra was my tennis
partner, as no one else would put up with him. All sorts of writers
came to tea—R. B. Cunninghame Graham, H. G. Wells, Yeats and
Lady Gregory, Wyndham Lewis. Violet Hunt had a parrot that
screamed 'Ezra! Ezra!' when we came in from tennis."

She said that Pound took her and her husband to a Yeats "evening."
He also "made dates for Skip with leading literary lights, and took me
around London while Skip kept them—even to Madame Tussaud's."

She added: "We never had a sentimental attachment, and so re-mained good friends for many years."

They met again in Paris.

Katherine Ruth Heyman was also in London that year. She com-posed a musical setting for Pound's "Apparuit" for piano and voice. On the manuscript copy of the score there is the following note in her hand: "This poem is written in the ancient Sapphic metre, and in the musical setting the rhythm has been accentuated. K.R.H. 1913—London." The poem, from the volume *Ripostes,* begins:

> Golden rose the house, in the portal I saw
> thee, a marvel, carven in subtle stuff, a
> portent. Life died down in the lamp and flickered,
> caught at the wonder.

This is the poem Pound showed Marsh at the little side table in the Chantecler; the versification is quantitative, not stressed as in Swin-burne's sapphics.

3.

Fletcher was happier with Miss Lowell. She shared his enthusiasm for modern French poetry. He asked permission to call by himself; when he did so, he read her a number of poems from *Irradiations.* She was "greatly impressed." They met often after that. She wrote Miss Monroe: "He writes in a style entirely his own, a sort of rhythmi-cal prose, dropping now and then into rhyme, and which he manages so skilfully that it is capable of extraordinary versatility." She thanked her for the letter to Pound: "I feel that in him I have not only gained a personal friend, but, through his kindness, a little wedge into the heart of English letters." She went to Paris, bearing introductions from Pound.

Pound wrote Miss Monroe in August: "I'm sending you our left wing *The Freewoman.* I've taken charge of the literature dept. It will be convenient for things whereof one wants the Eng. copyright held. I pay a dmd. low rate, but it might be worth while as a supplement to some of your darlings. So far Johns and Kilmer are about the only ones I care to welcome." The letter contained his first mention of Amy Lowell: "Miss Lowell is back from Paris, and pleasingly intelligent."

With his next he sent the poems by Fletcher. He wanted *Poetry* to use "the full sequence," but supposed it hopeless. "Of course one of Fletcher's strongest claims to attention is his ability to make a *book,* as opposed to the common or garden faculty of making a 'Poem,' and if you don't print a fairish big gob of him, you don't do him justice or stir up the reader's ire and attention."

Back in Brookline, Miss Lowell wrote to Miss Monroe:

"I have come back to my native land, having had a most interesting summer, and learned many things. Mr. Pound has more than lived up to his kindness when I first arrived." Pound told Frost: "When I get through with that girl she'll think she was born in free verse." He wrote her in Brookline: "I'd like to use your 'In a Garden' in a brief anthology *Des Imagistes* that I am cogitating—unless you've something that you think more appropriate."

Before leaving England she called on Henry James at Rye. The greatest of American novelists was seventy. Since she wanted to write, he had some advice to give her. Leaving his other guests at the tea table he led her into the garden. A "fierce and bitter" monologue followed.

"I have cut myself off from America, where I belonged," he told her, "and in England I am not really accepted. Don't make my mistake."[6]

Pound has recorded another scene, with another lady, in that garden, himself an onlooker, in Canto LXXIX, and in Canto VII there is a portrait in miniature of the great man in his habitat:

> The house too thick, the paintings
> a shade too oiled.
> And the great domed head, *con gli occhi onesti e tardi*
> Moves before me, phantom with weighted motion,
> *Grave incessu,* drinking the tone of things,
> And the old voice lifts itself
> > weaving an endless sentence.

There was one other poet Pound wrote to in connection with *Des Imagistes.* This was James Joyce, then residing in Trieste and struggling against poverty by teaching in the Commercial Academy and giving private lessons in English. It is probable that Pound first heard of Joyce through Yeats; but as a frequenter of Elkin Mathews's bookstore on Vigo Street he would have seen one of the slimmest volumes of verse ever to appear under a publisher's imprint—thirty-six poems on thirty-six unnumbered pages—with the title, *Chamber Music.* Mr. Mathews had published it in 1907 in an edition of 509 copies, price one shilling sixpence, and there were copies in abundance. The last poem in the volume is the now famous "I hear an army charging upon the land," and Pound asked Joyce for permission to include it in the collection he was making. Perhaps more important than Joyce's immediate acquiescence was the news he gave Pound of the book he was working on; but of this, more later.

The anthology that Pound was cogitating appears to have been a direct result of the successful launching of *Georgian Poets.* On June 22nd Marsh wrote to Rupert Brooke, who was in the United States:

"Wilfrid [Gibson] tells me there's a movement for a 'Post-Georgian' anthology, of the Pound-Flint-Hulme school, who don't like being out of G.P., but I don't think it will come off."[7]

When he wrote this, *Georgian Poets* was in a sixth edition.

4.

Des Imagistes. . . .

It is strangely effective, though not good French. What was he thinking of? (Unless, as Aldington has pointed out, the word "Anthologie" was assumed to precede it, as it does—in English—in Pound's letter to Amy Lowell.) Pound did not even know who was going to publish it, as the following will show.

In a shack on a slope of the Palisades in New Jersey, overlooking those mud flats which Pound had once visualized as the site of another Venice, there lived two artists, Samuel Halpert and Man Ray, who worked in a printing plant in downtown Manhattan. Halpert invited Alfred Kreymborg to spend a few days with them to escape the heat of New York. "He fell in love with the shack, the studio, the room they turned over to him and most of all with the view of the Jersey meadows, striped and streaked with the Passaic and Hackensack rivers." So wrote Mr. Kreymborg, in the third person, adding: "His hosts made no attempt to interrupt his dithyrambs—except to ask him to spend the rest of the summer with them."[8] They talked about poetry, they talked about art. Kreymborg had a vision. It concerned the greatest love affair in the world: a poet and a press.

One night Man Ray announced that his boss had promised to ship, to their very door, a discarded press. They began to think of titles for a new magazine. "The word, soil, constantly haunted their meditations," but finally, says Kreymborg, he came up with "glebe." He has described the scene. Halpert frowned and looked in the dictionary. "Is it a church you're founding?" he asked—like an Irisher. Said Ray: "Isn't the soil universal?" Said Kreymborg: "And art the one religion?"[9]

"Glebe, n. (Poet.) earth, land, a field; portion of land going with clergyman's benefice. [f. L *gleba* clod, soil]."

They had a title. They had a cover drawing—an abstract design by Man Ray. Letters went out to potential contributors, one of them to John Cournos in London.

Cournos was a young, thin, ascetic Russian-born journalist and poet from Philadelphia. Young he could not help being, thin he was born to be and still is—in his late seventies—but some of his asceticism was forced on him, for he fasted from time to time, not to see visions. He had chucked his job as art critic on the Philadelphia *Record* to go abroad. At the time Kreymborg wrote to him Cournos was interviewing English celebrities for any publication which would take them; this brought in something, but not much. It was thus that he had met Gordon Craig and become his friend, and through Craig, Pound.

Gordon Craig, the famous son of a famous mother, wanted to establish a school of theater arts. He formed a committee, with Cournos a member. The committee met regularly, first in the Leicester Galleries, later in John Street, Adelphi. Yeats, though a member, never came. Pound came at least once. Cournos was there with his fellow Philadelphian and friend, Henry Slonimsky. Cournos afterwards wrote:

"If you saw Ezra in the street for the first time, you'd notice him. And as he strode into the committee room—this tall distinguished looking young man with a shock of red hair flaming backward and his sharp red beard poised at a forward-downward angle and well-shaped features and deep-set blue eyes [sic]—Slonimsky and I nudged each other and exchanged glances, as much as to say: 'Now that's something like. Who is he, I wonder?' "[10]

When the meeting was over Cournos, Slonimsky, Ralph Hodgson and Pound went to a public house in the Strand. Cournos recalled:

"The salient impression I received as I watched him across the table in the public house was that of almost exuberant kindliness. And Ezra, as I had cause later to find out, was one of the kindest men that ever lived. He made no effort, as some do, to conceal the fact. It was there 'written all over him,' as the saying goes. He likewise revealed a keen interest in any stranger he met, casting upon him an appraising eye, taking prompt stock of the furnishings of his mind, annexing him if he proved worth while with a frank eagerness I never met in any one else."[11]

Cournos was "annexed." It is not surprising. He was—he is—a gentle soul and a talented writer. "Ezra Pound divined my loneliness and went a great deal out of his way to get me acquainted." He was introduced to Hueffer and Yeats, "and the young writers and painters who met at Mrs. Kibblewhite's house in Soho," among them Hulme and Flint. But when Pound asked him to go, as his guest, to a posh literary dinner at the Monico, Cournos demurred. He did not own a dinner jacket.

"Ezra overcame my objections. It was a poets' dinner, wasn't it? And, of course, poets were not the sort to be sticklers for dress."

He went.

"There must have been nearly a hundred poets there, unless some like myself were guests, and every one of them was in evening dress!"

He sat at a table with Edward Marsh, who wore a monocle; Sir Henry Newbolt; Maurice Hewlett, and Ernest Rhys, "an oldish man with a gray beard," who asked him if he wouldn't address the gathering.

"No! No! Quite impossible! I shouldn't know what to say! You must promise not to call on me!"[12]

Later, when he went to a hospital in the Italian quarter, "Ezra Pound came one visiting day and brought me a magnificent bouquet of yellow roses."

Cournos met Rhys again; Rhys suggested he write a book on American painting. Pound went over the first chapters. A marginal note by him next to a paragraph about William M. Chase reads: "Delightful.

The one possible way of presenting Chase." Pound thought so highly of the chapter on Sargent that he showed it to Yeats, "who liked it a great deal."

Pound wrote Alice Corbin Henderson, assistant editor of *Poetry:*

"I don't see where we're to find space for that prose of Cournos', but it *is* his own and is at least direct treatment of life. And he is a good chap who has risked physical comfort for the good of his soul in leaving a steady job."

Cournos told me: "One day he put three guineas in my hand." He "began to see something of Ezra himself in his small room at 10, Church Walk, Kensington, a room I inherited after he married Dorothy Shakespear and moved to a flat around the corner."

5.

To Church Walk, Cournos brought Kreymborg's letter asking for material for *The Glebe*. And in Brookline, Massachusetts, the postman delivered one to Amy Lowell from Fletcher. It consisted of four sheets covered on both sides in a sprawling hand which slanted every which way, with some words crossed out and others misspelled or written over, and in general displayed a nervous and sensitive temperament under great strain. It was dated Friday, September 7, 1913, from 4, Adelphi Terrace. Fletcher wrote:

"Dear Miss Lowell,

"I have a very important piece of news for you, which will excuse my writing thus bluntly. I want to advise you very strongly against going in Pound's proposed anthology.

"The anthology is not to be edited, really, by Pound. Aldington, the author of the silly sophomoric letter in the New Freewoman, is really the editor. The aim and object—not avowed, but secret—of the whole affair is to boom Aldington—to give him such a send-off in the United States that he and Pound will divide the country between them.

"If Aldington were really any good as a poet, I would not care. But I hate to see a rigged-up game being foisted on the public to boom a silly cub who deserves nothing but a licking.

"You see, the more names he has to act as satellites to his work, and

Life mask by Nancy Cox McCormack, Paris, 1921

"Hieratic head" by Gaudier-Brzeska, London, 1914

Portrait by Wyndham Lewis, undated. Reproduced by courtesy of the Trustees of the Tate Gallery, London

Dorothy Pound

Her mother: Olivia Shakespear

his wife's (he has just married H. D. another 'arriviste') the more likely his book is to be puffed. Therefore he wants yours. Also mine. He intends to use, of course, our weakest work, so his own will shine by comparison.

"He proposes to print, as a sort of annex, *parodies of himself,* and the letter mentioned above.

"You will say my letter is actuated by jealousy or spite. Not at all.

"I have refused, not once, but several times, to enter this anthology. And if I were starving on the streets I should continue to refuse. I will not let my name or my work stand as the support of a school with which [?of which] I disapprove.

"On the other hand, I believe you are sincerely trying to create great art. And there is a quality in your work—some of it—that I extremely admire, and that I rate higher than Aldington's or Pound's.

"You were also very nice to me, personally. I am not one of those who take favours from others, and then slip my knife in their backs."

He urged her to insist on being given more space, or to withdraw. Miss Lowell actually wrote to Pound, but received no reply; perhaps it was too late to do anything about it.[13]

Aldington wrote me: "The *animus* of Fletcher against me is quite unfounded. As a matter of fact, Ezra collected the poems without consulting me or showing them, and if the anthology was to boost anyone it was H.D., plainly labeled 'Imagiste' in her first contribution to *Poetry.* Certainly not me."

6.

Meanwhile, in the shack overlooking the Jersey meadows, Kreymborg and Man Ray awaited the printing press and the contributions they hoped would come. In the post office in the nearby village of Grantwood there arrived, one day, a package from London wrapped in what appeared to Kreymborg as the kind of heavy paper used by butchers. Inside was "a sheaf of manuscripts of various dimensions, edited with bold, marginal notes," together with "caustic instructions," *viz.*:

"Unless you're another American ass, you'll set this up just as it stands."

Kreymborg held in his hands poems by Aldington, H. D., Flint,

Cannéll, Miss Lowell, Williams, Joyce, Pound, Ford Madox Hueffer, Allen Upward and John Cournos. He wrote in *Troubadour*: "Man and Krimmie indulged in a delirious war-dance." Recovering, they decided to run the group as the first issue of *The Glebe*—as soon as the press came.

On a Saturday afternoon a small, horse-drawn cart driven by two elderly men appeared. In it was the printing press. As Kreymborg wrote, "It had come from downtown Manhattan, across the Fulton Street ferry, up the Jersey banks of the Hudson, over the Palisades and down to the shack without mishap." Then it happened. As the two elderly men struggled to get the press down, it slipped from their grasp and crashed to the ground. "An excited examination disclosed that only the most important parts were broken." But perhaps they could find an inexpensive printer in New York? Kreymborg told the whole story in a letter to Pound, who sent back a post card reading: "All right, we can wait."

Kreymborg did not find a printer, inexpensive or otherwise; he found a publisher—Albert and Charles Boni, in Greenwich Village. It is now necessary to correct some of the errors that crept into his account, and thence into *The Little Magazine: A History and a Bibliography*, the authors of which, having placed their reliance on Kreymborg's *Troubadour*, perpetuated his errors. For while Kreymborg wrote only a dozen years after the events he describes, it is probable that he, like others before him, has merged two periods—that of *The Glebe*, of which he was not the founder, and that of *Others*, of which he was. In a letter to Williams of December, 1913, Pound wrote: "I suppose you've seen Demuth about *The Glebe*—if not take my introduction to Alfred Kreymborg." If this means anything, it means that the publication was already under way when Kreymborg showed the Bonis the manuscript of *Des Imagistes*. Charles Demuth, the painter, had been a schoolfellow of Pound's and Williams's at Penn. Kreymborg became editor of *The Glebe* with its second number.

There were ten issues in all, each one, with the exception of *Des Imagistes*, given over to a single author. The series received its name from Adolf Wolff, a sculptor whose poetry under the title of *Songs, Sighs and Curses* adorned the first number. Albert Boni told me he was not crazy about *The Glebe* as over-all title, and the world has been extraordinarily silent about *Songs, Sighs and Curses*; Mr. Boni recalled only that the poems were of the "cosmic" order. The second number consisted of *The Diary of a Suicide,* by Wallace E. Baker, the third of a one-act play by Charles Demuth. The fourth was a play by Andreyev, the fifth *Des Imagistes;* Kreymborg is named as editor on the cover, but of course the real editor of that issue was Pound. The sixth contained Kreymborg's novelette, *Erna Vitek.* The seventh was *Collects* by Horace Traubel, the friend of Whitman, and the eighth *Poems* by George Cronyn, which Kreymborg gives as number one. The last two issues were devoted to translations of plays by Wedekind.

The Glebe was published at more or less regular monthly intervals, in paper covers, for sale at fifty cents, with a few copies bound in boards; subscription by the year, three dollars. *Des Imagistes, An Anthology,* consists of 64 pages, the last one blank and unnumbered. It is pleasant in format. There is a page advertisement of *Poetry* in the back, and an announcement of Kreymborg's forthcoming "novel." It was published at the shop of Albert and Charles Boni, 96 Fifth Avenue, in February, 1914. The issue is led off by Aldington's "Choricos," and in it Joyce's "I Hear an Army" received its first American publication.

7.

Two things strike a reader at once—the many poems, including four of Pound's six, which are adapted from the Chinese or formed on Chinese models, and the many, including Pound's other two, which are influenced by Greek art, thought and poetry. The six poems are: "Δώρια," "The Return," "After Ch'u Yuan," "Liu Ch'e," "Fan-Piece for Her Imperial Lord," and "Ts'ai Chi'h." Perhaps the pervasive Chinese tone is due not only to Pound but to Allen Upward, an English scholar and barrister who, inspired by Giles's *Chinese Poetry,* had been writing in that vein since 1900.

The poems of Flint are well worth reperusal, for they appear to have acted as source material for a more famous poet. I give two passages:

> I know this room,
> and there are corridors:
> the pictures, I have seen before. . . .

Tired faces,
eyes that have never seen the world,
bodies that have never lived in air,
lips that have never minted speech. . . .

Flint had translated Jean de Bosschère's *The Closed Door,* which
Conrad Aiken thinks influenced Eliot directly—"a cadenced, highly
colloquial verse, the unacknowledged fountain of a lot of that
period."[14]

Between the end of the anthology proper and the bibliography
there are some curious verses, with the title "Documents" (the
"annex" which Fletcher mentions). The first one is signed "R.A.,"
and appears to be a good-natured onslaught on another writer; Aldington, who had forgotten all about it, told me that it was meant to spoof
Ford Madox Hueffer. The second one, though unsigned, is obviously
by Pound. The second name in his title is that of Desmond Fitzgerald,
one of the Hulme circle, afterwards a member of the Irish Free State
government.

TO HULME (T. E.) AND FITZGERALD

Is there for feckless poverty
That grins at ye for a' that!
A hired slave to none am I,
But under-fed for a' that;
For a' that and a' that,
The toils I shun and a' that,
My name but mocks the guinea stamp,
And Pound's dead broke for a' that.

Although my linen still is clean,
My socks fine silk and a' that,
Although I dine and drink good wine—
Say, twice a week, and a' that;
For a' that and a' that,
My tinsel shows and a' that,
These breeks'll no last many weeks
'Gainst wear and tear and a' that.

Ye see this birkie ca'ed a bard,
Wi' cryptic eyes and a' that,
Aesthetic phrases by the yard;
It's but E. P. for a' that,
For a' that and a' that,
My verses, books and a' that,
The man of independent means
He looks and laughs at a' that.

One man will make a novelette
And sell the same and a' that.
For verse nae man can siller get,
Nae editor maun fa' that.
For a' that and a' that,
Their royalties and a' that,
Wi' time to loaf and will to write
I'll stick to rhyme for a' that.

And ye may prise and gang your ways
Wi' pity, sneers and a' that,
I know my trade and God has made
Some men to rhyme and a' that,
For a' that and a' that,
I maun gang on for a' that
Wi' verse to verse until the hearse
Carts off me wame and a' that.

The Glebe, Volume I, No. 5, created more of a stir than its predecessors in the series, and the Bonis announced it would be issued as a
book, at one dollar. It appeared in April, 1914, in blue cloth covers,
without *The Glebe* designation. Four hundred and eighty copies had
been ordered in advance. It was widely reviewed; Miss Lowell thought,
"very ignorantly." *Des Imagistes* was also published in London, by
the Poetry Book Shop, Harold Monro, prop. It fell dead there. Some
purchasers charged down Devonshire Street with the book in their
hands and demanded their money back.

CHAPTER VII

POUND AND ROBERT FROST

> And the days are not full enough
> And the nights are not full enough
> And life slips by like a field mouse
> Not shaking the grass.
> —Epigraph to *Lustra*

1.

Pound kept his mother and father fully informed of his activities, and his letters home are models of that type. He advised them what to read—occasionally "how." They, naturally, wanted him to return —he had been long away; but in the end it was he who prevailed— they went abroad to be near him in Italy. To judge by his own comments on them, his father's letters were more cheerful than his mother's, and he replied accordingly. His mother felt, and expressed, the usual concern which, however elegantly phrased, comes down at last to proper diet for an absent son. Perhaps she had learned of those days of "utter privation."

"Dear Mother: Your remarks on 'low diet and sedentary life' are ludicrously inappropriate—if that's any comfort to you. As to the cup of joy I dare say I do as well as most in the face of the spectacle of human imbecility.

"As to practicality. I should think with the two specimens you hold up to me, you'd be about through with your moralization on that subject. Surely the older generation (A. F. and T. C. P.) attended to the world's commerce with a certain assiduity, and camped not in the fields of the muses.

"I don't suppose America has more fools per acre than other countries, still your programme of the Ethical Society presents no new argument for my return."

The initials in his letter stand for his grandfather and grand-uncle, of whom more later. His mother went abroad to meet him, and he showed her Venice.

The pattern had been formed. It suited him. His reasons for staying in England were varied and valid. One may wish he had returned to his native land or, alternatively, whilst remaining in England, that he had confined himself to his own creations. But were not his discovery and championship of others a contribution to the culture of both countries? His impatience with the United States— to call it nothing worse—did not apply to its artists. Someone with leanings in that direction could abstract, from his critical writings and letters alone, a monumental tribute.

Fletcher commented, "The more I studied him, the more I was convinced that he was a queer combination of an international Bohemian and of an American college professor out of a job,"[1] to which Horace Gregory, when quoting this, added: "a minister of the arts without portfolio."[2]

Pound was indefatigable in his pursuit of original work, and seemed to thrive on discovery. A lesser man or poet might have seen only potential rivals in the men and women Pound presented to editors or helped to fame. It was, as he realized from time to time, a career in itself. He complained that other people's business was absorbing his time and energies; but he must have known when he complained that he could not do otherwise. From this point on there is even a crescendo in his *"creative* sympathy," as Wyndham Lewis was to term it.

He wrote to Alice Corbin Henderson, Miss Monroe's assistant:

"Have just discovered another Amur'kn. Vurry Amur'k'n, with, I think, the seeds of grace. Have reviewed an advance copy of his book, but have run it out too long. Will send it as soon as I've tried to condense it—also some of his stuff if it isn't all in the book."

He sent the review to Miss Monroe:

"Sorry I can't work this review down to any smaller dimensions!

However, it can't be helped. Yes it can. I've done the job better than I thought I could. And it's our second scoop, for I only found the man by accident and I think I've about the only copy of the book that has left the shop."

Both letters are dated March, 1913, days unspecified.

2.

In April, with twenty-eight pounds received from *Poetry* with "thanks, salaams, etc.," Pound went to Sirmione, the promontory on the Lake of Garda where Catullus lived, where Dante stayed. In May he was in Venice. He sent his mother photographs of a Donatello Madonna and an interior "which I don't think you saw. At least I wasn't with you if you did see it." He advised her to read Butler's *The Way of All Flesh.* He added a sentence or two of news: "The Doolittles are here, père et mère. Also Hilda and Richard."

He was back in London before the end of the month and plunged into editorship again. He wrote Miss Monroe: "I've been so fortunate as to get some prose from Hueffer." He asked her to "clear the decks for it, s.v.p." She did; it appeared under the title, "Impressionism."

In June he wrote his father:

"Dear Dad: Thanks for your cheerful letter. If there is any joy in having found one's 'maximum utility,' I should think you might have it, with your asylum for the protection of the unfortunate. As for T. C., it is rather fine to see the old bird still holding out, still thinking he'll do something, and that he has some shreds of influence.

"I'll try to get you a copy of Frost. I'm using mine at present to boom him and get his name stuck about. He has done a 'Death of the Farm Hand' since the book that is to my mind better than anything in it. I shall have that in the *Smart Set* or in *Poetry* before long.

"Whitman is a hard nutt. The *Leaves of Grass* is the book. It is impossible to read it without swearing at the author almost continuously. Begin on the 'Songs of Parting'—perhaps on the last one which is called 'So Long!', that has I suppose nearly all of him in it.

"We had a terribly literary dinner on Saturday. Tagore, his son and daughter-in-law, Hewlett, May Sinclair, Prothero (edt. *Quarterly Rev.*), Evelyn Underhill (author of divers fat books on mysticism), D. and myself."

"Sedentary" may have rankled: "Am playing tennis with Hueffer in the afternoons." It is in this letter that he refers to Rummel "playing at Mrs. Fowler's Friday, before his public concert."

As to "The Death of the Hired Man," Fletcher relates that Pound spoke to him "very highly" of Frost, and on a subsequent visit, "he picked up a typewritten manuscript lying on the table and proceeded to read it aloud. . . . to the last syllable with every mark of admiration." This nonplussed Fletcher, whose poetry—in particular, *Irradiations*—was so different and which had also been admired by Pound, despite some strictures. Fletcher asked: "Was it then that Ezra Pound was simply a chameleon, shifting his opinions from day to day as he shifted his coat; or did he frankly possess some touchstone of superior judgment which enabled him to admire equally poems so diverse as Frost's and my own?"[3]

3.

There are several versions of the way in which Pound and Robert Frost became acquainted; Frost is the source for all, varying the tale with advancing years. A synthesis is possible.

After the manuscript of *A Boy's Will* had been accepted Frost walked about London. On Devonshire Street, at nightfall, he saw a shop with a swinging sign displaying three torches on a blue field, its window full of books, broadsides and photographs. It was the Poetry Book Shop. It happened to be a night for a "poetry squash"; Frost entered, and found a place on the stair. Another latecomer, sitting just below him, remarked: "I can see by your shoes you are an American." The speaker was F. S. Flint, and in a moment the two were engaged in conversation. When Frost said that he wrote poetry, Flint asked him if he knew, or had heard of his countryman, Ezra Pound. Frost had not, which seems odd, and was cautioned not to tell Pound this when they met.

It would appear that Flint spoke about the other handsome American, for Frost received a card from Pound, with the following annotation: "At home sometimes." Months passed before Frost called. Gorham B. Munson, to whom Frost told the story, wrote in 1927:

"Piqued at first because Frost had been so leisurely in responding to his card, Pound soon warmed to his rugged caller with the boyish face and when he learned that possibly proof sheets of *A Boy's Will* might be secured at David Nutt's he insisted on going at once to the office. The proof sheets were ready, and the pair returned to Pound's studio. Frost was directed to occupy himself in some way while Pound turned immediately to reading the poems. Satisfied that here was sound poetry, Pound then dismissed his guest with the remark that he had a review to write, and in a short time the first salutation to *A Boy's Will* appeared in type over the distinguished name of Ezra Pound."[4]

When Frost told the story to John Holmes in 1936 he said Pound asked him if the book were already out, to which he replied that he knew nothing about it. Pound put on his hat and they went to 17 Grape Street, the Nutt office, where "Frost had the pleasure of seeing Pound buy a copy of the book he had not yet seen."[5]

That Frost called more than once is apparent from the nature of the review which Pound wrote; and additional evidence is provided by another visitor.

Ralph Fletcher Seymour, who had designed and was now printing *Poetry*, called on Pound with a letter of introduction from Harriet Monroe. There had already been some correspondence between the two men, for Seymour had branched into publishing, and it is he who is meant in Pound's first letter to Miss Monroe—"my Arnaut Daniel has gone to the publisher." So certain was Pound it would be published that in the following year, in the bibliography of his work appearing in *Des Imagistes,* he lists *The Canzoni of Arnaut Daniel,* R. F. Seymour & Co., Fine Arts Building, Chicago. But it never appeared. Mr. Seymour told me:

"I had a manuscript in this office for a year or more, returning it only because my then partner thought Pound bad business. It was a translation of a jongleur's chanson, and Walter Morse Rummel had transcribed the funny-looking musical notation into what I supposed was trustworthy modern notation."

Undiscouraged by the fact that Mr. Seymour had nothing definite to tell him about the Daniel, Pound gave him an account of *Patria Mia,* and followed up by sending him the manuscript. It disappeared. In 1950, it was found, still in its original envelope, and Mr. Seymour proceeded to publish it. There was a great stir over Pound's "lost essay," as it is designated in library indexes. A typist could have copied it from the files of the *New Age*.

The afternoon that he called on Pound Mr. Seymour found the downstairs door locked. As he stood there knocking, another man arrived and also knocked. "He was dignified, a little shabby, almost a small town schoolmaster, but much too awake and smart." This was Frost. A third man came—"short, rather thin, with dark hair and clean-cut, English features. His forehead was prominent, expressive eyes dominated his face. He was English." He was Cournos.

The door was finally opened by Mrs. Langley, the landlady, who had been mopping the stairs. She wiped her hands on a rag and let them in. The three men filed past her and ascended the narrow stairs to Pound's room. Seymour noted that "books were everywhere; old leather trunks bulged with them, the limp, wire-cloth couch seat was held up by dusty tomes shoved underneath." There was also, he observed, the latest issue of *La Vie Parisienne*.

Pound told them they were all expected at May Sinclair's for tea. "He strode there at the head of our small procession, tall, fair-skinned, blond, clothed in black with black, flat-rimmed hat, carrying a long, gold-headed cane."[6]

"Pound was really friendly to me," Mr. Seymour told me in 1959. "We went to some newsman's lunching clubs and to several bohemianish group meetings. Later, in Paris, as he was returning to London from a few weeks off up in the Swiss alps, he took the trouble to look me up and we loafed in a street café down in front of the Opera.

"Pound struck me as an amiable, distinguished, somewhat opinionated, thoroughly well informed, slightly nervous gentleman absorbed in establishing a background which would enable him to pay his bills, perfect himself in the romance languages, and express true virtues in his own writings. He was as interesting to look at as his photographs have almost unfailingly shown him to be. His manners were quiet and gentlemanly."

4.

Mr. Munson also heard from Frost of a luncheon with Pound, to which both had been invited by two ladies: "Pound disgusted by their shallow flow of talk on art, Pound rising, knocking his chair over as he did so, saying haughtily, 'I leave these ladies to you,' departing to Frost's consternation."

Mr. Munson also mentions "the jiu jitsu demonstration Pound made on Frost's person in a restaurant," possibly another occasion; and "Pound's challenge to Lascelles Abercrombie to fight a duel on the score that Abercrombie's articles were a public offense—and the amusing aftermath," which he omits. It was Abercrombie who had persuaded Frost to live with him and his family at Ryton, Gloucestershire, where Edward Thomas and Wilfrid Gibson were frequent visitors.

As to the duel: Abercrombie had written an article advising young poets to abandon realism and study Wordsworth. According to Fletcher, Pound wrote him as follows: " 'Dear Mr. Abercrombie: Stupidity carried beyond a certain point becomes a public menace. I hereby challenge you to a duel, to be fought at the earliest moment that is suited to your convenience. My seconds will wait upon you in due course. Yours sincerely, Ezra Pound.' For a moment this letter, recited gleefully to me by its author, seemed a clever thing; but it soon seemed to me that its indignation was far too strenuous. Whistler, under similar circumstances, would have contented himself with a contemptuous gibe."[7]

It would be interesting to know what seconds Pound had in mind; in the event, they were not required. Abercrombie, says Fletcher, took the challenge seriously, because a friend of his had told him that "Ezra was an expert fencer," forgetting that as the challenged party he could choose the weapon; but when this thought finally struck him, he replied to Pound, accepting the challenge, "but proposed that the parties concerned should mutually bombard each other with unsold copies of their own books," some commentators adding at fifteen paces, some twenty or thirty.

Cournos wrote that Abercrombie went to see Yeats about it, "and who should open the door to him but Ezra in person. If what I heard is correct, Abercrombie turned on his heels and fled."[8]

Cournos told me: "Pound was always there."

It was not only to talk or to listen that Pound came; he was teaching Yeats to fence; hence the Irish poet's stanza—

I thought no more was needed
Youth to prolong
Than dumbbell and foil
To keep the body young.

His biographer says that during the winter of 1912–1913 "his life in Woburn Buildings was only rendered tolerable by the assiduous attentions of Ezra Pound." He adds: "It was during one bout of indigestion that he worked himself into a fury against Wordsworth as a clumsy humbug."[9] Pound may have caught the fury from him; or vice versa.

"I shall never forget my surprise," Goldring wrote, "when Ezra took me for the first time to one of Yeats's 'Mondays' at the way in which he dominated the room, distributed Yeats's cigarettes and Chianti, and laid down the law about poetry. Poor golden-bearded Sturge Moore, who sat in a corner with a large musical instrument by his side (on which he was never given a chance of performing) endeavoured to join in the discussion on prosody, a subject on which he believed himself not entirely ignorant, but Ezra promptly reduced him to a glum silence."[10]

Association with Yeats led Pound to an interest in Irish affairs; or perhaps it was merely his gregarious nature. The Irish Literary Society, which Yeats had helped to found, and where he "constantly fought out our Irish quarrels," met in Bloomsbury Mansions; and thither went Pound and Hulme, and occasionally another member of their circle, F. W. Tancred. Padraic Colum told me of a "celidh," one of the informal gatherings that took place on Saturday night, at which Hulme and Tancred got up on the platform and did a clowning act, Hulme being big and Tancred little; and of another where Pound held forth on Irish themes. "Good tea" was served there, Colum said, "one of the best teas in London"—no doubt, Irish. (Mary Colum thought Pound "liked to be mixed up in everything that was going on around him." In her book—to which I will refer again—she tells of an "Irish race convention" in Paris, the organizers of which brought together prominent Continentals of Irish ancestry. It was presided over by the Spanish Duke of Tetuan. Pound, she says, escorted Yeats to it. He is also thought to have written one of the speeches.)

Those musical instruments Yeats's friends were always carting around—Miss Farr's psaltery, Sturge Moore's whatever it was, probably another psaltery, or possibly virginal—intrigued Pound. They had all come from the workshop of Arnold Dolmetsch, and a great desire to possess one himself came over him. He may have mentioned this to Alvin Langdon Coburn, the famous photographer, who was a friend of the Dolmetsch family, for they went to Haslemere together. Mrs. Dolmetsch wrote me: "Ezra Pound, then a budding poet, of rather flamboyant appearance, was immediately attracted to Arnold Dolmetsch; and through their continued intercourse he became deeply interested in the English music of former centuries. He delighted in listening to Arnold's performances on the *clavichord*. For this reason he became possessed of one." Pound, in fact, asked Dolmetsch to make him a duplicate of his own instrument, but was sold the original instead. He still has it; in 1959 he ordered new strings.

When Arnold and Mabel Dolmetsch visited him in Kensington, he showed them examples of his friends' art. "One thing which greatly amused us," she wrote, "was that he pulled out a drawing by one of his associates which was perfectly *normal*; and then showed us the finished version, wherein the same had been madly distorted, according to the fashion then in vogue. At sight of this Arnold was overcome with mirth."

When Pound showed Gaudier-Brzeska's "Embracers" to his landlord, that worthy remarked:

"Dew what you like with me, think of a man cuttin' that in stone!"

5.

Mr. Munson quotes a number of early reviews of Frost's work in an appendix to his little volume, but omits Pound's.

Pound's review of *A Boy's Will* appeared in *The New Freewoman* September 1, 1913. Two lines from the book served as epigraph:

> I had withdrawn in forest, and my song
> Was swallowed up in leaves,

from "A Dream Pang." The review began:

"There is another personality in the realm of verse, another American, found, as usual, on this side of the water, by an English publisher long known as a lover of good letters. David Nutt publishes at his own expense *A Boy's Will*, by Robert Frost, the latter having been long scorned by the 'great American editors.' It is the old story.

"Mr. Frost's book is a little raw, and has in it a number of infelicities; underneath them it has the tang of the New Hampshire woods, and it has just this utter simplicity. It is not post-Miltonic or post-Swinburnian or post-Kiplonian. This man has the good sense to speak naturally and to paint the thing, the thing as he sees it. And to do this is a very different matter from gunning about for the circumplectious polysyllable.

"It is almost on this account that it is a difficult book to quote from."

Nevertheless, he quoted; and, for a brief review, a great deal—two lines and the final stanza from "My November Guest," three lines from "Mowing," and a complete poem. It would appear that Pound and Frost talked intimately when they met.

"There is perhaps as much of Frost's personal tone in the following little catch, which is short enough to quote, as in anything else. It is to his wife, written when his grandfather and his uncle had disinherited him of a comfortable fortune and left him in poverty because he was a useless poet instead of a money-getter.

IN NEGLECT

> They leave us so to the way we took,
>   As two in whom they were proved mistaken,
> That we sit sometimes in a wayside nook,
> With mischievous, vagrant, seraphic look,
>   And *try* if we cannot feel forsaken.

"There are graver things, but they suffer too much by making excerpts. One reads the book for the 'tone,' which is homely, by intent, and pleasing, never doubting that it comes direct from his own life, and that no two lives are the same.

"He has now and then such a swift and bold expression as

> The whimper of hawks beside the sun.

He has now and then a beautiful simile, well used, but he is for the most part as simple as the lines I have quoted in opening or as in the poem of mowing. He is without sham and without affectation."

It remains a curious fact, as Mr. Munson pointed out in his book, that Frost left the United States in September, 1912, despairing of ever being published there, and that a month later Harriet Monroe launched *Poetry: A Magazine of Verse*. It is perhaps equally curious that with that publication functioning so well Pound did not store his ammunition. The United States, for all that it lay over the ocean, presented a broad target, and he fired away. His preoccupation with it, which never left him, was that of a lover who abuses his mistress through the mails and then wonders why she doesn't love him. He ended his review of Frost's second book in *Poetry* (December, 1914) as follows:

"It is natural and proper that I should have to come abroad to get printed, or that 'H. D.'—with her clear-cut derivations and her revivifications of Greece—should have to come abroad; or that Fletcher—with his *tic* and his discords and his contrariety and extended knowledge of everything—should have to come abroad. One need not censure the country; it is easier for us to emigrate than for America to change her civilization fast enough to please us. But why, IF there are serious people in America, desiring literature of America, literature accepting present conditions, rendering American life with sober fidelity—why, in heaven's name, is this book of New England eclogues given us under a foreign imprint?"

6.

One-half of Pound's correspondence is the history of poetry in our time and a curriculum for poets. Boswell has related how he trudged over half London in order to verify a single date; Pound was no less persevering as a literary impresario. He put no reliance on local critics: "I go about this London hunting for the real. I find paper after paper, person after person, mildly affirming the opinion of someone who hasn't cared enough about the art to tell what he actually believes." As for the poets themselves: "I'm sick to loathing of people who don't care for the master-work, who set out as artists with no intention of producing it, who make no effort toward the best, who are content with publicity and the praise of reviewers."

The other half seems a waste of spirit. The poet and teacher wrote to the editor of the Boston *Transcript:*

"Dear Sir: I don't know that it is worth my while to call any one of your reviewers a liar, but the case has its technical aspects and the twistings of malice are, to me at least, entertaining.

"I note in *Current Opinion* for June a quotation from your paper to the effect that my friend Robert Frost has done what no other American poet had done in this generation 'and that is, unheralded, unintroduced, untrumpeted, he won the acceptance of an English publisher on his own terms' etc.

"Now seriously, what about me? Your (?negro)[11] reviewer might acquaint himself with that touching little scene in Elkin Mathews' shop some years since.

"Mathews: 'Ah, eh, ah, would you, now, be prepared to assist in the publication?'

"E. P.: 'I've a shilling in my clothes, if that's any use to you.'

"Mathews: 'Oh well. I want to publish 'em. Anyhow.'

"And he did. No, sir, Frost was a bloated capitalist when he struck this island, in comparison to yours truly, and you can put that in your editorial pipe though I don't give a damn whether you print the fact. . . .'"

CHAPTER VIII

POUND AND YEATS

1.

The association between Ezra Pound and William Butler Yeats was long, intimate and beneficial to both. However different their outlook, both were dedicated men, and their friendship, nurtured at first by the younger man's attentions, was sustained by a mutual respect; with forbearance, when strains appeared, usually supplied by the older. But it was not in Woburn Buildings, on those atmospheric Mondays or other times, that their friendship ripened, but in Sussex—first— where they lived together, and afterwards as neighbors in Rapallo. The turn in their relationship came in 1913. On August 5th of that year Yeats wrote his father:

"Next winter I am taking a secretary though I shrink from the expense, believing that I shall be able to bear the expense because I shall be able to write. When my sec comes at the end of October you will find me a better correspondent as he will answer the business letters."

Pound wrote his mother before leaving London:

"My stay in Stone Cottage will not be in the least profitable. I detest the country. Yeats will amuse me part of the time and bore me to death with psychical research the rest. I regard the visit as a duty to posterity."

She sent him a birthday check, which he acknowledged as follows:

"Dear Mother: I plan to spend my birthday largesse in the purchase of four luxurious undershirts. Or rather I had planned so to do; if, however, the bloody guardsman who borrowed my luxurious hat from the Cabaret cloak room (*not* by accident) does not return the same, I shall probably divert certain shekels from the yaeger."

The "Cabaret" was the "Cabaret Club," on Beak Street, owned by Madame Strindberg (the playwright's third wife). It was the first night club in London. Epstein columns supported the ceilings, and the walls were decorated—or as Sir Osbert Sitwell put it, "hideously but relevantly frescoed"—by Wyndham Lewis. There was a pervasive pink, and the gathering frenzy of the eve of war was expressed by fashionable and artistic clients dancing the fox trot and the bunny hug. Perhaps the guardsman of Pound's letter saw the poet arrive, his bright hair topped by the big black flopping hat, and marked it for his own. "*Not* by accident." It must have been a ravishing sight and temptation to the guardsman, who perhaps could not help exclaiming over it. He was overheard, but not believed. The rest is silence.

Pound gave his mother a résumé of his activities:

"I seem to spend most of my time attending to other people's affairs, weaning young poetettes from obscurity into the glowing pages of divers rotten publications, etc. Besieging the Home Office to let that ass K – – – stay in the country for his own good if not for its. Conducting a literary kindergarten for the aspiring, etc. etc."

"Richard and Hilda were decently married last week, or the week before, as you have doubtless been notified.

"Brigit Patmore is very ill but they have decided to let her live, which is a mercy as there are none too many charming people on the planet."

He hoped it was definitely settled that his mother would come over in the spring. "If dad can't come then, we'll try to arrange that for the year after."

The Home Office reference concerns Harry Kemp, an American poet of that period, later known for his autobiographical *Tramping on Life*. He told me in 1924, with the same enthusiasm which had carried him across the ocean into trouble eleven years before, that he felt that he could not live another moment without seeing "the land of the English poets." He stowed away, and was arrested the moment he set foot on that sacred soil. His explanation, which was reported in the press, and the activities on his behalf by Pound, who got other poets to help, were to no avail, for Kemp had come upon officialdom; or perhaps it was the other way around; and he stayed in a room without a view until another ship took him back.

As for Brigit Patmore's charm, Cournos terms her one of the two most beautiful women he met in London. There is an excellent picture of her in his book; very pre-Raphaelite—indeed, she appears to be leaning on the gold bar of Heaven.

As for Mrs. Pound's visit, Cournos recollected that she came to London "in 1913 or 1914." She was not present at her son's marriage to Dorothy Shakespear in April, 1914. Cournos had tea with her and Pound in a Museum Street tea shop.

"Ezra tried to needle me into speaking against the United States and in praise of Europe, because his mother didn't want him to remain abroad," Cournos told me.

It is possible that both of Pound's parents came at least once, for D. H. Lawrence recalled both for an American friend. Standing beside the fireplace, his red beard glowing like another lick of the flame, he described the young Pound he had met—"and there stood a young, callow, swashbuckling Ezra, with an ear-ring in one ear, very affected and silly. Then came his parents to London to see him, after Ezra had the London drawing-rooms bewitched by his mannerisms and affectations; and they were good plain middle-western folks—and Ezra died away, and there were pa and ma, good and plain and middle-western, and poor Ezra not knowing what to do about them."[1]

2.

Stone Cottage, Coleman's Hatch, Sussex, stood on a heath with its back to the woods. There were four rooms. Yeats had found it while visiting the H. T. Tuckers in nearby Ashdown Forest. Mr. Tucker was a brother of Olivia Shakespear. His wife, the former Mrs. Hyde-Lees, had a daughter by her first marriage. It may be that Miss Hyde-Lees was as much of a reason for Yeats taking the cottage as the woods in which he enjoyed walking, for he afterwards married her.

Pound wrote Amy Lowell: "W. B. Y. and I are very placid in the country." He also told her: "I've resigned from *Poetry* in Hueffer's favour, but I believe he has resigned in mine and I don't know yet whether I'm shed of the bloomin' paper or not."

He wrote to Miss Monroe: "All right, but I do not see that there was anything for me to have done save resign at the time I did so. I don't think you have yet tried to see the magazine from my viewpoint.

"I don't mind the award as it seems to be Yeats who makes it, or at least 'suggests,' and as you have my own contrary suggestion for the disposal of the money made before I knew Lindsay had been otherwise provided for.

"For the rest, if I stay on the magazine it has got to improve. It's all very well for Yeats to be ceremonious in writing to you, a stranger, and in a semi-public letter. Nobody holds *him* responsible for the rot that goes into the paper."

Yeats had written to Miss Monroe:

"When I got the very unexpected letter with the prize of £50, my first emotion was how much it would have meant to me even ten years ago; and then I thought surely there must be some young American writer today to whom it would mean a great deal, not only in practical help, but in encouragement. I want you therefore not to think that I am in any way ungrateful to you, or in any way anxious to put myself into a different category to your other contributors because I send back to you £40. I will keep £10, and with that I will get Mr. Sturge Moore to make me a book-plate, and so shall have a permanent memory of your generous magazine. I vacillated a good deal until I thought of this solution, for it seemed to me so ungracious to refuse; but if I had accepted I should have been bothered by the image of some unknown needy young man in a garret."

Later, he wrote Miss Monroe again:

"I want to make a suggestion which you need not follow in any way. Why not give the £40 to Ezra Pound? I suggest him to you because, although I do not really like with my whole soul the metrical experiments he has made for you, I think those experiments show a vigorous creative mind. He is certainly a creative personality of some sort, though it is too soon yet to say of what sort. His experiments are perhaps errors, I am not certain; but I would always sooner give the laurel to vigorous errors than to any orthodoxy not inspired."

Pound wrote Williams, December 19th:

"I am very placid and happy and busy. Dorothy is learning Chinese. I've all old Fenollosa's treasures in mss.

"Yeats is much finer *intime* than seen spasmodically in the midst of the whirl. We are both, I think, very contented in Sussex. He returned $200 of that award with orders that it be sent to me—and it has been."

Poetry had announced an award of $250 for the best poem published during its first year. Pound's vote for "The Grey Rock" decided the issue. Miss Monroe then persuaded Albert H. Loeb, one of the original backers of the magazine, to offer a second prize of $100, which went to Lindsay for his "General Booth Enters into Heaven." Among the honorable mentions was "Choricos."

Some of the poems Yeats was writing during this sojourn in Stone Cottage appeared in *Responsibilities*. His father was pleased to learn that Yeats had returned to Irish legend, as in "The Grey Rock," though ostensibly addressed to the shades of the Rhymers' Club, particularly those of Ernest Dowson and Lionel Johnson; and "The Two Kings," which J. B. Yeats deemed "Homeric," but which Pound labeled something else. Yeats complained to his father, who wrote back:

"What the devil does Ezra Pound mean by comparing 'The Two Kings' with Tennyson's Idylls? 'The Two Kings' is immortal because of its *intensity* and *concentration*. In 'The Two Kings' there is another quality often sought for by Tennyson but never attained, and that is *Splendour of Imagination*—a liberating splendour cold as the sunrise. I do not agree with Ezra Pound. It is so full of the 'tears of things' that I could not read it aloud, and yet Ezra is the best of critics and writes with such lucid force, and I am only an amateur—but I have the advantage. I am longer in the world and have travelled further, and *intensity* and *concentration* are not Tennysonian."[2]

J. B. Yeats had another advantage—he was Irish.

Pound later reviewed Yeats's *Responsibilities,* in which "The Grey Rock" appears, in *Poetry*. It may have surprised the older poet to find that he, too, was writing "Imagisme." Pound said: "Mr. Yeats is a symbolist, but he has written *des Images* as have many good poets before him; so that is nothing against him, and he has nothing against them (*les Imagistes*), at least so far as I know—except what he calls 'their devil's metres.' "

Yeats, who was forty-eight—twenty years older—found Pound "a learned companion and a pleasant one." He wrote Lady Gregory: "He is full of the Middle Ages and helps me to get back to the definite and concrete, away from modern abstractions, to talk over a poem with him is like getting you to put a sentence into dialect. All becomes clear and natural." Pound read to him in the evenings: "Ezra never shrinks from work." But in a letter to Sir William Rothenstein, Yeats termed Pound's "a rugged and headstrong nature, and he is always hurting people's feelings, but he has I think some genius and great goodwill."

Good will was needed on both sides, all things considered. Yeats tried to read him, "struggling with my rhythms and saying they wouldn't do," Pound wrote Professor Schelling. "I got him to read a little Burns aloud, telling him he cd. read no cadence but his own, or some verse like Sturge Moore's that had not any real characteristics strong enough to prohibit W. B. Y. reading it to his own rhythm. I had a half hour of unmitigated glee in hearing 'Say ye bonnie Alexander' and 'The Birks o Averfeldy' *keened*, wailed with infinite difficulty and many pauses and restarts to *The Wind Among the Reeds*."

3.

Although Pound was engrossed in the Fenollosa manuscripts, London had attractions, too, and he was often there—to visit Dorothy Shakespear and her mother, to see his friends and, in general, keeping an eye on the literary scene. In the letter to Williams, from which I have already quoted, he wrote:

"Have just bought two statuettes from *the* coming sculptor, Gaudier-Brzeska. I like him very much. He is the only person with whom I can really be 'Altaforte.' Cournos I like also. We are getting our little gang after five years of waiting. You must come over and get the air—if only for a week or so in the spring.

"Richard is now running the *New Freewoman* which is now to appear as *The Egoist*. You must subscribe as the paper is poor, i.e.

weak financially. The *Mercure de France* has taken to quoting us, however."

Pound had persuaded Dora Marsden and Harriet Shaw Weaver that their leading article was sufficient for the suffragette cause. That left the rest of the bimonthly for literature. He had persuaded Fletcher to back it—for a time; and almost persuaded Amy Lowell to buy it. Aldington became assistant editor with the December 15, 1913, issue; January, the publication became *The Egoist,* and Joyce's *Portrait of the Artist as a Young Man* began to appear in it serially in February. When Miss Lowell asked if it could be brought over, Pound made a counterproposal: he, Hueffer, Lawrence and Joyce would edit the English section; she could have the American. She replied: "I don't know who Joyce is."

As for "*the* coming sculptor" Pound, accompanied by Mrs. Shakespear, had recently gone to an exhibition of Allied Artists at the Albert Hall. As they wandered in the upper galleries he became aware of a thin young man who reminded him of Williams. The young man had bright eyes, and he moved with a kind of animal grace; Pound thought "a well-made young wolf." He seemed to be listening to their banter about the art on display. Descending to the ground floor, they stopped before a group of figures. Pound was immediately interested, and turned to the catalogue to find the sculptor's name. Then he tried to pronounce it. The syllables would not come. He persisted. Suddenly he heard a voice saying: "Cela s'appelle tout simplement Jaersh-ka. C'est moi qui les ai sculptés." It was the young man, who promptly disappeared. Pound wrote to him, but he did not come until John Cournos brought him to 10 Church Walk.

The scene that took place has been described by both Pound and Cournos. "I was interested and I was determined that he should be," Pound wrote.[3] He decided that he would read to this young man poems that he had written when the same age—that is, about twenty. He read "Altaforte" and "Piere Vidal Old," both of which have French settings. Pound afterwards thought that "Altaforte" convinced the sculptor that he would be a fit subject for his art. He sat for Brzeska for a monumental bust and the portrait sketch which appears on his letterheads. Cournos recalled:

"When Gaudier and I left, the sculptor was enthusiastic because Ezra had dared to use the word 'piss' in a poem. When I told this to Ezra, he was delighted; actually, however, Ezra did not use the word in his poem, but some other quite innocent word which had a similar sound."[4]

Perhaps it was the last word in the first line of "Sestina: Altaforte."

Pound began to sit for his portrait shortly after his return from Stone Cottage. Gaudier-Brzeska had planned to use plaster, but Pound termed it "a most detestable medium." He purchased a half-ton block of marble. Poor Gaudier; he could not afford anything better, and he worked as a rule with stones found anywhere, with tools he had wrought with his own hands. On days when Pound accompanied him to his studio, a boarded-up archway of the Putney Railroad Bridge, he could hear the young man mutter "What a waste of good stone!" as their bus passed a cemetery. The long labor of cutting began, and with it the labor of reforging blunted chisels, which Gaudier-Brzeska performed himself.

On a shilling wooden chair, in the damp and drafty studio, with trains rushing overhead, Pound saw the massive stone take shape. But even before the image emerged from the marble there was an image of him in the heavy black lines Gaudier-Brzeska had drawn to guide his hand. He had seen Pound as a priest of the arts, and his vision was of a hieratic head. He told his sitter: "You understand it will not look like you, it *will . . . not . . . look . . .* like you. It will be the expression of certain emotions I get from your character."[5]

Two months passed. Pound thought that the bust of him was "most striking" two weeks before it was finished.

"I do not mean to say it was better, it was perhaps a *kinesis,* whereas it is now a *stasis*; but before the back was cut out, and before the middle lock was cut down, there was in the marble a titanic energy, it was like a great stubby catapult, the two masses bent for a blow. I do not mean that he was wrong to go on with it. Great art is perhaps a stasis. The unfinished stone caught the eye. Maybe it would have wearied it.

"He himself, I think, preferred a small sketch made later, to the actual statue, but in sculpture there is no turning back."[6]

He found the sculptor "the best company in the world."

"Some of my best days, the happiest and the most interesting, were spent in his uncomfortable mud-floored studio."

Pound saw Gaudier-Brzeska, with his bright black eyes and wisp of a beard, as a Renaissance man, "a sort of modern Cellini." It pleased him to sit gazing at the marble on its stand and at the sculptor with his head "out of the Renaissance" bobbing as he worked.

"I have now and again had the lark of escaping the present, and this was one of those expeditions. I knew that if I had lived in the Quattrocento I should have had no finer moment, and no better craftsman to fill it. And it is not a common thing to know that one is drinking the cream of the ages."[7]

They joked together of a time in the distant future when Pound would sell the bust to the Metropolitan for five thousand dollars, after which both would be able to live "at ease" for a year.

If their memoir-writing contemporaries are to be believed, the "hieratic head" was originally intended to be phallic. Epstein goes so far as to say that it was Pound who asked Gaudier-Brzeska to give it the outline of a phallus. Pound refers to the head in the seventh poem of "Moeurs Contemporaines."

The massive stone found a setting in Violet Hunt's front garden on Campden Hill, where it stayed throughout the war, disconcerting her when the moon shone full on it, and the neighbors who thought it was "a German *cache* for papers." Younger members of Pound's circle used to go to peep at it through the railings. Rain, mud, snails and pigeons streaked and slobbered it, and one day Pound gave it a swabbing, with a bucket and mop borrowed from Miss Hunt's gardener.

4.

Yeats and Pound separated over Christmas. Pound went to "Slowgh (more or less)"—as he termed it in a letter to his mother—to spend the holiday with Hueffer and Violet Hunt who had been married in Germany; but her claim to being Mrs. Hueffer was contested—successfully—in England by the first wife. The cottage they occupied had once belonged to Milton. Pound told his mother:

"Impossible to get any writing done here. Atmosphere too literary. 3 'Kreators' all in one ancient cottage *is* a bit thick.

"Xmas passed without calamity.

"Have sloshed about a bit in the slush as the weather is pleasingly warm. Walked to the Thames yesterday.

"Play chess and discuss style with F. M. H.

"Am not convinced that rural life suits me, at least in winter."

There were occasional expeditions when Pound and Yeats were together. Memorable was a trip to "Newbuildings," the home of Wilfrid Scawen Blunt, whose wife was Byron's granddaughter.

Rich and irascible, neglected as a poet, an opponent of British policy in the Sudan, and a breeder of Arabian steeds, Blunt at seventy-four felt his isolation keenly after a long and picturesque life. He knew Yeats, but not Pound. At the very moment he was writing in his diary, "I am alone just now here and in this dark world I am overwhelmed with woe. I see myself as one sees the dead, a thing finished which has lost all its importance,"[8] Yeats, Pound and Frederic Manning decided to give a dinner in his honor. Manning, an austere classicist, was not particularly friendly toward Pound. Pound termed him "envenomed," and Manning termed Pound "More like Khr-r-ist and the late James MacNeil Whistler every year." Five other poets agreed to join them. Blunt was astonished, and touched. He suggested that the poets come to him, but accepted Yeats's suggestion for the main course.

On January 18, 1914, the poets came—Yeats, Pound, Aldington, Flint, Manning, Sturge Moore and Victor Plarr, another survivor of the Rhymers' Club and the friend of Ernest Dowson and Lionel Johnson. Masefield, who had been in on the plan, found he could not attend, perhaps from an access of caution. Bridges, the Poet Laureate, declined at the start because of Blunt's politics.

They entered the dining room. Magnificent on the table, in full plumage, was a roasted peacock. The poets ate; it was worth while being a poet in those days. They all ate two helpings.

Pound read out the address which he had written for the occasion:

> Because you have gone your individual gait,
> Written fine verses, made mock of the world,
> Swung the grand style, not made a trade of art,
> Upheld Mazzini and detested institutions
>
> We who are little given to respect,
> Respect you, and having no better way to show it,
> Bring you this stone to be some record of it.

The "stone" was, in reality, a small marble box in which each of the poets had placed a manuscript poem. Engraved on the box was a bas-relief by Gaudier-Brzeska, which Blunt afterwards termed "terribly paulo-post-futurist" and turned to the wall.

"I really did not understand the address they read me," he said, "or perceive till afterwards that they had confused Araby with Mazzini in it."[9]

Yeats had told Pound that Lady Gregory thought the occasion should be given publicity, but Pound replied: "Tell her we hate the newspapers as Blunt hates the British Empire." Nevertheless, Yeats sent an unsigned report to *The Times*, and other papers picked it up. There was general indignation, particularly in Conservative circles.

Back at Stone Cottage, Yeats wrote a poem:

> What's riches to him
> That has made a great peacock
> With the pride of his eye?

In his upstairs room, Pound heard him hard at it—

> as it were the wind in the chimney
>   but was in reality Uncle William
> downstairs composing
> that had made a great Peeeeacock
>   in the proide of his oiye
>   had made a great peeeeeeecock in the . . .
> made a great peacock
>   in the proide of his oyyee
> proide ov his oy-ee
>   (Canto LXXXIII)

5.

While Yeats engrossed himself in "spiritistic" things, reading Boehme, Blake and Swedenborg, his "chief mystical authorities," Pound worked on the Noh manuscripts of Fenollosa.

These short, stylized plays, the players masked, in which gesture

and dance are more significant than speech, the folding and unfolding
of a cloth immemorial symbol, with the savors of centuries of tradition like invisible incense, challenged Pound's powers both as poet
and synthesist. The results are part of the literature of our time. The
effect on Yeats, leading him to write in an entirely new manner, in
an entirely new form, will be told later.

Their proximity brought mutual benefits. There is, in Pound's
versions of the Noh plays, with their warriors and priests, sacred
places, ghosts and old griefs, a kind of Celtic overtone. Perhaps it was
already there in the original, from which all verbiage had been
stripped away in the refining process of centuries; perhaps it was
Pound's avoidance of the speech created by the English dramatic poets,
with its "literary" flavors. But, quite possibly, Pound may have been
drawn to the kind of simple utterance which the writers of the Irish
renaissance had introduced with such magnificent results; and one of
them was his fellow lodger at Stone Cottage. He wrote to Harriet
Monroe, January 31, 1914, with a copy of *Nishikigi*:

"Here is the Japanese play for April. It will give us some reason
for existing. I send it in place of my own stuff, as my name is in such
opprobium we will not mention who did the extracting. Anyhow
Fenollosa's name is enough."

He had read the play to Mrs. Langley, and to his grocer, whose
name eludes me; such are the hazards of delivery by the front stairs.

"There's a long article with another play to appear in *The
Quarterly*. This *Nishikigi* is too beautiful to be encumbered with
notes and long explanation. Besides I think it is now quite lucid—
my landlady and grocer both say the story is clear *anyhow*."

He wrote again, on March 28th:

"No, the Fenollosa play can't wait. It won't do any harm to print
it with the Yeats stuff in May. Every number ought to be at least as
'sublimated' as such a number will be. If we can't stay that good we
ought to quit."

Nishikigi was printed in the May number.

I give two passages from it. The "Nishikigi" are "wands of medi-
ation" which suitors leave before a gate; a beautiful woman might
reap a thousand before selecting one, and the suitor who left it.
"Hosonuno" is the name of a local cloth which the woman weaves.
The chief characters in the play are the ghosts of the hero and his

beloved, kept apart in life, still separated in death, and a wandering priest.

WAKI [Priest]

That is a fine answer. And you would tell me then that Nishikigi and Hosonuno are names bound over with love?

SHITE [Pronounced *"Sch'tay"*: the hero]

They are names in love's list surely. Every day for a year, for three years come to their full, the wands, Nishikigi, were set up, until there were a thousand in all. And they are in song in your time, and will be. 'Chidzuka' they call them.

TSURE [Follower of the hero; the beloved]

These names are surely byword.
As the cloth Hosonuno is narrow of weft,
More narrow than the breast,
We call by this name any woman
Whose breasts are hard to come nigh to.
It is a name in books of love.

SHITE

'Tis a sad name to look back on.

TSURE

A thousand wands were in vain.
A sad name, set in a story.

SHITE

A seed pod void of the seed,
We had no meeting together.

The priest is persuaded to go to the tomb of the lover, a cave, where all his charm-sticks were buried with him. There, the Shite and the Tsure act out their tragedy, and through the Waki's piety win union and the promise of reincarnation.

SHITE

Look, then, for the old times are shown,
Faint as the shadow-flower shows in the grass that bears it;
And you've but a moon for lanthorn.

TSURE

The woman has gone into the cave.
She sets up her loom there
For the weaving of Hosonuno,
Thin as the heart of Autumn.

SHITE

The suitor for his part, holding his charm-sticks,
Knocks on a gate which was barred.

TSURE

In old time he got back no answer,
No secret sound at all
Save . . .

SHITE

. . . the sound of the loom.

TSURE

It was a sweet sound like katydids and crickets,
A thin sound like the Autumn.

SHITE

It was what you hear any night.

TSURE

Kiri.

SHITE

Hatari.

TSURE

Cho.

SHITE

Cho.

CHORUS
(*mimicking the sound of crickets*)
Kiri, hatari, cho, cho,
Kiri, hatari, cho, cho.
The cricket sews on his old rags,
With all the new grass in the field; sho,
Churr, isho, like the whirr of a loom: churr.

Fenollosa's own commentary on *Nishikigi* ends:

"Then follows a wonderful loom song and chorus, comparing the sound of weaving to the clicking of crickets; and in a vision is seen the old tragic story, and the chorus sings that 'their tears had become a colour.' 'But now they shall see the secret bride-room.' The hero cries, 'And we shall drink the cup of meeting.' Then the ghostly chorus sings a final song:

> How glorious the sleeves of the dance
> That are like snow-whirls."

Pound's version reads:

CHORUS

Shall I ever at last see into that secret bride-room, which
    no other sight has traversed?

SHITE

Happy at last and well-starred,
Now comes the eve of betrothal;
We meet for the wine-cup.

CHORUS

How glorious the sleeves of the dance,
That are like snow-whirls!

SHITE

Tread out the dance.

CHORUS

Tread out the dance and bring music.
This dance is for Nishikigi.[10]

6.

In March, while Yeats was in New York, Pound paid another visit to "Newbuildings," accompanied by Aldington. Blunt astonished the two young poets by appearing at dinner in the full regalia of an Arab sheik, with a brace of gold-mounted pistols in his sash. His toast was: "Damnation to the British government." They talked poetry. Blunt afterwards reported: "I am trying to persuade them both into some kind of sanity."

Pound wrote Miss Monroe:

"I have just come back from Blunt's, he is giving us a batch of stuff for July. I dare say he will send back the cheque for it; he seldom or never accepts payment."

In April he gave a poetry reading in Kensington Town Hall, "complete in velvet coat, flowing tie, pointed beard and a halo of fiery hair," says an eyewitness. "Lolling against the stage, he became very witty and fluent, and with his yankee voice snarled out some of his and Hulme's poems. Somehow, such a voice rather clowned verse." Hulme read a paper, and was supported by Wyndham Lewis; the eyewitness did not care for their delivery either.[11]

Pound may have been nervous—he was, after all, a bridegroom. J. B. Yeats wrote to Lily Yeats, March 24, 1914:

"On Sunday I was all day at Quinn's. Willie was there. . . . He mentioned that he has to hurry home for Ezra Pound's marriage. He is to marry Mrs. Shakespear's daughter. She is beautiful and well off and has the most charming manners."[12]

Pound's marriage to Dorothy Shakespear—due, perhaps, to his habit of secrecy where personal affairs are concerned—offers meager materials for a biographer. Even his mother was in the dark. A cabled announcement from London to the Philadelphia *Evening Bulletin* brought a reporter to the house in Wyncote on March 25th. Mrs. Pound said:

"My son has known Miss Shakespear for some years. Although I have not yet met her, we were waiting for the 'inevitable.' I do not know, definitely, whether members of the family will attend the wedding, but it is probable that instead we shall await the return of my son and his bride from their honeymoon and then visit them in London. I've been trying to persuade my boy to visit me in Wyncote, but his work and his close alliance with men of note in the literary and art world of London have thus far prevented his coming here for an extended stay."[13]

The *Evening Bulletin* stated that the event would "take place on Saturday April 18, and not on April 14, as first published." It also stated that the marriage would take place at the home of the bride's parents. The Philadelphia *Inquirer* carried a story on April 18th, dateline Wyncote, which began: "In London, England, tonight, Ezra Pound, the world-famous young American poet and critic, was married to Miss Dorothy Shakespear, daughter of Mr. and Mrs. Hope Shakespear, of No. 12 Brunswick Gardens." The story continued:

"In this brief announcement must be included all the details at this time known to the young poet's parents, Mr. and Mrs. Homer Pound, of Wyncote, and to the many friends of the bridegroom in Philadelphia and other Eastern cities. For, with the true eccentricity of real genius, the poet did not acquaint his parents with any of the details of the event—not even the name of the officiating clergyman, nor the number of guests, nor the names of the members of the bridal party."

A reporter, sent to the Pound residence to inquire about these details, was told by Pound's mother:

"I simply can't oblige you. Not that I do not want to, but Ezra has taken his wedding event very much as a matter of course, as an event which, ordinarily, takes place at some time in the lifetime of pretty nearly every man, and he has not told us much about it. There's the formal invitation—we received that a fortnight ago. I know that my daughter-in-law belongs to a distinguished English family—but I do not know a single thing about her gown, nor about her bridesmaids, nor of the guests."[14]

The marriage was solemnized at the parish church of Kensington—St. Mary Abbot's—on Monday, April 20, 1914, at 10:15 A.M. according to the rites and ceremonies of the Established Church, and was duly entered in the Register Book of Marriages (Entry No. 193): "Ezra Pound, 28, Bachelor, M.A., Poet; Dorothy Shakespear, 27, Spinster." His residence "at the time of marriage" is given as 5 Holand Place Chambers, hers as 12 Brunswick Gardens. Under "father's name and surname and rank or profession of father," the Register Book has "Homer Loomis Pound, Assayer, and Henry Hope Shakespear, Solicitor." The witnesses were Mr. Shakespear and H. T. Tucker.[15]

There were brief announcements in the London *Times* of April 20, 21 and 22. Amy Lowell sent a check as a wedding present. The Pounds were still in London in the summer, when Miss Lowell paid a second visit. In the winter Pound again joined Yeats in Stone Cottage. Yeats wrote his father from Coole Park, December 26, 1914:

"The week after next I go to the Sussex Cottage and Ezra Pound will be my secretary again for a couple of weeks. He brings his wife with him this time. She is very pretty (Mrs. Shakespear's daughter) and had a few years ago seven generals in her family all living at once and all with the same name—Johnson, relations of Lionel Johnson."

Mrs. Pound informs me they were "not all Johnsons."

CHAPTER IX

"THE GREAT ENGLISH VORTEX"

> An image of Lethe,
> and the fields
> Full of faint light. . . .
> —"The Coming of War: Actaeon"

1.

Miss Lowell returned to England in July, 1914, taking along a maid, a maroon automobile, and a chauffeur in maroon livery. Once more, she made the Berkeley Hotel her headquarters. She was not happy about *Des Imagistes*; after all, she had been represented by only one poem.

She found changes. Pound's group was different. There was a new movement afoot—he was at the heart of it. It was called "Vorticism," a word of his invention. It had its own publication—

BLAST
"A Review of the Great English Vortex."

Its editor was Wyndham Lewis.

Douglas Goldring has described the "inaugural tea party before publication, at which editorial policy was laid down and a list of the people to be blasted and blessed drawn up." It was held in Lewis's studio in Fitzroy Street. Pound was there; it was, in fact, presided over by Pound and Lewis. "The list of those whom we blessed begins with 'Bridget,' the beautiful, red-haired Bridget Patmore, for whom

Ford—and also, oddly enough, Violet—had a romantic admiration. Most of the others were either members of the South Lodge circle, 'blessed' to please Ford and Violet, or popular public figures." They included music-hall artists. "The list of the blasted appears to have been compiled from the eminent figures whose publicity was considered boringly excessive." They included "Beecham (Pills, Opera, Thomas), Croce, Bishop of London (Winnington Ingram) and all his "posterity' (he was unmarried), Marie Corelli, Clan Thesiger, Clan Meynell, Clan Strachey, A. C. Benson, Galsworthy, Sidney Webb and an unidentified lady named Ella, who may have been Wheeler Wilcox."[1]

The first issue was dated June 20, 1914. Aldington reviewed it in *The Egoist* of July 15th and that night the Vorticists gave a dinner at the Dieudonné restaurant, in Ryder Street, St. James's. Pound invited Miss Lowell. She came. She saw *BLAST*, size 12 ½ inches by 9 ½ inches, the title in enormous type zigzagging across the cover, the color of which Pound termed "magenta," but which Lewis called "puce." Much of its contents was in outsize capital letters—it, in fact, spluttered with them:

BLAST

years 1837 to 1900

it screamed.

Curse abysmal inexcusable middle-class
(also Aristocracy and Proletariat).

That took care of everybody generally. Specifically:

BLAST

pasty shadow cast by gigantic Boehm
(imagined at Introduction of BOURGEOIS
VICTORIAN VISTAS).
WRING THE NECK OF all sick inventions born in
that progressive white wake.

This may include a swipe at Marinetti and the Futurists, as well as the obvious one at industrial combines and statues.

> BLAST their weeping whiskers—hirsute
> RHETORIC OF EUNUCH and STYLIST—
> SENTIMENTAL HYGIENICS
> ROUSSEAUISMS (wild Nature cranks)
> FRATERNIZING WITH MONKEYS

That took care of Darwin.

> DIABOLICS—raptures and roses
>   of the erotic bookshelves
>   culminating in
>   PURGATORY OF
>   PUTNEY

That took care of Swinburne, about whom Pound had once rhap-
sodized in rhyme for many pages. For this typographical firecracker
was probably by Pound; it resembles another made years later in St.
Elizabeths Hospital. Lewis, for his part, went after Futurism directly.

The first Futurist manifesto had called for speed, praised machines
and war, glorified youth—as Mussolini was to do—and advocated
the destruction of museums. The Futurists hated the past, and reviled
Venice for its gondolas and canals; what was wanted instead, Marinetti declared, were "bridges leaping like gymnasts," and "the glid-
ing flight of aeroplanes, the sound of whose screw is like the flapping
of flags." Other manifestoes followed; one was entitled "Tuons le
clair de lune!"—now not an altogether unlikely prospect. Painters
and sculptors joined him, and there was an exhibition in Paris, London, Berlin, Amsterdam and Brussels. It was all a frenzy, meaning
absolutely nothing except, perhaps, the coming of war. Shortly before
Miss Lowell arrived, Marinetti gave two lectures at the Doré Gallery
in Bond Street, looking—as Goldring has described him—like "a
flamboyant personage adorned with diamond rings, gold chains and
hundreds of flashing white teeth." Lewis, Hulme and Gaudier-
Brzeska were present—as hecklers—at the second lecture, at which
Marinetti read his staccato poetry to the accompaniment of a bass
drum pounded in the wings.

He also read to a group at 18 Woburn Buildings. Aldington terms
it "one of the most difficult evenings" he ever spent with Yeats. He

and Sturge Moore and Pound acted as interpreters. After Yeats had read some of his own poems, he asked to hear some of Marinetti's. "Whereupon," Aldington says, "the Italian poet sprang up and declaimed, in a stentorian Milanese voice—

> 'Automobile,
> Ivre d'espace,
> Qui piétine d'angoisse,' "

et cetera. As the declamation continued, Yeats begged some of those present to ask Marinetti to stop—neighbors were pounding the walls.

Enter the billiard-cloth trousers.

"The 'costume' was worn only once and by me," Aldington told me. "It was invented by me, H. D., Ezra and Dorothy to wear at Marinetti's lecture on futurist clothing, which we knew was to be drably utilitarian, a single unit fastened by a zipper. M. noticed it and denounced young Passéists in the audience—I'd say he is pretty passé himself."

2.

In addition to his blast against the Victorian era, Pound contributed an essay entitled "Vortex," and twelve poems, one of which was "Fratres Minores." In the original it went:

> With minds still hovering above their testicles
> Certain poets here and in France
> Still sigh over established and natural fact
> Long since fully discussed by Ovid.
> They howl. They complain in delicate and exhausted
>   metres
> That the twitching of three abdominal nerves
> Is incapable of producing a lasting Nirvana.

It was transformed in *BLAST*. The first line is thoroughly and completely blacked out; so are the last two. In this formidable task, Iris Barry wrote, "young maidens were employed," presumably to fend off, at the last moment, seizure and suppression by the censor. This may account for the time lag in the dating of the issue and its celebration by the Vorticists. Someone in the New York Public Library has tried to decipher the blacked-out lines by patient scraping. It was not a success.

Pound's "Vortex" stated:

"Every concept, every emotion presents itself to the vivid consciousness in some primary form. It belongs to the art of this form. If sound, to music; if formed words, to literature; the image, to poetry; form, to design; colour in position, to painting; form or design in three planes, to sculpture; movement, to the dance or to the rhythm of music or verses."

Perhaps it was worth saying in 1914.

Many things were said at the dinner which were less lucid, less pleasant. Ford and Miss Lowell got into a dispute about "literary principles." She was still angry when she returned to the Berkeley. It could not have been an exchange of views; it must have been an attempt on one side or the other, or both, at violent conversion.

There are no schools, no movements; only artists. The list of contributors to *BLAST* is itself a refutation of a "movement," for it included such disparate creators as Lewis and Pound, May Sinclair, Ford Madox Ford; Gaudier-Brzeska, the painter Edward Wadsworth, and Jacob Epstein. Ford, in fact, always called himself an Impressionist, and his signature is missing from the Vorticist manifesto. The many reproductions tend to the abstract rather than the representational; but what had the artists in common except their enthusiasm? What had the writers?

"Vortex, n. Mass of whirling fluid, esp. whirlpool."

Lewis wrote Lord Carlow, with a copy of the magazine:

"Such things as *BLAST* have to be undertaken for the artist to exist at all. When you have removed all that is *necessarily* strident, much sound art-doctrine is to be found in this puce monster."

A notice in *BLAST* stated that copies could be obtained from "Mr. Wyndham Lewis, Rebel Art Centre, 38 Great Ormond Street, Queen's Square, W.C. (Hours 11 a.m. to 1 p.m.) and at 5 Holland Place Chambers, Church Street, Kensington." Violet Hunt had copies for sale in South Lodge. A lady whom Sargent had painted—Mrs. Leopold Hirsch—returned hers. Her letter suggested that Miss Hunt could "doubly benefit" the editor by reselling it to "someone who hadn't daughters." That poem by Pound—"she couldn't really have it lying about." It was probably a pristine copy, lines not blacked out.

3.

Miss Lowell, having met the contributors to *BLAST* in the Dieudonné, gave an *Imagiste* dinner in the same restaurant two nights later. Pound sent Aldington to help her with the arrangements. There were, inevitably, some duplications. Her guests were the Aldingtons, Cournos, Fletcher, Flint, Upward, Gaudier-Brzeska, Hueffer and Violet Hunt, and Pound and his wife. There were speeches, by Upward and Gaudier-Brzeska, who also answered questions from the floor. After all, he was a leading—perhaps the leading—Vorticist, only Pound excepted, and he too had a "Vortex" in the first issue of *BLAST*. It began:

"Sculptural energy is the mountain.

"Sculptural feeling is the appreciation of masses in relation.

"Sculptural ability is the defining of those masses by planes."

Pound credits Cournos with being "the first to see what Gaudier had got into his VORTEX"—that is, *"the whole history of sculpture"* (his italics).[2]

Upward's contribution to the evening had its awkward moments. Cournos had already felt "an undercurrent of hostility among the diners, and if not hostility, then condescension, toward the hostess," when Upward got up to speak. He took as his text Miss Lowell's poem in *Des Imagistes*. He was her guest; she was, as it were, a guest in England. He was not deterred. By the time he got through with the subject, a bath by moonlight, Miss Lowell was the bather, and everyone was doubled over with laughter, except the author, who sat as straight and stiff as her stoutness would permit, and clearly vexed by the performance.

There were occasional moments of gaiety. Pound snatched a tray from a waiter and juggled it. But Ford was glum throughout. His account of the dinner, in a piece about Gaudier-Brzeska in *The English Review,* has been termed by her biographer "probably the most violent attack on Amy Lowell in print." It is an understatement. It seems strange, then, to come upon him again in her company; but such was to be the case. She also saw Upward again.

She was happier in her own drawing room, in the suite at the Berkeley. She saw a great deal of the Aldingtons. She saw Fletcher. She wrote Cournos that she "liked Russians," and invited him over. He came. She went on a picnic with Upward; it rained. She went to see Gaudier-Brzeska in his studio. And like all the other poets, she turned up at the Poetry Book Shop. It was the afternoon of a poetry "squash," a hot July afternoon; shades were drawn and candles lit. In this atmosphere Rupert Brooke read his poems. "He read inaudibly, as he always did," Conrad Aiken, who was present, told me. From the back came a Bostonian female voice: "Louder!" Brooke paused. "Can't you hear me?" he asked, peering into the gloom. "Not one word!" answered Miss Lowell. Thereupon, Aiken said, "Brooke became completely inaudible."

Meanwhile, she was pursuing her plan, which was to win to her side those followers of Pound she wished to include in an *Imagiste* anthology of her own, with or without him; for she foresaw trouble. Her idea was simple—the same poets, if possible, as before, but the same amount of space for each, final selections controlled by vote of all. The Aldingtons were the first she mentioned it to; they joined up. Flint and Lawrence followed. Fletcher, who had resisted both Hulme and Pound, capitulated. There was some flirting with Ford, whose poem, "On Heaven," was much admired, but finally it was agreed it was not really an "Imagiste" poem, and he withdrew it. The other contributors to *Des Imagistes*—Cannéll, Cournos, Joyce, Upward and Williams—were thought to be not producing enough, and were not asked. It was soon apparent that the Aldingtons were Miss Lowell's chief aiders and abettors.

How many times has a certain July evening in her suite been described! It had been a sunny day; now, in her large private room, which she preferred to the dining room downstairs, where she felt self-conscious, waiters were setting out the dinner she had planned. Aldington was at a window, looking down on the traffic of Piccadilly and the golden haze over the Green Park. Across the street, at a corner of the Ritz Hotel, there was a poster over the newsstand—"GERMANY AND RUSSIA AT WAR, OFFICIAL." As he watched, another poster went up: "BRITISH ARMY MOBILISED." And then, at that moment, the door of Miss Lowell's suite opened and a tall, slender man with red hair and bright blue eyes entered, exclaiming:

"I say, I've just been talking to Eddie Marsh, and he's most depressing. He says we shall be in the war."

It was D. H. Lawrence. Marsh, the editor and sponsor of the *Georgian Poets,* was private secretary to the Prime Minister. Someone said: "Oh, nonsense."

"There are no schools, no movements." We do not know what the new movements in the arts, in France as well as in England, would have accomplished had they been permitted to run their course. I do not speak of disillusion, but death. Most of the talented men involved, being young, were killed in the 1914–1918 war. But, of course, among the survivors, there was disillusion. It was a double setback—as Henry James phrased it, "what the treacherous years were all the while really making for and *meaning.*" He wrote at the end of July, 1914: "With it all too is indeed the terrible sense that the people of this country may well—by some awful brutal justice—be going to get something bad for the exhibition that has gone on so long of their huge materialized stupidity and vulgarity. I mean the enormous national sacrifice to insensate amusement, without a redeeming idea or a generous passion, that has kept making one ask one's self, from so far back, how such grossness and folly and blatancy could possibly *not* be in the long run to be paid for."[3]

4.

Pound felt, not unreasonably, that as "Imagisme" was of his coinage, he had some rights in the name. He wished neither to be associated with the project nor to have the name used. It was something of a dilemma for him, all the same. He wrote Miss Lowell on August 1st:

"The present machinery was largely or wholly my making. I ordered 'the public' (i.e., a few hundred people and a few reviewers) to take note of certain poems.

"You offer to find a publisher, that is, a better publisher, if I abrogate my privileges, if I give way to, or saddle myself with, a dam'd contentious, probably incompetent committee. If I tacitly,

tacitly to say the least of it, accept a certain number of people as my critical and creative equals, and publish the acceptance.

"I don't see the use. Moreover, I should like the name 'Imagisme' to retain some sort of a meaning. It stands, or I should like it to stand for hard light, clear edges. I can not trust any democratized committee to maintain that standard. Some will be splay-footed and some sentimental."

Two weeks later he suggested a way out of the dilemma: "If you want to drag in the word Imagisme you can use a subtitle 'an anthology devoted to Imagisme, vers libre and modern movements in verse' or something of that sort."

There were some unhappy meetings between them. She wrote Harriet Monroe:

"You ask about the quarrel between Ezra and the rest of us. It is not a quarrel now, it is a schism.

"Do you remember, Ezra was very anxious to run the *Mercure de France?* He came to me at once as soon as I got to London, and then it transpired that he expected to become editor of said 'Review' with a salary. I was to guarantee all the money, and put in what I pleased, and he was to run the magazine his way. We talked over the cost of expenses, and we both thought that $5,000 a year was the least that such a magazine could be run on. As I have not $5,000 a year that I can afford to put into it, I based my refusal upon that fact, and it was most unfortunate that Ezra apparently did not believe it. Like many people of no incomes, Ezra does not know the difference between thousands and millions, and thinks that any one who knows where to look for next week's dinners, is a millionaire, and therefore lost his temper with me completely, although he never told me why, and he accused me of being unwilling to give any money towards art."

This was written after her return to Brookline; there is more to come. I have paused here because Pound's project was fraught with such possibilities. What *if* five thousand dollars a year had been forthcoming to finance a *Mercure de France* edited by him? He was an internationalist in the world of arts, and multilingual. What could he not have accomplished at the helm of that famous journal? The petty literary squabbles would have been spared him, his absorption with economics and politics might never have come about, and he might never have gone to Italy to live. But Aldington thought the whole project "one of Pound's delusions, or a misunderstanding on Amy's part." He told me: "No foreigner could possibly edit a French literary periodical. The French wouldn't have him."

She thought that the best way to help other poets, and also herself, was to republish the *Imagiste* anthology, with the same contributors, year after year, in the manner of *Georgian Poetry.* "Only Ezra was annoyed." She says he sent for the Aldingtons and told them they had to choose between him and her, "which was awful for them, as he is a very old friend, and has done much for them, and I was only a new friend. They behaved with the utmost honour in the matter. They told Ezra it was not a question of me at all, but a question of the principle, that they felt it only fair to let the poets choose their own contributions and to give each poet equal space. He then tried to bribe them, by asking them to get up an Anthology with him, and leave me out. This they absolutely refused to do.

"We had many consultations on the subject, in which Flint, Lawrence, and Ford Madox Hueffer joined us, and we all agreed that Ezra could not expect to run us all his own way forever, and that if he chose to separate himself from us, we would be obliged, although most regretfully, to let him."[4]

They had been talking among themselves. "Ezra is back from the country and looks terribly ill," Aldington wrote her in September. "He lies on a couch and says he has 'cerebral gout.' Poor devil, I wonder if Fat Hueffer was right? Perhaps Ezra is a little cracked. He doesn't seem to be able to talk of anything except himself and his work."

But Pound's letters of that month—to Douglas Goldring about *his* work and to Harriet Monroe about Masefield's and Eliot's—demonstrate the dangers of too great reliance on isolated remarks. Katherine Ruth Heyman naturally took Pound's side. But when she made some gibes at Miss Lowell's expense, Pound told her: "Don't make fun of Amy—she's the only hippopoetess in our zoo."

It was a quite different characterization from the one of the year before that Miss Lowell sent Miss Monroe: "He is very brilliant, but he does not work enough, and his work lacks the quality of soul, which, I am more and more fain to believe, no great work can ever be without."

Pound and his wife dined with her before she left England.
"We had a very pleasant and perfectly amicable evening."[5]
Her collection finally appeared as *Some Imagist Poets.*

5.

These occasional skirmishes, and attendant setbacks, failed to worry
Pound. He was, of course, very resilient, and Williams's characterization of him at college—"he is the essence of optimism and has a cast-
iron faith that is something to admire"—continued to hold good.
Optimism and faith were certainly needed where some of his schemes
were concerned.

"My problem is to keep alive a certain group of advancing poets,
to set the arts in their rightful place as the acknowledged guide and
lamp of civilization," he wrote Miss Monroe. "The arts must be supported in preference to church and scholarship. Artists first, then, if
necessary, professors and parsons." He was more explicit with Miss
Weaver: "I shall have a rather longish article, that is about a page to
a page and a half, announcing the College of Arts." Meanwhile, he
sent her a piece by John Rodker. "Here is some copy for which I take
no responsibility. Rodker has some reason or other for wanting his
essay printed as soon as possible. He always has. Miss Heyman's
article might precede Rodker's. Please do not put it next to mine."
Later, to Miss Monroe: "*No,* for gawd's sake, don't connect Violet
Hueffer with F. M. H. There have been enough suits for libel etc.
I can't go into the inner history at this moment, but refrain from
bracketing the two names."

The "Preliminary Announcement of the College of Arts" appeared
in *The Egoist* of November 2nd, and became the basis of the following prospectus, which Pound sent everywhere:

"It has been noted by certain authors that London is the capital of
the world, and 'Art is a matter of capitals.' At present many American students who would have sought Vienna or Prague or some
continental city are disturbed by war. To these the College of Arts
offers a temporary refuge and a permanent centre.

"We draw the attention of new students to the fact that no course
of study is complete without one or more years in London. Scholarly

research is often but wasted time if it has not been first arranged and oriented in the British Museum.

"The London collections are if not unrivalled at least unsurpassed. The Louvre has the Venus and the Victory but the general collection of sculpture in the Museum here is, as a whole, the finer collection. The National Gallery is smaller than the Louvre but it contains no rubbish.

"Without chauvinism we can very easily claim that study in London is at least as advantageous as study elsewhere, and that a year's study in London by no means prevents earlier or later study in other capitals.

"The American student coming abroad is usually presented with two systems of study, firstly, that of 'institutions' for the most part academic, sterile, professionial; secondly, instruction by private teachers often most excellent, often the reverse.

"The College of Arts offers contacts with artists of established position, creative minds, men for the most part who have already suffered in the cause of their art."

He listed a partial faculty, singling out Arnold Dolmetsch, whose position was unique; "all music lovers are so well aware of it, that one need not here pause to proclaim it." The others were: Henri Gaudier-Brzeska, still living at the time of the prospectus; Wyndham Lewis, Edward Wadsworth, Edmund Dulac, Reginald Wilenski, Felix Salmond, K. R. Heyman, Ezra Pound, John Cournos and Alvin Langdon Coburn. Cournos told me that he was slated to expound the Russian novelists.

Pound sent the prospectus to Harriet Monroe. "It embodies two real ideas," he wrote her. "A. That the arts, INCLUDING poetry and literature, should be taught by artists, by practicing artists, *not* by sterile professors. B. That the arts should be gathered together for the purpose of inter-enlightenment. The 'art' school, meaning 'paint school,' needs literature for backbone, ditto the musical academy, etc." He thought Chicago, with its millionaires, might take up the idea and "do a really big thing." In London, no one came; nothing came of it.

He had a curious experience this year, and in a poem of two lines, assisted by a title less fanciful than useful, embodied everything that he and his associates had claimed for imagism as a method ("An

'Image' is that which presents an intellectual and emotional complex
in an instant of time.") :

PAGANI'S, NOVEMBER 8

Suddenly discovering in the eyes of the very beautiful
Normande cocotte
The eyes of the very learned British Museum assistant.[6]

This was Laurence Binyon, poet, Orientalist and keeper of prints
and drawings at the British Museum, who devoted twenty years to his
translation of Dante's *Commedia,* the first part of which Pound was to
review in the *Criterion.* In the review Pound recalled his first glimpse
of Binyon "in 1908 among very leaden Greeks." There are also two
affectionate references to him in Canto LXXX.

He wrote H. L. Mencken on February 18th from Coleman's Hatch
(Mencken had succeeded Willard Huntington Wright as editor of
The Smart Set) :

"I send all that I have. I did it this morning. I think it has some
guts, but am perhaps still blinded by the fury in which I wrote it, and
still confuse the cause with the result."

This was a poem entitled "1915: February," which has remained
unpublished and uncollected. He had already sent a "war poem" to
Poetry, and it appeared in the March number. It is "The Coming of
War: Actaeon," which does not appear to have been dashed off in
a hurry.

Yeats, asked to write a poem to help the war effort, declined, but
wrote instead the poem beginning:

> I think it better that in times like these
> A poet's mouth be silent, for in truth
> We have no gift to set a statesman right. . . .

6.

There was only one more issue of *BLAST,* and that did not appear
until July, 1915. The previous March saw a Vorticist exhibition in
the Doré Gallery on Bond Street; among the exhibitors were Lewis,

Wadsworth, Gaudier-Brzeska and Jacob Epstein, who showed his "Rock Drill" sculpture to which, he has admitted, he was tempted to attach a live pneumatique drill; but as that would have been Futurist, not Vorticist, he desisted. (Pound remembered the name in *Section: Rock-Drill 85–95 de los cantares.*)

Gaudier-Brzeska considered Epstein "the foremost in the small number of good sculptors in Europe." Pound wrote his mother: "Epstein is a great sculptor. I wish he would wash, but I believe Michel Angelo *never* did, so I suppose it is part of the tradition." But in an outburst to Pound about Epstein's "sloth," Gaudier exclaimed: "Work!! Work? I know he does not work. His hands are clean!!" Pound reported this to Epstein, who remarked: "Ugh, so I do not work? Well. I hope he works to some advantage." Aldington said of Gaudier: "He was probably the dirtiest human being I have ever known." Pound wrote Quinn: "I haven't seen much of Epstein of late. He and Lewis have some feud or other which I haven't inquired into, and as Lewis is my more intimate friend I have not seen much of Jacob, though I was by way of playing for a reconciliation." It was Epstein who called Pound's attention to "the qualities of sculpture" in Lewis's drawing. "That set me off looking at Lewis." A year later, Pound still did not know what the quarrel was about, "save that Jacob is a fool when he hasn't got a chisel in his hand and a rock before him, and Lewis *can* at moments be extremely irritating."

To judge by the accounts of the principals, or accounts about them, there seems to have been a general frazzling of nerves. Hulme made his point in an argument with Lewis by holding him upside down on the railings of Soho Square, and Gaudier-Brzeska threatened to punch David Bomberg; Bomberg quarreled with Epstein, and Epstein had his quarrel with Lewis. And one day, when Pound and Gaudier called on Epstein to look at his "Rock Drill" drawings and figure, as Pound began to expatiate on the design, Gaudier rasped out: "Shut up. You understand nothing."[7] Epstein is also the source for a curious remark by Hulme. "Someone once asked him how long he would tolerate Ezra Pound, and Hulme thought for a moment, then said that he knew already exactly when he would have to kick him downstairs."[8] Michael Roberts notes that Hulme's relations with Lewis, as well as Pound, were sometimes strained, "but he always liked and admired Gaudier"; and Gaudier reciprocated by carving a knuckleduster, of solid brass, for Hulme, who no doubt had read Raleigh, and saw the superiority of persuasion over mere advice.

Pound posed for Lewis many times; in particular, for a painting which "seized the essential Ezra," according to Iris Barry. It was a little larger than life-size, the face "sculptural," she wrote; "the cat-look is, after all, that of an Egyptian cat, hair in long tongues of fire, the grey coat having wonderfully that perpetual air of majestic flowing and billowing, the inevitable ebony stick, the quizzical expression, the force and dangerousness and simplicity of the man were all in that." It has disappeared. Lewis said that he put it in the open end of a taxi, paid the driver and sent it off to an art shop to be varnished. Another portrait of his friend is in the Tate; Pound is seated in an armchair, in profile, wearing a black jacket and green shirt.

BLAST No. 2 carried the following brief notice, by Pound:

"MORT POUR LA PATRIE.

"Henri Gaudier-Brzeska: after months of fighting and two promotions for gallantry, Henri Gaudier-Brzeska was killed in a charge at Neuville St. Vaast, on June 5th, 1915."

When the Germans shelled Rheims, Gaudier-Brzeska felt he had to return to France. Pound lent him the fare.

He was twenty-four years old.

Pound wrote Professor Schelling: "We have lost the best of the young sculptors and the most promising. The arts will incur no worse loss from the war than this is. One is rather obsessed with it."

In Canto XVI which is a mourning roster of his friends, he wrote:

> And Henri Gaudier went to it,
>   and they killed him,
> And killed a good deal of sculpture,
> And ole T. E. H. he went to it,
> With a lot of books from the library,
> London Library, and a shell buried 'em in a dug-out,
> And the Library expressed its annoyance.

But in Canto LXXX, of himself at that time:

and a navvy rolls up to me in Church St. (Kensington End) with:
           Yurra Jurrmun!
To which I replied: I am *not*.
"Well yurr szum kind ov a furriner."

                            7.

To the second *BLAST* Pound contributed a cluster of poems, most
of them never reprinted by him. One, which was, made mischief. He
had written to Harriet Monroe in April: "Rupert Brooke is dead in
the Dardanelles. I have some of his work, and will send the Post
Mortem in a day or so, probably tonight. So it will reach you in time
for the June number." He added generously: "He was the best of all
that Georgian group."
    Then *BLAST* appeared, with the following:

               OUR CONTEMPORARIES

        When the Taihaitian princess
        Heard that he had decided,
        She rushed into the sunlight and swarmed
                        up a cocoanut palm tree,

        But he returned to this island
        And wrote ninety Petrarchan sonnets.

    This contribution, regarded as an attack on Brooke, was read with
resentment in Chicago as well as in London, where Edward Marsh,
in particular, was incensed by it. Pound defended himself in a letter
to Miss Monroe:
    "The verse contains nothing derogatory. It is a complaint against
a literary method. Brooke got perhaps a certain amount of vivid
poetry in life and then went off to associate with literary hen-coops
like Lascelles Abercrombie in his writings.
    "Brooke would have been amused by the lines, at least I hope and
suppose he was man enough to have been entertained by them. If he
wasn't, God help him in limbo."

Pound also contributed a prose series entitled "Chronicles." One of them was headed "On the Rage of Peevishness which Greeted the First Number of *BLAST*." Another expressed a personal peeve. He still heard the bells in his new abode.

"Let it then stand written," he wrote, "that in the year of grace, 1914, there was in the parish of Kensington a priest or vicar, portly, perhaps overfed, indifferent to the comfort of others, and well paid for official advertisement and maintenance of the cult of the Gallilean . . . that is to say of the contemporary form of that cult.

"And whereas the Gallilean was, according to record, a pleasant, well-spoken, intelligent vagabond, this person, as is common with most of this sect was in most sorts the reverse . . . their hymns and music being in the last stages of decadence.

"The said vicar either caused to be rung or at least permitted the ringing of great bells, untuneful, ill-managed, to the great disturbance of those living near to the church. He himself lived on the summit of the hill at some distance and was little disturbed by the clatter."

The date indicates that he had written the piece shortly after he had moved into 5 Holland Place Chambers. It was also believed by many that he wrote an abusive letter to the vicar—in Latin; the vicar had a sense of humor, and the letter was displayed in the vestry.

When Cournos moved into the room at 10 Church Walk he did not mind the bells. For him, "it was hard to imagine anything more quiet than this out-of-the-way corner; only the chimes of St. Mary Abbot would pleasantly at intervals break the stillness."

But nothing is perfect. There was, across the street, a noisy household where, on Sundays, nonconformist hymns were sung. To show his displeasure, Cournos placed a copy of *BLAST* where the singers could see it; its huge lettering filled an entire windowpane.

"Miraculously the noise stopped each time I tried this."[9]

CHAPTER X

POUND AND ELIOT

1.

> *. . . Tout passe. L'art robuste*
> *Seul a l'éternité*
> *Le buste*
> *Survit à la cité. . . .*

Almost as lasting is a fond memory, by purest fancy bred. Miss Monroe wrote in her autobiography: "The most exciting of those early introductions, after Lindsay and Sandburg, was that of a young Missourian in London, T. S. Eliot, whose 'Love Song of J. Alfred Prufrock,' printed in June, 1915, although an extraordinarily finished product to begin with, was his first appearance as a poet. The previous September Eliot had called on Pound, who wrote me (enthusiastically for him), 'I think he has some sense, though he has not yet sent me any verse.' When 'Prufrock' reached us via our Foreign Correspondent, its opening lines—

> Let us go then, you and I,
> When the evening is spread out against the sky
> Like a patient etherized upon a table—

nearly took our breath away. Here indeed was modern sophistication dealing with the tag ends of overworldly cosmopolitanism."[1]

Pound wrote again, September 30th:

"I was jolly well right about Eliot. He has sent in the best poem I have yet had or seen from an American. PRAY GOD IT BE NOT A SINGLE AND UNIQUE SUCCESS. He has taken it back to get it ready for the press and you shall have it in a few days."

The two men had talked at length. Said the Idahoan of the Missourian: "He is the only American I know of who has made what I can call adequate preparation for writing. He has actually trained himself *and* modernized himself *on his own*. The rest of the *promising young* have done one or the other but never both (most of the swine have done neither). It is such a comfort to meet a man and not have to tell him to wash his face, wipe his feet, and remember the date (1914) on the calendar."

Early in October he wrote Miss Monroe, enclosing "The Love Song of J. Alfred Prufrock": "Here is the Eliot poem. The most interesting contribution I've had from an American." He hoped she would "get it *in* soon."

November: "Your objection to Eliot is the climax."

Same month, another letter:

"No, most emphatically I will not ask Eliot to write down to any audience whatsoever. I dare say my instinct was sound enough when I volunteered to quit the magazine quietly about a year ago. Neither will I send you Eliot's address in order that he may be insulted."

January (from Stone Cottage): " 'Mr. Prufrock' does not 'go off at the end.' It is a portrait of failure, or of a character which fails, and it would be false art to make it end on a note of triumph. I dislike the paragraph about Hamlet, but it is an early and cherished bit and T. E. won't give it up, and as it is the only portion of the poem that most readers will like at first reading, I don't see that it will do much harm.

"For the rest: a portrait satire on futility can't end by turning that quintessence of futility, Mr. P. into a reformed character breathing out fire and ozone."

April: "*Do* get on with that Eliot."

"The Love Song of J. Alfred Prufrock" appeared in June, 1915; in September Pound wrote to Miss Monroe about her English counterpart, who had imported copies of *Poetry:*

"Monro discovered 'Prufrock' on his unaided own and asked me about the author when I saw him last night. I consider Harold is dawning."

October: "I have cabled my vote for Eliot. As you might have known. I see no other possible award of the prize."

Same letter: "No, if your committee don't make the award to Eliot, God only knows what slough of ignominy they will fall into—reaction, death, silliness! ! ! ! ! !"

Ditto: "The things to be avoided are, naturally, an award to Amy, Skinner, Fletcher, Lindsay or Aiken. Or even Ficke. If you don't give the £40 to Eliot, for God's sake award it to *yourself*."

December: "Yes, the prizes were peculiarly filthy and disgusting, the £10 to H. D. being a sop to the intelligent. However, I knew it would happen. I know just what your damn committee *wants*."

The committee "wanted" Vachel Lindsay, two hundred dollars' worth; Constance Lindsay Skinner, one hundred dollars.

2.

The first meeting between Eliot and Pound was arranged by Conrad Aiken, who no longer remembers where it took place and whether he was present. Mr. Eliot, in his published account of the introduction, makes it a year later. He wrote:

"I had kept my early poems (including 'Prufrock' and others eventually published) in my desk from 1911 to 1915—with the exception of a period when Conrad Aiken endeavoured, without success, to peddle them for me in London. In 1915 (and through Aiken) I met Pound. The result was that 'Prufrock' appeared in *Poetry* in the summer of that year; and through Pound's efforts, my first volume was published by the Egoist Press in 1917."[2]

In a letter to the *Times Literary Supplement* (June 3, 1960) Mr. Aiken states that he had brought the typescript of "Prufrock" to London in 1914—it had been given him in Cambridge, Massachusetts, the year before—and that he had sent it to Harold Monro, editor of *Poetry and Drama,* among others. "After it had been summarily rejected by everyone," Mr. Aiken wrote, "[I] gave it to Ezra Pound for *Poetry*, of Chicago." He had also shown "La Figlia Che Piange" to Monro at a poetry squash—with no better luck. Aiken told me:

"Later, as I was walking back to my boarding house on Bedford Place I began to wonder if Monro hadn't thought it was mine, so I mailed it to him with a note which said, 'It's really by Mr. T. S. Eliot.' It was again turned down. So I went to see Pound, who had digs in Kensington, a triangular-shaped flat."

Monro's observation about "Prufrock," Aiken recalled, was "absolutely insane."

Aiken's own encounters with Pound seem to have been baffling experiences. At a bus stop in Piccadilly one day, he climbed to the the top of a bus, "and there was Pound," who asked him if he knew Walter Lippmann who, like Eliot, was of the Class of 1910 at Harvard. (Aiken was 1911.) Pound told him, "I'm being interviewed for a new paper—the *New Republic,*" and suggested that Aiken accompany him, although the interview was to be over lunch. Aiken hesitated, but Pound insisted. "Come along," he said; "Lippmann can afford it." Aiken went. The three men lunched at the Hotel Russell, Russell Square. The meal was almost over, and nothing had been said about the job, Aiken recalled, when Pound asked about it. Lippmann said he was looking for a "general correspondent," and asked Pound if he had any suggestions.

"Yes," said Pound (in Aiken's recollection) and proposed himself.

Lippmann (ditto): "Any other suggestions?"

Pound wrote John Quinn:

"I saw and lunched with Lippmann when he was over here, but he didn't seem disposed to take any of my stuff. A poet, you know! ! ! Bad lot, they are. No sense of what the public wants. Even Cournos, who isn't exactly modern, met Lippmann and said: 'You've heard of English stodge? Well, there's one stodge that's worse. That's American stodge.' "

Probably, what it all comes down to, is: some men can say "I can do this, that or the other, better than anybody," and they can, and it is no use being offended when they say it. But, of course, everyone is.

Mr. Lippmann, the renowned pundit of the *Herald Tribune,* wrote me:

"I have no vivid recollections except a visual image of what Pound looked like and also a memory that he talked wildly and at length."

Aiken said that Pound took him to meet Ford, Yeats, John Lane, "but it invariably misfired—none of them were ever home." As for the famous introduction, he was certain that the three poets did not meet for this purpose, and that it was all done by letter, which is also Eliot's recollection.

The author of "Senlin," a poem which had stirred a whole generation and which, as Horace Gregory points out, "anticipated, at a measurable distance, the overtones of T. S. Eliot's *The Waste Land*," spoke matter-of-factly of the London era. It was all so long ago. "Senlin," he told me, was the only one of his early "symphonies" which he planned to include in his *Selected Poems*. It was at this interview that Mr. Aiken made the remark about de Bosschère's influence which appears on p. 114. A volume by Jane de Bosschère was on the table.

He recalled Pound's appearance: "He had a little sharp beard, and wore corduroys—pants and jacket in not-matching colors—and a big black hat. I liked him, but he was a dogmatic creature . . . opinionated . . . arrogant, conceited.

"His letters are wonderful. But after I reviewed one of his anthologies, Pound wrote a letter beginning, 'Jesus God, Aiken, you poor blithering ass.' I replied with a postcard picturing a fat lady on the beach, titled something like 'the only pebble on the beach,' writing only, 'O Ezrie, I thought you was dead.' Another letter from Pound said, 'I suppose when I get out my history of the world you won't even recognize it for what it is.' This evidently referred to the *Cantos*.

"Pound's tragedy is up here," Aiken continued, pointing to his head. "His mind wasn't good enough. I think it's rudimentary. Pound doesn't think; if he'd thought, he wouldn't have got into all the trouble he did. However, 'Hugh Selwyn Mauberley' is a wonderful thing. There's a curious resemblance between it and 'J. Alfred Prufrock.' The same person could have written the titles—there's a twentieth century quotidien comic character in both titles."

Mr. Eliot wrote me (June 10, 1959):

"Like Conrad Aiken I am a bit vague as to how my first visit to Ezra Pound was arranged. Aiken is certainly right when he says we met in 1914. One or two of the early letters in the book of selected letters by Pound confirm that was toward the end of the year. But

whether Aiken wrote to Pound about me or gave me a letter or merely
gave me Pound's address and urged me to show him my poems, I
cannot remember. I feel pretty sure that I and Aiken and Pound didn't
all meet together. The important point, and one on which Aiken and
I agree, is that it was through Aiken's instrumentality and at his urging
that I showed my poems to Pound. Aiken had attempted to place these
early poems elsewhere on a previous visit to London, but with no
success."

3.

Mr. Eliot has described Pound's new quarters at No. 5 Holland Place
Chambers as "a small dark flat in Kensington. In the largest room he
cooked, by artificial light; in the lightest, but smallest room, which
was inconveniently triangular, he did his work and received his
visitors." The Aldingtons lived on the same floor. H. D. reported:
"Ezra is doing Chinese translations—and some are very beautiful!
He comes running in four or five times a day now with new versions
for us to read."

Pound cooked, and served, in a flowing fawn-colored dressing
gown, when he did not take his dinner guests to Bellotti's, an Italian
restaurant on Old Compton Street. He gave Eliot the impression of
being "only a temporary squatter. This appearance was due, not only
to his restless energy—in which it was difficult to distinguish the
energy from the restlessness and the fidgets, so that every room, even
a big one, seemed too small for him—but to a kind of resistance to
growing into any environment. In America, he would no doubt have
always seemed on the point of going abroad; in London, he always
seemed on the point of crossing the Channel. I have never known
a man, of any nationality, to live so long out of his native country
without settling anywhere else."[3]

Despite a woman's hand, the triangular room sounds very much
like the one in Church Walk with an admixture of old and new
possessions. The little clavichord purchased from Dolmetsch was
regarded by Lewis "as a strange unaccountable sort of mouse-trap,"
Pound told Margaret Anderson, and "the charwoman (after four
months' service) spoke of it the other day as 'the little black table'

(observation the leading characteristic of the 'lower orders')." There were books, foils, a marble torso and "boy with a Cony" by Gaudier-Brzeska; a typewriter "of great delicacy" as Pound wrote exultantly to Williams—sculpture and machine purchased with the two hundred dollars returned by Yeats; Giotto's "Dante" in a gold frame; other pictures, family photographs and, of course, manuscripts here and there, his own and others'. Wyndham Lewis recalled: "Manuscripts always were lying around in his Kensington apartment, sent by divers strangers, who subsequently might appear in the flesh. Some, like Eliot, became habitués." And Iris Barry: "Only the postman knew how many tons of manuscript poured into his little flat."

Eliot's characterization of Pound at this period is a tribute: "No one could have been kinder to younger men, or to writers who, whether younger or not, seemed to him worthy and unrecognised. No poet, furthermore, was, without self-depreciation, more unassuming about his own achievement in poetry. The arrogance which some people have found in him, is really something else; and whatever it is, it has not expressed itself in an undue emphasis on the value of his own poems. He liked to be the impresario for younger men, as well as the animator of artistic activity in any milieu in which he found himself. In this rôle he would go to any lengths of generosity and kindness; from inviting constantly to dinner a struggling author whom he suspected of being under-fed, or giving away clothing (though his shoes and underwear were almost the only garments which resembled those of other men sufficiently to be worn by them), to trying to find jobs, collect subsidies, get work published and then get it criticised and praised."

Not overlooked by Mr. Eliot was Pound's "passion to teach. In some ways, I can think of no one whom he resembled more than Irving Babbitt—a comparison which neither man would have relished. Perhaps the backgrounds were not unlike; perhaps if Pound had stopped at home, and become, as he might have become, a professor of comparative literature, the resemblance might have been closer still."[4]

Pound's arrogance was "really something else," and Mr. Eliot did not pursue it. Lewis, writing—like him—many years later, attempted to pinpoint what it was:

"He did not desire to prove to the people he had come amongst that he was superior in physical strength, but that he was superior to all other intellectuals in intellect, and all poets in prosodic prowess. *They* were to be the spectators merely—they were of very little account. The feelings of dislike were mutual and immediate, as I could observe, and he never sought to hide the fact that he looked upon them as of very little consequence."[5]

It is the solitary student of Penn and Hamilton, and the teacher—plus, of course, the poet he had become, with an intense consciousness of his abilities. Perhaps the teacher in him or, in any case, the man forever seeking, forever demanding, the "master-work," the man talking about the classics and impatient with pallid imitations or products, rubbed listeners the wrong way, so that his lectures fell on deaf though well bred ears. Lewis adds: "The particular group in whose company I met him were apt to be learned too." But, of course, they were learned in the same way that they were well bred; there had been no struggle, and there was no passion.

Pound wrote about Ford in *Poetry:*

"In a country in love with amateurs, in a country where the incompetent have such beautiful manners and personalities so fragile and charming that one cannot bear to injure their feelings by the introduction of competent criticism, it is well that one man should have a vision of perfection and that he should be sick to death and disconsolate because he cannot attain it." Again: "Of course it is impossible to talk about perfection without getting yourself much disliked. It is even more difficult in a capital where everybody's Aunt Lucy or Uncle George has written something or other."

His poems provide an amusing commentary on his texts:

> Come, my songs, let us speak of perfection—
> We shall get ourselves rather disliked. . . .

and

> Upon learning that the mother wrote verses,
> And that the father wrote verses,
> And that the youngest son was in a publisher's office,
> And that the friend of the second daughter was
>   undergoing a novel,
> The young American pilgrim

Exclaimed:
> "This is a darn'd clever bunch!"

4.

Sometime between the two issues of *BLAST* Pound introduced Wyndham Lewis to Eliot, which brought together three of "the men of 1914," Joyce being the fourth encompassed by Lewis's famous phrase.

James Joyce was in his thirty-second year when *A Portrait of the Artist* began to appear serially in *The Egoist*. The story of his privations, so often told, can be epitomized in the two words and dates placed by him at the end of the completed manuscript: "Dublin, 1904. Trieste, 1914." He at once began the composition of *Ulysses*. By 1915 the probability of Italy entering the war on the side of the Allies turned to certainty; active in bringing this about was a young Socialist editor named Benito Mussolini. Trieste became a city of perpetual harassments, caught between sympathy for Italy and its commerce with Austria. Joyce's students fell away, his writing all but ceased. It was then that two noblemen, students of his, interceded for him with the Austrian authorities, and Joyce and his family were permitted to leave for neutral Switzerland. In Zurich he at once advertised for pupils; a new round of drudgery began, and *Ulysses* was continued in his spare time. At this juncture Pound again took a hand.

"Damn! Why haven't I a respectable villa of great extent and many retainers?" he had recently written Williams. One may easily imagine the "academy" of writers and artists under his own roof which would have resulted, were the roof but broad enough. Something else was needed in Joyce's case, and Pound took his idea to Yeats. Yeats, of course, had known Joyce; in London, in 1902, he had introduced him to Arthur Symons and tried to find him some work. On Tuesday, July 6, 1915, Yeats wrote to Edmund Gosse:

"I have just heard that James Joyce, an Irish poet and novelist of whose fine talent I can easily satisfy you, is in probably great penury through the war. He was at Trieste teaching English and has now arrived at Zurich. He has children and a wife. If things are as I believe, would it be possible for him to be given a grant from the Royal Literary Fund? What form should the application take? I am sorry to trouble you but I know in a case of hardship you do not think anything is trouble." A postscript stated: "I would like to show you some of Joyce's work."

Yeats had *Chamber Music, Dubliners* and issues of *The Egoist;* he also had "letters and statements about James Joyce" gathered by Pound. The latter he sent on to the Secretary of the Royal Literary Fund with a covering letter—"if more particulars are needed you could perhaps get them from Mr. Ezra Pound, 5 Holland Place Chambers, Kensington, who has been in fairly constant correspondence with Mr. Joyce and arranged for the publication of his last book. I think that Mr. Joyce has a most beautiful gift. There is a poem on the last page of *Chamber Music* which will, I believe, live. It is a technical and emotional masterpiece. I think that his book of short stories *Dubliners* has the promise of a great novelist and a great novelist of a new kind. There is not enough foreground, it is all atmosphere perhaps, but I look upon that as a sign of an original study of life. I have read in a paper called *The Egoist* certain chapters of a new novel, a disguised autobiography, which increases my conviction that he is the most remarkable new talent in Ireland today."

A month and three weeks after Yeats's first letter to Gosse, Joyce was awarded £75.[6] It was, of course, a godsend. He wrote Yeats from Zurich: "I have every reason to be grateful to the many friends who have helped me since I came here, and I can never thank you enough for having brought me into relation with your friend Ezra Pound who is indeed a miracle worker." Pound also helped him directly; Joyce received from him, as coming from an anonymous donor, £25, and an additional two pounds a week for thirteen weeks from the Society of Authors, sent at Pound's instigation.[7] Lewis afterwards wrote:

"It is to take nothing away from that admirable and self-denying Quaker lady to point out that it was not Miss Weaver, after all, who came across Joyce's novel, *The Portrait of the Artist,* and recognised its value: as a result of which recognition and warm support it was serialised in her review, *The Egoist.* (Nor was Eliot's verse, nor my novel, *Tarr*—which she likewise serialised—material dependent on her editorial initiative, but work brought to her notice by Pound.) In a word, Ezra Pound 'sold' the idea of Joyce to Miss Harriet

Weaver. Subsequently that lady set aside a capital sum, variously computed but enough to change him overnight from a penniless Berlitz teacher into a modest rentier; sufficiently for him to live comfortably in Paris, write *Ulysses,* have his eyes regularly treated and so forth. These *rentes* were his—I know nothing beyond that— until he had become a very famous person: and the magician in this Arabian Nights Tale was undoubtedly Ezra."[8]

5.

The magician and miracle worker was closely observed at a literary tea given by May Sinclair by a young woman afterwards well known for her own novels. She was Phyllis Bottome. She saw "a tall, slight young fellow, with the face of a scholarly satyr, red-gold hair and pointed beard." She had heard he was vain, but thought, rather, that he was proud. He was "obviously nervous," and she carried away an image of "an electric eel flung into a mass of flaccid substances." She wrote of him later:

"You could not tell whether he would fall off his chair or remain on it, and he gave the impression of sharing the observer's doubts. He cleared his throat constantly, as if he thought life itself a thing to be got rid of. He spoke in short staccato sentences like the bark of an angry dog. He wore his brain outside of him like a skin; and that terrific exposure made him always vulnerable and frequently hostile."

They met again. Miss Bottome was living with her mother, and Pound urged her to break free, "to give up my domestic securities and live in economic independence upon the fruit of my wits." But while she lacked the courage, as yet, to meet life head-on, "his salutary push freed me from a good deal of inner servitude."

She was grateful to him for two other experiences. In his Kensington flat "he introduced me to the first really good meal I had ever tasted, and I think he gave it to me at a time when providing good meals for other people must have involved a certain amount of personal privation. This meal was a work of art. Hitherto my experiences of food had been rudimentary and religious. Religious in the sense that my mother thought it wrong to like it; and rudimentary in the sense that she knew nothing whatever about it. Throughout my life

Ezra Pound's meal has stood before me as an incentive, and a stand-ard."

What could it have been? She does not tell.

The other experience: "he gave me the first objective literary criticism I had ever listened to." He also laid down the literary law, and that so forcefully, that "three of Ezra Pound's searchlight exactitudes stick in me with the faithful rigidity of St. Sebastian's arrows." These were:

" '1. A work of art is the honest reproduction of a concrete image. Imagination is the faculty which finds out all about this image, and never the revelation of the feelings aroused by it.

" '2. Why are you not content with saying that a man stepped intentionally upon a kitten? It is surely not necessary to add that he was not a humane man.

" '3. If you think rightly you will act rightly. It is never honest to have a thought which does not become a part of your experience.' "[9]

Nothing untoward, apparently, ever happened at his own dinners, but meals in other people's houses seemed to have been for Pound occasions for singular behavior. Aldington recounts an instance of a *"gaffe"* the same year, same place, but a dinner instead of a tea: "One evening in 1915 we dined with May Sinclair. On this occasion Ezra distinguished himself by alternately leaning forward to spear potatoes with his fork from a dish in the middle of the table, and then lolling back to munch his capture."[10]

6.

Here it may be useful to take a closer look at "the men of 1914," together with one or two subsidiary figures, since all of them were important, it may be thought, in influencing if not in shaping Pound's beliefs. I leave Joyce out, for he alone of the major figures encomp-assed in Lewis's phrase remained aloof from any movement, whether artistic or political. As many of their ideas came from the anti-roman-ticist, neo-classicist revolt in France, it will be necessary to touch on it here.

In *Definition of Culture,* Eliot wrote: "The governing élite, of the nation as a whole, would consist of those whose responsibility was inherited with their position and affluence." *Quis custodiet ipsos custodes?* is a natural retort, and has been made before.[11] The idea of a "governing élite" with heritable trappings was much discussed by men without position or affluence in the days preceding and following World War I, among them the writers with whom we are dealing. Their contradictions were not apparent to them, and therefore need not concern us overmuch. Hulme translated Sorel's *Reflections on Violence* and Bergson's *Introduction to Metaphysics,* the latter with Flint's help, Aldington suggests, while Pound intimates in a 1937 letter that Hulme had both Flint's and Mrs. Kibblewhite's help on both volumes. Hulme was a great admirer of Bergson, who reciprocated by getting him readmitted to Cambridge, whence he had been "sent down" for brawling. He did not stay long the second time either. It would appear impossible for a philosopher enamored of Bergson to admire Maurras, that arch-reactionary whose followers threatened Bergson with execution and whose ideas and actions kept France in turmoil and contributed to her tragedy; but this Hulme was able to do. I have already quoted Aldington and others on his coarseness where women were concerned, and it cannot have escaped a post-World War II reader that a contempt for women always accompanies authoritarian reveries. Lewis shared this contempt, and his books, fiction and nonfiction alike, are sown with observations which seem incredible from a man who was also contemptuous of homosexuals. He, too, had praise for Maurras, as did Eliot, who afterwards found some of the Frenchman's ideas "deplorable."

In France, as in England, men who wrote well too often showed that this did not necessarily stand for thinking clearly or behaving with detachment or decorum. There, the revolt against romanticism was not confined to books, but transferred to polemics, and then was taken from the library into the street, where the neo-classicist intellectual became a bully and brawler in company with other bullies and brawlers, not all of them even literate, but muscular and armed. Maurras and his followers called for "order"—a word often to be found in the writings of Eliot, Pound and Yeats—specifically an order based on State and Church, and created nothing but disorder in a land which had not yet recovered from the convulsions of the Dreyfus affair, in which the Church had been routed, the State all but overthrown. The Maurrasians dreamed of a leader, the inheritor of the Forty Kings of France, who if but restored would restore order, by crushing democracy and the Jews; for, together with the anti-feminist, anti-democratic hysteria, there was always, in the authoritarian revery, the drug—or poison, rather—of anti-semitism. The Jews were behind democracy; they were also behind Protestantism. "Le protestant procède absolument du Juif," Maurras wrote, which may appear startling to Protestant Americans and Britons, but was, in fact, an old idea in Catholic countries. It failed to startle Pound, since he alludes to it. Miss Heyman became anti-semitic, too, her friends recall.

This question, of anti-semitism, is not, it seems to me, a "Jewish" problem at all, as he and others have conveniently termed it, but a Christian one. It is perhaps impossible to be an entire Christian without some anti-semitism, for it is inculcated at once, and inculcated early, and the two appear inextricable, or have been for so long that no amelioration is to be looked for. The poison is merely more virulent in some than in others. *De mortuis,* and so forth; alas, the phrase itself must have been designed because it was sometimes necessary to disregard its injunction. Gaudier-Brzeska had all the public promise of a supreme artist, but like many anti-semites, a private illness. A reader of his notebooks will be shocked by his hatreds, a reader of his letters disgusted by infantile fantasies about the woman whose name he had attached to his own and who passed as his sister and behaved like one, so that both their wretched lives were made more wretched by the frustrations of an abnormal relationship. But private illness is not the real point. The real point is: what is the Christian religion, whether Catholic or Protestant, that can fill a child with such hatred that when grown he or she is receptive to the methodical slaughter of unarmed men, women and children—of a mother with an infant in her arms, of the son with his bed-ridden mother on his back, carried into the pit where the machine guns were set up to annihilate the townspeople of a town? "I am twenty-three," a Jewish girl remarked to a foreign observer standing beside Himmler as she followed them, with others, in the pause between bursts of firing. And as though, when these horrors were past, the world had not yet had enough of them, there attached himself to Pound, in his latter days, another young man, who had never, I believe, had any idea in his head before, and who stepped from the portals of St. Elizabeths Hospital to fill the South with dissension and strife.

Great is the responsibility of poets and priests.

7.

As regards "the men of 1914" and their friends, the truth may lie in the fact that all were uprooted—even Yeats; for of all those who met and talked of an "elite order" only Hulme was native-born. Perhaps they wanted a stabilizing influence—a leader—for themselves, although they spoke and wrote of it as more desirable for others, the despised masses of men and women. Eliot wrote: "At the moments when the public's interest is aroused, the public is never well enough informed to have the right to an opinion."[12] But the choices made by the intellectuals, including those under discussion, in the decades which shattered the Western world are sufficient refutation.

In addition to the men who dreamed of an order whereof they would be the intellectual leaders, or in any case of their number, there were others with visionary schemes and fierce ambitions to drive the modern money-changers from the Temple or, better still, from the banks, so they could take over with printing presses of their own; they already had charts and diagrams for the distribution of "scientific" currency. One was Alfred Richard Orage, the Guild Socialist and editor of *The New Age,* through whom Pound met C. H. Douglas, the Scots engineer who was the inventor of Social Credit. Orage and Douglas convinced each other—they, in fact, wrote a book together about it—and afterwards convinced Pound, that the "real credit" of a nation resides in its people and their capacity to produce needed goods, but that a perversion had set in, due to the "cornering" of money, so that "financial credit" actually controlled "real credit," to the profit of a few. Enter, of course, the Rothschilds, the de Wendels, the Comité des Forges, and so forth. Enter anti-semitism.

As for Douglas, one might suppose an engineer to be immune to ideas which obscure the real objective, but I can only refer my readers to Thoreau's definition of a reformer. What kept Douglas, and his associates, warm in the face of cold indifference was the hot lamp of anti-semitism; it became their religion, as Communism was to be to some, as Monarchy and Church were to others. This man, who was going to reform the financial structure of the world, and usher in an age of dignity, plenty and peace, delivered himself of sentiments worthy of the lowest rabble-rouser concerning "the existence of great secret organizations bent on the acquisition of world-empire"—

Jewish, of course.[13] His followers, some of whom had hardly the brains to understand compound interest—I judge, of course, only by their writings, those gleetable effusions with which they comforted each other—understood this, and poor as they were, likewise generated heat to keep them warm. The *Social Creditor,* organ of the Douglasites, recommended to its readers "The Protocols of Zion," a notorious forgery, afterwards used by Hitler.

How, then, did second- and third-rate ideas—corrupting ideas— find such fertile soil in Pound's brilliant and sensitive mind?

Pound's mind is essentially a feminine one. Although he is himself a forceful personality, he has encountered personalities more forceful than his own, of whom the first was Hulme. Orage was another, Douglas a third. Frobenius and Mussolini were to be a fourth and fifth. Pound is—certainly he appears to have been—extremely susceptible to the intellectual or emotional pressures of other men. He has absorbed and been influenced by the ideas of others; some commentators, among them intimate associates of his, have flatly declared that he does not have, and never has had, ideas of his own, which appears far-fetched. But it is true that the ideas on which he has expended most time and energy—his creative work aside—have been the ideas of others. But ideas which may be fruitful in the field of aesthetics can be something else again in other areas. One thing is clear: the Leftists saw Mussolini and Hitler more clearly—particularly after Spain—as the enemies of mankind they turned out to be. The Rightists —I use both terms somewhat loosely, for on both sides there were men and women of good sense and good will who would spurn either label—saw in these uneducated and evil men symbols of order. Hence Lewis's praise of Hitler—he wrote books supporting him, but afterwards modified his views; hence Pound's praise of Il Duce in his *Jefferson and/or Mussolini,* and the later elegy on his death. William Rothenstein wrote in his memoirs: "If ever the Fascist party should come into power in England, I imagine Wyndham Lewis as the chief state artist; as Poet Laureate, Ezra Pound."[14] He wrote this when Sir Oswald Mosley's brawlers were in the streets of London, particularly in Whitechapel, assaulting Jews at the behest of a knight.

I will say nothing about Pound's dress, although colorful, although —in Mrs. Dolmetsch's phrase—flamboyant. He told Douglas Paige in St. Elizabeths that, so far as his early days in London were concerned, corduroy jackets and trousers were cheap and durable, and he could not afford more expensive materials. But he also added that others who bought such bohemian accoutrements were not courageous enough to don them; he was.

8.

Pound published three books in 1915. As editor of the *Poetical Works of Lionel Johnson,* he wrote:

"Mr. Elkin Mathews wanted, I think, some definite proof that Lionel Johnson was still respected by a generation, or, if you will, by a clique, of younger poets who scoff at most things of his time. Now Lionel Johnson cannot be shown to be in accord with our present doctrines and ambitions. His language is a bookish dialect, or rather it is not a dialect, it is a curial speech and our aim is natural speech, the language as spoken. We desire the words of poetry to follow the natural order. We would write nothing that we might not say actually in life—under emotion. Johnson's verse is full of inversions, but no one has written purer Imagisme than he has, in the line

Clear lie the fields, and fade into blue air.

It has a beauty like the Chinese."

"Curial"—"of a curia; of the Papal court." Johnson was a convert to Catholicism. Pound praises "the dozen places where this stately and meticulous speech is moved by unwonted passion." Again: "One thinks that he had read and admired Gautier, or that at least, he had derived similar ambitions from some traditional source. One thinks that his poems are in short hard sentences. The reality is that they are full of definite statement."[15]

Included in Pound's preface were Johnson's notes on some of his contemporaries; as Pound remarks, the judgments were "stark naked," some of the men judged were still living, and the *Poetical Works* had to be withdrawn. It was reissued without the preface.

It will be recalled that Lionel Johnson was a relation of the Shakespears; it may even be that it was at their instigation that Pound undertook to bring out a collected edition. "I am accustomed to meeting his friends," he wrote in the preface, "and his friends, with the sole exception of Mr. Yeats, seem to regard him as a prose writer who inadvertently strayed into verse." Yeats, of course, was a survivor of the Rhymers' Club whose two chief luminaries—leaving him to his own special place—were Lionel Johnson and Ernest Dowson. Another was Victor Gustave Plarr, author of *In the Dorian Mood*, who was forty-nine or fifty when Pound met him. In 1914 he published a book about Ernest Dowson, in which Pound is mentioned:

"Young Mr. Pound, to whom Dowson is a kind of classical myth, just as the ancients are a myth to us all, tells me a story, told him in turn by a good recorder, of how Dowson went to see poor Wilde in Dieppe after the débâcle, and how he endeavoured to reform his morality by diverting it at least into a natural channel. It is at best a smoking-room anecdote, not fit for exact repetition."

The "good recorder" happened to be Yeats, who has told the story in that section of his autobiography called "The Tragic Generation."

At the time Pound knew him Plarr was Librarian of the Royal College of Surgeons in Lincoln's Inn Fields, and compiling its catalogue. Plarr had been born in Strasbourg; his family settled in England after the Franco-Prussian War. Hence Pound's characterization of him:

> Among the pickled foetuses and bottled bones,
> Engaged in perfecting the catalogue,
> I found the last scion of the
> Senatorial families of Strasbourg, Monsieur Verog.
>
> For two hours he talked of Gallifet;
> Of Dowson; of the Rhymers' Club;
> Told me how Johnson (Lionel) died
> By falling from a high stool in a pub . . .

Galliffet: he led one of those famous charges, magnificent but not war, at the Battle of Sedan. Johnson, in one of his less "stark naked" notes had found Plarr "delightful, a kind of half-French, half-Celtic Dobson with nature and the past and dying traditions and wild races for his theme," and so Pound found him,

> out of step with the decade,
> Detached from his contemporaries,
> Neglected by the young,
> Because of these reveries.

I shall have occasion to return to this poem or, rather, section of a long poem.

Cathay was the second book. The first poem in it—"Song of the Bowmen of Shu"—has curious overtones, echoes even, of "The Return." The book, "for the most part from the Chinese of Rihaku, from the notes of the late Ernest Fenollosa," contains the well known "The River-Merchant's Wife: A Letter." A short poem, "The Jewel Stairs' Grievance," has a long note:

> The jewelled steps are already quite white with dew,
> It is so late that the dew soaks my gauze stockings,
> And I let down the crystal curtain
> And watch the moon through the clear autumn.

Note.—Jewel stairs, therefore a palace. Grievance, therefore there is something to complain of. Gauze stockings, therefore a court lady, not a servant who complains. Clear autumn, therefore he has no excuse on account of weather. Also she has come early, for the dew has not merely whitened the stairs, but has soaked her stockings. The poem is especially prized because she utters no direct reproach.

Cathay was published in April; Pound sent two copies to Quinn, the first in March, inscribed: "To John Quinn, Life Fellow to the Metropolitan Mausoleum of Art. Complimenti bring 'em to life. Forever Ezra Pound." In the other: "I rather like the 'Exile's Letter.' Yrs. E. P." In June, Yeats sent a copy to Robert Bridges.

The third book published by Pound in 1915—it appeared in November—was *Catholic Anthology,* in which nine of his own poems—"Contemporania"—appeared, and which he says he decided to edit with the idea of "getting sixteen pages of Eliot into print at once." The collection is led off by Yeats's "The Scholars," followed by Eliot's

"Love Song," "Portrait of a Lady," "The Boston Evening Transcript,"
the prose-poem entitled "Hysteria" and "Miss Helen Slingsby."

There is also a curious work entitled "Poem: Abbreviated from the
Conversation of Mr. T. E. H.," with the subtitle, "Trenches: St.
Eloi," a description of behind-the-lines in France. Hulme had been
wounded, and was in a war hospital in England, where Pound visited
him and made notes of his talk. He went back, and was killed. Others
in the anthology include Douglas Goldring, John Rodker, Harold
Monro, Harriet Monroe, Williams, Sandburg, Masters, Kreymborg
and Upward. The title was a misnomer and was resented in orthodox
circles. Mathews, who published the book, asked Pound: "Why, why
will you needlessly irritate people?" and Pound wrote Kate Buss
in the United States: "The Jesuits here have, I think, succeeded in
preventing its being reviewed. . . . Having forged the donation of
Constantine (some years since) they now think the august and tolerant
name belongs to them, a sort of apostolic succession."

The same year, in Grantwood, New Jersey, Alfred Kreymborg
began to issue a magazine with the title *Others,* from his manifesto:
"The old expressions are with us always, and there are always others."
His contributors included Williams, who helped out editorially,
Conrad Aiken, Richard Aldington, H. D., Marianne Moore, Mina
Loy, Skipwith Cannéll, Amy Lowell, Fletcher, Wallace Stevens, Eliot
and Pound.

9.

By 1916, Pound was ready to go to press with his versions of the Noh
plays made from Fenollosa's manuscripts. Yeats's excitement was perhaps greater than his own. Yeats wrote Lady Gregory: "I believe I
have at last found a dramatic form that suits me." He wrote to John
Quinn: "I hope I am not incoherent but I am tired out with the excitement of rehearsing my new play—*The Hawk's Well* in which masks
are being used for the first time in serious drama in the modern
world."

At the Hawk's Well was the first of Yeats's plays to be written in
the dramatic form founded on the Japanese Noh. There were only
three characters—Cuchulain, an Old Man, and the Guardian of the

Well played by Michio Ito, a traditional dancer, who was to be seen daily at the London Zoo flapping and prancing as he imitated the motions of hawks in preparation for his role; Yeats was often with him, watching in rapt admiration. People stared. (He also turned up in Pound's flat where, on the clavichord Dolmetsch had made, "Ezra persuaded Arnold to accompany a Japanese dancer with old English dance music," Mrs. Dolmetsch told me. "The effect was somewhat grotesque!")

The first performance was in Lady Cunard's drawing room, Cavendish Square, Sunday afternoon, April 2, 1916. Costumes and masks were designed by Edmund Dulac, who also made them. The audience was select—lovers of poetry, members of the government, "a few pretty ladies." Pound brought Eliot, unmatched corduroys flanked by bowler and tightly rolled umbrella. It was a memorable experience—for Eliot, one that changed his view of Yeats. He afterwards wrote:

"Yeats was well-known, of course; but to me, at least, Yeats did not appear, until after 1917 [read 1916], to be anything but a minor survivor of the '90s. (After that date, I saw him very differently. I remember clearly my impression of the first performance of *The Hawk's Well,* in a London drawing-room, with a celebrated Japanese dancer in the rôle of the hawk, to which Pound took me. And thereafter one saw Yeats rather as a more eminent contemporary than an elder from whom one could learn)."[16]

Dulac was added to the Pound circle. They became close friends. Dulac made a seal for Pound "in the Chinese manner," like Whistler's, and Pound began to sign his letters with it. His wife's view of Dulac was another matter. She was herself a talented artist. Pound wrote Quinn:

"My wife, trying to find a formula of words, said 'No . . . ah . . . no, Dulac *isn't* an artist.'

"I: 'What?'

"She: 'No, he's something else, he is different' (that means different from Lewis, me, Gaudier, Eliot, etc.). 'He is a . . . dilettante.'

"Which is probably the answer. He is a nice chap to dine with and probably better at conversation or anything else than at ART."

Certain Noble Plays of Japan, "from the manuscripts of Ernest Fenollosa. Chosen and finished by Ezra Pound, with an Introduction by William Butler Yeats," was published September 16, 1916, at the Cuala Press, Churchtown, Dundrum, in an edition of 350 copies. Pound wrote to Quinn:

"I think I am justified in having spent the time I did on it, but not much more than that."

10.

Lustra of Ezra Pound appeared the same year. A note on a flyleaf explained the title: "DEFINITION: LUSTRUM: an offering for the sins of the whole people, made by the censors at the expiration of their five years of office, etc. Elementary Latin Dictionary of Charlton T. Lewis." The book has a curious publishing history. Pound wrote Iris Barry in May:

"If you have a passion for utility, and if by any chance you intended to get my new volume of poems *Lustra* when it comes out, then do for God's sake order your copy at once and UNABRIDGED.

"The idiot Mathews has got the whole volume set up in type, and has now got a panic and marked 25 poems for deletion. Most of them have already been printed in magazines without causing any scandal whatever, and some of them are among the best in the book. (It contains Cathay, some new Chinese stuff and all my own work since Ripostes.)

"The scrape is both serious and ludicrous. Some of the poems will have to go, but in other cases the objections are too stupid for words. It is part printer and part Mathews.

"At any rate if you were going to want the book, do write for it at once, *unabridged*.

"The printers have gone quite mad since the Lawrence fuss. Joyce's new novel has gone to America (AMERICA!) to be printed by an enthusiastic publisher. Something has got to be done or we'll all of us be suppressed, à la counter-reformation, dead and done for."

Yeats, called in to mediate, quoted Donne to Mathews.

Pound wrote Miss Barry again in June:

"Poor Mathews can't send you the unabridged *Lustra* yet as it ain't printed. However, he has been persuaded into doing 200 copies unabridged for the elect and is allowed to have the rest of the edition almost as modest as he likes—God knows, the whole thing is innocent enough, but the poor man has had an awful week of it.—I suppose he has some right to decide how he'll spend his money.

"Monro is called up on Saturday so that stifled my shifting the book to the Poetry Book Shop."

The book did not appear until October. There were two editions—a trade edition and a private one limited to two hundred numbered copies. The limited edition contained eight poems not in the trade edition. These were: "Salutation the Second," "Commission," "The New Cake of Soap," "Epitaph," "Meditatio," "Phyllidula," "The Patterns," and "The Seeing Eye." "Commission" had disturbed Miss Monroe. "The New Cake of Soap" names a living person—

> Lo, how it gleams and glistens in the sun
> Like the cheek of a Chesterton—

two lines which might have pleased him. "Meditatio" and "The Seeing Eye" are about dogs; I give the latter as being superior and amusing:

> The small dogs look at the big dogs;
> They observe unwieldy dimensions
> And curious imperfections of odor.
> Here is a formal male group:
> The young men look upon their seniors,
> They consider the elderly mind
> And observe its inexplicable correlations.
>
> Said Tsin-Tsu:
> It is only in small dogs and the young
> That we find minute observation.

"Phyllidula" was a shocker of sorts (before Miller, Mailer, Kerouac and Co.):

> Phyllidula is scrawny but amorous,
> Thus have the gods awarded her,
> That in pleasure she receives more than she can give;

> If she does not count this blessed
> Let her change her religion.

There were also two editions in New York the following year.
Alfred A. Knopf published a trade edition which contained a number
of poems not in the London ones, including a section entitled "Poems
published before 1911," and a private edition of sixty copies, forty
of these being for John Quinn and not for sale. The private edition
contains one poem not in the trade edition: "The Temperaments."
This, apparently, stopped everyone but Quinn:

> Nine adulteries, 12 liaisons, 64 fornications
>   and something approaching a rape
> Rest nightly upon the soul of our delicate friend
>   Florialis,
> And yet the man is so quiet and reserved in demeanour
> That he passes for both bloodless and sexless.
> Bastidides, on the contrary, who both talks and
>   writes of nothing save copulation,
> Has become the father of twins,
> But he accomplished this feat at some cost;
> He had to be four times cuckold.

11.

In 1916, Newark, New Jersey—population 400,000—celebrated the
250th anniversary of its founding. Some $400,000 were spent on the
year-long festival, one dollar per head, so to speak, in which sum was
included thirteen cash awards for poems hailing the city—to wit, a
first prize amounting to $250, a second, $150, a third of $100, and
ten prizes of $50 each. The competition opened in January and closed
in December with some nine hundred entries received. The judges
were as follows: Hon. Frederic Adams, Judge of the Circuit Court,
State of New Jersey; Hon. Thomas L. Raymond, Counsellor-at-Law,
and Mayor of Newark; Miss Margaret Coult, Head of the English
Department, Barringer High School, and William S. Hunt, Associate
Editor, *Newark Sunday Call*. These were all from Newark. There

were also three "judges at large": John C. Van Dyke, Professor, History of Art, Rutgers College; Thomas L. Masson, author and editor of *Humorous Masterpieces of American Literature,* and Theodosia Garrison, author of *The Joy of Life and Other Poems.*

Poems submitted for the competition were not to contain more than a thousand words, a stipulation which may indicate fear of the long and wandering line. They were to bear a fictitious name or distinctive mark, and be enclosed in sealed envelopes. In another sealed envelope bearing the fictitious name or distinctive mark would be the author's name and address.

Like everyone else who had ever had a poem published, Pound received the circulars of the Newark poetry competition. He submitted a poem. Perhaps his distinctive mark was the Chinese seal made by Dulac. His poem flattered no one, least of all Newark.

TO A CITY SENDING HIM ADVERTISEMENTS

But will you do all these things?
    You, with your promises,
    You, with your claims to life,
Will you see fine things perish?
Will you always take sides with the heavy;
Will you, having got the songs you ask for,
    Choose only the worst, the coarsest?
Will you choose flattering tongues?

    Sforza . . . Baglione!
Tyrants, were flattered by one renaissance,
    And will your Demos,
Trying to match the rest, do as the rest,
The hurrying other cities,
Careless of all that's quiet,
Seeing the flare, the glitter only?

Will you let quiet men
                    live and continue among you,
    Making, this one, a fane,
    This one, a building;

Or this bedevilled, casual, sluggish fellow
Do, once in a life, the single perfect poem,
   And let him go unstoned?

Are you alone? Others make talk
      and chatter about their promises,
Others have fooled me when I sought the soul.
And your white slender neighbor,
      a queen of cities,
A queen ignorant, can you outstrip her;
   Can you be you, say,
    As Pavia's Pavia
And not Milan swelling and being modern
      despite her enormous treasure?

If each Italian city is herself,
   Each with a form, light, character,
To love and hate one, and be loved and hated,
      never a blank, a wall, a nullity;
Can you, Newark, be thus,
         setting a fashion
But little known in our land?
           The rhetoricians
Will tell you as much. Can you achieve it?
You ask for immortality, you offer a price for it,
   a price, a prize, and honour?

You ask a life, a life's skill,
        bent to the shackle,
        bent to implant a soul
     in your tick commerce?
          Or the God's foot
     struck on your shoulder
     effortless,
     being invoked, properly called,
     invited?
I throw down his ten words,
      and we are immortal?

In all your hundreds of thousands
                    who will know this;
Who will see the God's foot,
                    who catch the glitter,
The silvery heel of Apollo;
                    who know the oblation
Accepted, heard in the lasting realm?

If your professors, mayors, judges . . . ?
                    Reader, we think not . . .
Some more loud-mouthed fellow,
                    slamming a bigger drum,
Some fellow rhyming and roaring,
        Some more obsequious back,
Will receive their purple,
                    be the town's bard,
Be ten days hailed as immortal,
        But you will die or live
        By the silvery heel of Apollo.

One of the judges remarked that it was "captious, arrogant, hyper-critical, but [has] some merit." Another refused to consider it. Nevertheless, it won a $50 prize. The first prize went to Clement Wood for "The Smithy of God," a poem so flawlessly awesome that a mere extract can hardly do it justice:

        I am Newark, forger of men,
        Forger of men, forger of men—
        Here at a smithy God wrought, and flung
        Earthward, down to this rolling shore,
        God's mighty hammer I have swung,
        With crushing blows that thunder and roar,
        And delicate taps, whose echoes have rung
        Softly to heaven and back again;
        Here I labor, forging men.

A book entitled *The Newark Anniversary Poems,* including Pound's, was printed by Laurence J. Gomme, of the Little Book Shop Around the Corner.

CHAPTER XI

LETTERS TO A YOUNG POET

1.

There was, in 1916, in a wartime job in the General Post Office in Birmingham, a correspondence clerk named Iris Barry. Pound had seen her poems in Harold Monro's *Poetry and Drama,* and on April 17th he wrote her to send him some of her unpublished work—perhaps he could place it in Harriet Monroe's *Poetry.* The poems came, and he wrote back:

"I am not quite satisfied with the things you have sent in, still many of them seem to have been done more or less in accordance with the general suggestions of imagisme, wherewith I am too much associated. The main difficulty seems to me that you have not yet made up your mind what you want to do or how you want to do it. I have introduced a number of young writers (too many, one can't be infallible) ; before I start I usually try to get some sense of their dynamics and to discern if possible which way they are going.

"With the method of question and answer: Are you very much in earnest, have you very much intention of 'going on with it,' and mastering the medium, etc.? Or are you doing vers libre because it is a new and attractive fashion and anyone can write a few things in vers libre?"

He offered some individual criticisms:

"In some of the 'regular' stuff, you fall too flatly into the whole 'whakty whakty whakty whakty whak,' of the old pentameter. Pentameter O.K. if it is interesting, but a lot of lines with no variety won't do."

"Re cadence: 'Some loving thoughts still linger here with me,' seems rather a flat hobby horse sort of movement, that we've all heard till we're dead with it. So many of your pentameter lines seem all in one jog, whereas the metre skilfully used *can* display a deal of variety."

He returned to metre: "What they call 'metre' in English means for the most part 'jambic.' They have heard of other metres and tried a few, but if the music of the words and the feel of the mood are to have any relation, one *must* write as one feels. It may be only an old hankering after quantitative verse that is at the bottom of it. All languages I think have shown a tendency to lengthen the foot in one way or another, as they develop."

He agreed with her suggestion: "You are quite right, it is much easier to go at such points in talk than by letter. However."

2.

In June he wrote her that he was sending William Carlos Williams seven of her poems. Williams was now associated with Kreymborg in editing *Others;* Pound explained what it was—"a harum scarum vers libre American product, chiefly useful because it keeps 'Arriet,' (edtr. *Poetry*) from relapsing into the Nineties."

Their talk was put off.

"I am sorry about your holidays, also you should have a chance to see Fenollosa's big essay on verbs, mostly on verbs. Heaven knows when I shall get it printed. He inveighs against 'IS,' wants transitive verbs. 'Become' is as weak as 'is.' Let the grime *do* something to the leaves."

She decided to come.

"Dear Miss Barry: I believe the underground runs from here to Wimbledon. At least I have a map with black lines on it, moving in that direction, and I think it implies some form of conveyance. I will enquire with due diligence. Also as to time consumed in transit. Place of arrival, whether two or six stations in Wimbledon, etc.

"As to marks of identification in case there be two males loose on

the platform??? Do you wish any, or will you trust purely to instinct?
And I?

"It would be a shame to pass in silence for the want of a bouton-
niere. Perhaps a perfectly plain ebony staff, entirely out of keeping
with the rest of the costume will serve. Perfectly plain, straight,
without any tin bands, etc. at the top of it. Emphatically not a country weapon."

It is a little like one of his poems—"Villanelle: The Psychological
Hour":

> I had over-prepared the event,
> > that much was ominous.
> With middle-ageing care
> > I had laid out just the right books.
> I had almost turned down the pages. . . .

He concluded: "And what am I to look for?"
She did not tell him. She told me (1959):
"I don't think I had any distinguishing signs. I was just a young
person in a black suit, with, I think, a hat with flowers, which had cost
my family a lot of money: it was up to me to recognise Pound, not
he me."

Under the hat with flowers was the rather serious face of a young
woman "fairly fresh out of a convent: an only child and a solitary
one, very romantic." Her blue eyes were sometimes greenish-gray,
with "emphatic black eyebrows," and her "middle brown" hair was
done up in two long plaits coiled over the ears, "very tidy and circum-
spect." She was of medium size and not, as she had pretended, twenty-
two but "not quite seventeen." Her grandfather had known Blake,
"which perhaps explains why the family let me go to London and
didn't discourage my writing."

She and Pound met, as arranged, and walked across Wimbledon
Common, Pound talking all the time, beginning with Hulme, and how
it happened that Hulme's poems had been included in *Ripostes;* then
about the state of literature and the arts generally at the moment. A
wind was blowing—"it hurled the words away from Pound's lips"—
and she did not hear everything he said. She was also baffled by his
speech—"it takes time to get used to it."

"Pound talks like no one else," she was to write. "His is almost a wholly original accent, the base of American mingled with a dozen assorted 'English society' and Cockney accents inserted in mockery, French, Spanish and Greek exclamations, strange cries and catcalls, the whole very oddly inflected, with dramatic pauses and *diminuendos*."

She was also "too agitated" to grasp much, in any case, "now that I found myself striding along beside the Spirit of Revolt itself."

Forty-three years later his image was still vivid in her mind: "I am glad you see I was right about the green eyes, for goodness sake don't forget the cat-like cries too and the elegant black stick and somewhat voluminous overcoat, flying hair. . . ."

3.

For his part, Pound must have been agreeably surprised. He had taken her intelligence for granted, or he would not have written her in the first place in his role of editor and "impresario." He set out to educate her. His letters, when she returned to Birmingham, became more frequent; they also became longer. He headed one "KOMPLEAT KULTURE":

"Catullus, Propertius, Horace and Ovid are the people who matter. Catullus most. Martial somewhat. Propertius for beautiful cadence though he uses only one metre. Horace you will not want for a long time. I doubt if he is of any use save to the Latin scholar. I will explain sometime viva voce."

Virgil was "a second-rater, a Tennysonianized version of Homer," Pindar "the prize wind-bag of all ages. *The* 'bass-drum,' etc." For the rest: "There was poetry in Egypt; I have seen a small book of interesting translations and forgotten the name. *Cathay* will give you a hint of China, and the 'Seafarer' on the Anglo-Saxon stuff. Then as MacKail says (p. 246) nothing matters till Provence.

"After Provence, Dante and Guido Cavalcanti in Italy.

"Very possibly ALL this mediaeval stuff is very bad for one's style. I don't know that you have time to live through it and? ? ? ? to survive? (If I have survived.)

"The French of Villon is very difficult but you should have a copy of Villon and not trust to Swinburne's translations (though they are very fine in themselves); they are too luxurious and not hard enough."

She wrote that she had most of Villon "by heart," likewise Heine. He resumed his course: "Théophile Gautier is, I suppose, the next man who can write. Perfectly plain statements like his 'Carmen est maigre' should teach one a number of things."

He commended Flaubert and Stendhal. "Sometime, certainly, you must have the soufflé of contemporary French poets." Voltaire: "Perhaps you should read all of the *Dictionaire Philosophique.* Presumably no other living woman will have done so." Landor: "There is a whole culture." English poetry: "Ugh. Perhaps one shouldn't read it at all. Chaucer has in him all that has ever got into English." The Elizabethans: "Everybody has been sloppily imitating the Elizabethans for so long that I think they probably do one more harm than good." Wordsworth: "a dull sheep." "Byron's technique is rotten." Browning: "The hell is that one catches Browning's manner and mannerisms. At least I've suffered the disease." Spain had "nothing," Italy had Leopardi, "the only author since Dante who need trouble you, but not essential as a tool."

He offered to mail her some of the books mentioned. He told her the essence of style: concision and necessity. "It is as simple as the sculptor's direction: 'Take a chisel and cut away all the stone you don't want.' " He thought it over. "No, it is a little better than that." He left it there.

Landor had impressed him. "Yeats and I spent our last winter's months on Landor." They had gone right through him—ten volumes —reading to each other. "I don't quite know whether you will like much of it," he told Miss Barry. "Perhaps you had better keep it till later." He also wrote Williams advising him to "reread 'Sordello' and then get the ten vols. of Walter Savage Landor. Converse with no one until you have read all save a few of the dialogues on politics & orthography. He is the best mind in English literature. Don't hand this on to the mob yet."

That Pound should not have read Landor before that 1915–1916 winter at Stone Cottage is a criticism not of him but the curricula of the schools. Still, his "discovery" is a little breathless, considering his age. He need not have worried; the "mob" would never "go for that stuff." And Williams did not, to judge by his work.

4.

She is now "Dear Iris Barry." In reply to her inquiry: "Your poems are on the other side of a floor I have just stained and it is too wet and sticky to cross. You shall have them in a few days." He thinks the list of French poets can wait: "You can't have got to the end of the other lists." He sends it along, anyway: "Remy de Gourmont, De Régnier (a very few poems), Francis Jammes, Jules Romains, Chas. Vildrac, TRISTAN Corbière, Laurent Tailhade, Jules Laforgue, (dates all out of order), Rimbaud. I'll make out a list of books, when you are really ready, also send you *L'Effort Libre* anthology of the younger men. There's no hurry about returning the things you have."

She wanted to know if he liked music. "Je connus the London mondo musicale, at least the concert-hall, recital part of it." She is now "Dear Iris." He sent her a copy of the limited edition of *Lustra*. She exclaimed over his portrait by Coburn, and he wrote back: "The portrait is there to make junior typists clasp their hands ecstatically. Or as Yeats says: *'That'll* sell the book.' " (His landlady, whom he called in to show it, exclaimed: "Oh—the first that ever did you justice." She added: "Eh, I hope you won't be offended, sir, but, eh It-is-like-the-good-man-of-Nazareth, isn't-it, sir?") Miss Barry wanted him to receive a poet, whose "heart's desire" was to meet him. "Chère Iris: I believe in everyone's having their heart's desire at the earliest possible opportunity. . . . Still, you might have told me his name was Reginald."

She was thinking of writing her life:

"Beautiful Evelyn Hope: By all means write your autobiography. I would suggest that you do it as a series of letters to me. Under seal. It will be much easier than trying to write it all at a sitting, and it will keep the style simple and prevent your getting literary or attempting to make phrases and paragraphs. I know when I tried to do a novel based more or less on experience I wrote myself into a state of exhaustion doing five chapters at one sitting, arose the next day, filled reams, and then stuck."

She was thinking of marriage. "If you must marry, do follow your excellent ancestress's precedent. Marry and govern the state. Don't marry three servants and a villa in Birmingham. It is not a short cut to leisure." (Miss Barry told me: "The 'excellent ancestress' was more or less an invention of Pound's—namely Madame Du Barry whose husband was a vague relative of my family: hence no ancestress!") She thought of retiring to a farm to write. "The soul is more than flesh, etc. You had better much come up to London." But what would she live on? Tending bar? "I believe being a bar maid would be no obstacle, BUT one would be obliged to conceal the fact." He inquired about a room for her. "You can come to tea, and be took out to see someone or other some evening, and come in to meet some-one else. God knows who is in London at the moment, and divers circles are non-extant from war. Still you can put in your spare time somehow." He recommended a restaurant: "The cheapest clean res-taurant with a real cook is Bellotti's, Ristorante Italiano (NOT Res-taurant D'Italie) 12 Old Compton St." He sent directions "for life in the capital":

"NOT to use the competent and defensive air. (In really Lofty circles an amiable imbecility is the current form. . . .)

"General instructions: Ask questions. Everyone likes to be asked questions. Super-strategy: Ask questions showing knowledge of or sane interest in something of interest to interlocutor."

He signed himself, "Yours, Polonius."

5.

She came. She got a job with the Ministry of Munitions. She met Pound's wife and their friends. She became assistant librarian at the School of Oriental Studies. She was film critic and literary critic of *The Spectator*, film editor of the *Daily Mail*, a founder of The Film Society; and afterwards Librarian of the Museum of Modern Art in New York City and curator of its film library. She published a good deal of poetry, fiction and articles. Fifteen years after that memorable encounter at Wimbledon she published an article en-titled "The Ezra Pound Period."[1] In it, she summarized his activities and presented the notable cast of men and women who surrounded him, sometimes at home, where he "turned from cooking dinner (one of the things he does to perfection) wrapped in a flowing and worn fawn dressing-gown to the clavichord Dolmetsch made for him," but chiefly "at an inexpensive restaurant first in Soho and then—when the first proprietor could stand the air-raids no longer—in Regent Street, where there were weekly meetings." It was a Chinese restaurant, and they met there on Thursdays:

"Into the restaurant with his clothes always seeming to fly round him, letting his ebony stick clatter to the floor, came Pound himself with his exuberant hair, pale cat-like face with the greenish cat-eyes, clearing his throat, making strange sounds and cries in his talking, but otherwise always quite formal and extremely polite.

"With him came Mrs. Pound, carrying herself delicately with the air, always, of a young Victorian lady out skating, and a profile as clear and lovely as that of a porcelain Kuan-yin."

The cast—it was wartime, and there were soldiers on leave now and again in the weekly gatherings around the table:

"Semi-monstrous, bulging out his uniform, china-blue eyes peering from an expanse of pink face, pendulous lower lip drooping under sandy moustache as he boomed through endless anecdotes of Great Victorians, Great Pre-Raphaelites, Henry James, and somebody no one else had ever heard of and hardly believed in even then, was Ford Madox Hueffer—of particular interest to some of us when we realized he had once been the little William Tell boy in the Rossetti painting."

Again: "The young man in uniform who looked like a farmer was Aldington, home on leave from France."

Again: "Lewis, back from the Front, ghastly pale under his black hair and after silences that seemed, at least, to denote some suspicion of his fellow creatures, proving full of inimitable conversation, riotous song, and an unequalled play of humour."

The women: "Taller and more silent even than Mrs. Pound and looking, somehow, haunted, was Aldington's wife, the poetess H. D. A small lady, almost always dressed in raspberry pink, with acute dark eyes and a crisp way of speech and sharpness of phrase that, somehow, one would not have expected from her at first sight, was May Sinclair. Another regular diner was Mary Butts, with her long white Rossetti throat and vermilion-red hair strikingly like her ancestor, Henry VIII's tutor, and just married to John Rodker at the other end of the table. And who was the lady sitting up so very straight with her severe hat and nervous air—she might have been a bishop's daughter, perhaps? *That* was the lion-hearted Miss Harriet Weaver." (Miss Barry wrote me: "To me the heroine of the epoch was certainly Miss Harriet Weaver, the Quaker lady who published *The Egoist* and Joyce and Eliot, etc. She even gave *me* a hot bath and dinner once a week.")

In their midst: "Tall, lean and hollow cheeked, dressed in the formal manner appropriate to his daytime occupation in Lloyd's Bank—that was T. S. Eliot, generally silent but with a smile that was as shy as it was friendly, and rather passionately but mutely adored by the three or four young females who had been allowed in because of some crumb of promise in painting or verse.

"Chattering with a sublime disregard for practically everything, distraught golden hair, obviously a beauty of the Edwardian era, Violet Hunt often proved disconcerting to some of these same young women, for the way she pounced on them and asked questions and was at once good-natured and sharp-tongued."

Other men: "I never knew what drew Edgar Jepson to the group, except that both Pound and his close friend Edmond Dulac (a regular member of the group) were both passionately fond of jade, and Jepson collected it. He used to pass pieces of it about the table: Pound would finger each piece long and lovingly.

"Arthur Waley, pale and scholarly in appearance, with almost inaudible, clipped speech and incredible erudition, was there almost weekly—he had just begun those fine translations from the Chinese and Japanese that show the influence of Pound so clearly.

"Now and then Yeats appeared with his famous lock falling into his eyes. He was devoted to Pound."

The talk: "Round the table went the story of Miss Lowell's amazing descent upon London, of the opening of London's first night club by Madame Strindberg with her troop of little monkeys, of what young Nevinson had said to annoy in the Café Royal, of Saint Augustine and his mother's death, of Rihaku and Catullus, of Keats and the *Edinburgh Review,* of the big munition works which (so rumour had it every month or so) had been blown up by Zeppelin bombs overnight. Mixed in would be someone's account (Pound's, I think) of a row of houses discovered intact in Earl's Court outside the front door of each of which was a pair of stone dogs, large as life and no pair alike or even of the same species. There would be news of a restaurant where you could get more meat than ration cards properly allowed. There was mourning for the theft of the Dulac dog. To the accompaniment of air-raids without, we younger ones heard for the first time of Proust and the Baroness Elsa von Freytag Loringhoven, of Negro music and Chinese poetry, of the Oedipus complex and Rousseau the Douanier and Gertrude Stein.

"The effect, all too little realized at the time, was as though something that mattered very much had somehow and rather miraculously been preserved round that table when so much else was being scattered, smashed up, killed, imprisoned or forgotten."

Such, more or less, was the group which gathered about Pound in Regent Street on Thursdays. On Mondays there was a smaller group, which he took along "to sit at the feet of Yeats in his flat."

"Pound," Miss Barry wrote me, "was everybody's schoolmaster and more—he really bothered as to whether his 'disciples' had enough to eat or read the right books or met the appropriate elders."

6.

"His letters alone would have made a good magazine," Margaret Anderson wrote, and published those sent to her. Miss Anderson, editor with Jane Heap of the *Little Review,* had been corresponding with Pound for several years when he wrote her offering his services as foreign editor. "We hailed the occasion." Neither her autobiography[2] nor his *Letters* contains the letter with his proposal; the next one, however, is in both, undated by her, but dated by Pound's editor "January" with a question mark. The year is 1917.

"Dear M. C. A.," he wrote. "*The Little Review* is perhaps temperamentally closer to what I want done??????

"DEFINITELY then:

"I want an 'official organ' (vile phrase). I mean I want a place where I and T. S. Eliot can appear once a month (or once an 'issue') and where Joyce can appear when he likes, and where Wyndham Lewis can appear if he comes back from the war.

"DEFINITELY a place for our regular appearance and where our friends and readers (what few of 'em there are), can look with assurance of finding us."

In a signed editorial in the May issue he stated his position for readers of the *Little Review* and Harriet Monroe:

"My connection with *The Little Review* does not imply a severance of my relations with *Poetry* for which I still remain Foreign Correspondent, and in which my poems will continue to appear until its guarantors revolt.

"I would say, however, in justification both of *Poetry* and myself, that *Poetry* has never been 'the instrument' of my 'radicalism.' I respect Miss Monroe for all that she has done for the support of American poetry, but in the conduct of her magazine my voice and vote have always been the vote and voice of a minority."

The work that he had proffered began to appear, including his own. He enlisted Quinn's financial help. In a letter to Douglas C. Fox, Pound said: "The N. Y. office saw to printing and Quinn sent me 750 dollars a year for two years/thus permitting small payment to contributors." That "kindest, most generous, most irascible" of men was the way J. B. Yeats characterized Quinn, on which Pound commented to Miss Anderson: "I have never known anyone worth a damn who wasn't irascible." His next letter was a demonstration:

"Dear Margaret: What the ensanguined lllllllllllllll is the matter with this BLOODY goddamndamnblastedbastardbitchbornsonofaputridseahorse of a foetid and stinkerous printer??????

"Is his serbo-croatian optic utterly impervious to the twelfth letter of the alphabet????

"JHEEZUSMARIAJOSE!!! Madre de dios y de dios del perro. Sacrobosco di Satanas.

"OF COURSE IF IF IF bloodywell IF this blasted numero appears with anything like one twohundredandfiftieth part of these errors we are DONE, and I shall never be able to cross the channel or look a French ecrivain in the face."

It was not included in Pound's *Letters*.

Joyce's *Ulysses* appeared in the magazine; Pound, forwarding the first chapter, warned that there might be difficulties with the censors. There was. John S. Sumner, Secretary of the Society for the Prevention of Vice, served the Washington Square Book Shop with a summons for selling a copy, and the charge against the *Little Review* for publishing "obscenity" was pressed home by a father who feared that his daughter's morals might be impaired: that formidable *cliché*.

Pound wrote Joyce: "The only thing to be done now is to give Quinn an absolutely free hand."

The trial was held before three judges in the Court of Special Sessions, John Quinn defending. He naturally brought forward several prominent authors and editors to state why they considered *Ulysses* literature. John Cowper Powys said that he considered the novel "a beautiful piece of work, in no way capable of corrupting the mind of a young girl," whereupon Miss Heap whispered to Miss Anderson: "If there is anything in the world I fear it is the mind of a young girl." The verdict was "Guilty." The editors were fined one hundred dollars. An additional ignominy: the ladies were finger-printed, not without a struggle.[3]

7.

The London editor continued to send in work, by *les jeunes* as well as established writers: "The Iris Barry and Rodker stuff is not a compromise but a bet. I stake my critical position, or some part of it, on a belief that both of them *will* do something." He gave advice: "The one use of a man's knowing the classics is to prevent him from imitating the false classics." Again: "The strength of Picasso is largely in his having chewed through and chewed up a great mass of classicism; which, for example, the lesser cubists, and the flabby cubists have not." A poet (Maxwell Bodenheim) complained about him: "CRRRRHist JHEEZUS when I think of the hours of boredom I have put up with from people MERELY because they have in an un-guarded and irrecoverable and irresponsible moment committed a good poem, or several!!!!!!" And there was always Miss Lowell: "Is there any life into which the personal Amy would not bring rays of sunshine? Alas! and alas only, that the price, i.e., equal suffrage in a republic of poesy, a recognition of artistic equality, should come be-tween us." He warned: "If London and particularly Mayfair, is going to take up the magazine, we must be more careful than ever NOT to have in too much Amy, and suburbs." He compared: "Bill Wms. is *the* most bloody inarticulate animal that ever gargled. BUT it's better than Amy's bloody ten-cent repetitive gramophone, perfectly articulate (i.e. in the verbal section)." He wrote Williams:

"If you had any confidence in America you wouldn't be so touchy about it.

"I thought the – – – – millenium that we all idiotically look for and work for was to be the day when an American artist could stay at home without being dragged into civic campaigns, dilutations of controversy, etc., when he could stay in America without growing propagandist. God knows I have to work hard enough to escape, not propagande, but getting centered in propagande.

"And America! What the hell do you a bloomin' foreigner know about the place? Your père only penetrated the edge, and you've never been west of Upper Darby, or the Maunchunk switchback. Would Harriet, with the swirl of the prairie wind in her underwear, or the virile Sandburg recognize you, an effete Easterner, as a REAL American? INCONCEIVABLE!!!!"

He lectured Miss Anderson:

"A work of art, one ought almost to call it an 'act of art,' is enjoyable in proportion as the maker has made it to please himself. . . .

"When the idea of duty comes in, pleasure ceases. This simple statement is as true of art as amours.

"Precisely, a work of art made to please the artist may be comic (unintentionally comic), it may be agreste, barbaric, even stupid (as Montaigne and Dürer and Montecelli are, often, stupid) but it will not be *dead*. It will not have the distinguishing moribund character of a review in the *Times,* or of the poems in my volume, *Canzoni.*"

The typewriter "of great delicacy" was receiving a battering. There were times when even Pound faltered before it. One day he wrote Miss Anderson:

"Chère amie, I am, for the time being bored to death with being any kind of an editor. I desire to go on with my long poem; and like the Duke of Chang, I desire to hear the music of a lost dynasty. (Have managed to hear it, in fact.) And I desire also to resurrect the art of the lyric, I mean words to be sung, for Yeats' only wail and submit to keening and chaunting (with a *u*) and Swinburne's only rhapsodify. And with a few exceptions (a few in Browning) there is scarcely anything since the time of Waller and Campion. And a mere imitation of them won't do."

8.

Yeats, with good reason, cherished his father's letters. The mere thought that one of them might go astray was disturbing to him (J. B. Yeats had sent one to Woburn *Place* instead of Woburn Buildings). "I value the letters very much. I send them to be typed the moment they come." He was contemplating a selection from them for his sister's press at Churchtown. He wrote his father:

"I am handing the letters over to Ezra Pound, who is to make a first small volume of selections for Lollie's press, I thought he would make the selection better than I should. I am almost too familiar with the thought, and also that his approval, representing as he does the most aggressive contemporary school of the young, would be of greater value than my approval, which would seem perhaps but family feeling."

The 60-page book—*Passages from the Letters of John Butler Yeats, Selected by Ezra Pound*—was published at The Cuala Press in May, 1917, in an edition of four hundred copies.

In New York, old J. B. Yeats, who used to worry that his son would run off with a ballet dancer, had begun to worry that he would never run off with anyone. He began to frequent fortune tellers to learn, if possible, what his chances were of becoming a grandfather. He also inquired into the probable looks of his future daughter-in-law.

Lady Gregory was also concerned about Yeats's bachelorhood, and she occasionally drove down from London to Stone Cottage—sometimes when Pound was there—accompanied by personable young women who were well off. After the Easter uprising Yeats again thought of asking Maud Gonne to marry him, but their talks led nowhere, and he fell in love with her daughter, Iseult. "Oh, who is she?" Lady Cunard exclaimed when he brought her to call. "Never in my life have I seen such a complexion." In Normandy, he proposed to Iseult: like mother, like daughter. On his return, he wrote Lady Gregory:

"I don't think I can come to Coole just now. Mrs. Tucker has asked me down where she and her daughter are. I am, however in rather a whirlpool. Maud Gonne and the harmless Iseult have been served with a notice under the defence of the realm forbidding their landing in Ireland."

This was on September 18, 1917. He added—prophetically, as it turned out: "Maud Gonne will certainly do something wild." He wrote Lady Gregory again the next day: "I wrote you a very disturbed letter yesterday. Since writing I have decided to be what some Indian calls 'true of voice.' I am going to Mrs. Tucker's in the country on Saturday or Monday at latest and I will ask her daughter to marry me. Perhaps she is tired of the idea. I shall however make it clear that I will still be friend and guardian to Iseult." He concluded: "All last night the darkness was full of writing, now on stone, now on paper, now on parchment, but I could not read it. Were spirits trying to communicate?" He could not tell.

Yeats and Georgie—or George, as he preferred to call her—Hyde-Lees were married at the Harrow Road register office, London, on October 21, 1917. Pound was best man. They were now related by marriage. Yeats sent his wife's photograph to his father: "She permits me to say that it flatters her good looks at the expense of her character. She is not so black and white, but has red-brown hair and a high colour which she sets off by wearing dark green in her clothes and earrings, etc." A week after their marriage, she surprised him by her gift for spirit-writing.

CHAPTER XII

FAREWELL TO LONDON

1.

Some time in 1917 Pound turned to a rendering in contemporary speech of certain passages in Books II and III of the Elegies of Propertius. There are a number of references to this poet, the friend of Virgil and Ovid, in Pound's letters before 1917, and it was no sudden enthusiasm that led him to undertake the work. There are even points of similarity between the Roman and the American which cannot be overlooked—enormous erudition and respect for the past, combined with a varied yet vigorous modern style. The texts of Propertius have come down in fragmentary, garbled and disordered form, and his poems are, to some extent, reconstructions themselves. Vain, foppish, yet eager for general approbation, Propertius moved in the best circles, literary and social, in the Rome of Maecenas. Although he mentions many contemporaries, he does not mention Horace, who is likewise silent about Propertius, which suggests a feud. The masters he acknowledges are Callimachus and Philetas—not, it will be perceived, Roman ones. His first book of poems, inscribed to his mistress, established his reputation. She was a courtesan, and lived in Tibur. Her name was Hostia, the "Cynthia" of his poems.

It is only in recent years that Pound's intention has been understood, and the triumph of his method appreciated. He wrote to Professor Schelling: "No, I have not done a translation of Propertius. That fool in Chicago took the Homage for a translation, despite the men-

tion of Wordsworth and the parodied line from Yeats. (As if, had one
wanted to pretend to more Latin than one knew, it wdn't have been
perfectly easy to correct one's divergencies from a Bohn crib. Price
5 shillings.)" He also wrote to Orage: "There was never any question of translation, let alone literal translation. My job was to bring
a dead man to life, to present a living figure." Four sections of his
"Homage to Sextus Propertius" appeared in *Poetry,* and brought down
the wrath of the academic world, and in particular of Professor
William Gardner Hale, a friend of Harriet Monroe's, who attacked
Pound in the pages of her magazine. "Hale," Pound wrote, "pretends to read Latin, but has apparently never *understood* anything
but syntax." The battle spilled over onto the pages of the Chicago
Tribune, but the poem has survived.

> Shades of Callimachus, Coan ghosts of Philetas
> It is in your grove I would walk,
> I who come first from the clear font
> Bringing the Grecian orgies into Italy,
>   and the dance into Italy.
> Who hath taught you so subtle a measure,
>   in what hall have you heard it;
> What foot beat out your time-bar,
>   what water has mellowed your whistles?
>
> Out-weariers of Apollo will, as we know, continue
>   their Martian generalities,
>   We have kept our erasers in order.
> A new-fangled chariot follows the flower-hung horses;
> A young Muse with young loves clustered about her
>   ascends with me into the aether, . . .
> And there is no high-road to the Muses.
>
> Annalists will continue to record Roman reputations,
> Celebrities from the Trans-Caucasus will belaud
>   Roman celebrities
> And expound the distentions of Empire,
> But for something to read in normal circumstances?
> For a few pages brought down from the forked hill
>   unsullied?

> I ask a wreath which will not crush my head.
> > And there is no hurry about it;
> I shall have, doubtless, a boom after my funeral,
> Seeing that long standing increases all things
> > > regardless of quality.

Eliot omitted the poem in his selection of Pound's work, explaining:

"If the uninstructed reader is not a classical scholar, he will make nothing of it; if he be a classical scholar, he will wonder why this does not conform to his notions of what translation should be. It is not a translation, it is a paraphrase, or still more truly (for the instructed) a *persona*."[1]

There were some pot shots through the years. Aldington called "night-dogs" a schoolboy howler for *nocte canes,* but the drunks in Pound's line take care of any midnight yodeling. Pound took the *suggested* word, and enlarged the image—

> > crowned lovers at unknown doors,
> Night-dogs, the marks of a drunken scurry;

but, as he has remarked, he was not translating. "My job was to bring a dead man to life."

> > Midnight, and a letter comes to me from
> > > our mistress:
> > > Telling me to come to Tibur:
> > > > > *At* once! !

and again:

> > If she with ivory fingers drive a tune through the
> > > lyre,
> > > We look at the process.
> > How easy the moving fingers; if hair is mussed on
> > > her forehead,
> > If she goes in a gleam of Cos, in a slither of dyed
> > > stuff,

There is a volume in the matter; if her eyelids sink
    into sleep,
There are new jobs for the author;
And if she plays with me with her shirt off,
    We shall construct many Iliads.
And whatever she does or says
    We shall spin long yarns out of nothing.

The poem is in twelve sections. It is full of gossip of the antique
world, and the poet's role in that world:

Varro sang Jason's expedition,
    Varro, of his great passion Leucadia,
There is song in the parchment; Catullus the highly
    indecorous,
Of Lesbia, known above Helen;
And in the dyed pages of Calvus,
    Calvus mourning Quintilia,
And but now Gallus had sung of Lycoris.
    Fair, fairest Lycoris—
The waters of Styx poured over the wound:
And now Propertius of Cynthia, taking his stand
    among these.

It is an old preoccupation—

About my head be quiuering mirtle wound,
And in sad louers heads let me be found,

and

Not marble, nor the guilded monuments
Of princes, shall outlive this powerful rhyme—

Ovid, translated by Marlowe, and Shakespeare imitating Ovid.
Every long poem is a kind of stock-taking—"These fragments I
have shored against my ruins." To a man immersed in the classics
the war, which had shut each nation in on itself, each man in on
himself, was only a repetition of ancient disorders and follies. It

had all happened before, even the names were the same; that realization makes Pound's rhythms stride with giant steps, and there are great gulps of air instead of mere caesurae in the clash of syllables:

> When, when, and whenever death closes our eyelids,
> Moving naked over Acheron
> Upon the one raft, victor and conquered together,
> Marius and Jugurtha together,
> > one tangle of shadows.

> Caesar plots against India,
> Tigris and Euphrates shall, from now on, flow at his bidding,
> Tibet shall be full of Roman policemen,
> The Parthians shall get used to our statuary
> > and acquire a Roman religion;
> One raft on the veiled flood of Acheron,
> > Marius and Jugurtha together.

Only art has survived those hosts in their tangles—at least, that art which the hosts have not demolished in the sack and pillage of the world:

> Flame burns, rain sinks into the cracks
> And they all go to rack ruin beneath the thud of the years.
> Stands genius a deathless adornment,
> > a name not to be worn out with the years.

This preoccupation with the poet's role, the poet's place, was to lead him, in a few years, to consider his own place in twentieth century letters. A pervasive bitterness, akin to the melancholy of Propertius, will be found in the later poem.

2.

Miss Monroe's acceptance of only four sections of his "Propertius" was galling to his pride as a craftsman. He wrote a new correspondent who was sending him fresh work from New York:

"One buys leisure to work by selling one's stuff for what one can. Harriet (Monroe) is too old to learn. Thank heaven I have conducted some of her funds to a few authors who needed emolument. I have repeatedly resigned. And it took a six months' struggle to get her to print Eliot's 'Prufrock.' I have nothing but my name on the cover. And the prospects of a very mutilated piece of my Propertius appearing in her paper, because it would be criminal for me to refuse £10/10; and because it don't matter. It don't matter in the least what appears or does not appear in that magazine. The elect will see, ultimately, the English publication of the series.

"(All of which is for your ear and no other. The woman is honest, and can not help her obfuscations.)"

The whole of "Homage to Sextus Propertius" appeared in successive issues of Orage's *New Age,* beginning June 19, 1919. It was published in book form in *Quia Pauper Amavi* by The Egoist, Ltd., in October of that year in two editions—one hundred copies on handmade paper, signed, and a trade edition on ordinary paper. The book also contained the original drafts of Cantos I, II, and III. The same month John Rodker printed, on Japanese vellum, at the Ovid Press, forty copies of "The Fourth Canto." Pound wrote to Quinn:

"*Quia Pauper Amavi* is at last out. Eliot has done a dull but, I think, valuable puff in the *Athenaeum*; granite wreaths, leaden laurels, no sign of exhilaration; but I daresay it is what is best in that quarter.

"He has shown in earlier articles the 'English Department' universitaire attitude: literature not something enjoyable, but something which your blasted New England conscience makes you feel you *ought* to enjoy.

"Have had two opulent weeks as dramatic critic on *The Outlook,* and have been fired in most caddish possible manner. Have had my work turned down by about every editor in England and America, but have never before felt a desire for vengeance."

He was no longer "bored to death with being any kind of an editor." Good new work could always be relied on to take him out of the doldrums. Now it was the woman in New York. He was curious about her:

"Your stuff holds my eye. Most verse I merely slide off of (God

I do ye thank for this automatic selfprotection), BUT my held eye goes forward very slowly, and I know how simple many things appear to me which people of supposed intelligence come to me to have explained.

"Thank God, I think you can be trusted not to pour out flood (in the manner of dear Amy and poor Masters).

"I wish I knew how far I am right in my conjecture of French influence; you are nearer to Ghil than to Laforgue, whose name I think I used in The Future. My note in the L. R. was possibly better.

"O what about your age; how much more youngness is there to go into the work, and how much closening can be expected?"

He invited her to submit a manuscript for book publication, and offered his experience in arranging the table of contents, which he deemed important. "I have got Joyce, and Lewis, and Eliot and a few other comforting people into print, by page and by volume. At any rate, I will buy a copy of your book IF it is in print, and if not, I want to see a lot of it all together. You will never sell more than five hundred copies, as your work demands mental attention. I am inclined to think you would 'go' better in bundles about the size of Eliot's *Prufrock and Other Observations.*"

He placed her poems in the magazines which he served. He got her first book published by The Egoist Press. He told her: "I doubt if I will ever return to America, save perhaps as a circus."

Her name was Marianne Moore. They did not meet until 1939.

3.

On Armistice Day he wandered for hours to observe the people of London reacting to the news. In Trafalgar Square boys stripped the war posters from the Nelson column and set them afire. In Piccadilly he found himself within two feet of the royal carriage, and observed at first hand "the general enthusiasm for George on his drive through the drizzle in an open carriage, with no escort save a couple of cops." He caught a cold, which he still had when he wrote Quinn about it four days later.

The men who came back from the war resumed their interrupted activities. Pound's letters tick them off: "Lewis' new show opening

Thursday," "Manning again in circulation," "Fat Madox Hueffer in last evening," "Wadsworth and Lewis in town, more or less free," "Aldington at 'front' educating Tommies."

The artists and writers fared better than their less gifted brothers-in-arms; they still had an occupation and a goal. They returned to their old haunts in Kensington, Soho and Bloomsbury. But now there was a subtle and vexing difference in the groups that met in restaurants and "at homes." Those who had served were different not only by reason of their service, but by their shared experience. This experience Pound had missed. It was no longer important that during the war his presence in London had given them a "base" to return to and that on their leaves they had sought him out to renew themselves with talk of art and letters. He had done more: he had kept the men at the Front informed of literary and artistic developments, and to judge by one account, there were moments when mail call, because of him, meant a thrilling experience. Ford wrote Margaret Anderson after the war:

"I will tell you of one of the happiest that comes back to me. It was when, during the heaviest days of the war, in France, our Ezra sent to me, cut off by ages and miles from all remembrance of ever having written anything and from all seeming possibility of ever again writing anything—when, then, our Ezra sent me in France, the copies of *The Little Review* in which you were serialising something of mine."

Aldington was one of the last to be demobilized. Like the others, he too sought out Pound. It was not a happy meeting, and Aldington's record, though written later, is suggestive of noncommunication and strain:

"Ezra I found still in the same small apartment in Kensington, rather overwhelmingly obstructed with one of Dolmetsch's spinets and a quantity of poor Gaudier's statues. For some reason Ezra had become violently hostile to England—perhaps those 'night dogs' were biting him. At any rate he kept tapping his Adam's apple and assuring me that the English stopped short there. I thought at first he meant that he had been menaced by returning troops as a slacker, but it eventually came out that he was implying that the English had no brains." He added:

"Yet there were compensations even for this calamity. One of them was T. S. Eliot."[2]

4.

The emergence of Eliot marked another turning point for Pound; or perhaps it only appears so in retrospect. For a time they benefited each other by their discussions, then for a time they ruled the world of English and American poetry together, and it is hard to imagine that world without one or the other. It would have been a different world. And whatever it was that Pound was striving for, outside of good work—his own and others'—there was no rivalry between the two masters. It would have been foreign to the character and intentions of both men.

Pound wrote of Eliot in Mr. Eliot's *Criterion*:

"He displayed great tact, or enjoyed good fortune in arriving in London at a particular date with a formed style of his own. He also participated in a movement to which no name has ever been given.

"That is to say, at a particular date in a particular room, two authors, neither engaged in picking the other's pocket, decided that the dilutation of *vers libre*, Amygism, Lee Masterism, general floppiness had gone too far and that some counter-current must be set going. Parallel situation centuries ago in China. Remedy prescribed 'Émaux et Camées' (or the Bay State Hymn Book). Rhyme and regular strophes.

"Results: Poems in Mr. Eliot's *second* volume, not contained in his first ('Prufrock,' *Egoist,* 1917), also 'H. S. Mauberley.'

"Divergence later."[3]

Eliot, in the essay from which I have quoted, said:

"Half of the work that Pound did as a critic can be known only from the testimony of those who have benefited from his conversation or correspondence. At a certain moment, my debt to him was for his advice to read Gautier's *Émaux et Camées*."

Aldington wrote of both:

"Ezra started out in a time of peace and prosperity with everything in his favor, and muffed his chances of becoming literary dictator of London—to which he undoubtedly aspired—by his own conceit, folly and bad manners. Eliot started in the enormous confusion of war and post-war England, handicapped in every way. Yet by merit, tact, prudence, and pertinacity he succeeded in doing what no other American has ever done—imposing his personality, taste, and even many of his opinions on literary England."[4]

But was Pound "aspiring" to this particular role? There was a vacuum, and he filled it; there simply was not anyone else around who could have done so, or done better what he did. Johnson himself never sought the role of "The Great Cham of Literature"—it was thrust upon him, and then he gave quite a performance while it lasted, which was a very long time. But Johnson was an Englishman, at home in his own country. He was feared as well as admired, but not resented. In time, many of those Pound had helped found their admiration for him grown dim as their gratitude. An entire chapter might be composed on this, for many bitter letters and revised judgments exist, his own as well as theirs.

"I hope I shall not seem sensational if I say that looking back I cannot see him stopping here very long without some such go-between as Ford Madox Hueffer," wrote Wyndham Lewis in 1948.

The way of the literary dictator is not easy. Burke said of Dr. Johnson: "It is well, if when a man comes to die, he has nothing heavier upon his conscience than having been a little rough in conversation."

Sir Osbert Sitwell has provided a glimpse of Pound during this period after the 1918 Armistice. Every Thursday evening they were in London he and his brother dined at a restaurant in Piccadilly Circus where Eliot, Herbert Read, Pound and Wyndham Lewis met. Each sat, back to the wall, at a separate table. It made conversation "self-conscious or desultory."

Sir Osbert said: "Ezra Pound was inclined to mumble into his red beard, a habit perhaps brought on by his defensiveness, the result, in turn, of attacks delivered on himself during the years of his domicile in England. He was particularly a type the English do not understand or appreciate."[5]

He also points out that Pound was even less appreciated after World War II.

5.

Pound has recorded his own disappointed hopes in England in the note appended to "Hugh Selwyn Mauberley," subtitled—perhaps ironically—"Life and Contacts," and in the poem itself. Whatever the title may suggest, particularly in juxtaposition with Eliot's "J. Alfred Prufrock," the character of the title is not comic. There are several learned commentaries on this important work which, when it appeared in 1920, took an immediate place as one of the few major poems of our time, and it has held that place since with uncontested authority. It is not an "easy" poem, but no poem of worth that is more than eight lines—the limit marked by Samuel Butler, after which the poet grew faint, he thought—is "easy" since it exists on several levels, as does any work of art. The commentaries are rather for the young poet, who can learn a great deal from Pound's literary roots as well as the flowering which is the poem itself. I therefore leave them to a footnote,[6] except for one flight which struck me as extraordinary, and return to Pound's note to the poem in the enlarged *Personae*, where it occupies pages 185-204. It reads:

"The sequence is so distinctly a farewell to London that the reader who chooses to regard this as an exclusively American edition may as well omit it and turn at once to page 205."

This is patently in a bitter vein—at the very least, an impatient one. It is why certain portions of the commentaries do not satisfy, for the note is explicit about an experience, and it would appear all but impossible to turn that experience into something else; but this the commentators have all but succeeded in doing. Mr. Eliot, who wrote without benefit of their views, since he wrote before they did, goes as usual to the heart of the matter about the poem:

"It is compact of the experience of a certain man in a certain place at a certain time; and it is also a document of an epoch; it is genuine tragedy and comedy; and it is in the best sense of Arnold's worn phrase, a 'criticism of life'."[7]

The sequence consists of eighteen poems. The "tone" is Corbière rather than Laforgue, as in Eliot. There is a Latin motto from Nemesianus—"The heat calls us into the shade"—a title from Ronsard, a line from Homer, in Greek—"For we know all the things which are in Troy"—a line from Villon, and several paraphrases and annotations from Henry James, Remy de Gourmont and Gautier, particularly the last. There is also an adaptation of a rhythmic sequence by Bion (from the lament for Adonis). Yet it is all clear, all of a piece; the eclecticism is modern, and crowns the eclecticism of Pound's earlier work. One may ask, however, why he brought in a doomed hero: Capaneus, one of The Seven Against Thebes, whom Zeus destroyed for his pride. Pound told Professor Schelling: "Of course, I'm no more Mauberley than Eliot is Prufrock," and "Mauberley is a mere surface."

Of course, when a poet is through with a poem, the poem exists as "a mere surface" of the poet. He has other fish to fry; or, to revert to an earlier and more elegant phrase, he is a phoenix. He may now write a quite different poem, with a quite different structure, the structure however being of the greatest importance. Thus, almost everything in "Mauberley" had been prefigured in "Homage to Sextus Propertius"—everything, that is, except the bitterness; that, and the "rhyme and regular strophes," the versification of a master. As the text of "Mauberley" is easily available I shall quote only such passages as illustrate Pound's experience and views of the contemporary scene. The first poem in the sequence is entitled "E. P. Ode Pour L'Election de Son Sepulchre." The personal tone is immediately conveyed:

> For three years, out of key with his time,
> He strove to resuscitate the dead art
> Of poetry; to maintain "the sublime"
> In the old sense. Wrong from the start—
>
> No, hardly, but seeing he had been born
> In a half savage country, out of date;
> Bent resolutely on wringing lilies from the acorn;
> Capaneus; trout for factitious bait;
>
> Ἴδμεν γάρ τοι πάνθ', ὅσ' ἐνὶ Τροίῃ
> Caught in the unstopped ear;
> Giving the rocks small lee-way
> The chopped seas held him, therefore, that year.
>
> His true Penelope was Flaubert,
> He fished by obstinate isles;
> Observed the elegance of Circe's hair
> Rather than the mottoes on sun-dials.

Unaffected by "the march of events,"
He passed from men's memory in *l'an trentiesme*
De son eage; the case presents
No adjunct to the Muses' diadem.

Villon's "Great Testament" begins with the line quoted by Pound,
who has substituted "son" for "mon." Villon disappeared shortly after
his thirtieth year, banished from Paris, where he had been twice under
sentence to be hanged. If that lank, sun-dried vagabond did not
starve to death in his wanderings, he was probably hanged on a
provincial gibbet; the landscape was studded with them. The same
thing occurred in the case of Rimbaud, who disappeared at eighteen
although, to be sure, he was afterwards found; but he had stopped
writing verse. Thus, there are at least two adjuncts to Pound's case,
if by "the case" he means his own. If his fame was undergoing an
eclipse, it is not apparent from his productions. We are left with the
man himself. In a recent revision (*Diptych,* 1958, consisting of
"Propertius" and "Mauberley"), "trentiesme" has become "tren-
tuniesme," which places the composition in 1916, and makes the
opening line *circa* 1913, when he was indeed "resuscitating" poetry.

6.

If the first poem is a portrait of the poet—Eliot's "certain man"—
the second is the setting—the "certain place at a certain time." The
setting is of almost equal importance, for had it been different the
portrait might not have been attempted; probably would not. In the
second poem the intellectual atmosphere of the time is given:

> The age demanded an image
> Of its accelerated grimace,
> Something for the modern stage,
> Not, at any rate, an Attic grace;
>
> Not, not certainly, the obscure reveries
> Of the inward gaze;
> Better mendacities
> Then the classics in paraphrase!

The "age demanded" chiefly a mould in plaster,
Made with no loss of time,
A prose kinema, not, not assuredly, alabaster
Or the "sculpture" of rhyme.

In the twelfth poem, the landscape itself appears:

Conduct, on the other hand, the soul
"Which the highest cultures have nourished"
To Fleet St. where
Dr. Johnson flourished;

Beside this thoroughfare
The sale of half-hose has
Long since superseded the cultivation
Of Pierian roses.

The third poem is a bridge between the poet's ideal, the classic past, and the tin-plated present:

All things are a flowing,
Sage Heracleitus says;
But a tawdry cheapness
Shall outlast our days.

Four and five are unrhymed, as though his indignation could not be contained; they are harsh and bitter denunciations of the war in which some of his friends died, from which others returned

home to old lies and new infamy;
usury age-old and age-thick
and liars in public places.

Daring as never before, wastage as never before.

The war, dislocating the world, had dislocated time, and now the poet turns his gaze to an earlier time and early admirations. The sixth poem is full of evocations of the Tate Gallery, where the eyes of Rossetti's wife and model peer out

> Thin like brook-water,
> With a vacant gaze.

From the pre-Raphaelites he comes to the Nineties, and introduces Victor Plarr as "M. Verog," like himself "out of step with the decade," in the poem from which I have already quoted. It would appear that there is a hint in the title of the poem to Plarr's removal from Strasbourg and his settlement in London—"Siena Mi Fe' Disfecemi Maremma"—"Siena made me, Maremma undid me"—a line from Dante of which Eliot also has made use. Pound's respect for the man from the Nineties is in contrast, in the two poems that follow, to his views on a brace of successful contemporaries—"Brennbaum" (Max Beerbohm) and "Mr. Nixon" (Arnold Bennett). But impressive though the portrait of Beerbohm is as a metrical exercise, it remains superficial from a basic flaw—Pound did not really know his sitter:

> The heavy memories of Horeb, Sinai and the forty years,
> Showed only when the daylight fell
> Level across the face
> Of Brennbaum "The Impeccable."

It is not "The Incomparable Max." But if not, what is it? (In 1955, in Rapallo, Sir Max told S. N. Behrman: "I am not Jewish. I cannot claim that.") What in Pound made him devote four lines of an eight-line poem to a Jewishness in his subject which was not even there? He is more successful in the characterization of Bennett:

> "I never mentioned a man but with the view
> Of selling my own works.
> The tip's a good one, as for literature
> It gives no man a sinecure.
>
> And no one knows, at sight, a masterpiece.
> And give up verse, my boy,
> There's nothing in it."

There is a third contemporary for whom Pound has only affection:

> Beneath the sagging roof
> The stylist has taken shelter,
> Unpaid, uncelebrated,
> At last from the world's welter
>
> Nature receives him;
> With a placid and uneducated mistress
> He exercises his talents
> And the soil meets his distress.
>
> The haven from sophistications and contentions
> Leaks through its thatch;
> He offers succulent cooking;
> The door has a creaking latch.

It is Ford Madox Ford, in retirement in Sussex, who has also recorded Pound's visit:

"Mr. Pound appeared, aloft on the seat of my immensely high dogcart, like a bewildered Stuart pretender visiting a repellent portion of his realms. For Mr. Pound hated the country, though I will put it on record that he can carve a suckling pig as few others can."[8]

Ford underwent an even lengthier eclipse in later years, from which his best work is now emerging. With this portrait, so personal and sympathetic, it is impossible to go along with even so eminent a commentator as Professor Kenner—who merits the *imprimatur* of New Directions and Faber and Faber, and thus speaks with authority —when he says:

"J. Alfred Prufrock is not Mr. Eliot, but he speaks with Mr. Eliot's voice and bears intricate analogical relations with the later Eliot persona who is the speaker of *Four Quartets*. Hugh Selwyn Mauberley, on the other hand, does not speak with Mr. Pound's voice, and is more antithetically than intimately related to the poet of the *Cantos*. . . . he is a parody of Pound the poet with whom Mr. Pound is anxious not to be confounded."[9]

Echoes of "Prufrock" occur in the twelfth poem (the first two lines are from Gautier):

"Daphne with her thighs in bark
Stretches toward me her leafy hands,"—
Subjectively. In the stuffed-satin drawing-room
I await The Lady Valentine's commands,

Knowing my coat has never been
Of precisely the fashion
To stimulate, in her,
A durable passion;

Doubtful, somewhat, of the value
Of well-gowned approbation
Of literary effort,
But never of The Lady Valentine's vocation:

Poetry, her border of ideas,
The edge, uncertain, but a means of blending
With other strata
Where the lower and higher have ending;

A hook to catch the Lady Jane's attention,
A modulation toward the theatre,
Also, in the case of revolution,
A possible friend and comforter.

7.

Another "borrowing" must now be accounted for.

There is, three-fourths of the way through the sequence, an
"Envoi" of great beauty dated 1919. If the five poems which follow
are taken as grace-notes to the poems which precede it, no difficulties
can occur; but the commentators have raised them to expound their
own particular theories. Lacking theories, the ordinary reader may see
in the poems which follow the "Envoi" Pound's continued preoccupation with the work he has created, even to the point of "lifting" lines
from the earlier poems, which he now gives other settings. Example:

> "His true Penelope
> Was Flaubert,"
> And his tool
> The engraver's.

He also lifts titles—"The Age Demanded"—and directs the reader:
"Vide Poem II. Page 188," already quoted. Hence,

> For this agility chance found
> Him of all men, unfit. . . .

and

> Ultimate affronts to
> Human redundancies;

> Non-esteem of self-styled "his betters"
> Leading, as he well knew,
> To his final
> Exclusion from the world of letters.

The "Envoi" is the masterpiece of the sequence, for which all the
poems provide a setting and on which they all converge. "For three
years, out of key with his time," as well as other passages, falls better
on a modern ear perhaps; its ambiguities let "bright young things"
ring changes and critics neither young nor bright pour forth their
profuse strains of exegesis. But the "Envoi" is impervious to all such
aids:

ENVOI (1919)

> *Go, dumb-born book,*
> *Tell her that sang me once that song of Lawes:*
> *Hadst thou but song*
> *As thou hast subjects known,*
> *Then were there cause in thee that should condone*
> *Even my faults that heavy upon me lie,*
> *And build her glories their longevity.*

Tell her that sheds
Such treasure in the air,
Recking naught else but that her graces give
Life to the moment,
I would bid them live
As roses might, in magic amber laid,
Red overwrought with orange and all made
One substance and one colour
Braving time.

Tell her that goes
With song upon her lips
But sings not out the song, nor knows
The maker of it, some other mouth,
May be as fair as hers,
Might, in new ages, gain her worshippers,
When our two dusts with Waller's shall be laid,
Siftings on siftings in oblivion,
Till change hath broken down
All things save Beauty alone.

I give Waller's "Song" here for convenience; it was set to music
by Henry Lawes.

SONG

Go lovely Rose,
Tell her that wastes her time and me,
That now she knows
When I resemble her to thee,
How sweet and fair she seems to be.

Tell her that's young,
And shuns to have her Graces spy'd,
That hadst thou sprung
In Desarts, where no men abide,
Thou must have uncommended dy'd.

Small is the worth
Of Beauty from the light retir'd;
Bid her come forth,
Suffer her self to be desir'd,
And not blush so to be admir'd.

Then die, that she,
The common fate of all things rare,
May read in thee
How small a part of time they share,
That are so wondrous sweet and fair.

I asked Pound in 1959, "Who sang you once that song of Lawes?"
He wrote from Rapallo: "Your question is the kind of damn fool
enquiry into what is nobody's damn business."

Hugh Selwyn Mauberley by E. P. was published by The Ovid
Press, April 23, 1920, in an edition of two hundred copies, of which
fifteen were on Japanese vellum, numbered and signed and not for
sale; twenty numbered from 16 through 35 and signed, and the
remainder numbered but unsigned. In June of the same year appeared
Umbra—"the early poems of Ezra Pound. All that he now wishes to
keep in circulation from Personae, Exultations, Ripostes, etc. With
translations from Guido Cavalcanti and Arnaut Daniel and poems by
the late T. E. Hulme." There were two editions: "100 copies printed,
numbered and signed by the author," and a trade edition. It was the
last of Pound's books under the imprint of Elkin Mathews.

8.

New work, or a new publication in which he could have a hand, could
always rouse him. From his flat at 5 Holland Chambers a new letterhead went forth—a large sheet with his address at top right, and all
down the left-hand side this announcement: "THE DIAL, Edited by
Scofield Thayer, 152 W. 13th St., New York, will print during
1920–21 the inedited writings of REMY de GOURMONT and has al-.
ready received either acceptable manuscript or promises of collaboration from Julien Benda, Marcel Proust, Benedetto Croce, Miguel

Unamuno, W. B. Yeats, Paul Valéry, Ford Madox Hueffer, T. S. Eliot, James Joyce, Wyndham Lewis, Jean de Bosschère, Ezra Pound, Guy Charles Cros, Joseph McCabe, Albert Mochel, André Spire, Paul Morand, May Sinclair, Louis Aragon, Alexander Aroux, Jean Giraudoux, Fernand Divoire, Richard Aldington, André Salmon, Philippe Soupault, W. C. Williams, Mina Loy, O. W. de Lubiez Milosz, Ludwilla Savitsky, Fritz Vanderpyl, Arthur Symons, Michael Arlen, H. D."

Pound had become the London correspondent of *The Dial*, whose first issue appeared January, 1920, and he was again indefatigably rounding up contributors. Although he was to write later, "E. E. Cummings was undoubtedly the white-haired boy for that outfit," it is difficult to imagine the subsequent careers of Eliot, Marianne Moore, Williams and himself without that unmatched and unmatchable forum, Eliot's *Criterion* excepted.[10]

Why did he do it? It augmented his income. Perhaps he felt, as in the case of the truncated "Propertius," that he had no right to turn down an offer which brought some cash with it. Perhaps he needed something of the sort to bolster his position, if not his ego. But, above all, he knew that he could be useful to other writers— probably, in his own mind, and probably correctly, more useful than another correspondent would be if he declined Thayer's proposal. He wrote T. E. Lawrence on April 20th:

"I have just taken the job and can't, I'm afraid, give you much indication of what they *do* want, save that I am asked to provide 'em with Mrs. Meynell, Lowes Dickinson, Lytton Strachey, Yeats, Eliot, myself in homeopathic (very) doses, etc."

And Lawrence replied from All Souls College, Oxford, with a great blot in the middle of his letter:

"O E-P!

"For twenty days I have been faced by your letter: each day I read a new name of a contributor to *The Dial*: but there is surely no place for me in that galaxy? Of course Joyce can write (and does, just occasionally): you can write (and do): T. S. Eliot . . . perhaps: but the people I like are so different, Hodgson: Sassoon: D. H. Lawrence: Manning: Conrad: I suppose that blot means you fainted, so I won't go on: but do you see the point? I'm academic idyllic, romantic; you breathe commas and exclamation marks."[11]

Pound appears to have followed up his letter with a visit, for Robert Graves has recorded a meeting with him in Lawrence's rooms at All Souls. Graves wrote: "From his poems, I had expected a brawny, loud-voiced, swashbuckling American; but he was plump, hunched, soft-spoken and ill-at-ease, with the limpest of handshakes." When Pound left, Graves asked Lawrence: "What's wrong with that man?" Lawrence replied: "Pound has spent his life trying to live down a family scandal—he's Longfellow's grand-nephew."[12]

That spring, Pound reviewed *Economic Democracy* by C. H. Douglas in the *Little Review*. The meeting between him and the father of Social Credit had taken place, through Orage. When its results are considered, it may appear significant that Pound embraced their view of economics when he was deeply dissatisfied, and perhaps deeply disturbed. Social Credit was to draw to its ranks, on both sides of the Atlantic, men with visions of a better world; and the forlorn of both sexes, the misfits with private frustrations and hatreds, all those who needed the bolstering shoulder of a "cause." They also needed to "belong." The same phenomenon occurred in the ranks of the English and American Communists. That year Yeats wrote:

> The best lack all conviction, while the worst
> Are full of passionate intensity.

9.

In 1920, Williams published *Kora in Hell: Improvisations*. In the prologue he defended the American school—himself, Sandburg, Kreymborg and Bodenheim—against the international school— Pound and Eliot. "All my gripes to other poets, all my loyalties to other poets are here." He termed Pound "the best enemy United States verse has," and sent him a copy of the book. Pound reacted violently, as was natural:

"My dear old Hugger-scrunch: Un po' di giustizia!! Or rather: you're a liar. Precisely I am an 'enemy of American verse.' "

The letter is long, and full of justifications which the reader of this book can do without. It is the first of three on the subject; Pound wrote immediately after reading the prologue, and wrote again when he was going through the text. He took exception to the account of his conversation with Williams's father, as related earlier. He told Williams he would "welcome your candid re both *Homage to S. Prop.* and *Mauberley* if you have the texts. Nobody tells me anything about 'em that I don't know already." There is a suggestion of regret that he and his earliest poet friend could not have worked side by side:

"Possibly lamentable that the two halves of what might have made a fairly decent poet should be sequestered and divided by the – – – – buttocks of the arse-wide Atlantic Ocean."

Their friendship had withstood many crises. Perhaps the ocean helped, that ocean across which Pound peered often in his thoughts but which he could not bring himself to cross.

"AND now that there is no longer any intellectual *life* in England save what centres in this eight by ten pentagonal room; now that Rémy and Henry are gone and Yeats faded, and NO literary publication whatever in England, save what 'we' print (*Egoist* and Ovid Press), the question remains whether I have to give up every shred of comfort, every scrap of my personal life, and 'gravitate' to a New York which wants me as little now as it did ten or fifteen years ago. Whether, from the medical point of view it is masochism for me even to stay here, instead of shifting to Paris. Whether self-inflicted torture ever has the slightest element of dignity in it?

"Or whether I am Omar.

"Have I a country at all . . . now that Mouquin is no more, and that your father has no more goldwasser, and the goldwasser no obescent bonhomme to pour it out for me?

"Or you who sees no alternative?

"All of which is, as you have divined, in relation to your prologue."

It was a time for stock-taking. Once he had written with finality:

> I have weathered the storm,
> I have beaten out my exile.

CHAPTER XIII

ROOTS AND FOREBEARS

1.

For the seventh time in his life Pound was in Venice. He stayed a day or two in a cramped room at the Albergo Bella Venezia, then ensconced himself in a more expensive one—"much too expensive," he felt—in the Albergo Pilsen-Manin. It was April. A time for stocktaking. What was he doing there? What did it mean to be an American?

"There is blood poison in America," he had written Williams from London; "you can idealize the place (easier now that Europe is so damd shaky) all you like, but you haven't a drop of the cursed blood in you, and you don't need to fight the disease day and night; you never have had to. Eliot has it perhaps worse than I have—poor devil.

"You have had the advantage of arriving in the milieu with a fresh flood of Europe in your veins, Spanish, French, English, Danish. You had not the thin milk of New York and New England from the pap; and you can therefore keep the environment outside you, and decently objective."

It was not nationality that bothered him—nationality meant nothing to him. It was race. "Race is probably real. It is real." And he belonged to the American race that had wrested a continent from Nature, the Indians and the English. Two hundred Loomis ancestors had fought in the Revolution, and there were countless others. But, of course, that early American race was really English, or more properly, British; those were English voices in the wilderness, and it was English minds that had framed the Declaration of Independence and the Constitution. In leaving England, he was leaving "race" behind for the second time. He might have gone back to the United States, even if only briefly, to confirm or modify certain views about his country, as in a recent poem—

> The thought of what America would be like
> If the Classics had a wide circulation
> Troubles my sleep. . . .

He went, instead, to Venice.

He wished to learn "whether, in the development and attrition of one's faculties, Venice could give one again and once more either the old kick to the senses or any new perception." Venice had meant a great deal to him in the past, and "some sort of salvo must be allowed the habitat where one's first recueil was printed—for it is, after all, an excellent place to come to from Crawfordsville, Indiana, whatever it may be as a point of arrival from London." He recalled his first visit with his great-aunt-in-law; he was thirteen then. "Without her I might not have been here. Venice struck me as an agreeable place—as, in fact, more agreeable than Wyncote, Pa., or '47th' and Madison Avenue. I announced an intention to return. I have done so. I do not know quite how often. By elimination of possible years: 1898, 1902, 1908, 1910, 1911, 1913, 1920." It was with her, when they went to Tunis, that he bought the green robe, described earlier.

But even Venice could not supply, a seventh time, either the "old kick" or a "new perception." Whether he knew it or not, he was seeking an answer to the enigma of himself. For his preoccupation was not Venice at all, but his American heritage. That freightage he had carried with him from London. In the too expensive room, with pen dipped in a patent Italian inkwell "designed to prevent satisfactory immersion," he began a chronicle of himself. He was thirty-five years old.

"It is one thing to feel that one could write the whole social history of the United States from one's family annals, and vastly another to embark upon any such Balzacian and voluminous endeavour."

He did not embark on it. He wrote something, however; better than nothing. I shall eke it out, from other sources. He called it *Indiscretions or, Une Revue de Deux Mondes.* It has style, and it is entertaining. It is a portrait of an American.

2.

Pound was, and has remained, American to the core. His mother's forebears, the Westons, came to America on the *Lion,* the ship that brought Roger Williams and his bride. Weston is a place name in Connecticut as well as Massachusetts. Through Joseph Wadsworth, who stole the Connecticut charter and hid it in "Charter Oak," the Westons were related to Henry Wadsworth Longfellow whose poetry, however, did not impress the subject of this book. Of three Pounds traced in the 1630's two went to "Connecticut or Rhode Island," another—with "body servant"—to Virginia. His paternal grandmother, Pound wrote in *Indiscretions,* was "of the family Loomis, who were reputedly horsethieves." He preferred the reputation to the records in the family Bible which "reported them to have been county judges and that like in Upper New York State; but an old lady whom I met in Oneida County said they were horse-thieves, charming people, in fact, the 'nicest' people in the county, but horse-thieves, very good horse-thieves, never, I think, brought to book."

The old lady was right; they were horse-thieves. (He met her while he was attending Hamilton.) In view of the fact that Angevine Loomis's grandson has used her family name as his middle name more often than that of his mother, it may be useful to delve briefly into Loomis annals.[1] The name, incidentally, is pronounced "Lummis" in upstate New York.

Daniel Loomis, father of the gang's "founder," fought in the Revolution, one of many of that name or ilk. His son, George Washington Loomis, 1779–1851, may have been born in Windsor, Connecticut, where there is to this day a famous school for boys bearing the family name. But it was from Vermont that he came, around 1802, to York State. He built a farmhouse on a hill overlooking a broad sweep of the Chenango River and cleared 385 acres. This was on the west side of the Nine Mile Swamp near Sangerfield, in Oneida County. He was in good repute as a neighbor and was admired for his horsemanship. He really loved horses. In 1810 a kind of secondary Loomis talent cropped up—he was arrested, with five others, on a charge of passing counterfeit money. Three of the men went to prison; Loomis himself paid one hundred dollars to one of his victims for the return of a counterfeit bill. Counterfeit money recurs in annals of the Loomis Gang, but it was never suggested that a Loomis printed any.

George Washington Loomis served in the War of 1812, and returned from it to the farm west of the Nine Mile Swamp, where he and his family flourished mightily and, as through a spy-glass, darkly. When he died, direction of the family and its confederates in neighboring counties fell to his son and namesake, called "Wash." There appear to have been seven or perhaps even eight other offspring. If some of the accounts are to be believed, mother and daughters were as talented as the sons. Horses were the prime booty, and with them saddles and harness, often of exquisite workmanship. Carriages also found their way to Nine Mile Swamp, and thence to Canada and Pennsylvania. By the end of the Civil War the Prison Association of New York sent a report of the gang's depredations to the State Legislature. It begins:

"There is a family residing in Oneida County, who, according to common fame, have followed the profession of thieving for nearly twenty years. They have grown rich by their unlawful practices. Their children are educated in the best and most expensive seminaries. They dress genteelly, their manners are somewhat polished, and they appear tolerably well in society. Their operations are carried on through the counties of Oneida, Oswego, Otsego, Madison, Chanango, Schoharie, Delaware and Sullivan. They have numerous well trained confederates in all those counties."

The report is long, and the Legislature had other business to attend to. It did nothing, but at length the victims did. The Loomises were "brought to book" by an enormous posse, with attendant shootings, hangings and barn burnings.[2] The women were unharmed. Two of them married into the Pound family.

3.

> All things are a flowing,
> Sage Heracleitus says. . . .

"Family traits were very strong in Pound," Williams told me. "He was bound to his family." He added that Pound's interest in credit "stems from Thaddeus Pound," the poet's grandfather, who made a great deal of money, and also ran through it.

A biographical sketch of Thaddeus Coleman Pound was written in 1870 by the grandfather of Horace Gregory, who called it to my attention. Gregory wrote me:

"I first heard of the Pound family through reading a last edition (it had been through several) of my grandfather's book, *Industrial Resources of Wisconsin* (1870)—'A New and Vastly Improved Edition' to which he added biographies of public men. This edition of the book was dedicated to Lucius Fairchild, then governor of the State of Wisconsin, and his lieutenant-governor was Thaddeus Coleman Pound. My grandfather knew both men, for John Gregory was civil engineer for the city of Milwaukee during the administration of the city's first mayor, Solomon Juneau—and the Pound family stopped over in Milwaukee in 1847. Politically both Fairchild and T. C. Pound were Republicans. Earlier, according to John Gregory, young Pound was a 'tariff Whig.' Under Fairchild, Pound was 'a Republican of the most radical type. He believed in the political equality of all men and women.'

"John Gregory (1783–1879) was scarcely less adventurous than Pound. He came from Trinity College, Dublin, where he was sent by well-to-do cousins, the Gregorys of Coole Park. At Trinity he wrote several books on mathematics and astronomy, and knew Robert Emmet; he designed the bridges in Phoenix Park, Dublin. He ran a school of mathematics and engineering in Dublin. In the mid-1840's he was sent by Trinity to the United States to write a book on U.S. economics for emigrating, famine-stricken Irish. The result was *Industrial Resources of Wisconsin*. His first wife died in Ireland. He had grown children in Ireland—only one son came over with him. He met my grandmother, daughter of a British scientist, and her father on the boat to this country. He married her and they settled in Milwaukee.

"When I met William Butler Yeats in Dublin in 1934, he told me he 'had a vision of my grandfather on the stairs of Trinity College.' "

John Gregory's account of Grandfather Pound is written in the proper panegyric style. It appeared first in *Western Monthly*. The subject was "one of the noted lumbermen of that section of the country where lumbermen are the mighty merchants of the land, eminent in the politics of his State, quite notably distinguished among the public men of the great Valley of the Upper Mississippi" and—not least—"he has acquired all he has, and become what he is, notwithstanding early poverty." He had been a member—and Speaker—of the State Assembly, and was afterwards a delegate to the Republican National Convention in Philadelphia in 1872, and three times elected to Congress. His grandson says he entered Congress a rich man, and left it a poor one, and wonders "what prodigy of rectitude these opposed statements may have."

Thaddeus Coleman Pound, son of Elijah Pound, was born in a log cabin in 1832 in Elk, Warren County, Pennsylvania, whither his Quaker parents had removed from Rochester, New York. Ten years later Elijah Pound brought his family back to Rochester, the land having proved unyielding. There, father and sons went to work in a wool factory, Thaddeus receiving a shilling a week for "assorting wool." He also earned some additional coins by washing buggies in the Genessee River. John Gregory's account continues: "The 'hard times' of this period [it was in the magistracy of James K. Polk] are a matter of general recollection. Poverty knocked at the door of Elijah Pound's home. He determined to try his fortune in the western lands." In May, 1847, he took his family to Milwaukee, Wisconsin, on a lake steamer, and rented a farm in Rock County, "about ten miles from the now beautiful and flourishing city of Janesville." That winter, Thaddeus, who had regularly attended the district school, was made the teacher by "vote of the pupils," his predecessor having been dismissed (cause unspecified).

Thaddeus returned to Rochester to marry. There was a double ceremony, his brother Albert marrying Sarah Loomis. In the winter of 1855 Thaddeus and Angevine Pound taught high school in Cale-

donia, New York, "making enough money, less twenty dollars borrowed," wrote John Gregory, to take them to Chippewa Falls, Wisconsin, which became their permanent home. Thaddeus Pound's
rise in the world dates from this removal. He found employment as
a bookkeeper in a lumbering firm, and learned all phases of the business. He started his own firm. His wife helped—as their grandson
has reported, she "supervised the kitchen, not as a spectator, but in
order to prepare the meals for about forty lumbermen."[3] Of his
grandfather he wrote: "The frontier aristocracy was, of necessity, a
physical aristocracy. The others either died or weakened. My grandfather used to wrestle with his lumberjacks not only for sport, but
to maintain his prestige."[4]

At the time John Gregory published his account, Thaddeus Pound
was president and "chief business manager" of the Union Lumbering Company, "whose business, amounting to more than a million
dollars annually, is conducted over a vast expanse of territory, and
embraces the lumber trade in all its branches—from getting the new
material from the forest, to landing it, in boards, shingles, and laths,
on the wharfs of the Mississippi River cities; merchandizing in about
all of its branches; agriculture in all its forms."

In addition, Thaddeus Pound built the first railway from Eau
Claire to Chippewa Falls, and from Abbotsford to St. Paul, and from
Camp Douglas to Hudson, later extended to Superior.

"The statement ought not to be omitted," wrote Mr. Gregory,
"that Mr. Pound's brother, Albert, has always been associated with
him in business, and is now the secretary of the Lumber Company.
They have never kept any accounts with each other; have never
quarreled, and the one is just as well off as the other."

The Union Lumbering Company issued its own scrip. A specimen
reads:

STATE OF WISCONSIN

Union Lumbering Company
Chippewa Falls

Will pay to the bearer on demand

FIFTY CENTS

IN MERCHANDISE OR LUMBER

It looks like legal tender, and passed for such in the mills and stores of the Union Lumbering Company. It bears the signature of Albert Pound, secretary. His grand-nephew commented on it in 1934: "good when money was issued against commodities. E. Pound, Rapallo." The Federal government thought otherwise, and the company ceased to compete with the United States Treasury.

4.

Thaddeus Coleman Pound died in Chicago in 1914, leaving two children, Mrs. Florence Foote and Homer Loomis Pound, father of the poet, both of whom were then residing in Philadelphia. Homer Pound had been born in Wisconsin, "probably the first white male child born in the northern part," his son was to write, and he had an Indian for nurse. He attended a military school in Minnesota and was destined for West Point, but got off the train half-way to it and returned to Wisconsin where he went to work in a company store. He began to think of marriage. He was tintyped—i.e., photographed —with, among other belles of the West, Ella Wheeler, afterwards Wilcox, who was to achieve renown as the "Poetess of Passion." (I have heard that she was the first to review Ezra Pound's work in the United States, but God knows where.) Homer went to Washington to visit his father, was invited to New York, and met the Westons and his future bride, Isabel.

A job was indicated.

Thaddeus Pound having become the owner of silver mines in the Territory of Idaho, thought the best way of protecting his property in that period of "jumped claims" was through the establishment of a Government Land Office. It was established in Hailey, on the Big Wood River in south central Idaho, altitude 5,342 feet. The Sawtooth Mountain range, north of Hailey, is now a national forest; Ernest Hemingway has vacationed there. Hailey, laid out in 1881, was incorporated as a village in 1903, as a city in 1909; population in 1885, around two thousand. It became a trading center for mining (silver and lead), a livestock area and a summer resort.

The Government Land Office was "opened" by Homer Pound, Recorder, by appointment of President Arthur. Miners came from as far away as two hundred miles to file their claims and have their ore assayed. He became an expert assayer. He did not neglect his personal affairs—correspondence with the East, and the building of the first plastered house in the new settlement.

The house is a large frame building, with three bedrooms, living room, "music room," dining room, kitchen and large pantry. The land on which it stands belonged to John Hailey, for whom the town was named; he deeded it to the Idaho and Oregon Land Company, got it back and deeded it to Homer L. Pound, on June 21, 1884, for five hundred dollars. There is a good-sized lawn to the south and west of the house. On September 15, 1886, the house was deeded by the Pounds to Homer Stull, the next Recorder of the U.S. Land Office, both the first and second Recorders being named Homer, which seems worthy of notice. The house is now occupied by a former mayor of Hailey. The outside is the same as when Homer Pound built it, except for a bay window, off the living room, which was eliminated by the present occupants. To this house, Homer Pound brought his bride after a honeymoon at Niagara Falls and Chippewa Falls.

Hailey at this time consisted of one street lined with saloons—forty-seven of them—one hotel, and a newspaper.

"Oh! Homer, how could you bring my daughter to *such* a place?" said the bride's mother arriving for a look at her grandson. She stayed at the hotel, and was horrified to find there was no lock on the door. Homer Pound told his son later:

"Lock! Lock! You wouldn't, a man wouldn't, lock his door out there [they were living in Wyncote then]. If you locked your door, they'd suspicion you."

The only thing Homer Pound's wife had against the place was the high altitude. She finally had to leave because of it.

Fortunes were still being made, though not by government employees. Homer Pound hired a man to saw wood for him; a week later he asked the sawyer to repeat. The sawyer said:

"Saw wood? Homer, saw wood? Say, do you want to go East and sell a mine for me?"[5]

Ezra Pound has also recalled how he met "a quiet little man" in Paris in 1919, "ambassador at the time," whom his father remembered "in the act of reaching for a revolver to help out his partner" in 1884.[6]

5.

Ezra Pound was born October 30, 1885, in the plastered house. There was no bureau of vital statistics, hence no official record. At eighteen months he was taken to the Weston home at 24 East 47th Street, New York City. The trip was made during the Great Blizzard of 1887, behind the first rotary plow, the inventor of which was on board the train. To this circumstance Pound says he owes his life, for he was suffering from a severe case of croup, which the inventor cured with lumps of sugar dipped in kerosene. His mother did not at all like the suggested remedy, but was persuaded to try it after her infant had had yet another night of wracking cough. It worked. From New York City the Pound family went to Wisconsin to the great-grandfather's farm—Elijah Pound was still alive—where Thaddeus also lived; and finally, in June, 1889, to Philadelphia, where Homer Pound became assistant assayer of the United States Mint, then located at Jupiter and Chestnut Streets. It had a Greek façade. Civil War veterans used to gather in the rotunda or in the shade of its pillars; occasionally they explored the interior, as did the infant Ezra. In the first of his "Money Pamphlets" he has recalled how duped Americans brought their "gold bricks" to his father to be assayed. "This was the period of the free coining of gold, and any one had the right to have his own metal coined. So, the stories of these dupes have been familiar to me, through personal experience, since I was five years old."[7]

The Pound family resided first at 208 South 43rd Street, and two years later moved to Wyncote. In 1901 father and son visited the Royal Mint in London, which they found more formal than the establishment in Philadelphia. The son wrote:

"We did not 'saunter' and dodge about among stamping presses, or try our strength on apparently trifling but utterly unliftable sacks of gold. There was none of the genial 'You can have it if you will carry it out,' with which the, I think, 10,000 dol. size bag used to be treated."[8]

He described his father as "the naivest man who ever possessed good sense." He described himself in London on this visit as "a lanky whey-faced youth of 16, presence unexplained save by consanguinity."[9] It was on the eve of his enrollment at the University of Pennsylvania. His account stops there.

He was an only child.

It was a whimsy of his, when he came to write *Indiscretions* in Venice in 1920, to give his forebears and himself whimsical names. No reading of nontechnical matters is so difficult as a genealogical account; here the difficulty is magnified by the author's caprice. For the benefit of such readers as may wish to examine the original[10] the following *dramatis personae* may prove useful, if kept handy:

Thadeus Cuthberton Weight: Thaddeus Coleman Pound, paternal grandfather.

Selina Loomis: Angevine Loomis, paternal grandmother.

Euripides Weight: Homer Loomis Pound, father.

Hermione Easton: Isabel Weston, mother.

Gargantua, or "The Infant Gargantua": Ezra Pound.

The great-aunt-in-law who first took him to Venice is also there, bulking large, with a handshake for President Grant and formidable in brocade and wreathed smiles at other inaugurals; but her name eludes me, as does her precise relationship to the poet's family— she had, after all, three husbands, only one of whom—the middle one—was a Pound. *Indiscretions* is, for all that, a charming work, evocative of the American past, and not too long; the kind of chronicle by precocious offspring of interesting families which *The New Yorker* was to make into a dependable fixture. Its model, or inspiration, is Henry James's *A Small Boy and Others*. It appeared serially in Orage's *New Age* beginning with the May 27, 1920, number, and was published in book form in Paris three years later.

For Pound, after much soul-searching, having already decided not to stay in England, decided not to go back to the United States.

CHAPTER XIV

POUND IN PARIS

"Le premier événement d'importance pour la littérature américaine des années 20 fut l'emigration d'Ezra Pound de Londres à Paris."
—William Bird, *Les Années Vingt.*

1.

No one who was not young in Paris in the Twenties will be able to understand the excitement which the mere mention of Pound's name aroused, over the saucers and carafes, in the innumerable still lifes with figures of the cafés. And there was another excitement—reported and listened to with awe—the excitement of having glimpsed him striding in the street in his flopping hat and flapping coat or cloak, or sitting at a concert, the red-crested head thrown back, the beard outthrust, and the eyes half-closed or closed in thought or dreaming. The whole modern movement in art and literature seemed to be embodied in that tall, handsome, strenuous and ungainly figure, that innovator to whom all the innovators paid homage, that bearded adventurer who dealt in masterpieces, not like a merchant but a prince, shuttling them back and forth across the Channel and the Ocean Sea. And indeed he looked like a prince, with his regal features and Grand Seigneur beard, as the life mask made in 1921 so clearly shows.

Perhaps the aura which the young beheld and felt was due to this —that he was the embodiment of a force for artists as well as art:

he did not praise them, then leave the rest to chance. But, of course, his own achievement had something to do with it, and his fame, after all, was linked to the emergence of great names or names growing in renown. In Paris, the back-biting and squabbles of literary London were unknown, at least to the new generation. And to that generation Pound's books, aside from his verse, were an academy. It was not only the forgotten and exotic literatures he had revivified in translation or adaptation, though it ought in fairness to be remembered what their impact was when their impact was fresh. "A sad name, set in a story," and "a name not to be worn out with the years"; the birds and budded branches of Provence, crackling with light and cries; "the mosses, the different mosses" of Cathay. As much as anyone, but earlier than anyone, he had brought Henry James to the fore—first in the pages of the *Little Review*, now in *Instigations*, published in New York by Boni and Liveright, a volume of classic studies—dedicated to his father—which also contained his homage to Remy de Gourmont. And there was also the growing intimation, the bruit, of a major work in progress, the dedicated attempt of a modern poet to achieve an epic form. A year after *Instigations* Boni and Liveright published *Poems 1918–1921*, which included Cantos IV-VII.

2.

He had chosen Paris, although for another year he merely went back and forth across the Channel. What seems clear is that he had no intention of returning to the United States. All the same, he toyed from time to time with the idea of a lecture tour which would give him enough money for leisure afterwards. In this, he was encouraged by Williams, who naturally wanted Pound back in "God's country." But Pound was taking no chances. He wrote "Deer Bull":

"Re travel. I rather want to take a solid year in Paris. But if 'they say' anything solid—i.e. expenses guaranteed and ??? (couple) of thousand (??? £) $ over, i.e. guarantee of leisure for a year after the whirlwind campaign—I will listen to the stern voice of duty and save as much of the country as is ready to be snatched from the yawning maw of gum shoes, Y.M.C.A., Chubb, e tutti quanti.

"I had rather you came to Paris, but should be glad of 'further information.' I went to Newcastle year before last for one lecture—I suppose coming to U.S. would be like doing that for a year???"

There is no eagerness in it.

From Venice he went to Desenzano to meet Joyce. He wrote Quinn from Paris, June 19, 1920:

"I came out of Italy on a tram-car, and reckon the next man will come out in a cab.

"Joyce finally got to Sirmione; don't yet know whether he has got back to Trieste. Strike started half an hour after I got to Milan, and many trains stopped where they were on the stroke of 12."

Mussolini was to make the trains run on schedule, among his other accomplishments.

He described the author of *Ulysses*:

"Joyce—pleasing; after the first shell of cantankerous Irishman, I got the impression that the real man is the author of *Chamber Music*, the sensitive. The rest is the genius; the registration of realities on the temperament, the delicate temperament of the early poems. A concentration and absorption passing Yeats'—Yeats has never taken on anything requiring the condensation of *Ulysses*."

(Joyce told Herbert Gorman that "he suspected that Pound had been disappointed in him at their first meeting, and considered him pretty much of a hopeless bourgeois.")

Pound added: "His next work will go to the *Dial*."

He had also talked to other potential contributors in Italy: "Linati, translator of Synge and Joyce, is to send Italian notes."

As for Paris: "Here I suspect the war is still effective. Impression the people are being affable to each other (in literary circles) in hope of maintaining the illusion that Paris is still the hub of the universe. However, have only been here 3 days and may yet dig up something of mild interest.

"After Gaudier, Lewis, Joyce, one wants something a bit meaty to excite one."

Pound had persuaded Joyce that Paris would be the best place for him. It may have taken some doing, for even Villon had not been so poor or so hungry as Joyce had been in his first bitter stay there, when he wrote to his mother on his twenty-first birthday: "Your order for 3/4 of Tuesday last was very welcome as I had been with-

out food for 42 hours. Today I am twenty hours without food." Some
concentration—some absorption—which can enable one to send such
knowledge to one's mother! Pound, who was staying at the Hôtel
Elysée on the rue de Beaune, found an apartment for Joyce and his
family at 9 rue de l'Université. He then went around Paris with
copies of *A Portrait of the Artist*. He persuaded John Rodker's
mother-in-law, Mme. Ludwilla Bloch-Savitsky, to translate it into
French.

Joyce was thirty-eight years old—tall, thin as a pole, with gray
streaks in his hair and a tuft of beard on his chin. He appears to have
held on to the long overcoat, narrow and down to the ankles, of his
previous sojourn in Paris, and he wore tennis shoes. When Pound returned to London, he sent, by Eliot and Lewis, a package for Joyce
so intricately tied up that untying it became a ceremony of exaspera-
tion, Joyce becoming impatient under the curious gaze of the visiting
writers. At length, with the help of nail scissors, the strings were cut,
and from a jumble of brown wrapping paper and an assortment of
old clothes a pair of old brown shoes emerged. "Oh!" said Joyce.

Pound was present when Joyce met the future publisher of *Ulysses*.

3.

Pound already knew Sylvia Beach. With his wife he had gone to
Shakespeare and Company, that famous book shop which was to become the club and college of the expatriates. The shop was then on
the rue Dupuytren; Miss Beach recalls that he looked "just as he did
in his portraits." He was wearing a velvet jacket and "open-road
shirt." His works were in plain view; before opening the shop, she
had gone to London where she called on Elkin Mathews who, it will
be recalled, was a bookseller as well as publisher, and from him had
ordered the works of Pound, Yeats and Joyce. She found "the
acknowledged leader of the modern movement not bumptious"—he
did not talk about books, not even his own. He surprised her by talking about his carpentry. Did she have anything around the shop
that needed mending? "He mended a cigarette box and a chair. I
praised his skill."

Mrs. Pound was concerned about the location of the shop. That obscure little hilly street—would people really be able to find it? She said she would make a little map for Miss Beach to put on the back of her library circular. "This map, signed 'D. Shakespear,' guided many a customer to Shakespeare and Company."

With her friend, Adrienne Monnier, Miss Beach went to a supper party at the apartment of the poet André Spire in the rue du Bois de Boulogne. She afterwards wrote: "I worshipped James Joyce, and on hearing the unexpected news that he was present, I was so frightened I wanted to run away, but Spire told me it was the Pounds who had brought the Joyces—we could see Ezra through the open door. I knew the Pounds, so I went in."[1]

Pound, "stretched out" in a big armchair, was wearing a blue shirt which, she thought, matched his eyes. (Later, when she described him in an article in the *Mercure de France,* he wrote her that "he had never had blue eyes at all.") Mrs. Pound was talking to Nora Joyce, a tall woman with reddish curly hair and eyelashes. The shout of "À table!" told that supper was ready, and all present sat down. Joyce appeared from the library. Miss Beach observed him closely. "He gave an impression of sensitiveness exceeding any I had ever known." Spire poured wine for everyone, except Joyce, who turned his glass upside down—he had made a resolution not to drink anything till evening. Pound, seeing this, collected all the bottles on the table and lined them up in front of Joyce. "He got very red." In the original draft of this chapter in her book, Miss Beach wrote: "A blush spread over his face and neck and he appeared so embarrassed that I pitied him and avoided looking his way." When supper was over, Joyce again disappeared into the library, and there Miss Beach sought him out. They talked. She told him about Shakespeare and Company. He began to appear there. He appeared there every day. He was worried about the fate of his book, as yet unfinished. One day she said to him:

"Would you let Shakespeare and Company have the honor of bringing out your *Ulysses?*"

He was delighted.

"Undeterred by lack of capital, experience, and all the other requisites of a publisher, I went right ahead."

Robert McAlmon sought subscriptions in bars. Gide came in and signed. Ernest Hemingway—"my best customer"—signed for several copies. And Pound "made a sensation when he deposited on my table one day a subscription blank with the signature of W. B. Yeats on it." When Shaw refused to subscribe—as Joyce had predicted—Pound took up where Miss Beach left off. Shaw wrote back: "Do I have to like everything you like, Ezra? As for me, I take care of the pence and let the Pounds take care of themselves." He had written to Miss Beach: "If you imagine that any Irishman, much less an elderly one, would pay 150 francs for such a book, you little know my countrymen."[2]

Miss Beach photographed Pound in her book shop. He is standing in a corner by a window, a smooth stick with a tassle under his right arm, the tassled top pointing like an arrow to two fat volumes entitled *Poetry and Drama*. His gloved hands are resting on an open book, to the left of which reposes his hat with an enormous band. He has on a loose-fitting jacket and an "open-road" shirt. His mop of hair seems thicker than ever, but straggly, like a wig, his sideburns broad and long as side-whiskers. His expression is pensive. He appears to have been asked to look up from the book he was reading in order to be photographed, and his gaze is neither on the book nor out the window but, as it were, halted and unseeing, and perhaps a little self-conscious—a man hemmed in by books who has been interrupted in his reading.

4.

In the spring of 1921, Alfred Kreymborg, who had guided *Des Imagistes* through the press seven years before, and Harold Loeb, co-editor with him of the newly launched *Broom,* stopped off in Paris on their way to Rome. From the Hotel Jacob, Kreymborg sent a note to Pound suggesting an immediate meeting. Pound wrote back inviting him and Loeb to the Café des Deux Magots, (for luncheon, Kreymborg recalled; for drinks, wrote Loeb, who says it was the Café du Dôme). There were two women at a table on the *terrasse* when Kreymborg and Loeb arrived. The younger one rose at their approach and introduced herself as Mrs. Pound, then introduced them to her mother. Pound had gone for cigarettes, and Kreymborg started out to find him. Coming toward him across the Boulevard Raspail was "an athletic figure in velveteens, wide-open collar and flowing tie." Although they had never met, Kreymborg recognized Pound, and turning his cane upside down made several swipes at an imaginary golf ball, climaxed with the cry of "Fore!" as Pound came up. A look of amazement crossed Pound's face; then, with a jerk of his head, he proffered his hand, and said, "This must be *Others*." He led the way back to the *terrasse*.[3] (Loeb has also described Pound on this occasion, "dressed like one of Trilby's companions. He wore a black velvet jacket and fawn-colored pants. He used a walking stick and a pointed goatee to emphasize his words.")[4]

His words were "an instantaneous tirade on *Broom*," Kreymborg wrote. When a list of potential contributors was laid on the marble-topped table, Pound took a pencil and crossed out name after name, "usually with some cutting remark." Very few survived. According to Kreymborg, Pound kept addressing him and Loeb as "you Americans."

"There was never any doubt as to his contempt for the land of his birth," Kreymborg wrote. "Nor for the land of his recent adoption—England. France was his country now."

Loeb "just watched and listened." He saw Pound on another occasion; perhaps this was at the Dôme. Writers, painters, sculptors joined the group, and the *garçon* brought more chairs. "Of a sudden Ezra wasn't there. A dark, tall sculptor confided that Ezra usually made off without warning, thereby evading the formal round-the-table handshake customary on the boulevards."

He was meeting the "new men." He was "inclined to like" Braque. He found Cocteau and Picabia "intelligent." He wrote Marianne Moore to tell Williams that Cocteau "looks more like him than even his own brother Ed."

He met Gertrude Stein. It was Amy Lowell all over again; but this was an Easter Island Amy. She wrote in *The Autobiography of Alice B. Toklas*:

"He came home to dinner with us and he stayed and he talked about japanese prints among other things. Gertrude Stein liked him but did not find him amusing. She said he was a village explainer, excellent if you were a village, but if you were not, not. Ezra also talked about T. S. Eliot. It was the first time any one had talked about T. S. at the house. Pretty soon everybody talked about T. S."

Pound called again, accompanied by Scofield Thayer, co-owner and editor of *The Dial*:

"This time it was worse than japanese prints, it was much more violent. In his surprise at the violence Ezra fell out of Gertrude Stein's favourite little armchair, the one I have since tapestried with Picasso designs, and Gertrude Stein was furious. Finally Ezra and the editor of The Dial left, nobody too well pleased. Gertrude Stein did not want to see Ezra again. Ezra did not quite see why."

Others have suggested it was because Pound plumped himself in the armchair and snapped off a leg. (Thomas Wolfe did the same thing in Peter Monro Jack's apartment; but Jack did not mind.)

5.

Scofield Thayer wrote Alyse Gregory, just before she became managing editor of *The Dial*, a post in which she was succeeded by Marianne Moore:

"Gertrude Stein is five feet high and two feet wide and has a dark brown face and small, wise, old Jewess eyes. She curls up in the corner of a divan and falls over like a doll in trying to receive editors. She possesses the homely finish of a brown buckram bean-bag. In conversation she put it all over Ezra, who got back by saying all sorts of things on the way home."

Kensington and Easter Island encountered each other near the Luxembourg Gardens. He told her: "But I do want to come to see you." She replied: "I am so sorry, but Miss Toklas has a bad tooth and beside we are busy picking wild flowers." She commented in the *Autobiography*: "All of which was literally true, like all of Gertrude Stein's literature, but it upset Ezra and we never saw him again."

She had done the same thing to Picasso, but that estrangement lasted only a year. How it was possible for them to avoid running into each other, in that whirl and swirl of artists and writers whom they knew in common, is something to ponder. For he took the "solid year" in Paris. He "took" four of them. When Thayer reached Paris, in July of 1921, Pound was staying at a hotel on the rue des Saints Pères, his wife being on a visit to England. The famous studio on the rue Notre Dame des Champs may already have been spoken for, but they had not yet moved in. Perhaps he had crossed the Channel in order to meet Thayer; if so, he stayed on and they were frequently together. Thayer told Miss Gregory:

"Ezra Pound, of whom I have been seeing more rather than less, is a queer duck."

There is the inevitable description: "He wears a pointed yellow beard and an elliptical pince-nez and open Byronic collar and an omelette-yellow bath robe."

In a restaurant: "One has observed him so awkward as unintentionally to knock over a waiter and then so self-conscious as to be unable to say he is sorry. But like most other people he means well and unlike most other people he has a fine imagination. At close quarters he is much more fair in his judgments than his correspondence and his books would warrant one to believe."

Pound at home: "When one arrives at his hotel on the street of the Holy Fathers, one usually learns from the young lady that Mr. Pound is *au bain*. But the young lady consents to go upstairs to see Mr. Pound and to inquire if Mr. Pound will see guests. Mr. Pound receives, beaming and incisive."

Thayer was staying at the Hotel Continental on the rue Castiglione, a different kettle of fish. One night, Pound went to see him. With Thayer was a young American poet whose poems in the first number of the rejuvenated *Dial* had brought him instant fame. His name was E. E. Cummings. Late that night, through Paris streets woven of lamps and mist, Pound and Cummings walked back together, as far as the Place St. Michel, where the two poets parted. Thirty-eight years later (in 1959) Cummings wrote me:

"During our whole promenade Ezra was more than wonderfully entertaining:he was magically gentle, as only a great man can be toward some shyest child."

6.

Pound's permanent address in Paris was 70 *bis* rue Notre Dame des Champs, the street where Whistler had lived as a young man. The studio was in the courtyard *pavillon*, ground floor, rental thirty dollars a month. The books, the pictures, the statuary gathered in Lon-

don, reappeared; the University of Pennsylvania fencing foils, buttons up, were propped in a corner above adjoining bookcases, and a
new piece of furniture, made by Pound, was added to the old array.
It was the table on which he wrote. The studio remained somewhat
sparsely furnished, and Pound set himself to making other pieces.
Later, there were other odds and ends of sculpture—"of the school
of Brancusi," said Ford—strewn about the floor, Pound's handiwork.
"He acquired pieces of stone as nearly eggshaped as possible, hit
them with hammers and then laid them about on the floor." He also
tried painting.

As a result, the studio often looked like an art gallery; there were
Dorothy Pound's pictures, and "exhibitions" of unknown or emerging artists.

There was also a cat.

As poet, as editor and correspondent, as host to writers and artists,
Pound in Paris was not much different from the tireless Kensington
instigator. There was, indeed, a kind of repetition, or in any case, an
unbroken continuation, of his way of life—ameliorated of course by
French touches and embellishments, not least the cafés, although he
was himself an abstemious drinker, bordering on teetotalism, and an
infrequent smoker. From a distance of forty years one sees, as it were,
a newer photograph superimposed on the other—the London one—
and despite a blur of weather and plane trees, a familiar pattern
emerges. For once again, Ford was just down the street; Aldington
turned up; and there was even a sculptor into whose work and
aesthetics Pound plunged as of old.

The sculptor was Constantin Brancusi, that lovable, bearded and
bright-eyed man from Rumania whose metal bird was to soar out of
the U.S. Customs into the consciousness of the world. By the spring
of 1921 Pound was working as hard for Brancusi as he had ever
worked for Gaudier-Brzeska.

"Am taking up the *Little Review* again, as a quarterly," he wrote
Wyndham Lewis, "each number to have about twenty reprods of
ONE artist." He began with Brancusi. There was no hesitation what-
ever, as the accompanying essay reveals:

"No critic has a right to pretend that he fully understands any
artist; least of all do I pretend, in this note, to understand Brancusi
(after a few weeks' acquaintance) even as well as I understood

Gaudier (after several years' friendship); anything I say here effaces anything I may have said before on the subject, and anything I say the week after next effaces what I say here—a pale reflection of Brancusi's general wish that people would wait until he has finished (i.e., in the cemetery) before they talk aesthetics with or about him."

But he did understand:

"Where Gaudier had developed a sort of form-fugue or form-sonata by a combination of forms, Brancusi has set out on the maddeningly more difficult exploration toward getting all the forms into one form."

He was enchanted by Brancusi's studio in the Impasse Ronsin, the cul-de-sac off the rue de Vaugirard that was the scene, a decade or so before, of a sensational double murder. He was not alone in this—many visitors have described it, as well as Brancusi's routine when he was giving a party: the morning marketing, the working day, the plates, the silver, and the napkins laid out when guests began to arrive, the chicken soup begun on the clay stove he built himself, then the chicken grilled over coals; Brancusi talking all the while, smoking his hand-rolled cigarettes, replenishing glasses; and then the coffee grinder, ground in the midst of his company. Pound wrote:

"Brancusi can spend most of his time in his own studio, surrounded by the calm of his own creations, whereas the author of this imperfect exposure is compelled to move about in a world full of junk-shops, a world full of more than idiotic ornamentations, a world where pictures are made for museums, where no man has a front-door that he can bear to look at. . . ."

He was away from his as often as possible. Kathleen Cannéll, now separated from her husband, said he dropped in at all hours, even midnight, to take her to a dive in the rue du Lappe, to the Bal Bullier, or to a party. "He always arrived at parties when they were in full swing."

7.

Eliot turned up, and departed, leaving a manuscript for Pound to look over. What else he did is best told by Eliot himself.

"It was in 1922 [read 1921]," he afterwards wrote in the essay from which I have been quoting, "that I placed before him in Paris the manuscript of a sprawling chaotic poem called *The Waste Land* which left his hands, reduced to about half its size, in the form in which it appears in print."[5]

There was a good deal of correspondence between the two men, not all of which has yet been published, and the manuscript itself shuttled back and forth between Paris and London. This is indicated by the first communication on the subject which appears in Pound's *Letters,* dated "Paris, 24 Saturnus, An 1," or 24 December, 1921. (This, I take it, is Pound's way of marking his first year away from England; it, in any case, has nothing to do with his Fascist-style dating of letters from Rapallo. The "March on Rome" did not take place until October 28, 1922.) The letter begins, "Caro mio: MUCH improved." Again: "The thing now runs from 'April . . .' to 'shantih' without a break. That is 19 pages, and let us say the longest poem in the English langwidge. Don't try to bust all records by prolonging it three pages further." Again: "My squibs are now a bloody impertinence. I send 'em as requested; but don't use 'em with *Waste Land.*" Eliot replied, addressing Pound as "Cher Maître": "Criticisms accepted so far as understood, with thanks."

Eliot had thought of using "Gerontion" as a preface to the poem, and of dropping the passage about Phlebas the Phoenician; Pound advised against both procedures. Among the queries which he forwarded to Eliot was one by Dorothy Pound "about some natural phenomenon," not otherwise identified, alas—the poem is full of them. Pound also sent his unstinted praise:

"Complimenti, you bitch. I am wracked by the seven jealousies, and cogitating an excuse for always exuding my deformative secretions in my own stuff, and never getting an outline. I go into nacre and objets d'art." He enclosed a poem entitled "Sage Homme":

> These are the poems of Eliot
> By the Uranian Muse begot;
> A Man their Mother was,
> A Muse their Sire.
>
> How did the printed Infancies result
> From Nuptials thus doubly difficult?

If you must needs enquire
Know diligent Reader
That on each Occasion
Ezra performed the Caesarian Operation. . . .

Eliot replied: "Complimenti appreciated, as have been excessively depressed." He added that he had written to Scofield Thayer "asking what he can offer for this." He afterwards wrote in his essay about Pound:

"I should like to think that the manuscript, with the suppressed passages, had disappeared irrecoverably: yet, on the other hand, I should wish the blue pencilling on it to be preserved as irrefutable evidence of Pound's critical genius."

It must now be apparent to all that the transitions—or lack of them —in *The Waste Land,* which Eliot's imitators made into a vogue, were due to the editor. The original construction of the poem may have owed something to Pound's methods in the sequence of Cantos already published.

8.

To Pound, *The Waste Land* was "a masterpiece; one of the most important 19 pages in English." He could not understand why the author of those pages should have to work in a bank when he could be writing other masterpieces. He did something about it. Had he been rich, he would have done it more directly. For he was now alarmed not only for Eliot's work, but for Eliot himself. Eliot had had one breakdown (he wrote the poem during his convalescence in Switzerland, and the mélange of foreign phrases at the beginning was not, as some critics afterwards said, portents of the collapse of Western civilization, but the talk of patients); now, back at Lloyd's Bank, he was on the verge of another.

It was March, 1922.

Pound conceived a plan. He discussed it. He typed it up, making carbon copies, and sent the copies around.

"There is no organized or coordinated civilization left," he wrote, "only individual scattered survivors.

"Aristocracy is gone, its function was to select.

"Only those of us who know what civilization is, only those of us who want better literature, not more literature, better art, not more art, can be expected to pay for it. No use waiting for masses to develop a finer taste, they aren't moving that way."

His plan was to have thirty persons contribute ten pounds (fifty dollars) per year to support a deserving artist. "T. S. Eliot first name chosen." Pound himself, and Richard Aldington, started the list with guarantees of ten pounds. "If they can afford it others can." They were joined by May Sinclair. The project was given a name— "Bel Esprit." Pound again drew up a circular, this time printed by John Rodker. It went out on a stream of letters. Pound wrote Williams: "I have been on the job, am dead tired with hammering this machine." In the same letter: "One might, after freeing Eliot, run a yearly trip from America. Or at least you one summer, Marianne another, etc. when there was someone worth it. At present, although the necessary 30 for Eliot haven't been found, I can I think offer you a summer home."

Wyndham Lewis offered himself as a candidate; Pound wrote him from Siena in April: "Try New York: I mean emigrate. England is under a curse." He wrote Williams from Venice in May:

"My studio won't hold three, but my spouse goes to Eng. about July 15th. I can therefore offer you a room for 6 weeks or 2 months." The room was above the studio occupied by the Pounds. "You wd., during the 6-8 weeks, have the inconvenience of my presence below you, balanced by the convenience of getting yr. breakfasts ready made and not having to struggle with charwomen."

Back in Paris in July, Pound wrote Harriet Monroe:

"I shall hang out myself until the U.S. is ready to start a ministry of Beaux Arts, and put me in charge. They won't do that until nearly the end of the hecker era, and the crepuscule of the boobs. Also they will have to digest one or two facts, stated in the elementary geography books, but never digested by the pupils."

He heard from Aldington—that Amy Lowell had refused, and wrote her:

"Auw shucks! dearie, aint you the hell-roarer, aint you the kuss."

9.

He translated Cocteau's long poem, "The Cape of Good Hope"—
"translated it remarkably," Miss Anderson wrote—for the *Little Review*. He translated *The Natural Philosophy of Love* by Remy de
Gourmont and drew up a "memorandum of agreement" with H. B.
Liveright for further translations. It is an interesting document,
bearing the date "4 Jan. a.d. 1922" and alternately "4 Saturnus An 1":

"Mr Liveright agrees from this date Jan 4th 1922 until Jan 24th
1924 to pay to Ezra Pound the minimum of five hundred dollars
yearly as an advance on [overline: "payment for"] whatever translations from French into English Mr Pound shall make at Mr Liveright's
request. Mr Pound undertakes to translate such books as Mr Liveright
chooses to the best of his ability and with reasonable promptitude.
The rate of payment to be computed roughly on that paid for the
translation of Gourmont's 'Physique de l'Amour.' Mr Pound is not
to forfeit right to said five hundred dollars should Mr Liveright fail
to select or accept any french works for translation and publication.

"It is further understood that Mr Pound will probably be unable
to undertake more than one thousand dollars worth of translation in
any one year.

"Mr Liveright agrees not to demand Mr Pound's signature on the
translation of any work that Mr Pound considers a disgrace to
humanity or too imbecile to be borne."

Figures afterwards added to the "memorandum" show that he
received a total of five hundred dollars.

He worked on his "opera."

He and his wife dined with Yeats and his wife and James and
Nora Joyce. Douglas Goldring stopped off to see him and took him
out to dinner. "I was able to reward some of Ezra's many kindnesses
by giving him dinner and providing a bottle or two of drinkable
champagne." The singer, Yves Tinayre, came to tea. They had met in
London where, as the music critic "William Atheling," Pound had
heard and praised his voice. Now—it was 1922—he was on the way
from London to Milan; "just passing through Paris," Tinayre told
me. As he and his wife were walking on the Boulevard Montparnasse
he became aware that someone was running after him, calling his

name. Just in front of the Dôme Pound caught up with him and said, "Come along to tea, I have an opera for you—I wrote it for you." Tinayre and his wife accompanied Pound to the rue Notre Dame des Champs, stopping first at a pastry shop on the way where Pound bought "a lot of pastries." They had tea on a packing case over which a cloth had been spread, sitting in the chairs Pound had made. They were like Renaissance chairs, stiff and ungainly, with hard pillows which, Tinayre said, "looked like *something.*" Pound told him: "I couldn't afford to buy furniture, so I made some." Mrs. Pound poured. There was only one spoon, which was passed around. After tea, Pound showed Tinayre the score of his opera.

"The conception was entirely novel to me," Tinayre told me. "At that time I was a concert and opera singer, and I had not yet done any medieval research. Pound's idea struck me as fine—for words, Villon's ballades, for music a few trombones and troubadour-like songs. The music was longitudinal and linear. He showed me the 'Heaulmière' first, terming it the 'fireworks' of the piece. Then he sang it."

The reader will perhaps recall that Pound, like Yeats, had no ear— for music, that is.

He was ubiquitous. He was present at the opening of the "Jockey," a night club at the corner of the rue Campagne Première and the Boulevard Montparnasse—not, no, certainly not to be confused with *the* Jockey Club—and a photograph made outside it on this occasion shows him in the center of a group of notables. From left to right: Man Ray, photographer and painter, with a tiny camera and long cigarette holder in his left hand, right hand in the pocket of his overcoat and looking for all the world as though about to whisk forth a revolver to shoot the other photographer dead; Hilaire Hiler, painter and piano-thumper at the "Jockey," and beside him the jockey Walter Miller, for whom the place was named, with a bowler or billycock on his head and his overcoat over his arm; Pound; another bowlered gent, the folk singer, Les Copeland; two other Americans, both handsome, one of them once the lightweight champion of the United States Army; and seated on the pavement, Tristran Tzara, the daddy of Dada, monocled, of course, and beside him, elegantly hatted and spatted, the famous hands sheathed in knitted gloves, a young and grinning Jean Cocteau. Pound had on an outsize beret which did not so much sit on his head as float on his mass of upbrushed hair, a velvet jacket over which the enormous points of his shirt collar seem spread-eagled, a loose sweater underneath, his right hand clutching a cane on which he is bearing down, and on his face an amused and happy smile as he gazes off into the distance where amused Parisians have gathered to watch the picture-taking.

That beret, those flapping hats. It was like Whistler, "personage étrange, le Whistler, au chapeau bizarre"; and the descriptions of him in du Maurier's *Trilby* could be applied to Pound—"vain, witty, eccentric in attire" and "the most irresistible friend in the world as long as his friendship lasted."

10.

The same year—1923—saw the publication in Paris, at The Three Mountains Press, of *Indiscretions or, Une Revue de Deux Mondes,* Pound's autobiography up to his sixteenth year, written in Venice three years before. It was the first volume in a series entitled by him "The Inquest." Pound wrote Williams, inviting him to submit something:

"There's a printer here wants me to supervise a series of booklets, prose (in your case perhaps verse, or whatever form your new stuff is in). Gen. size about 50 pages (??? too short for you). Limited private edtn. of 350 copies, 50 dollars down to author, and another 50 later."

The printer was William Bird.

In an appendix to the book, Pound wrote:

"As an experiment it needs no justification, but to reprint it? Re? Because it is rather unavailable; and to print it in the first place? There is a gap—between, that is, the place where the Great H. J. leaves off in his 'Middle Years' and the place where the younger writers try to start some sort of faithful record. One offers one's little contribution to knowledge, and one stops (A), because there is something else one wants, more intensely, to do, and (B) because there are prosateurs ready to do this sort of record with more vigour and enthusiasm, and probably with more interest in prose than one has oneself.

"At any rate my title fits the whole series, to which my fragment is (without any of the succeeding authors being in the least to blame) a sort of foreword. They have set out from five very different points to tell the truth about *moeurs contemporaines,* without fake, melodrama, conventional ending."

The other five volumes were: *Women and Men,* by F. M. Ford; *The Great American Novel,* by W. C. Williams; *England,* by B. M. G. Adams; *Elimus* by B. Cyril Windeler, with twelve illustrations by Dorothy Pound; and Hemingway's *In Our Time.* The Guffey first edition of Hemingway's book has the following inscription:

"This book was printed and published by Bill Bird who had bought an old hand press and set it up on the Isle Saint Louis in Paris it came out about a year after it should because I introduced Bill to Ezra Pound and Ezra suggested a series of books—'There'll be me and old Ford and Bill Williams and Eliot and Lewis' and some others Ezra said 'and we'll call it an inquest into the state of English prose.' Eliot didn't include—nor did Lewis and finally Ezra had five titles—Bill said, 'What about Hem?'

" 'Hem's will come sixth,' Ezra said. So when they were all printed and this one gotten out it was later than the Three Stories and 10 Poems although Bill had the manuscript long before McAlmon had the other set up."

All this while, in addition to contributing verse and prose to an array of magazines almost dizzying in their variety, Pound was writing his renowned "Paris Letter" for *The Dial,* which, together with Eliot's "London Letter," in Marianne Moore's perceptive phrase, "italicized their poetry" for American readers. Pound was succeeded as Paris correspondent by Paul Morand, which may account, in part, for some of the acerbity with which he always mentions the Frenchman's name.

Gilbert Seldes, an editor of *The Dial,* wrote me in 1959:

"I met EP only once. I remember he ate as if he'd never had a meal before—at a very good restaurant near the Odéon—and I hadn't enough cash left to take a taxi all the way home.

"EP left Paris shortly after I arrived. Hemingway thought I had him fired from *The Dial*—actually I was commissioned to find a French correspondent but tried to keep EP on until he went to Italy. The coincidence of my arrival and the supplanting of EP as *The Dial's* Paris representative was unfortunate—Hemingway never forgave me."

11.

Hemingway was often to be found in the *pavillon* in the courtyard. "A big young man with intent eyes and a toothbrush mustache was there when I arrived," wrote Malcolm Cowley, "and Pound introduced him as Ernest Hemingway; I said that I had heard about him. Hemingway gave a slow Mid-western grin. He was then working for the International News Service, but there were rumors that he had stories in manuscript and that Pound had spoken of them as being something new in American literature. He didn't talk about the stories that afternoon; he listened as if with his eyes while Pound discussed the literary world. Very soon he rose, made a date with Pound for tennis the following day and went out the door, walking on the balls of his feet like a boxer."

Cowley was one of *les jeunes*—poet, critic, a "little magazine" editor, lugging "copy" all over Europe for Harold Loeb, to the cities swirling with paper money, where printing was cheapest. He had just returned from Berlin, where a dollar was the equivalent of two thousand paper marks "or an all-wool overcoat"; an issue of *Broom* had been printed there. After Hemingway left, Pound went on talking ("continued his monologue," Cowley wrote in *Exile's Return*).[6]

" 'I've found the lowdown on the Elizabethan drama,' he said as he vanished beard-first into the rear of the pavillion; he was always finding the lowdown, the inside story and the simple reason why. A moment later he returned with a worm-eaten leather-bound folio. 'It's all in here,' he said, tapping the volume. 'The whole business is cribbed from these Italian state papers.'

"The remark seemed so disproportionate that I let it go unchallenged, out of politeness. 'What about your own work?' I asked. Pound laid the book on a table piled with other books. 'I try not to repeat myself,' he said."

He had on a red dressing gown. His red beard "jutted out like that of an archaic Greek soldier," Cowley thought, but afterwards he revised this to "a fox's muzzle." Pound was now pacing up and down, the dressing gown swirling about him. He said that he had written the "Ballad of the Goodly Fere" at twenty-two. "Having written this ballad about Christ, I had only to write similar ballads about James, Matthew, Mark, Luke and John and my fortune was made." He went to England instead. "He was still convinced that he had been right to leave America. America was England thirty years before. America was England without the fifty most intelligent men. America didn't print his poems in magazines until they had been collected into books in England."

He thought that he had lost "many of his English readers" when *Ripostes* appeared. "The public doesn't like to be surprised and the new poems had been surprising, even a little shocking." The public was disconcerted to find he "wasn't merely an author of masculine ballads or a new Browning who brought medieval characters to life in medieval phrases." He lost more readers with *Lustra*—"they hadn't liked his use of colloquial language or the frankness with which he described the feelings of *l'homme moyen sensuel.*" The same thing happened when he published *Mauberley* and the early *Cantos*—"he had always outdistanced his audience."

He talked about Wyndham Lewis—"the real Vorticist, a man of amazing intellectual force." He said Lewis had visited New York in 1917 "and two weeks later"—Cowley says Pound paused for emphasis—"the United States had declared war on the Central Powers."

He talked about Gaudier-Brzeska, Joyce, Eliot and "dozens of gifted writers" whom he had helped. "Now he was thirty-seven years old and it was time for him to stop doing so much for other men and for literature in general, stop trying to educate the public and simply write. It would take years for him to finish the *Cantos;* he wanted to write an opera and he had other plans. To carry them out it might be best for him to leave Paris and live on the Mediterranean, far from distractions, in a little town he had discovered when he was in *villeggiatura.* . . ."

Wyndham Lewis also found Hemingway in Pound's studio when he called (there was no answer when he rang the bell, and he opened the door himself):

"A splendidly built young man, strip to the waist, and with a torso of dazzling white, was standing not far from me. He was tall, handsome, and serene, and was repelling with his boxing gloves—I thought without undue exertion—a hectic assault of Ezra's. After a final swing at the dazzling solar plexus (parried effortlessly by the trousered statue) Pound fell back upon his settee. The young man was Hemingway."

Lewis found the Paris studio "a great change from the dark Kensington quarters." He also thought that Pound was "much more in his element in Paris." He enjoyed one of Pound's meals: "I actually believe he cooked better in Paris than he did in London."[7]

12.

How did he find time for it all; where did he get the energy? For, despite his talks and walks, his circulars, his letters, and his ubiquity, the work he had undertaken went steadily forward. The "Eighth Canto" had appeared in *The Dial* for May, 1922, and the following year, July, 1923, *The Criterion* published Cantos IX-XII—the "Malatesta Cantos"—which were seen through the press by Richard Aldington, substituting as editor in Eliot's absence. It led to another falling out with Pound.

"When I read the proof," Aldington wrote, "I discovered that Ezra had called the Pope a s.o.b. The law of libel in England is severe; Roman Catholics are sensitive; and anyway I didn't think it urbane to call the Pope a s.o.b. So I cut it out; whereupon Ezra promptly transferred the epithet to me by mail."[8] The passage is in Canto X:

> So that in the end that pot-scraping little runt Andreas
> > Benzi, da Siena
> Got up to spout out the bunkum
> That that monstrous swollen, swelling s. o. b.
> > Papa Pio Secundo
> > Aeneas Silvius Piccolomini
> > da Siena
> Had told him to spout, in their best bear's-greased latinity—

with examples. Yet Pius II was a scholar and a poet—at the court of Frederick III, poet laureate—and a patron of poets, but this was before he took holy orders; after which, says a historian, "those who surrounded the Pope were almost all Sienese, and of these Sienese, the majority were Piccolomini," which may account for the canto's emphasis.

He wrote Professor Schelling: "Perhaps as the poem goes on I shall be able to make various things clearer. Having the crust to attempt a poem in 100 or 120 cantos long after all mankind has been commanded never again to attempt a poem of any length, I have to stagger as I can."

He told Harriet Monroe it would take him forty years to complete the poem he was working on—an uncanny forecast, something like Stendhal's. He also let her know that he had written some music and was now at work on an opera about Villon. He explained that he had made "an intensive study" of medieval music for years, and that it had "far greater rhythmic variety than modern laws of music admit." The opera was practically done, he said; he and George Antheil were getting it down on paper.

13.

George Antheil, twenty-two, lived above Shakespeare and Company (and sometimes—when he forgot his key—used its swinging sign to get up to his window, which was right over its door). The apartment was tiny. Sharing it with him was a young Hungarian student he had met in Berlin. Her name was Boski.

Antheil had been on a concert tour when, quite suddenly, he decided to become a composer. In the middle of his tour he gave up the piano, for which he had shown a virtuoso's ability and, taking Boski along, settled in Paris. The date was June 13, 1923. That evening they attended Stravinsky's "Les Noces," by invitation. Antheil has described what they wore.

"Boski's Berlin gown was a black velvet tight-fitting low-cut affair, setting off her jet-black hair and that brown-blue glint which all Hungarians seem to flash from their otherwise white epidermis." She was eighteen and "really in love."

"I personally looked ridiculous. I was dressed in an expensive full-dress suit which Hanson had specially tailored for me in London. I also wore a soft hat and a *cape of my own design* [Antheil's italics] tailored by the same Berlin tailor who had made my silken padded revolver holster for my left armpit."⁹ They were married some years later.

It was an age of showmanship, of the exploitation of looks and clothes, reflected in Man Ray's famous photograph of Antheil: the round blond head with bangs, the—to Miss Beach—"interesting but wicked-looking eyes," the pretty mouth. It did not hurt to be attractive in Paris then, whatever one's sex. Margaret Anderson, whom Antheil had known in the United States, invited him to a tea at which she and Georgette LeBlanc were the guests of honor. At this party, at an unspecified place in the St. Germain quarter, Antheil met Erik Satie "and a Mephistophelian red-bearded gent who turned out to be Ezra Pound." Pound, he afterwards wrote, was "unusually kind and gracious" to him and asked for his address, saying he would call on him one day. He called early the next morning, "in a green coat with blue square buttons; and his red pointed goatee and kinky red hair above flew off from his face in all directions." Pound told him that he had come to hear some of his music, and as there was no piano there, they went to a friend's apartment, probably Adrienne Monnier's. Antheil says he played for hours, and then Pound returned home with him. Pound asked if he had written anything about his musical aims, and as it happened he had. Pound borrowed the manuscript. Weeks and months passed. Sylvia Beach told Antheil that Pound was working on a book about him.

Perhaps Pound saw in Antheil another Gaudier-Brzeska—young, talented, possibly a genius; and with his way to make. Aaron Copland once said: "When I first went to Paris I was jealous of Antheil's piano playing—it was so brilliant; he could demonstrate so well what he wanted to do." But was the young man from New Jersey a composer? Pound decided he was. He took Antheil in tow.

Since Paris, at that time, was a place where good notices could be had for a price, real reputations were established by the salons. To the salons on the Left Bank that he knew so well, Pound presented the very presentable newcomer, then took him to meet Jean Cocteau, who was the impresario of the salons on the Right. And thus he was launched.

Pound also introduced Antheil to his lifelong friend, Olga Rudge, a concert violinist. "She was a dark, pretty, Irish-looking girl, about twenty-five years old," Antheil wrote, "and, as I discovered when we commenced playing a Mozart sonata together, a consummate violinist. I have heard many violinists, but none with the superb lower register of the D and G strings that was Olga's exclusively." Miss Rudge, he adds, although born in Boston, had been raised in England and Italy, and spoke English "with a decided British accent" and Italian "flawlessly." At Pound's request he wrote two violin concertos for her.

When Yves Tinayre saw Pound again, it was in Olga Rudge's apartment, 2 rue Chamfort. And the last time he saw the chairs Pound had made for the studio in the rue Notre Dame des Champs—which he seems never to have forgotten—Miss Rudge had them. This, of course, was after Pound and his wife had moved to Rapallo.

14.

Harriet Monroe took her first vacation from *Poetry* in 1923. She went again to London, where she attended some "squashes" at Harold Monro's Poetry Book Shop, a recital by Edith Sitwell at the Aeolian Hall, and a P.E.N. dinner. She renewed acquaintances with May Sinclair and Ernest Rhys. She also met Aldington and Iris Barry. In Edinburgh she visited Ernest Walsh, a young poet whom she had befriended in the United States, and his new friend and benefactress, Ethel Moorhead, who was somewhat older. Miss Monroe then crossed the Channel to France.

She met Pound for the first time. She met his friends. She went, of course, to Sylvia Beach's book shop, where she met Joyce. In Pound's studio, and in the studios of his friends, she met an ever-widening circle of writers, painters, sculptors and composers. She was sixty-three years old. She made notes of three conversations.

In Brancusi's studio, Erik Satie told her that "the future of civilization rests with America, Russia and China." She was astonished; he explained that his view was based on the things they had in common—"geography and richness of race" and "the continental scope of these three nations." She could not believe that China, which she had visited in 1910, and was to visit again, belonged in the same category with America and Russia.

"Ah, but there is an enormous sleeping strength there," Satie said. "China is like a great dog dozing by the fire, whom we have been irritating out of its slumber, and who will stand up before long and, in shaking itself awake, will shake the world."

She called on Ford Madox Ford—"who has definitely dropped the *Hueffer* from his name"—in his apartment on the Boulevard Arago. He had another wife now—not Violet Hunt. Over tea in his medieval garden, Ford said the only hope for civilization was France. "If France goes under we are all done for."

Pound put Italy above France.

"Italy has civilized Europe twice," he said, "and it may be that she has spiritual force enough in her to do it again. At any rate, she is very much alive just now to every manifestation of the modern movement that is going on anywhere in the world."

Miss Monroe was impressed by his "artistic heroism." He was out "to start civilization again—nothing less. For a minor detail of his new start he thinks artists should be endowed, as in Italy of the Renaissance." He was not discouraged because the "Bel Esprit" project was moving slowly. But for Eliot to be "imprisoned in a bank," or for Joyce to have to "bother about shillings and pence" was "the cardinal crime of an age which sees ill-advised millionaires expend thirty thousand dollars for a pamphlet by Poe the starveling, and an hundred or two thousand for some canvas by the impecunious Rembrandt or Millet or Cézanne."[10]

Another visitor to the *pavillon* that year—one with a different view of Pound—was Margaret Anderson. With Jane Heap, of the *Little Review,* she had met Yeats—one of their earliest contributors —at Quinn's West Side apartment in New York City. Yeats talked about Pound and Joyce, and Miss Anderson felt, she afterwards wrote, that she had "found the key to my present discontent. It was time to go to Europe." She went. Miss Heap joined her in Paris, and together they called on their foreign editor.

"He was living in one of those lovely garden studios in the rue Notre Dame des Champs," Miss Anderson wrote. "He was dressed in the large velvet beret and flowing tie of the Latin Quarter artist of the 1830's. He was totally unlike any picture I had formed of him. Photographs had given no idea of his height, his robustness, his red blondness—could have given no indication of his high Rooseveltian [T.R., not F.D.R.] voice, his nervousness, his self-consciousness. After an hour in his studio I felt that I had been sitting through a human experiment in a behaviorist laboratory. Ezra's agitation was not of the type to which we were accustomed in America—excitement, pressure, life too high-geared. It gave me somehow the sensation of watching a large baby perform its repertoire of physical antics gravely, diffidently, without human responsibility for the performance."

She was puzzled, she says, by "other characteristics." It was only later that she was able to explain them to herself. She thought he shared in common with other expatriates "slowness on the up-take, the tendency to personalize the impersonal—interpreting in terms of politeness or of policy what should be kept in terms of ideas, the tendency to orientalize one's attitude toward women." She found him "fairly patriarchal in his attitude to women," whom she kissed on the forehead or drew upon his knee, which she herself found distasteful. She concluded: "It will be more interesting to know him when he has grown up."[11]

15.

The arrival of John Quinn in Paris was a notable event—he was, after all, "l'avocat new yorkais, défenseur de Margaret Anderson lors du procès qui lui fut intenté après la publication de *Ulysses* dans 'The Little Review.' " The Pounds gave a reception for him, and he was photographed with Pound, Joyce and Ford. On this occasion, Pound wore a matching suit, although the jacket appears to have been cut from an original design, loose and short in the waist, leaving an open space for the deployment of the hands in trouser pockets. He is sitting in a French upholstered chair which is almost too small for him, the crested head being just above the timber line, body deep-sunken or slouched, legs far forward and crossed. He appears lost in thought, not looking at anyone or anything. Behind him—"long, lean, burning like a coal with passion," as Ford has described him—stands Quinn, in a long, loose coat, waistcoat showing, one hand on hip, gaze directed at the photographer. Ford, seated in a stiff wooden chair, is looking good-naturedly at a piece of Pound's sculpture, which is balanced on his right knee, and Joyce, in an outsize replica of the stiff wooden chair, likewise has fixed his gaze on the *objet d'art*. His expression is deadpan and enigmatic. On a shelf above are the University of Pennsylvania foils.

In another part of the studio that day Hemingway was "shadow-boxing" in front of a Chinese silk portrait. Pound told Ford: "He's an experienced journalist. He writes very good verse and he's the finest prose stylist in the world." When Ford objected that only the day before Pound had termed *him* the finest prose stylist, Pound, he says, exclaimed: "You! You're like all English swine."

In his account of the reception Ford adds: "Ezra a few years before had been called the greatest bore in Philadelphia, so ceaselessly had he raved about London and Yeats and myself to uninterested Pennsylvanians. Now he was Anglophobe." (For "a few years" read "thirteen.")

Pound was recommending Hemingway to Ford; he had already persuaded Ford to start a magazine. "It's just like you to miss the chance of a sub-editor like that," Pound exclaimed in Quinn's hearing, and, Quinn murmured to Ford: "Poor fellow. . . . Poor fellow. . . . I'm sorry for you."

Pound to Quinn: "I'd never think of letting Ernest engage himself under those English diarrhoeas."

Quinn to Ford: "Poor fellow. . . . You're an honest man. . . . I hate to see you in that position."

Pound to Quinn: "The damfool deserves it. . . . He can't see the difference in merit between Arnault Daniel and Guillem de Cabestann. . . . He *prefers* Guillem. . . . What could you expect?"

Quinn to Ford: "I just *hate* to see you in that position."

Ford to Quinn: "It is not as uncomfortable as it looks." Ford to the reader: "The chair I was in had been made by Mr. Pound during his cabinet making stage. It was enormous, compounded of balks of white pine and had a slung canvas seat so large that, once you sat down, there you lay until somebody pulled you out."

Joyce, apparently, said nothing.

With Quinn as a backer, Ford launched the *Transatlantic Review,* assisted, first, by Basil Bunting, then by Hemingway, who was also a contributor, as were Pound, Robert McAlmon, Gertrude Stein, Joyce, Williams, Dos Passos and E. E. Cummings. Hemingway did not care for Cummings, but he went in all the same.

"In the case of Ezra," Ford wrote a decade later, "in the days of the *English Review* I read three verses of his *Goodly Fere* [read "Sestina: Altaforte"]; in that of Mr. E. E. Cummings I had decided after reading ten lines of his that I would open the *Transatlantic Review* with the poems he sent me."[12]

The review was published from the gallery over the great wine cave which served as William Bird's printery at 29, Quai d'Anjou, on the Ile St. Louis. Beneath leaded windows flowed the Seine. After the first issue, Ford began to give parties there. They started as teas. "But you never saw such teas as mine were at first. They would begin at nine in the morning and last for twelve hours." That was on Thursdays. "They began again on Friday and lasted till Saturday." Ford recalled, ruefully, that if all the would-be contributors and gate-crashers had bought a copy, the *Review* would have made a fortune. "Not one did."[13]

16.

On Wednesday, January 9, 1924, William Carlos Williams sailed for Europe, and a number of babies in the vicinage of Rutherford, New Jersey, missed the honor of being delivered by him. He was accompanied by his wife. Pound was in Italy, and they were shown around Paris by Robert McAlmon. Together, they peered in the window of Shakespeare and Company and saw some of his books, "looking somewhat dusty."

They called on Brancusi, who talked about Pound's opera. Williams exclaimed: "Pound writing an opera? Why, he doesn't know one note from another." Brancusi was "furious." They dined with James and Nora Joyce at the Trianon; McAlmon, who was host, raised his glass. "Here's to sin!" he said, but Joyce said: "I won't drink to that," and nobody did. They went to the Dingo, where they ate Portuguese oysters and listened to Hilaire Hiler play the piano. They met George Antheil. They dined again at the Trianon, this time with tables pushed together for the Joyces, Fords, Harold Loeb and his friend Kitty Cannéll, Antheil, Marcel Duchamp, Man Ray, Mina Loy and one of her two handsome daughters, Sylvia Beach, Louis Aragon and William Bird, the bearded publisher of the Three Mountains Press. They went to Brancusi's studio again, and partook of his beefsteak, Rumanian style. He walked part of the way home with them, in sabots. They were staying at the Hotel Lutetia.

The night before they left Paris for the south, they had dinner with Mina Loy and both her handsome daughters. After dinner they went to a party at Ford's, in the garden apartment described by Harriet Monroe. Williams liked Ford; Ford had "a mind wonderfully attractive to me," he afterwards wrote. But "there were too many people in the place," and Williams and his wife left. There followed a month in the south—Carcassone, Toulouse, Villefranche, Nice, Monte Carlo—McAlmon their guide. Nancy Cunard came to see them in Villefranche, and they thought of going to Rapallo to see Pound. They went instead to see Nancy Cunard in Monte Carlo. There Williams saw a copy of *Tulips and Chimneys,* E. E. Cummings's first book of poems, published the year before, and he read it that night. Back in Villefranche, he met Djuna Barnes and her beautiful companion, Thelma Wood. William Bird arrived. There was much talk of literature, and more of wines.

In March they went to Italy. They met Norman Douglas in Rome. They went to Austria. They started back. William and Sally Bird had invited them to Dijon for the wine-tasting festival, and thither they went. They tasted quite a bit, and as Williams says, he learned "to appreciate and differentiate, to suck air in over the tongue with a mouthful of those beautiful vintages!" They "dozed" their way to Paris, where McAlmon had found them rooms at the Hotel Unic, and the new rounds began. They ran into Joyce in the street, went to a concert, and then "for drinks"—Harold Loeb, Mary Butts, the Birds, McAlmon, Mina Loy and one of her daughters—met Hemingway on a bicycle and passed Joyce in a taxi. McAlmon's wife, Bryher, who had been traveling around Europe with H. D., appeared with H. D. At the Dôme, among the berets and the beards, a notable slummer was glimpsed—T. S. Eliot, in top hat, cutaway coat and striped trousers. Williams thought the get-up "was intended as a gesture of contempt," and says the gesture was received as "just that."

Williams played tennis with Hemingway and Loeb, then went to lunch at Nancy Cunard's, on the Quai d'Orléans, where he saw Gaudier-Brzeska's "Faun"; George Moore, who had been in love with Lady Cunard, now friends with her daughter, was also expected, but "didn't want to come." Loeb went to Spain with Hemingway and a few others, and became Robert Cohn in *The Sun Also Rises*. Williams supped with McAlmon and Bryher—"H. D. having been finally shaken"—and then returned to the Quai d'Orléans for a party. Two days later: "Good talk with H. D. over old times, Ezra's sudden interest in music." A few nights later there was a "memorable" supper at Adrienne Monnier's, who served chicken prepared from a secret recipe. Also present were Sylvia Beach, McAlmon, Bryher, H. D. Outside, on the rue de l'Odéon, there was a shout—Pound announcing his return from Rapallo. Miss Monnier called out an invitation, but he refused to come up, and Williams ran down. "He looked thinner but otherwise just as always." Pound gave him his address and went on.

17.

Williams went to see Pound two days later. Near the rue Notre Dame des Champs he passed a woman who, by the erectness of her walk, her hat and shoes, he guessed to be Dorothy Pound, but he was not certain and did not greet her. There were roofers at work on the *pavillon*. Pound talked about his appendix, and Williams listened with clinical interest. Then Pound launched into music—"renaissance music, theory of notation, static 'hearing,' melody, *time*." Later, Williams wrote:

"I have always felt that time was Ezra's chief asset as a music appreciator. A man with an ear such as his, attuned to the metrical subtleties of the best in verse, must have strong convictions upon the movements of the musical phrase. His praise of music and his interest in it, though, were to me always suspect. It was necessary for Ezra, in self-defense, though it was far beyond his natural abilities or capabilities, to include music in his omniscience concerning the modalities of the arts. Tones, I am certain, meant nothing to him, can mean nothing. His interest lay in the melody, the musical 'sentence,' the time variants (as in Antheil, when he could be listened to), renaissance music, the early composers, before Bach. Ezra could be listened to with profit in that field. Let him go on. It was worth it."[14]

But something of his original amazement and distrust, that had made him exclaim in Brancusi's studio, lingered in Williams's mind.

"It must infuriate Ezra to know there is *something* in the world of which he is not the supreme master," he wrote.

When Dorothy Pound came in, he saw that she was the woman he had passed on the street. He had not seen her for fourteen years, since his 1910 London visit, and then "her mother had been the more prominent in Ezra's life." Pound was all for preparing lunch over an alcohol lamp on a "shaky-looking" table, but Williams declined and they went instead to a resturant near the Odéon; Mrs. Pound stayed behind. In the afternoon Mrs. Williams appeared with a new hat, and at teatime "the Maestro himself officiated" over the alcohol lamp. Of Mrs. Pound's conversation, Williams recalls only that she did not care for Paris people or Paris winters, but praised Italy. She made them a present of a painting, of rocks on the Dartmouth moors; he thought it "cubistic in feeling, flat and cold."

Just before leaving Paris Williams was taken on a "cultural trip" by Pound to the home of Natalie Clifford Barney in the Faubourg St. Germain. Miss Barney's Friday *salon* was a famous one. She was "l'Amazone" of Remy de Gourmont's *Letters to an Amazon,* but while she rode horseback in the Bois every morning, she was, nevertheless, very feminine, dressing all in white. But she was surrounded by women with stiff collars and monocles as well as writers and officers of the Legion of Honor. Williams found her "extremely gracious and no fool." He admired "her lovely garden, well kept, her laughing doves, her Japanese servants." He couldn't stomach the masculine women, however, and is quite ribald about them on page 229 of his *Autobiography.*

Hemingway's view of Pound's musicianship was more tolerant than Williams's:

"Pound is among other things a composer and has done a splendid opera on Villon. It is a first rate opera. A very fine opera.

"But I feel about Ezra and music something like about M. Constantin Brancusi and cooking. M. Brancusi is a famous sculptor who is also a very famous cook. Cooking is, of course, an art but it would be lamentable if M. Brancusi would give up sculpture for it or even devote the major part of his time to cookery.

"Still Ezra is not a minor poet. He has never been troubled by lack of energy. If he wants to write more operas he will write them and there will be plenty of force left over."[15]

18.

Antheil and the Treatise on Harmony appeared November, 1924 (not 1923, as the subject of it states in his autobiography) and was a publication of Three Mountains Press, William Bird, prop. It consists of three sections: an elaboration by Pound of Antheil's views on harmony, and his own; something about Antheil himself (Pound considered him the only composer in sight), and a compilation, selected, edited, and commented on—by Antheil—of William Atheling's (i.e., Pound's) music criticism in the *New Age*, 1917-1920. The book is rather formless, but full of good things, and helped Antheil more than it did Pound. Antheil was not particularly grateful. He wrote in his autobiography:

"I still do not know why I permitted Ezra to issue his book about myself. Perhaps it was because at that moment I could see no other way of blasting into the otherwise tight-as-a-drum salons. In any case my error and lack of judgment were to cause me a lot of future grief—grief which has not been entirely dispelled even today [he wrote in 1945, when Pound was in trouble].

"Ezra's flamboyant book, couched in language calculated to antagonize everyone first by its ridiculous praise, then by its vicious criticism of everybody else, did me no good whatsoever; on the contrary, it sowed the most active distaste for the very mention of the name 'Antheil' among many contemporary critics, prejudiced them before they had even so much as heard a note of mine.

"Nobody could have been a tenth as good as Ezra made me.

"All this was not even necessary. Less than three months later Satie himself would take up the cudgel for me, this at my first concert in the great Champs Elysées Theater."

There was, of course, a riot, a prefiguring, as it were, of the great riot to come when his "Ballet Mécanique" was performed. The music itself that night—"Sonata Sauvage," "Airplane Sonata" and "Mechanisms"—found its way into the larger work. Satie, says Antheil, cried out: "Quel precision! Quel precision! Bravo! Bravo!" There were a number of arrests.

"I felt for the automatic under my arm and continued playing. I had gone through riots in Germany, but this promised to really become something," Antheil wrote in *Bad Boy of Music*, his autobiography, but has little to say of Pound's efforts to find him an audience.

There were other concerts featuring Pound's music. Miss Beach has recorded one, by invitation from "M. et Mme. Ezra Pound," to a private concert in one of the smaller chambers of the Salle Pleyel. The program, which consisted of works by Antheil and Pound, was headed: "Musique Américaine: (Declaration of Independence): performed by Olga Rudge & George Antheil." Among those present were Joyce and his son, Georgio; Margaret Anderson and Jane Heap; Ernest Hemingway; Djuna Barnes; Sylvia Beach and Adrienne Monnier.

And one evening, in a small assembly room in Montparnasse, Antheil included in his program a sonata for drum and piano. There were perhaps one hundred persons in the audience, about half of them American tourists, the rest young French men and women of the *avant-garde*. Among the Americans was a college professor who told me:

"Antheil, an excellent musician, was, I am sure, improvising, and the drummer—whiskers, gray tweeds—was obviously trying to communicate some sort of narrative with his drumming—maybe a battle, maybe the love act, maybe an encounter of wit. He employed many tempi and I could distinguish no definite rhythmic pattern. The performance was heard respectfully. I recall hoping that the evening might end in a riot. Not so. Pound's seriousness of mien in beating his big bass drum won the day."[16]

There was still another concert on which Pound "walked out," disgusted by Antheil's sudden excursion into "neo-classicism." Antheil afterwards claimed his symphony was not "neo-classic," but it was not until 1928 that he got a chance to tell Pound so. Still, in the welter of reminiscences, pro and con, many of them written by interested parties, it is not always easy to understand what was going on, or precisely what attitudes were adopted or displayed. When it came to the writing, everyone naturally wanted to look good.

19.

Pound told Mary and Padraic Colum when they called at the *pavillon*: "One has to keep going east to keep one's mind alive." He said "there was not a soul on the banks of the Thames who knew anything about anything." Now he was tired of France, too. Certain ideas were taking hold, and it was no longer enough for him to consort with artists and writers. Lincoln Steffens was scheduled to give a lecture on Soviet Russia in a friend's apartment, and Pound asked the Colums to accompany him. It was the last thing in the world Mary Colum wanted to do. They went. She wrote in *Life and the Dream:*

"Ezra listened to it with rapt attention, his eyes glued to the speaker's face, the very type of a young man in search of an ideology, except that he was not so very young. He seemed to have an intense interest in new political and economic ideas, and after Steffens was finished he rose to his feet and started talking about the Douglas plan, to which he had tried to convert Arthur Griffith and through him the new Irish state. He had begun the writing of those letters of his to every prime minister in Europe on this subject. Maybe if they had listened to him it might have done something for Europe; at least it couldn't have done as much harm as the ideas that the prime ministers themselves cherished."[17]

Some snippets of Steffens's talk appear in the *Cantos*—

> No use telling 'em anything, revolutionaries,
> Till they're at the *end,*
> Oh, absolootly, AT the end of their tether—

and what a banker told him (for "Baymont" read Lamont):

> And Tommy Baymont said to Steff one day:
> "You think we run it, lemme tell you,
> "We bought a coalmine, I mean the mortgage fell in,
> "And you'd a' thought we could run it.
>
> "Well I had to go down there meself, and the manager
> "Said: "Run it, of course we can run it,
> "We can't sell the damn coal."

> (Canto XIX)

Mrs. Colum noted: "Unlike Eliot, he had a pronounced American accent of the middle-western provenance, and in spite of the ducal Renaissance beard would have passed anywhere as a slightly eccentric middle-western professor."[18] The last bit sounds like Fletcher's characterization. When Padraic mentioned they were returning to New York, Pound asked: "Who is there to talk to there?" (He said it again in a letter after J. B. Yeats died: "Who is there to talk to now?") Colum told me Yeats's father was "the type of talker Pound was always looking for." He had a question of his own. "How do you find time to help others?" he asked, and Pound replied: "Well, what is there for a Protestant to do, except good works?" Colum told me: "I have a real affection for Pound, but he disturbs me, he is disturbing, but perhaps that was what he was intended to be."

Colum appears in Canto LXXX with the tribute of a quoted line, and Griffith in LXXVIII with—presumably—his reply to Pound: "Can't move 'em with a cold thing like economics."

Mina Loy has recorded an unusual view of Pound—a man of fads: "He was like a child, and an old professor at the same time. His craze then was endocrine glands. He would talk about it a great deal —very learned discussion. Glands," she added, "were the latest thing at the time."

Speaking of him twenty years after her sojourn in Paris, she said: "He was a sensitive man who didn't think other people were sensitive. One of his friends said he had brought from America the faults of America, and none of the virtues.

"He probably found Italy a very seductive place—simple-minded Italian peasants, everything quite heavenly."[19]

Something was driving Pound—eastward as it happened, but the United States was out of his calculations, and eastward was the only direction he could go. Perhaps he was running from something— himself, most probably. There is a hint of frenzy in the Paris records and memoirs, and what does not appear in most of them, an addition to his London repertoire of assorted accents, exclamations in foreign languages, strange cries and catcalls, of Anglo-Saxon words which Ford and Aldington almost alone have hinted at. And there were outbursts which literally terrified some of his friends.

Perhaps he was running from the accelerating bustle and din of modern life. In *The Exile*, No. 2, he wrote:

"The carrefour by the Dome in one year, or two years, about 1922-3 had rather the air of a suburban strawberry festival in the America of my youth. A couple of years later this same carrefour had rather the air of Eighth Avenue, New York, on a Saturday night in or about 1910, except for the gaiety of the paper lanterns, in place of that of the metal street lamps."

But, in addition to all else, he was not well. In the sanity hearing held in the District Court of the United States for the District of Columbia in 1946 one of the doctors who had examined him testified:

"His health was not too good at that time. He submitted to two or three operations. I do not remember whether they were all carried out in Paris or whether it was finished in Italy, but he had been to Italy on those occasions."

He wrote William Bird from Rapallo "Re Studio":

"If Hem doesn't want it, can yr. friends find 2000 fr. recompense for beds, cookstoves, electric wiring? Or how much *can* they find?

"I don't suppose the landlord (lady) will accept the same franc rent again, but equivalent in $'s. It is now only $15 a month; it *was* $30 when we took it. Also do yr. friends want the *cat?*"

20.

In April of 1924 he was in Florence and Assisi, in May in Rome, but the end of the year found him in Rapallo again. Christmas was spent in Taormina; thence he traveled to Siracusa and Palermo. This was in January. By February, 1925, he and his wife had settled in Rapallo. And as though to crown the Paris period now definitely at an end there appeared, in the spring of 1925, the first number of a brilliant new magazine entitled *This Quarter,* edited by Ernest Walsh and Ethel Moorhead, and dedicated to "*Ezra Pound* who by his creative work, his editorship of several magazines, his helpful friendship for young and unknown artists, his many and untiring efforts to win better appreciation of what is first-rate in art comes first to our mind as meriting the gratitude of this generation." The issue also contained signed tributes by Miss Moorhead and Walsh, and by James Joyce and Ernest Hemingway. Joyce, who was not interested in other people's writing, had nothing to say about Pound's work and merely acknowledged the help he had received:

"I owe a great deal to his friendly help, encouragement and generous interest in everything that I have written, as you know there are many others who are under a similar debt of gratitude to him. He helped me in every possible way in the face of very great difficulties for seven years before I met him, and since then he has always been ready to give me advice and appreciation which I esteem very highly as coming from a mind of such brilliance and discernment."[20]

Hemingway's "Homage to Ezra" (from which I have already quoted) reached Walsh from Spain:

"So far, we have Pound the major poet devoting, say, one fifth of his time to poetry. With the rest of his time he tries to advance the fortunes, both material and artistic, of his friends. He defends them when they are attacked, he gets them into magazines and out of jail. He loans them money. He sells their pictures. He arranges concerts for them. He writes articles about them. He introduces them to wealthy women. He gets publishers to take their books. He sits up all night with them when they claim to be dying and he witnesses their wills. He advances them hospital expenses and dissuades them from suicide. And in the end a few of them refrain from knifing him at the first opportunity."

Miss Beach has told in her book how Pound came to make the acquaintance of Ernest Walsh. Walsh was sick in a hotel in Paris, and sent her a letter saying he was broke. She was too busy to go herself, and sent a friend. "Luckily for Walsh, he had a letter to Pound also, and Ezra, who made a business of rescuing poets, hurried round."[21] Miss Moorhead wrote:

"I have only met Ezra Pound twice. The first time was when he came to see Ernest Walsh who was sick. In a small hotel room myself and another were sitting on the floor for lack of chairs. The big man sat on the bed awkwardly with legs dangling, trying to get balanced. He didn't look at us but seized a book lying on the bed and looked at that. Terribly conscious of the big personality on the bed, the insignificant ones on the floor said nothing and with the selfishness of the invalid the invalid left it to those on the floor. There were disturbing vibrations of only awkwardness in that room. I reacted to that and left the room. The other one was on the floor another five minutes, then we met outside that room, angry at the lost opportunity of hearing golden words from the poet. He hadn't uttered a word but we hadn't said anything idiotic—that was something."

All the same, she carried away a vivid impression: "If a psycho-analyst or mesmerist had afterwards said familiarly 'Ezra?' I would not have answered: *Poems, cantos, sonatas!* I would have said: "Eyes . . . color . . . cadmium . . . amber . . . *topaz in Chateau Yquem!*"

The second time she saw him was on a Left Bank boulevard. It was after lunch, and Pound looked "merry." This time she felt "vigorous and courageous vibrations." Pound, she says, had been ill, and she asked him if he were better now. He replied: "I was ill. I am better." Her reaction was, "great man pompously accurate—not pretty girl." And once more she carried away the impression his eyes had given her, which she repeats.[22]

Walsh wrote:

"Not everyone likes him. No man of character has ever been a universal favorite. I like Pound. He is the most sensitively generous of men. He is a man. Not a married man. Nor a literary man. Nor a public man. He is plain honest-to-God-man. It isn't so little a thing to be in this world of about every other kind of genius."

Her words, which had gushed forth under the emotional impact of their brief encounters, were afterwards much regretted. The memory of his words plagued and tortured him as he lay dying a year after they were written.

21.

That summer of 1925, in Bologna, where they were visiting the poet Emanuel Carnevali, Walsh and Miss Moorhead saw Pound again. "We were then arranging for the second number of *This Quarter*," she afterwards wrote. "Ezra Pound was very keen about it, but we had not asked him to contribute. (We had asked him for a contribution for our first number but he had not enough belief in the unknown editors to risk a manuscript.) Enthusiastic as he then was (at Bologna) about *This Quarter*, Ezra Pound's bogey was that we would ask him for some CHARITY for *This Quarter*. I use his own word CHARITY. He repeated often that he had 'done so much for CHARITY' and that 'he could do no more for CHARITY!'"

She and Walsh "came to the conclusion that Ezra Pound was really hard up. And so we put our heads together and planned to buy a

canto of Ezra Pound's for our second number." They paid contributors thirty francs a page, and naturally were "flabbergasted"—Miss
Moorhead's word—when Pound asked for forty pounds; but by then
Pound's cantos had appeared in *The Dial, Poetry, The Criterion* and
the *Transatlantic Review,* and whatever the others paid, *The Dial*
paid two dollars a line. Miss Moorhead speaks in the singular: "We
received it on agreeing to pay, and it appeared in our second number"; but what appeared in the second number (Summer, 1925)
were Cantos XVII-XIX—that is, three of them—which filled twelve
pages.

A "friendly correspondence" with Pound followed; some months
later, on another visit to Italy, they stopped off in Rapallo to call on
him. In a poem which appeared in the third issue of *This Quarter,*
entitled "Sonnet for E. P.," Walsh recalled this visit:

I remember Italy as a place where the sea touched me as the
Fingers of a woman who understood and the moon was her breast
And there was a poet who said I ought to go to bed early
I will always remember that man he blossomed in the eye

Miss Moorhead's version is different; she says that Pound was full
of suggestions for *This Quarter,* "but afterwards, because his advice
and suggestions were not taken up, his friendship cooled." She also
says that Walsh sent Pound a group of poems, asking for criticism,
and that Pound did not reply. "Ernest Walsh greatly valued Pound's
opinion and he was worried during those last sad months of his illness that Pound had not replied. But he was thoroughly disillusioned
about Ezra Pound before he died and spoke bitterly of him as an
exploiter." The poems reached Miss Moorhead after Walsh's death.
She says Pound wrote *"that* HE *couldn't do anything about the poems.*
HE *couldn't suggest any publisher who would handle them,* HE
couldn't advise anything," and comments that "this presumption is
characteristic of Ezra Pound:—his anticipation of a request and the
warning that it is no use to make it!"

I have been quoting from her editorial in the third number of
This Quarter, written in the full tide of grief over the untimely death
of Ernest Walsh, and with the fury of a woman redressing a supposed wrong. I say "supposed," for it must be apparent to all that

whatever change of sentiment Miss Moorhead—and, by implication, Walsh—had undergone, Pound had not changed, and in Rapallo was not only out of touch with events in Paris, but had undertaken a publication of his own which consumed his time and energy. Miss Moorhead's editorial, entitled "Ezra Pound and *The Exile*," gives the name of his publication, about which I shall have more to say. She is bitter because Pound did not mention Walsh in his magazine: "A tribute to Ernest Walsh would have given value and interest and life to *The Exile*. Ernest Walsh was so much alive, that he is alive now and will not die, and writers who write about him must be alive too. Perhaps this is why Ezra Pound does not write about him." Her editorial ends:

"I herewith take back that dedication. I have said before that Ernest Walsh was disillusioned about Ezra Pound before he died. *We* take back our too-generous dedication."

Hemingway's tribute to Pound ends:

"Many people hate him and he plays a fine game of tennis. He would live much longer if he did not eat so fast. Young men in the years after the war coming over from America where Pound was a legendary person to Paris where they found him with a patchy red beard, very accessible, fond of tennis and occasionally playing the bassoon, decided there could not be anything in the Pound legend and that he was probably not a great poet after all. As the army rhyme used to say: hence criticism in America.

"Like all men who become famous very young he suffers from not being read. It is so much easier to talk about a classic than to read it. There is another generation, though, in America that is replacing the generation that decided Ezra could not be a great poet because he was actually alive and kicking, and this generation is reading him. They come to Paris now and want to meet him. But he has gone to Italy.

"As he takes no interest in Italian politics and does not mind Italian cookery he may stay there some time. It is good for him to be there because his friends cannot get at him so easily and energy is thus released for production."

22.

As was the case with London, Pound and his wife went back and forth between Rapallo and Paris before settling down. They lived for several months in the Albergo Pernizotti on Mont' Allegro, above Rapallo, and for a time in the Albergo Rapallo, on the sea front; here, their apartment was over the café. One day the hieratic head arrived, uprooted at last from Violet Hunt's garden in Kensington; and there being no place to put it, it went into the window of the café, where passers-by could see it, then into the lobby, where it stayed until the Pounds moved to the apartment they were to keep for more than a quarter of a century. This was on the Via Marsala, number 12, five flights up. The rooms opened onto a roof garden, and from it they could see "Rapallo's thin line of broken mother-of-pearl along the water's edge," as Yeats, who saw it often, was to phrase it. The bust was placed in a commanding position at one end of the roof garden, and cast a cold eye on many a meditation, and many a *conversazione*.

On Thursday, May 6, 1926, Pound was in Rome, at the Sala Sgambati; Olga Rudge was violinist, Alfredo Casella at the piano. The program, in three parts, included compositions by Satie and Ravel; in the third, there was a composition by Pound entitled "Hommage Froissart."

On Saturday, June 19, 1926, "Ballet Mécanique" was performed at the Théâtre des Champs-Elysées, Vladimir Golschmann conducting. "Getting there early," Lincoln Steffens wrote home, "I stood outside and saw, I think, all the queer people in Paris, French and foreign, men and women. Wild hair, flannel shirts, sticks, no hats and big hats for both men and women, and, note well, many intelligent faces."[23] Late-comers had difficulty getting to their seats. In a box was Joyce, a patch over one eye. T. S. Eliot arrived, escorting Princess Bassiano. Up in the top gallery, says Miss Beach, surrounded by friends of the Left Bank, was Pound, prepared to smother hisses and other unfriendly manifestations; but I saw him below.

There were eight pianos and a player piano on the stage (with Antheil at the player piano). There were xylophones, electric bells, whistles and loudspeakers. There was also an airplane propeller. "I have only used these sounds because they are part of the musical sound of our modern life," Antheil afterwards explained; but then it was too late. The din of the pianos stunned that vast audience, which began to heave in anger, as though struck simultaneously by the same blow. Cries of "Enough!" filled the theater, and the aisles were instantly thronged by people trying to get at the musicians or to get out, but impeded by Antheil partisans, while hisses rained on them. And suddenly the centerpiece on the stage, which had appeared to be merely a modernistic decoration, unnoticed by most, began to whir. It was the airplane propeller. A blast, as from the Arctic, blew straight down the middle of the theater, and there was a gasp of surprise, followed by a groan of discomfort. More people got up, and as they could not get into the aisles, began to climb over seats. Fights broke out everywhere, and elegantly dressed men and women were seen striking strangers with their sticks and umbrellas, and were struck in return. Above the roar rang Pound's voice; according to Sylvia Beach, he was even seen "hanging head downward from the top gallery."

Ten days later, Pound's opera was performed.

23.

The full title of the opera is *The Testament of François Villon, A Melodrama by Ezra Pound, Words by François Villon, Music by Ezra Pound*. Portions of it were first performed in 1924, Yves Tinayre being accompanied by Olga Rudge. In 1926, at the old Salle Pleyel, where Lizst and Chopin had played, it was performed somewhat more elaborately. The printed invitation reads:

"M. et Mme. Ezra Pound

vous invitent à une audition privée

Parole de Villon

Arias and fragments from an opéra

LE TESTAMENT

Texte de Villon   Musique par Ezra Pound

à la Salle Pleyel

22, Rue Rochechouart

Le Mardi Soir

29 Juin 1926

(à 9 heures 15)."

There was a clavichord and brass, a French *corne,* and Olga Rudge played the violin. Once more, Yves Tinayre sang the tenor role, and Robert Maitland was the bass. Tinayre told me that Pound wanted "a buzzi-buzzo comic bass that goes down in the cellarage," and he recommended Maitland with whom he had sung the Bach B Minor Mass in Paris. Maitland, he told me, was a tall Englishman "with a round nose and vacant stare." Pound immediately engaged him. During rehearsals Antheil played jazz "heavily" on the clavichord.

One of the mysteries of the performance was the unnamed singer who sang the role of "La Belle Heaulmière." Even the music critic, Virgil Thomson, who was present, never found out. The singer was Tinayre, who told me he put a shawl over his head and disguised his voice—"I made it a weepy voice"—and sang the part as an old woman. He termed *Villon* "an extraordinarily fine musical feat. It was for only two voices, tenor and bass, and there was a real alternation of voice." In his Riverside Drive apartment he sat down at the piano and illustrated with snatches of his own tenor and Maitland's bass. The opera, he said, was "a success of surprise." Thomson told me: "It wasn't a professional job, Pound was not a professional musician; but he handled verbal values very prettily." He still recalled with pleasure the "rather majestic sound" of the *corne,* a five-foot horn made of real horn, which cost Pound a great deal of trouble to find. It was capable of only two notes, separated by an interval. Thomson said: "The low note was hard to blow, but rather grand." The other note was a fifth above it. This mediaeval instrument was played by Tinayre's brother Paul. Tinayre said it was because of this horn that he devoted the next twenty years to research in mediaeval music.

In his *Autobiography,* Williams says that when he talked with

Tinayre the singer "could hardly stop laughing over some of the effects that turned up" in the opera. But when I talked with Tinayre, he told me he had not laughed at the opera but only in telling about Pound's rendition of the "Heaulmière" passage from it. "Pound," he said, "has no ear, and he sang it rhythmically."

Pound's interest in music went back, of course, not only to his earliest childhood, when he had seen his mother at the piano, but to his early London days—to his friendship with Kitty Heyman and Walter Rummel, when many of the poets, Yeats among them, saw in music a possible source of new verse rhythms, influenced, perhaps, by Pater's dictum: "All art constantly aspires towards the condition of music." As regards poetry, it had worked in earlier times; but then, to be sure, poets were musicians; musicians, poets; and gentlemen were a little of both.

Tibor Serly said to Pound: "Look, I am learning about literature from you—how could you possibly be sitting down and writing operas?" and Pound replied: "I've been looking to see which composers can set words to music, music to words. I'll have to do it myself."

"Speaking of notation as an aid to memory," Pound told a visitor at St. Elizabeths, "that's the way I did my opera *Villon*. I have the only copy in existence over there in my room. BBC put it on in 1932 [read 1931] and they had some copies, but lost them. Too bad they didn't make a record of it, because I wrote out the *motz el sons* just the way the old troubadours did, just as an aid to memory. I used the modern notation in the old simple shorthand way, and I can read it, but nobody else can without hearing it first—I could hum it or whistle it to 'em. I don't have much of a voice to carry a tune, singing, but whistling or humming, I could make it clear to the musicians."[24]

The text of the opera was only in part his own, the parts to be sung being drawn entirely from Villon's "Great Testament" and other ballades. Pound appears to have finished the opera in 1924, and this may account for Villon's age in his text, thirty-nine, Pound's age that year.

Pound also wrote a violin sonata for Olga Rudge, which she afterwards performed with great skill. Serly, who arranged Pound's "Sonate," told me:

"What I did was take the single-line voice and amplify the composition by extensions, occasionally, here and there, by adding more bars—but only by extending the material itself, not adding any new material at any time. I merely divided the sections in proper order so that it has a better continuity of form.

"I avoided adding any actual harmonies to the original, but fortified and filled in such harmonies as I found there. So that, in its whole, it becomes a kind of scherzo-like work of several parts, which was transcribed for a complete, full-string orchestra.

"In this garb, the attempt was made to retain, or maintain, the whole primitive melodic structure, while cautiously adding a modern garb so that it may be compatible with the music of today.

"I asked Pound if he wished it to be published, and he thought it wasn't worth while."

Serly has the original manuscript.

Either before or after the Salle Pleyel performance of *Villon* Pound called on John Cournos, curious, Mrs. Cournos told me, to see whom his old friend had recently married. Cournos and his wife were staying at the Hôtel Cayre on the Boulevard Raspail.

"Pound came and sat down and put his feet right up on the desk where John had been writing a moment before," Mrs. Cournos said.

They adjourned to a neighboring café.

24.

Two other events of this year should be noted. Pound's published letters contain no mention of the first.

"My dear Olivia," Yeats wrote to Mrs. Shakespear on September 5, 1926, from Dublin, without indicating the source of his information. "I hear that you are to be a grandmother and that the event is taking place in the usual secrecy. You are probably furious, but you will find a grandchild a pleasing distraction in the end. It is an ideal relationship, for your business will be unmixed indulgence. I congratulate you upon it. Dorothy being doubtless still more furious will make an excellent mother."

He wrote again, September 24th:

"My dear Olivia: I divine that you have already adopted the grandchild. When do you and he arrive in London?"

Omar Shakespear Pound was born in the American Hospital in
Paris on September 10, 1926, and registered as an American citizen,
his mother being American by marriage. Olivia Shakespear told Cournos that Pound had remarked, when reeling off her grandson's name:
"Just note the crescendo."

And in New York, the new and enlarged *Personae* appeared, under
the imprint of Boni and Liveright. Its subtitle was misleading: "The
collected poems of Ezra Pound. Including Ripostes, Lustra, Homage
to Sextus Propertius, H. S. Mauberley." So was the note before the
contents: "Edition to date of all Ezra Pound's poems except the unfinished 'cantos.' " It was merely a *selection,* and many poems, admired of others, but no longer admired by Pound, were left out; some
of these, Mr. Eliot was to put back in his selection, but he omitted
the "Propertius," for reasons which I have given elsewhere.

It was a time for new directions, but Pound took an old one. He
wrote to Cournos, November 10, 1926:

"No fool like an old fool. Am thinking of a small infrequent but
regular-appearing review. DOES anyone want it or need it. Damn the
public . . . I mean does anyone need it to PRINT stuff in; short misfits,
that no one else will print, and that have absolootely NO commercial
value. They have to be short as there is no money to pay printer for
LONG stuff. If you have nawthing but nuvvles it is no use to you.
Wotterbaht les jeunes, do they still sprout?"[25]

He wrote Cummings the same day:

"Three weeks of bad weather, driving one off the tennis court and
the general spread of Vinalism thru the 'field of murkin licherture,'
possibly resurgence of early and pernicious habit, have driven me to
consider a infinitestimal review as 'outlet.' "

He wrote Miss Monroe on the 15th:

"Have been looking through your last 18 or more numbers, find
many of 'em uncut.

"My impression is that you have tried ladies' numbers, children's
numbers, in fact everything but a man's number . . . Fraid I will
hav to take the bad boys off your hands and once again take up the
hickory."

But he was already whisking it about. A section of *Finnegan's Wake*
reached him that month, and he wrote Joyce:

"All I can do is to wish you every possible success. I will have another go at it, but up to the present I make nothing of it whatever."

More letters went out. One of them appeared in the December, 1926, issue of the *New Masses* under the heading "Pound Joins The Revolution!" He had written:

"I find five numbers of New Masses waiting for me here on my return from Paris, and have read most of the text with a good deal of care. For the first time in years I have even gone so far as to think of making a trip to America; so you can take the blame for that if for nothing else.

"If it's not too much trouble, send on any material about Passaic. John Reed's Ten Days That Shook the World, [Scott] Nearing's *Dollar Diplomacy,* or whatever you think most necessary for my education."[26]

There were also copies of *The American Mercury.* He wrote Samuel Putnam, a Covici editor, afterwards author of *Paris Was Our Mistress:*

"I have just read your Mercury article: 'Chicago, an obituary'; perhaps more carefully than you intended it to be read. If your interest in the subject has lasted past getting the matter off your chest, I can, if you like, supply you with a few data, or explanations of various things you mention as 'miracle' or miraculous, etc.; i,e, various causes, dates of birth and demise, and even a possible remedy (belated in all probability, but still.)"

Putnam was, naturally, interested, and Pound sent a seven-page letter. In it, he took some credit for himself for the success of *Poetry* and the *Little Review,* with "data"; but, chiefly, it was a "plug" for the writers he believed in, some of whom, he hoped, Covici would publish. "The NEW elements in this list are Rodker and McA. [McAlmon] and my 'Antheil' wd. at least be up to date, or nearly so. Williams's 'Great American Novel' ought to be imported."

The letters are all dated the old-fashioned way, that is, with dates, and there are, as yet, no mottoes or a portrait on the letterhead, which merely carried his name and Rapallo address in bold blue capital letters on typewriter-size paper. As before, there are two or three or more spaces between words.

CHAPTER XV

THE EXILE

1.

The hickory firmly held, Pound switched with a good will. Most of the stripes fell on a dunce that neither knew nor cared. The dunce was very provoking. It loomed larger and ever more stupid in his mind, magnified by bright thousands of miles and uncharted fathoms of air. Besides, it never listened.

It was the United States.

As in 1920, there were some thoughts of a visit to the homeland he had not seen for three lustra (fifteen years). He was even toying with the idea, again, of a whirlwind lecture tour which—perhaps— would reap a golden harvest. He confided to Miss Monroe:

"I have not, at the moment, any strong objection to visiting Amer‚ ica. I shall probably be HORRIFIED if or when I do get there. It is probably infinitely worse than anything I am prepared for, despite my being prepared for ANYTHING within the range of my imagination."

The implication was clear enough.

"As to the lecture tour: the question is simply: what wd. it pay? I can not afford to do it on the cheap. If I blow all that energy, I have got to have a few years free from worry AFTER it.

"Poverty here is decent and honourable. In America it lays one open to continuous insult on all sides, from the putridity in the White House down to the expressman who handles one's trunk."

In 1926, the United States was under the magistracy of Calvin Coolidge, and in an era of prosperity. A view of the country at this particular juncture, booming before the bust, would have displayed at their best the virtues he had praised in *Patria Mia*: American vigor, American openness, American generosity; American love of the big and the tall and the high, mountains and skyscrapers, talk and deeds. There was also the broadening cultural phenomenon—music, museums and book clubs. Of course, there was also Prohibition. All these things might have given him a new perspective and new insights. He chose, instead, to remain abroad, in a place infinitely remoter than London or Paris had been, so far as any real knowledge or news of the United States was concerned.

The first mention, first praise, of Mussolini occurs in this letter to Harriet Monroe:

"I personally think extremely well of Mussolini. If one compares him to American presidents (the last three) or British premiers, etc., in fact one can NOT without insulting him. If the intelligentsia don't think well of him, it is because they know nothing about 'the state,' and government, and have no particularly large sense of values. Anyhow, WHAT intelligentsia?" He answered her question: "England gives small pensions; France provides jobs. . . . Italy is full of ancient libraries; the jobs are quite comfortable, not very highly paid, but are respectable, and can't much interfere with the librarians' time.

"As to 'betterness,' if I were a citizen of any of these countries I wd. have some sort of appui, which is unthinkable in America. As for professorships? ? ? I have not been overwhelmed with offers."

The new review provided a classroom, and a platform from which to lecture. There was also a correspondence course by mail.

2.

The word "exile" seems to have had an extraordinary fascination for Pound and his contemporaries. In the same year both Cournos and Aldington published collections of verse respectively titled *In Exile* and *Exile and Other Poems*. But, of course, the note had been struck earlier, by Joyce, in that famous sentence near the end of *Portrait of the Artist*: "I will not serve that in which I no longer believe, whether it call itself my home, my fatherland or my church: and I will try to express myself in some mode of life or art as freely as I can and as wholly as I can, using for my defence the only arms I allow myself to use, silence, exile and cunning."

Pound called his new review *The Exile*. The first number, Spring, 1927, printed in Dijon, started off with a portion of Canto XX, pages 1 to 6. Other contributors were John Rodker, with a big chunk of a novel which took up most of the issue; Richard Aldington, and "E. W. Hemingway," whose contribution was entitled "Neo-Thomist Poem," and consisted of the following lines:

> The Lord is my Shepherd,
> I shall not want him for long.

Pound commented in his editorial: "Mr. Hemingway's POEM refers to events in what remains of the French world of letters." So much for France. (In *The Exile,* No. 3, Pound wrote: "We refuse to recognize France as a contemporary part of civilization so long as kow-tow to paper forms, faddle of passports and cartes d'identité remains an integral part of the outward manifestations of her internal imbecility." Incidentally, he always wrote "Poet" on his passports and *cartes d'identité.*)

"As to an editorial program:

"The republic, the res publica means, or ought to mean 'the public convenience'. When it does not, it is an evil, to be ameliorated or amended out of, or into decent, existence. Detailed amendment is usually easier, and we await proof that any other course is necessary. But in so far as America is concerned, we should like to know whether there is *any* mental activity outside the so called 'revolutionary elements', the communescents, etc."

He concluded:

"The American view as expressed by the leading American intelligentzia is that America is *the* most colossal monkey house and prize exhibit that the astonished world has yet seen."

What "intelligentzia"? They numbered two: H. L. Mencken and George Jean Nathan, whose monthly feature in *The American Mercury* held up to laughter and to scorn the boobosities of Americans, chiefly legislators, both state and national.

The red cover, the editorial onslaught, gave the United States Customs a chance to exhibit its own special brand of boobery: literary criticism, it having distinguished itself in the realm of art criticism. *The Exile,* No. 1, was held up; in No. 2, Pound purports to quote from a New York correspondent, who may have been a distributor: "An assistant customs appraiser grabbed my arm the other day and said, 'Say, the fellow that wrote that stuff in your magazine must be a narcotic fiend! Nobody has thoughts like those except under the influence of drugs! We don't want stuff like that here—we're going to have to defend our women and children against the Bolsheviks pretty soon!!'" (In No. 3, he states that the issue was held up because it was dated "Spring 1927" instead of "April 1927," which made it a book instead of a magazine, if I understand Pound and the Port of New York, whom he is quoting.) It led Pound to the further comment:

"As to Mr. Coolidge's economic policy, I have one further suggestion—namely, that he can completely eliminate the cost of lunatic asylums by dressing the present inmates in customs uniforms and placing them in ports and along the frontiers. This will dispense with the present employees entirely and the public will be just as well served."

The Exile, No. 2, was published in Chicago, Pascal Covici, publisher. "But for Mr. Covici undertaking to print this second issue, the editors would have desisted." Mr. Covici, that highly respected publisher, had just brought out Pound's *Antheil,* an advertisement of which appears in this issue. There is some more of Rodker's novel, a poem by Ralph Cheever Dunning, poems by Carl Rakosi, a story by Robert McAlmon, and a chapter from Joe Gould's "Oral History," which was chiefly about E. E. Cummings. There is also a "Prolegomena" by Pound which begins: "The drear horror of American life can be traced to two damnable roots, or perhaps it is only one root: 1. The loss of *all* distinction between public and private affairs. 2. The tendency to mess into other peoples' affairs before establishing order in one's own affairs, and in one's thought." More interesting is a page with the over-all title, "Modern Thought." It consists of quotations from Mussolini, Lenin, De Gourmont and McAlmon, and I give them in the order listed:

"We are tired of government in which there is no responsible person having a hind-name, a front name and an address."

"The banking business is declared a state monopoly. The interests of the small depositors will be safeguarded."

"The duty of being is to persevere in its being and even to augment the characteristics which specialize it."

"People are not charming *enough.*"

The last page has a "Notice to Contributors," meaning future and aspiring ones:

"Anybody attempting to contribute to this periodical ought to know at least two languages. If intending collaborators do not already know French, I suggest that they learn it first and submit manuscript after they have."

3.

Meanwhile, in New York, the editors of *The Dial,* to which he had contributed less and less, decided to honor him by its award for 1927, which brought with it two thousand dollars. *The Dial* Awards were not prizes, as there was no competition; they were given for proved merit. The first recipient had been Eliot for *The Waste Land,* 1922; the second Marianne Moore, for her *Observations,* 1924; the third E. E. Cummings, 1925, and the fourth William Carlos Williams, 1926. Miss Moore, managing editor of *The Dial* when the award was offered to Pound, told me (1959): "He was well enough known to have received the first *Dial* award, and it was a concession to accept it. Still, I thought he was quite brusque, and his attitude unbecoming. If you accept anything, why not accept it graciously, instead of grudgingly?"

The Dial for January, 1928, carried the following announcement, written by James Sibley Watson, editor and co-owner:

"The DIAL AWARD for 1927 was recently offered to Mr. Ezra Pound, and we are most happy to announce that he accepted it—with this proviso:

" 'It is impossible for me to accept an award except on Cantos or on my verse as a whole. . . .

" 'It wd. be stupid to make the award on prose-basis as my prose is mostly stop-gap; attempts to deal with transient states of murky imbecility or ignorance.' [In his *Letters,* this phrase is printed, probably correctly, as "Murkn Imbecility."]

"We agree to the provisio without hesitation, indeed we had never any different notion about it. But as people who know more about verse are going to discuss Mr. Pound's in these pages, we should like to draw attention briefly to another service of his to letters which many are aware of and which many seem anxious to forget.

"Writers are the most ungrateful animals. They suck their orange as dry as they are able to, and forever after it disgusts them to have to think about that orange at all. The innumerable little contemptuous paragraphs uttered by the younger (up to 60) Parisian writers when Anatole France drew attention to himself by being buried are an exaggerated example of this disgust.

"One uses a Parisian example because things are always clearest cut in Paris where the writers outside the Academy exhibit the charming unanimity of flying fish. Perhaps the only similarity between Mr. Pound and Anatole France is that they both encouraged new writers. Where Anatole France encouraged mostly bad ones, it can be said that Mr. Pound has never made a mistake."

The number led off with "Part of Canto XXVII," and was followed by Eliot's essay, "Isolated Superiority," a review of *Personae: The Collected Poems of Ezra Pound.* Eliot's tribute began:

"By publishing his 'collected poems'—a collection remarkable because it represents also a rigorous selection and omission—Mr. Pound provokes us to another attempt to estimate his work. I am doubtful whether such a valuation is, or will ever be, quite possible for our generation; but even if not, it is worth while at least to enquire into the nature of our difficulty in criticizing his work.

"Pound has had, and has an immense influence, but no disciples. For the absence of the latter, I think he is to be felicitated."

The money, to Pound, meant help to writers. He wrote Cournos:

"Investment of Dial prize is due to yield about one hundred bucks per annum. The first 100 has already gone, discounted in three lots, one ten guinea s. o. s. earlier this week, and from most unexpected source.

"I think you better regard the enclosed as advance payment for something to be written for Exile, when the skies are clearer. No hurry. What have you on hand unsaleable elsewhere?"

He also told Cournos, who had recently undergone an operation: "Have had four slits made in my own anatomy during last 15 months. Do you want any advice from the experience?"[1]

4.

It was the next issue of *The Exile*—Spring, 1928—which justified Pound's new venture into editing. The first six pages consisted of poems by William Butler Yeats, beginning with "Sailing to Byzantium." Pages 7 to 27 are taken up by Louis Zukofsky's "Poem Beginning 'The' " consisting of dedicatory notes and 330 numbered lines; when Pound reprinted it in his *Active Anthology,* 1933, notes and numbers were omitted.

"I don't suppose anybody dares print this," Zukofsky wrote when he sent the poem, "but if anybody does, it will be you."

Dorothy Pound also read it, for she made an ink drawing of three cats for the Third Movement, subtitled "In Cat Minor"—

> The prowl, our prowl,
> Of gentlemen cats
> With paws like spats—

which Pound forwarded to Zukofsky, who still has it.

The poem contains numerous Pound or Eliot overtones; a quarter of a century later, in St. Elizabeths, Pound read another long poem by Zukofsky and wrote him: "I note that you got OUT of influence of E. P. and Possum/NO longer the trace of linguistic parisitism that I noted with surprise on rereading some early Zuk." I shall have more to say about Zukofsky, in 1928 one of the youngest of *les jeunes,* whom Pound "annexed."

"Part of Canto XXIII" also appeared, with this note: "The opening of this canto is too obscure to be printed apart from the main context of the poem." Rodker's novel, *Adolphe 1920,* is concluded. Dunning has a story, and Pound an article about Dunning. His editorial concludes: "Quite simply: I want a new civilization."

That spring, Pound spent a little of the *Dial* award money on himself. He went to Vienna. As he was passing a café he heard his name shouted. It was Antheil; with him was his wife. Antheil thought there was a moment's hesitation before Pound joined them, and ascribed this to his late excursion into neo-classicism. "Moreover his recent spotty correspondence continued to emphasize that I no longer knew what I was doing."[2] So wrote Antheil in his autobiography; but I venture the guess that Pound had gone to Vienna to hear Antheil's music. Antheil says he assured Pound that he was through with neo-classicism "forever," and the subject was dropped. They became gay; Pound wanted to have fun, and his idea of fun, according to Antheil, was "visiting literary people." Boski said: "Would you like to visit Schnitzler? He's some sort of uncle of mine." Even Antheil had not known this, and he dared her to telephone. She did. They were asked. They went, by streetcar, to a suburb. A maid let them in, saying Herr Schnitzler would be right down.

"He came downstairs looking exactly like the photograph in *Vanity Fair,* a large, warm, roundish face accentuated by a heavy dark beard. He looked vaguely like that eternal photograph of Brahms playing the piano smoking a cigar. He was about sixty-five, was dressed in a skiing sweater, and came down the steps three at a time, swinging his short, stubby self along by grasping the two handrails."[3]

And the meeting between the two famous writers? I find Antheil's account unsatisfactory. He is so eager to be amusing, and it is always difficult to be amusing if eager:

" 'I am a writer too, Herr Schnitzler.'

" 'Ah so?' replied Schnitzler. He was the picture of the older successful writer beaming upon, and offering inspiration to, the younger but yet unsuccessful writer. 'And have you published anything, Mr. Pound?'

" 'Seven or eight books,' Ezra answered."

By the spring of 1928, when this colloquy supposedly took place, Pound had published thirty-five books, if one or two anthologies and translations be included, and among the books was *Antheil and the Treatise on Harmony.*

What other literary lights they saw in Vienna, Antheil does not say. Nor does he describe, this time, what he and Boski had on. Pound was wearing the coat with large square blue buttons. He was still in Vienna in May, when he wrote the famous long letter—in French— to René Taupin, who was at work on *L'Influence du symbolisme français sur la poésie Américaine (de 1910 à 1920)*. Pound answered questions about the Imagists, and offered to read the manuscript before it went to press.

From Vienna he went to Frankfurt, once more probably because of an Antheil concert there; and there, at the Forschungesinstitut für Kulturmorphologie, he called on Leo Frobenius, whom he had long admired.

5.

Cournos, McAlmon, Williams and Zukofsky contributed to the fourth and final number of *The Exile,* Autumn, 1928, published in New York with the imprint of Covici Friede. There are five articles by Pound— in effect, lectures on "root ideas," bureaucracy, Article 211 of the U.S. Penal Code and the city of the future, which appears to forecast throughways, by him termed "speedways." Under "Article 211" he commented: "One has to go on reprinting this, otherwise no one will believe it exists. Legislators made it. Le style c'est l'homme." He had included it in *Instigations*. His letters are full of references to it, and his astonishment and rage over it never diminished. It begins: "Every obscene, lewd or lascivious, and every filthy book, pamphlet, paper, letter, writing, print, or other publication of an indecent character and every article or thing designed, adapted, or intended or preventing conception or producing abortion," etc. It created a censorship at the ports of entry, thus barring important literary and medical works at the whim of a customs underling, who read—as a rule—only the "funnies."

Pound lectured Mencken on it: "Also *you*, confound you, with your columns on asinine legislation ought to dig out Article 211, U.S. Penal Code." And in *The Exile* he wrote:

"If we must have bureaucrats, by all means let us treat them humanely; let us increase their salaries, let us give them comforting pensions; let them be employed making concordances to Hiawatha, or in computing the number of sand-fleas to every mile of beach at Cape May, but under no circumstances allow them to do anything what bloody ever that brings them into contact with the citizen." Again: "The job of America for the next twenty years will be to drive back the government into its proper place, i.e., to force it to occupy itself solely with things which are the proper functions of government." He was translating from the Chinese again, and advised: "The higher bureaucrats should be grounded in the TA HIO and in the analects of Confucius."

Pound's *Ta Hio: The Great Learning*, "Newly Rendered into the American Language," was published this year as one of the University of Washington Chapbooks. He asked Glenn Hughes, the editor, to state in the prospectus, "In this brochure (or chapbook) Mr. Pound does for the first of the Confucian classics what he did, in *Cathay*, for Rihaku," and withdrew his preface. "Most of what I had written wd. merely raise irrelevant issues re state of America, demnd perversion of Constitution, sonsovbitches in office, of collapse of Xtianity, god-damnability of all monotheistic Jew, Mohammed, Xtn. Buncomb, etc."

In London, Wyndham Lewis read with increasing astonishment his old friend's effusions, particularly as represented by *The Exile,* and announced to the world his own view of him and them. It created a sensation. He termed Pound "a genuine naif . . . a sort of revolutionary simpleton!"

The four issues of *The Exile* were distributed in New York by the Gotham Book Mart, a shop specializing in the moderns, particularly Pound, whose portrait adorned the premises. Its proprietor was Frances Steloff, a woman of deep faith and unswerving loyalties.

CHAPTER XVI

POUND AND YEATS IN RAPALLO

1.

To Yeats, Rapallo was "the little town described in the Ode on a Grecian Urn." He was enraptured by its mountains and the bay, the low vines and the tall trees. He had gone there for his health. He wrote Olivia Shakespear from the Albergo Rapallo on February 23, 1928: "George has this very moment started for Switzerland with Michael who is to be left there at school. She returns on Friday week. I remain here in Dorothy's and Ezra's charge. We have made great changes of plans and intend now to take a flat here."

"Ezra and Dorothy," he told her, "seem happy and content, pleased with their way of life, and Dorothy and George compare their experience of infancy and its strange behaviour—George instructing Dorothy out of her greater store." His wife was overjoyed to see her "cousin" again: "If we carry out our plans and settle here they will renew all their old friendship and to George at any rate that will be a great happiness."

He wrote Lady Gregory the next day: "Ezra Pound has been helping me to punctuate my new poems, and thinks the best of all is a little song I wrote at Cannes just before I was ordered to stop work." He spoke of Rapallo as "an incredibly lovely place—some little Greek town one imagines—there is a passage in Keats describing just such a town. Here I shall put off the bitterness of Irish quarrels."

In the morning he walked by the sea—where Aldington saw him

from his hotel window which overlooked the esplanade; in the afternoon he took to his bed, and in the evening visited with the Pounds, "from 7 to 9 or 10." Sometimes Pound accompanied him on walks at night through Rapallo's narrow streets. By April he was able to work again, giving last touches to *A Vision* and at the same time composing an essay about his contemporaries, chiefly Pound, with a poem by Cavalcanti as text. He told Lady Gregory:

"Have you read Wyndham Lewis? He attacked Ezra Pound and Joyce in *Time and Western Man,* and is on my side of things philosophically. My essay takes up the controversy and explains Ezra Pound sufficiently to keep him as a friendly neighbor, for I foresee that in the winter he must take Russell's place of a Monday evening."

Yeats destroyed the essay because it seemed to him unclear and unreadable; it was to have formed part of *A Packet for Ezra Pound,* with which later editions of *A Vision* opens. His private view of Pound appears in the letter to Lady Gregory:

"He has most of Maud Gonne's opinions (political and economic) about the world in general, being what Lewis calls 'the revolutionary simpleton.' The chief difference is that he hates Palgrave's *Golden Treasury* as she does the Free State Government, and thinks even worse of its editor than she does of President Cosgrave. He has even her passion for cats and large numbers wait him every night at a certain street corner knowing that his pocket is full of meat bones or chicken bones."

"I remember almost the last time I met Yeats," Sir Osbert Sitwell wrote, "I mentioned that I had seen Pound in Italy, and he remarked, 'Anyone *must* like Ezra, who has seen him feeding the stray cats at Rapallo.' "[1]

In *A Packet for Ezra Pound* Yeats described the ritual of the cats: "Sometimes about ten o'clock at night I accompany him to a street where there are hotels upon one side, upon the other palm-trees and the sea, and there, taking out of his pocket bones and pieces of meat, he begins to call the cats. He knows all their histories—the brindled cat looked like a skeleton until he began to feed it; that fat gray cat is an hotel proprietor's favourite, it never begs from the guests' tables and it turns cats that do not belong to the hotel out of the garden; this black cat and that grey cat over there fought on the roof of a four-storied house some weeks ago, fell off, a whirling ball of claws and fur, and now avoid each other."

Back in his own rooms in the Albergo Rapallo, Yeats pondered the scene he was setting down on paper. It was not enough that he had seen the nightly ritual of kindness; there was a hidden significance for which he probed. And then he wrote: "Yet now that I recall the scene I think that he has no affection for cats—'some of them so ungrateful,' a friend says—he never nurses the café's cat, I cannot imagine him with a cat of his own." How, then, was the ritual to be explained? "Cats are oppressed, dogs terrify them, landladies starve them, boys stone them, everybody speaks of them with contempt. If they were human beings we could talk of their oppressors with a studied violence, add our strength to theirs, even organise the oppressed and like good politicians sell our charity for power." The parallel with Maud Gonne occurs again:

"I examine his criticism in this new light, his praise of writers pursued by ill-luck, left maimed or bedridden by the War; and thereupon recall a person as unlike him as possible, the only friend who remains to me from late boyhood, grown gaunt in the injustice of what seems her blind nobility of pity: 'I will fight until I die,' she wrote to me once, 'against the cruelty of small ambitions.' "

2.

In November of 1928 Yeats and his wife settled in Rapallo, No. 12 Via Americhe, eight flights up. On the 23d he wrote to Olivia Shakespear:

"The furniture arrived this morning and George is at the flat settling things in order. We move in next Tuesday and have tried to persuade the Pounds to join us in a vigorous house-warming but Dorothy seems to classify champagne with steak and onions and badger's flesh, and other forms of tinsel of this world. I write each morning and am well, much better than I ever am at home and am already sunburnt. I am finishing a little book for Cuala to be called either *A Packet* or *A Packet for Ezra Pound*. It contains first a covering letter to Ezra saying that I offer him the contents, urging him not to be elected to the Senate of his country and telling him why. Then comes a long essay already finished, the introduction to the new edition of *A Vision* and telling all about its origin, and then I shall wind up with a description of Ezra feeding the cats ('some of them are so ungrateful' T. S. Eliot says), of Rapallo and Ezra's poetry—some of which I greatly admire, indeed his collected edition is a great excitement to me."

Writing on the same day, Pound told Marianne Moore that Yeats "is now reading my august works, for whatever ultimate benefit the world may derive from that phenomenon."

"United by affection" though they were, Yeats was puzzled by Pound, and he expressed it from time to time, in letters to Lady Gregory and others, though not to Mrs. Shakespear. He expressed it in conversation with Richard Aldington who, in the winter of 1928, was in Rapallo, where Pound entertained him at his tennis club. Pound wrote to Harriet Monroe in December: "Aldington seems to have awakened from his slumbers. I may be sending you something of his, before long." Aldington says Pound was "his usual genial and modest self." His hotel window had a view of the esplanade, and he could see Yeats "taking his daily constitutional." Yeats wrote Mrs. Shakespear: "If one had not to take exercise life would be perfect, but 3.30 when I must go out for mine has just come—at 4.30 it will be the chill of evening."

Aldington invited Yeats and his wife to dinner at his hotel. Upon learning who his guests were to be, the hotel manager provided a private room—"I fear," Aldington wrote, "because Yeats was an Irish senator, but I hope because he was a great poet." Yeats, having lost his gloves, arrived with his hands thrust into gray woollen socks. Over the spaghetti, Yeats suddenly asked:

"How do you account for Ezra?"

There was a pause.

"Here is a man," Yeats continued, "who produces the most distinguished work and yet in his behaviour is the least distinguished of men. It is the antithetical self."

Aldington confesses he did not see the antithesis.

"In his work," he wrote, "Ezra can be abrupt and barbarous; when he wants he can be a pleasant companion and the most generous of men. He is sensitive, highly strung, and irascible. All this throwing down of fire-irons and sputtering of four-letter words is merely Ezra's form of defence against a none too considerate world. I should say

Ezra has had to put up with far worse annoyances from other people than they ever have from him."[2]

Aldington noted another arrival, when "for a day Ezra vanished. Meeting him after lunch next day I asked where he had been, and he answered importantly that he had been 'in conference' with Antheil."[3]

"When I got there," Antheil wrote, "I saw that although Ezra and I had made up in Vienna, he was no longer as cordial as in the early days."[4]

The thread of Antheil's sojourn in Rapallo reappears in Yeats's letters, which probably means that Pound was friendly enough, for he introduced them. Yeats wrote Mrs. Shakespear on March 2, 1929:

"To-night we dine with Ezra—the first dinner-coated meal since I got here—to meet Hauptmann who does not know a word of English but is fine to look at—after the fashion of William Morris. Auntille— how do you spell him?—and his lady will be there and probably a certain Basil Bunting, one of Ezra's more savage disciples."

Antheil wrote: "Ezra now introduced me to a number of persons who habitually sat at the only free table of Rapallo's only decent restaurant, the Hotel Rapallo Café. Two of them were Nobel Prize winners, William Butler Yeats and Gerhart Hauptmann."[5] Two other habitués of the table were Franz Werfel and Emil Ludwig.

In the same letter to Mrs. Shakespear "Auntille" becomes "Antille," but by the next mention of it Yeats is spelling it correctly, probably because Antheil was now writing the music for *Fighting the Waves*. "If he persists, and he is at present enthusiastic, it means a performance in Vienna in the autumn. He has a great name there since his setting of Oedipus a few months ago." Yeats attempted to describe him for Lady Gregory: "He is about 28 and looks 18 and has a face of indescribable innocence." Antheil's music for Yeats's play appears in *Wheels and Butterflies*. The play was produced at the Abbey, together with Shaw's *The Apple Cart*.

3.

Yeats wrote to Lady Gregory:

"I see Ezra daily. We disagree about everything, but if we have not met for 24 hours he calls full of gloomy and almost dumb oppression."

They did not always discuss poetry. In *A Packet for Ezra Pound* Yeats termed Pound's art "the opposite of mine," while his criticism "commends what I most condemn." He was "a man with whom I should quarrel more than with anyone else if we were not united by affection." But they were in agreement on other matters. Yeats wrote T. Sturge Moore in April, 1929:

"Ezra Pound has just been in. He says 'Spengler is a Wells who has founded himself on German scholarship instead of English journalism.' He is sunk in Frobenius, Spengler's German source, and finds him a most interesting person. For Frobenius suggested the idea that cultures (including arts and sciences) arise out of races, express those races as if they were fruit and leaves in a preordained order and perish with them." (Douglas C. Fox, Frobenius's assistant, told me this was an excellent summary.)

As for himself, Frobenius "has confirmed a conception I have had for years, a conception that has freed me from British Liberalism and all its dreams."

On the terrace overlooking the sea Yeats asked and Pound answered questions about the *Cantos*. He wrote in *A Packet for Ezra Pound*:

"For the last hour we have sat upon the roof which is also a garden, discussing that immense poem of which but seven and twenty cantos are already published. I have often found there brightly painted kings, queens, knaves, but have never discovered why all the suits could not be dealt out in some quite different order. Now at last he explains that it will, when the hundredth canto is finished, display a structure like that of a Bach Fugue. There will be no plot, no chronicle of events, no logic of discourse, but two themes, the Descent into Hades from Homer, a Metamorphosis from Ovid, and mixed with these, mediaeval or modern historical characters."

Yeats found the explanation difficult to follow, and Pound took an envelope from his pocket and scribbled "certain sets of letters that represent emotions or archetypal events—I cannot find any adequate definition—A B C D and then J K L M, and then each set of letters repeated, and then a new element X Y Z, then certain letters that never recur, and then all sorts of combinations of X Y Z and J K L M and A B C D and D C B A, and all set whirling together." It was still not clear and they went inside, where Pound pointed to a photograph on the wall. It was a mural by Cosimo Tura, "in three compartments, in the upper the Triumph of Love and the Triumph of Chastity, in the middle Zodiacal signs, and in the lower certain events in Cosimo Tura's day [the fifteenth century]. The Descent and the Metamorphosis—A B C D and J K L M—his fixed elements, took the place of the Zodiac, the archetypal persons—X Y Z—that of the Triumphs, and certain modern events—his letters that do not recur—that of those events in Cosimo Tura's day."

Pound also explained the poem by means of alphabetical combinations in a letter to his father:

"A. A.   Live man goes down into world of Dead
"C. B.   The 'repeat in history'
"B. C.   The 'magic moment' or moment of metamorphosis, bust thru from quotidien into 'divine or permanent world.' Gods, etc."

Homer Pound was also puzzled.

Meanwhile, Pound continued his correspondence course with old and new correspondents; to one of the latter he sent a circular entitled "Program 1929," *viz.:*

"1. Government for utility only.

"2. Article 211 of the Penal Code to be amended by the 12 words: *This statute does not apply to works of literary and scientific merit.*

"3. Vestal's bill or some other decent and civilized copyright act to be passed. Footnote: instead *everybody's* going to New York, ten or a dozen bright lads ought to look in on the national capital. We need several novels in the vein of Hemingway's *The Torrents of Spring* dealing not with helpless rural morons but with 'our rulers.' "

He sent the scorching letter to the alumni secretary of the University of Pennsylvania, given earlier. He wrote the State Department protesting against the absence of addresses on consular stationery. In December he wrote to Williams: "Since my progenitors cum over here, I don't see any god damn American magazines cos nobody sends 'em. *And* I shd. like to see the advertisement of one of those latest smallest lightest printing presses again."

Pound's parents eventually took over the Yeats flat in the Via Americhe. Sir Max Beerbohm, who had met Pound several times in Rapallo, without knowing that he had written a poem about him, also met his parents. He told S. N. Behrman: "He idolized them, and they idolized him."

4.

There are only four letters in Pound's published correspondence for the year 1930. He wrote to Cummings in March, and then there is a gap until October, when he wrote to Harriet Monroe. But he was still in Rapallo in April, when Yeats wrote Lady Gregory from the Via Americhe:

"Ezra Pound arrived the other day, his first visit since I got ill— fear of infection—and being warned by his wife tried to be very peaceable but couldn't help being very litigious about Confucius who I consider should have worn an Eighteenth Century wig and preached in St. Paul's, and he thinks the perfect man."

Earlier, Yeats had written Olivia Shakespear:

"To-day I met Ezra for the first time—you know his dread of infections—seeing me in the open air and the sea air, he sat beside me in front of the café and admired my beard, and declared I should be sent by the Free State as Minister to Austria, that Austria would alone perfectly appreciate my beard." Yeats added: "Certainly I need a new career for I cannot recognize myself in the mirror."

By June 1st, when Yeats wrote to Mrs. Shakespear again, the Pounds had left Rapallo, had been to London, and were in Paris. Yeats wrote, "My dear Olivia: The children are here and are—now that Dorothy and Ezra are gone—our only event." He related in detail the doings and sayings of Anne and Michael, in a letter full of an elderly father's delight, and added: "What a lot Dorothy is missing by leaving Omar in London!"

In Paris, the Pounds had dinner with Ford. Willard R. Trask, Ford's literary secretary, and Trask's wife were living with Ford in a big apartment at 32 rue de Vaugirard; it was just before Ford's final marriage to the young American painter, Janice Biala. It was an informal household, with a *femme de ménage* who cooked the midday meal, while dinners were served up either by Ford or the Trasks, all three being good cooks. The night the Pounds were to come Ford was very excited; Mary Trask[6] told me he did not react like this with other guests.

"Pound is coming," Ford kept repeating.

The Trasks had not met Pound before. Mrs. Trask described him as "a very large man, very American, talking like an American, somewhat pompous, with red hair and red beard." She said of Mrs. Pound: "She was very fair, with blue eyes, the most unadorned looking woman I've ever seen—no lipstick, no make-up, hair merely drawn back, and absolutely beautiful, beautiful with authentic beauty." The Pounds, sitting side by side on the sofa, "looked devoted."

Ford said before they came that Pound had told him once that Dorothy was the only woman he had ever met who could say *anything,* and it "would be all right, she was such a lady."

Ford's reception by Pound, two years later, was a less agreeable event.

That August saw the publication in Paris, at the Hours Press, of *A Draft of XXX Cantos,* in an edition of 212 copies. There were two copies on vellum, not for sale.

CHAPTER XVII

POUND AND *LES JEUNES*

1.

While some of his contemporaries achieved a kind of stable fame or a particular niche, and others sank into obscurity, Pound continued to occupy a unique position, never wholly forgotten, and for the young a perennial new discovery. It was as though time could do nothing to him. The young hardly bothered to find out how many years he had held such sway. They wrote to him eagerly, and read his replies greedily; they kept in touch with one another because he advised them to do so; and together they read and discussed his poetry and pronouncements. His criticism ranged from a single word to entire essays, accompanied by letters of advice and encouragement to those he thought worthy, and there were separate letters to others to lend them a hand either with money or by publication. He also dipped into his own purse. This concern for them gave him an enormous hold over the young who were poets, or intellectuals, or both. Above all, perhaps, he was their teacher. He had not only discovered and explored new areas of literature; he took the trouble to show them *How to Read,* in the book of that title, published in 1931. It became their Bible.

There was living, at this time, in New York City—Harlem, to be precise—the young man who had sent him "Poem Beginning 'The.'" "Wafer-thin," said Michael Arlen of one of his characters; pencil-thin might be said of Louis Zukofsky, an intellectual poet with a whispering voice, the antithesis of the hearty romantic variety, sharing with his friend Williams a horror, or cold rage, about that ilk. Zukofsky also knew the composer Tibor Serly, and had recently met Basil Bunting, now residing in New York. For Pound never left anything to chance; having become interested in Zukofsky, he not only wrote to him, but sent him introductions, and even told visitors to the United States to look him up. One such visitor was Lauro de Bosis, a young Italian poet, author of a poem about Icarus. One day, Zukofsky received an invitation from the Italy America Society and the Casa Italiana of Columbia University to a concert of early Italian music. On the invitation was the following note:

"Dear Mr. Zukofsky

"3 months ago, before coming to America, my dear friend Ezra Pound told me that you were the only intelligent man in America. Do come—I must know you. Or ring me up (Cathedral 0935) and come to lunch with me.

"Yours sincerely
"L. de Bosis"

De Bosis returned to Italy. He flew over Rome in a rented plane, dropping anti-fascist leaflets. His plane was swept from the sky by Fascist planes and pursued out to sea. He was never seen again.

2.

Zukofsky had appeared as a poet in the third number of *The Exile*, and as a critic of poetry in the fourth and last. He was now at work on a study of Pound's *Cantos*—the first, he told me, ever attempted. It pleased Pound:

"Dear Z.

"THE irony is that the Dial tried for ten years to boost the idea that criticism wuz a serious operation related to writing. Also Eliot once intented the Criterion for a critical review. What I propose to do is to have yr. article on me translated into french and if poss. wangle it into the Mercure.

"Fer various reezuns.

"1. No decent crit. of me in french.

"2. ten years too soon to print the thing in England or America. So far as I know no one else has writ. a crit of me AFTER reading the work. This method has advantages. Also so far as I know you are the first writer to credit me with an occasional gleam of intelligence or to postulate the bounds or possibility of an underlying coherence."[1]

But when Zukofsky complained that he preferred poetry to criticism, even his own, Pound agreed—with certain reservations:

"Am cheered to know you don't like writing cri'zism. That's as it shd. be. However its up to blokes like us to do it. The inspired lunatics can't. There are very few inspired lunatics.

"It is also up to us to kill off the sonzabitchzzs that LIKE to write it (crizism).

"How much pleasanter it wd. be on the bright Oct. p.m. to be writing 3 pages of Canto."

Above all there was the problem of making a living. It was solved, temporarily, when Zukofsky accepted a teaching post in the University of Wisconsin, which led Homer Pound to recommend a trip to Chippewa Falls to look up some of his old friends. Pound himself wrote:

"Dear Z

"As you are in a ninstitoot of learning so called cd. you by any stretch of imagination go to the Dept. of Economics (or history or whatever) and try to find out if the more enlightened members of same THINK there is anyone in the U.S. now writing, who knows his arse from a bung hole or any other rudimentary etc . . . about economics, or government, OR the constitution of the U.S.A. or legal principle."

He added: "Of course NORMAL professors will regard themselves as (and of a right orter be) ignorant of EVERYthing not included in some course of the curry/ticlem."

And Homer Pound wrote when the essay appeared:

"Am very much pleased with your essay on his Cantos. . . . let me say that yours is about the most understanding of them all and you seem to have 'met the enemy and he is yours'. . . . . E. P. seemed pleased. I wish I could read the one you have in French but alas I have no language except the English."

3.

Zukofsky was not happy as a teacher, either. He gave up his teaching job and returned to New York. He evolved, with his friends, the theory of Objectivist poetry. Williams explained it thus: "The poem, like every other form of art, is an object, an object that in itself formally presents its case and its meaning by the very form it assumes. Therefore, being an object, it should be so treated and controlled— but not as in the past. For past objects have about them past necessities—like the sonnet—which have conditioned them and from which, as a form itself, they cannot be freed."[1] The Objectivists admired Dante and Pound, and hardly anyone else, unless it was each other. Shakespeare's poetry was "too explanatory and verbose," Zukofsky told an interviewer, Whitman was "modern though without culture or learning."

Pound persuaded Miss Monroe to let Zukofsky edit an Objectivist issue of *Poetry*. Later, there was an Objectivist Press—Pound, Zukofsky and Williams its advisory board. It published a few books before folding; one of them was Williams's *Collected Poems*. "The suggestion to collect my poems was a lovely gesture from my own gang and I was deeply moved by it. Louis Zukofsky did most of the work of making the collection."[3] Wallace Stevens wrote the introduction. There was also an *Objectivist Anthology*, edited by Zukofsky and dedicated to Pound "still for the poets of our time the most important."

Acceptances, encouraging letters, introductions were all very well. But what Zukofsky wanted above all else was a chance to get to Europe and meet Pound. He applied for a Guggenheim Fellowship. He was backed by Pound, of course; and Pound got Harriet Monroe and Eliot to back him, too. (Eliot wrote Pound: "I agree he is a man of parts, and I shall have more pleasure in recommending him than anyone yet—by the way, I don't think anyone I have sponsored has got in yet.") Zukofsky did not get in, either. When Pound learned of it, he exploded. The first part of his letter to Zukofsky is unquotable, except for two sentences:

"I saw their punk list (prob. not complete) in Paris Herald."

"The rejection will probably improve your style."

On the second page he wrote:

"I shd. be glad to see you but can't pay yr/ boat fare. Been short of cash for three years: due to bein such a godd damn fool as to try to do a decent job over the Cavalcanti.

"Am in very bad temper and see no likelihood of anything occurring that will alter that state of things.

"On the whole, nothing to be done but to write a li'l good poetry from time to time.

"The period during which capitalist syfilization cd. cooperate in the ahts is evidently sinkin' to its last pozzo nero."

But Pound was nothing if not logical. If he believed this about America, could he in conscience leave a promising poet, one with brains to boot, in that doomed land? On November 22, 1931, he wrote Zukofsky:

"Damn it all, how badly do you want to get to Europe, if AT all? And what is the extreme limit of degradation to which you wd. submit, in the way of menial servitude etc. . . . ? ?"

And on the same day, to Williams:

"*If* in yr. judgement he ought to have a breathing spell, can we in any way manage it? Has he *any* resources (fiscal)?"

Pound was himself short of cash. The fifty pounds just received from the B.B.C. for *Villon* "were useful," he told Zukofsky, "though not [enough] to wipe out all indebtedness." In the same letter: "I can't employ you at an eating wage. Z' a mystery how I bloody live ennyhow. Mebby on imagination." But Zukofsky continued to occupy his thoughts. He was now addressing him as "Filius delectus mihi" and kept him posted about himself:

"Merejkowsky, Stefan Zweig, Pirandello, yours very truly and some lesser lights are asked to orate at the gran/ Fiera del Libro in Firenze this month, representin' internashunal licherchoor. . . . Me first offishul honours."

"Had amiable jaw with Marinetti in Rome and have come bak

loaded with futurist and fascist licherchoor: most of the futurist stuff
dated before 1924."

And he sent a picture postcard of himself. He is standing with
the critic and editor Gino Saviotti on the waterfront near the Albergo Rapallo, dressed in a light jacket and white flannel slacks
and white shoes. There is a cane in his right hand, in his left a
white straw hat which he apparently has just doffed for the photographer. Saviotti has dispensed with hat and jacket. He has on a
white shirt open at the collar and light slacks, right hand pocketed,
in his left a cane. Behind them is the glitter of the sea.

Meanwhile another young poet, Robert Fitzgerald, wrote to Pound.
He was in Switzerland; could he call? In the apartment on the Via
Marsala he felt that "the bearded and cat-eyed man had about him
the hero light of the Irish." Pound showed him his copy of *Ulysses*,
with a long inscription, and a letter in which there was a snapshot
of a tanned Hemingway grinning beside a shark he had caught in
the waters off Cuba. He remarked that in that very room he had
taught Yeats to fence. Fitzgerald was impressed by Pound's work-
room, where he had "an active filing system"—cords strung overhead
from which dangled envelopes and sheafs of manuscript.

In the afternoon they walked on the *lungomare*. Pound had on a
cape and wide-brimmed hat, which he doffed cavalier style to other
promenaders. They had dinner at the Albergo Rapallo. Fitzgerald
found Pound less positive in talk than in his writing. Of their conversation he remembered three things. Pound showed him a trecento
or quattrocento seal, and said: "Here was a culture that got into every
detail of life."

"Later on, I suppose in answer to some remark, he said in a
troubled and reluctant way, as if to himself and as if it were an admission, 'I live in music for days at a time.' He did not mean the word-
less music of the composers—Vivaldi, Antheil—who then interested
him, but the music within himself, a visionary music requiring words.
I knew that this applied to the Cantos."

The remark troubled Fitzgerald. "His tone when he said that he
lived in music might have warned me that in that beautiful intelligence all was not going well." He was also troubled by a suggestion
that he—Fitzgerald—should write a review of Pound's *Cavalcanti*
for the *Criterion* or the *New English Weekly*. "My position was that
one did not interest oneself in reviews of one's work."[4]

Pound's *Guido Cavalcanti: Rime* was published in Genoa, Edizioni Marsano, "Anno IX" (1931). He had done the "decent job" he set out to do—more, he had achieved masterpieces of translation. The following is from Cavalcanti's "Canzone," which does not appear in the earlier *Sonnets and Ballate:*

> *Immaginar nol puo hom che nol prova*
> > *E non si mova*
> > > *perch' a llui si tirj*
> *E non si aggirj*
> > > *per trovarvi giocho*
> *E certamente gran saver nè pocho:*
>
> *Da ssimil tragge*
> > > *complessione e sghuardj*
> > *Che fà parere*
> > > *lo piacere*
> > > > *piu certo*

> None can imagine love
> > > that knows not love;
> Love doth not move, but draweth all to him;
> Nor doth he turn
> > > for a whim
> > > > to find delight
> Nor to seek out, surely,
> > > > great knowledge or slight.

> Look drawn from like,
> > delight maketh certain in seeming

4.

Ford came. It was August, 1932. They talked. Olga Rudge was present. The talk appeared in *Il Mare;* later, she translated it. As Pound has included it in *Pavannes and Divagations,* it is probably his work. He—or Miss Rudge—termed Ford "grandfather of con-

temporary English literature." She—or Pound on her behalf—
added: "We were present when his friend Pound attacked him, ver-
bally." To judge by the printed text of the conversation, Pound had
something to do with the editing, certainly as regards the words in
parenthesis:

"*Pound:* What authors should a young Italian writer read if he
wants to learn how to write novels?

"*Ford:* (Spitting vigorously) Better to think about finding himself a subject.

"*Pound:* (Suavely, ignoring Ford's irritation) Well, suppose he
has already had the intelligence to read Stendhal and Flaubert?

"*Ford:* A different curriculum is needed for each talent. One can
learn from Flaubert and from Miss Braddon. In a certain way one
can learn as much from a rotten writer as from a great one.

"*Pound:* Which of your books would you like to see translated
into Italian and in what order?

"*Ford:* I don't trust translations; they would leave nothing of my
best qualities. Some writers are translatable.

"*Pound:* What are the most important qualities in a prose writer?

"*Ford:* What does 'prose writer' mean? The Napoleonic Code
or the Canticle of Canticles?

"*Pound:* Let us say a novelist.

"*Ford:* (In agony) Oh Hell! Say philosophical grounding, a
knowledge of words' roots, of the meaning of words.

"*Pound:* What should a young prose writer do first?

"*Ford:* (More and more annoyed at the inquisition) Brush his
teeth.

"*Pound:* (Ironically calm, with serene magniloquence) In the
vast critical output of the illustrious critic now being interviewed
(changing tone) . . . You have praised writer after writer with no
apparent distinction (stressing the word 'apparent' nearly with
rage). Is there any?

"*Ford:* There are authentic writers and imitation writers; there
is no difference among the authentic ones. There is no difference
between Picasso and El Greco.

"*Pound:* Don't get away from me into painting. Stick to literary
examples."

And so forth. Perhaps Ford could not read Italian; perhaps he
never saw it. They were photographed together.

5.

In the fall of 1932 Pound sent Zukofsky passage money—a check for $112 drawn on the Jenkintown Bank & Trust Company, of Jenkintown, Pennsylvania. It was in this bank that, long before, Homer Pound had deposited a sum on which his son could draw without explanation, provided each withdrawal was under one hundred dollars. Some of the checks must have resembled the famous figures of a famous soap. Zukofsky did not use the check Pound sent; the following year he accepted a smaller sum, for Williams and Serly also chipped in. He nevertheless was reluctant to part with so unique a souvenir, or 'association item," in booksellers' parlance, and told Pound who wrote back:

"I imagine if you wish to give free rein to sentiment and 'frame it' that honour and saftey wd. be both sa'sfied by cutting a long V into the right hand end (eliminating the series number and the figures of the amount; but conserving date and signature and the written sum). You cd. return the V. to me."

Here, Pound made a drawing of a check, indicating the two places where the deletions could be scissored.

Zukofsky, who had been deeply touched by Pound's generous gesture, wrote a poem about it and sent it to Pound, who replied: "Your incomprehensible pome will be in the next number [of *Il Mare*]. You will snort at my adjective. What indeed is comprehensible. Basil's latin is poss. more so."

Basil Bunting was now living in Rapallo. Zukofsky's poem, Bunting's Latin version of it, duly appeared. I give the opening lines of each:

in that this happening	quia id quod accidit
is not unkind	non est immitis
it put to	pudebat omnia
shame every kindness. . . .	mitiora. . . .

There is no pleasure unalloyed. Zukofsky's name appeared minus the "s."

Full of good will where the young were concerned, Pound's mood could change in a trice. There was January lightning.

William Rose Benét, having conceived the idea of an anthology in which the poets themselves could choose what they thought their best poem, with comments, wrote Pound asking him to contribute; Pound refused. Benét, thinking that the fee he had offered was insufficient, cabled that he would raise it. Pound replied, January 23, 1933, from Rapallo:

"Dear Mr. Benét: I appreciate your kindness in cabling but I am afraid I shall have to be even more explicit in my answer.

"I think you have done too much harm, as asst. edtr. of the *Sat. Rev. Lit.*, from year to year pouring poison into or onto the enfeebled or adolescent Amurkin mind; or at any rate doing yr. and Canby's damndest to preserve mildew." [Henry Seidel Canby was the editor of the *Saturday Review of Literature,* as it was then called.]

The letter concluded:

"The foetor of the *Sat. Rev.'s* critical effort to uphold the almost-good and the not-quite-dead and the fear of facing the demands made in my *How to Read!!*

"How the deuce do you expect me to swallow all that for the sake of a small sum of money?"

6.

"Anno IX."

Writing to friends in England and the United States, Pound had begun to date his letters as well as his books Fascist style, from the "March on Rome," 1922. There were also mottoes on the letterheads—now adorned with the Gaudier-Brzeska portrait—some of his own phrasing, one by Mussolini:

"A tax is not a share."

"A nation need not and should not pay rent for its own credit."

"Liberty is a duty not a right."

He met Mussolini in 1933 for the first and—it is believed—only time. It was in the Mappo Mundo room of the Palazzo Venezia in Rome, the big room with the desk at the far end behind which Il Duce watched his visitors approach. On the desk lay a copy of *A Draft of XXX Cantos,* perhaps one of the two copies printed on vellum by the Hours Press. Pound was naturally delighted when

Mussolini pointed to the handsome volume. He was even more delighted when Mussolini remarked: "But this is amusing." It is recorded in the opening of Canto XLI:

> "MA QVESTO,"
>   said the Boss, "é divertente."
> catching the point before the aesthetes had got there. . . .

It is unusual for Pound to begin a canto with capitals; here they
are Roman and imperial, hence the "v" instead of a "u." It is a
pretty compliment, dated "XI of our era." Mussolini is mentioned
in half a dozen cantos. Fletcher was of the opinion that Pound admired the Italian leader because he was a go-getter and success.
He was "the Boss."

Not much more is known about their meeting. Some Italian writers
think that Pound proposed the planting of Brazil nuts to improve
the lot of the natives; Mussolini, they say, listened, frowned, and
then a functionary, appearing with precision, put an end to the
interview. It did not put an end to Pound's admiration. In April that
year there appeared in England a book entitled *Ezra Pound's ABC
of Economics* (a title which brings Cowley's observation to mind:
"he was always finding the lowdown, the inside story and the simple
reason why"). A postscript to the book is signed *"E. P. Feb.* 12, *anno
XI dell' era Fascista"*—that is, Lincoln's birthday, in the eleventh
year of the Fascist era, 1933, a concatenation which very few besides
Pound found pleasure in. The text is an attempt to interest the lay
reader in the Social Credit program of Major C. H. Douglas, and
Pound's impatience with those who cannot see it his way breaks
through everywhere:

"There are four elements; and it is useless trying to function
with three:

"1. The product.

"2. The want.

"3. The means of transport.

"4. AND the certificates of value, preferably legal tender and
'general,' in the sense that they should be good for wheat, iron,
lumber, dress goods, or whatever the heart and stomach desire. . . ."

It could have been a summary of any monetary system in the

world, if one had sufficient knowledge of money to fill in the woolly spaces. It might even be a description of the program which the Technocrats had for the United States in the same period. Money was very hard to get hold of in 1933, and had been hard to get hold of for several years; and everyone who pondered the subject came up with a printing press. "AND the certificate of value, preferably legal tender." More interesting, in the light of subsequent events, was Pound's conclusion:

"The brains of the nation or group to be used in discerning WHAT work is most useful, what work is less necessary and what is desirable even though not strictly necessary."

Perhaps it was all clear in his own mind; but I am not alone in failing to comprehend what was intended, apart from Fascism or a similar authoritarian order. This is an observation, not a stricture. Pound's involvement with economics was due to his concern for people, for the ordinary man struggling against economic odds, a fact which I hope this book will help to make clear.

7.

Zukofsky went abroad in June, 1933. He was met at Cherbourg by René Taupin. In Paris he stayed at the Hotel Périgord, near the Bibliothèque Nationale, where Pound himself had often stayed. He called on the sculptor Brancusi and the painters Léger and Masson —at Pound's suggestion. From Paris he went to Budapest to join Tibor Serly. A reporter for *Pesti Napló* interviewed him in a coffeehouse on the Danube waterfront. The photograph that appears with the interview shows a long, narrow, earnest face, brown eyes peering intently from behind horn-rimmed glasses, thick, dark brown hair parted on the left side. He was twenty-eight years old. The interviewer noted that he spoke "in a quiet almost whispering tone." Basil Bunting, in a red jacket, met him in Genoa to escort him to Rapallo. They arrived in time for lunch, which they had with Pound and his wife at the Albergo Rapallo. Pound, Zukofsky said, was very paternal. He chided Zukofsky about a recent essay. "Perhaps three people understood your Henry Adams, but only two will understand your Apollinaire. How do you expect to live?" Pound, Zukofsky told me, didn't care for Apollinaire anyway, saying Joyce and Williams had done his sort of thing earlier.

Zukofsky was quartered with Homer and Isabel Pound in Yeats's old apartment on the Via Americhe, where a whole gallery of photographs of Ezra, from childhood on, vied with Yeats's Blakes for attention; included in the gallery were photographs of Omar Pound who was being brought up in England. Zukofsky thought Pound's mother aristocratic in appearance and carriage. "She held herself like Queen Mary." He was given a room which had its own bathroom. "The rooms were enormous," he told me. "I was lost in mine." He was supposed to take his meals with the Buntings, for which Pound paid, but sometimes, when he tried to slip out to have breakfast by himself, Homer Pound, towering above him, would bar the exit.

"In Idaho," he would say, "if anyone tried to refuse hospitality —."

He left the sentence unfinished. But it sufficed. Zukofsky usually breakfasted with Homer and Isabel Pound.

Ezra he saw in his own apartment. "He was extremely nice to me." Every day, whether they had seen each other previously or not, Zukofsky went to tea on the Via Marsala, accompanied by Bunting. The teas lasted for hours; Pound, apparently, loved Italian pastries and consumed them with relish and ardor. The only other person present, as a rule, was Dorothy Pound. "She was beautiful, just sitting there like a beautiful ornament, silent most of the time."

One day, Zukofsky said to Pound: "I'd like to hear you read." Pound took up the volume of *Cantos* and turned to XXX. "It needs voice," he said, "you have to have the voice for it." He swaddled the words with breath, breathing heavily between words. Zukofsky read it back to him, "very quietly and clearly" in his whispering voice. He thought Mrs. Pound liked the way he read it.

Pound's study, Zukofsky said, contained very few books, chiefly James and the classics. "I had the feeling the old books there were the books he had listed in *How to Read*—Divus's *Odyssey,* Golding's *Metamorphoses,* Gavin Douglas's *Aeneid.*" Pound's desk was near a window, really a French door, leading to the terrace, and there was a club chair, for visitors, beside it. The chair he sat in was a swivel chair—at least Zukofsky recalls he was "always swiveling." The Dolmetsch clavichord was there, too; Zukofsky asked him to play,

and Pound without a moment's hesitation sat down and played—
"very fluidly."

Once he accompanied Pound "up the hill towards Santa Mar-
gharita," to hear some Pergolese sung by a singer of Pound's acquaintance. On the way back, Pound expatiated on the superiority
of Pergolese over Wagner, and began to imitate Wagner with
groans and grunts, whistles and catcalls, amid much gesturing and
cavorting.

Sometimes, when Zukofsky went sailing with Bunting, they would
see Pound far out, rowing strenuously seaward on a *pontone,* a raft
consisting of two pontoons and a board for seat. He liked to swim by
himself. This was in July; in August, Serly arrived from Budapest,
bringing the interview.

8.

The interview was headed "Louis Zukofsky: American Vanguard
Poet." Perhaps he had already told Pound about it, perhaps Serly
brought the subject up. Pound was intrigued. He sat down at his
typewriter and typed the interview while Serly translated and Zukofsky listened. What follows is from Pound's own typescript, made
that August day in Rapallo, question and answer in dialogue form,
with some inessential phrases omitted. The reporter asked Zukofsky:

"How do you like Europe? Don't misunderstand me, I don't mean
as a tourist but as a poet."

"To speak candidly," Zukofsky had replied, "Europe does not interest me very much. In America we have grown out of this interest
in Europe. We take and have taken only the best that Europe possessed. I came here chiefly to meet the master of American poetry and
in a sense its father, Ezra Pound, who has now been living for several years in Rapallo."

"Is there a definite group in America who acknowledge Pound
and have definite characteristics?"

"Yes and no. They have broken with the known, customary, successful, banal forms. Each of the group tries in his own way to find
means of expression and this very independence holds the group together. Among the most important are William Carlos Williams,

René Taupin, Basil Bunting and Carl Rakosi, who will probably interest you seeing he is a Hungarian. I might also mention Charles Reznikoff, Kenneth Rexroth and Forrest Anderson."

"Much as we regret it, we have not yet had the opportunity of making the acquaintance of any of them."

"I can relieve you of some of the regret by saying that few in America know of them."

Zukofsky went on to term Pound's *How to Read* "a fundamental work, in which he states that this and that in particular is fit and meet to be read and a foundation for modern poetry." His interviewer remarked: "If anything of ours were to be spoken of in this manner we would say it was dogmatic." Zukofsky continued: "Beside this, the volume *Cantos* has been published. This is the representative masterwork of modern poetry." Asked what he meant by "modern," he said (in Serly's translation): "Modern to me is Dante with whom, at bottom, modern poetry began since it was he who freed poetry from static clichés and created a simultaneous historical poetry." Of his own group, he said: "We tend to write an expressive and musical verse rather than a magniloquent one. We seek the plasticity of words and their interrelations and musical connections rather than their denotations. We look for actual beauty (value) and not for atmosphere. We do not accept this business of atmosphere."

Only one thing marred Pound's pleasure in his new friend. He failed to make an economics major out of Zukofsky. On the morning Zukofsky left Rapallo, Pound walked with him to the station.

"Go with God," he said, "if you like the company."

Zukofsky went, and Serly stayed. Gerhart Münch, Luigi Sansoni, Olga Rudge were in Rapallo, and Pound organized concerts in the town hall. Williams thought that Pound's interest in music sprang from his "extraordinary" sense of time, but Pound's intense involvement was, of course, something more. He is one of the discoverers of Vivaldi in our time, and it is because he had the Vivaldi works in Dresden copied for him that they have been preserved. The originals were destroyed by Allied bombings. As for the concerts, Pound went about organizing them with all his drive, and all his immense knowledge of and appreciation for the composers of past centuries. The concerts continued for years, and became a part of the cultural life of

Rapallo. His fellow townsmen came, and there were visitors from Rome and elsewhere, many of them distinguished by their profession or their rank. Often he dipped into his own pocket to make them possible.

Pound wrote Zukofsky:

> "Three whoops for the TiborRRRRRR
> conductorrr of orchestrorrr."

He also wrote Professor J. H. Rogers, of Roosevelt's "Brain Trust," under the date "18 Sept Anno XI":

"I don't care what you DO, so long as it isn't on my conscience that you are an Abroaded innocent/ trusting in British vipers, Genevan mandrakes, and ignorant of Douglas, and ras moneta (stamp scrip). I am prob/ younger 'n you are, tho' not much, but by god I'll spit on yr/ tombstone if some attention isn't given to contemporary economics." He signed himself "cordially yrn/" and enclosed a form for reply. This was never used, and it may be found, together with Pound's letter, in the Yale University Library. Pound afterwards explained in print ("Money Pamphlet, Number Four"). The London Economic Conference also got nowhere.

9.

Another visitor came—William Butler Yeats. One sees Pound holding forth on all occasions, and to all who cared to listen; but some did not care. Some had other matters on their minds which concerned them more nearly and which they, naturally and innocently, supposed that Pound might like to discuss with *them*. Such a one was Yeats, who has recorded the story of his strange pilgrimage to Rapallo, and its alarming result.

"A year ago," he wrote in 1934, "I found I had written no verse for two years; I had never been so long barren; I had nothing in my head, and there used to be more than I could write."

He turned first to the discipline which had stood him in good stead throughout his career; but this time he also decided to seek advice, as many a younger man has done, although seldom from one younger than himself: "I wrote the prose dialogue of *The King of the Great Clock Tower* that I might be forced to make lyrics for its imaginary people. When I had written all but the last lyric I went a considerable journey partly to get the advice of a poet not of my school who would, as he did some years ago, say what he thought."

Yeats saw Basil Bunting first, whether by design or chance he does not tell. Their talk, so far as Pound was concerned, was discouraging. Pound's opinions, he learned, were unchanged: "Phidias had corrupted sculpture, we had nothing of true Greece but certain *Nike* dug up out of the foundations of the Parthenon, and that corruption ran through all our art; Shakespeare and Dante had corrupted literature, Shakespeare by his too abounding sentiment, Dante by his compromise with the Church." That night, Yeats asked Pound to dine with him. He told his friend and kinsman by marriage:

"I am in my sixty-ninth year, probably I should stop writing verse, I want your opinion upon some verse I have written lately."

He waited expectantly for Pound's invitation to him to read what he had brought. It did not come. Pound, in fact, would not talk about literature at all.

"He said, apropos of nothing 'Arthur Balfour was a scoundrel' and from that on would talk of nothing but politics. All the modern statesmen were more or less scoundrels except 'Mussolini and that hysterical imitator of him Hitler.' When I objected to his violence he declared that Dante considered all sins intellectual, even sins of the flesh, he himself refused to make the modern distinction between error and sin. He urged me to read the works of Captain Douglas who alone knew what caused our suffering [Yeats apparently did not know the captain had been promoted]."

Yeats told Pound that he found all that he wanted of modern life in detective stories and stories of the Wild West. As for serious reading, he was just then re-reading Shakespeare, and planned to go on to Chaucer. Hearing this, Pound denounced Dublin as "a reactionary hole." On this note they parted, Pound taking Yeats's manuscript with him.

The next day he brought it back to the hotel where Yeats was staying and pronounced judgment. It was a single word: "Putrid."[5]

The play was produced at the Abbey Theatre on July 30, 1934, and turned out to be the most popular of Yeats's dance plays. Writing to Mrs. Shakespear in August, Yeats said: "Send the enclosed cutting [from the *Times*] to Dorothy to show to Ezra that I may confound him. He may have been right to condemn it as poetry but he condemned it as drama."

Another caller fared worse. He was a young English bibliophile, bearing a letter from Wyndham Lewis, who received one from Pound. "What happened I never knew," Lewis afterwards wrote. "His letter contained the savage axiom: 'There's only one thing to do with an Englishman—kick him in the teeth.' "

There were other times when Pound's behavior alarmed his friends. Hemingway, who saw Pound for the last time in Paris in 1934, later recalled that Joyce asked him to come along to dinner with Pound as he—Joyce—was convinced Pound was "mad" and he was "genuinely frightened of him." Hemingway went to the dinner, and throughout Pound spoke "very erratically."[6]

10.

These fits were of temporary duration. He could be completely charming when he wished to be. Still another visitor came to Rapallo, after calling on Gertrude Stein in Paris. He was James Laughlin IV, a personable and well-to-do young man, as tall as Thomas Wolfe, but slender, who wired Pound from Paris that he would like to call on him. Pound replied: "Visibility high." Laughlin stayed in Rapallo through Christmas, 1934, and returned the following year. He told me he lunched with Pound and his wife every day, had tea with them, then dined out, usually at the Albergo Rapallo. Pound, he said, had a name for the people coming to see him; it was "the Ezuversity." Pound gave him books to read, aroused his interest in Italian literature and Social Credit, and took him to the movies. "He was quite a movie fan." Mrs. Pound never went. Laughlin also accompanied Pound to the Salzburg Festival, and there they met Douglas C. Fox, another young and personable American, Frobenius's assistant. Fox told me:

"Pound's spoken German was not good, but he could read it well enough. He was continually writing to the Forschungesinstitut für Kulturmophologie to obtain more information on one point or another. However, since his letters were what they were, no one with only a conventional knowledge of English and practically no knowledge of Pound could understand what they were all about. So I, as the only American there, was made special correspondent for Pound. Sometimes I did not get what E. P. was driving at either—particularly insofar as his continual allusions to people and events, with whom and with which I was unfamiliar, were concerned. But, we communicated, and Pound apparently got the feeling that here was someone who understood. I was not so certain.

"Pound was going to the Salzburg Festival that summer and suggested that I meet him there. And so, one damp summer noon, Pound, James Laughlin and I lunched in the Peterskeller hard by the graveyard at the foot of the hill on which the castle stands. I liked the man but could not follow his conversation, which was much like his writing—*staccato*—leaping from one subject to another, so that by the time I had figured out one allusion I was two or three more behind."

11.

Heads of states seemed to fascinate Pound. If he could not meet them, he wrote to them. He wrote twice to President Roosevelt in 1934. It is difficult to see why in either instance, except through his own view of himself as a man with a mission. On April 27th, "anno 11," but really "anno 12," on stationery with the Gaudier-Brzeska portrait, he wrote:

"Dear Mr Roosevelt
"Frank Morley [of Faber and Faber, Christopher Morley's brother] has just sent me a copy of 'On Our Way' with what looks like a genuine autograph but with an inscription apparently faked by the sportive F. V. M.
"I am reviewing it with what temperance my conscience permits, and with considerable doubt as to my criticism passing the printer. This note is probably long out of date. I think there is a misprint on p. 162, *willing,* line 10, where you mean *unwilling* or *not willing.* This has doubtless been called to yr/ attention, but if by any

chance it has escaped until now, I shall feel justified in sending this note.

"With best wishes and . . . . . convictions that you have not yet publicly shared."[7]

It is a curious fact, considering the typographical whopper it was, that the error referred to by Pound had not been caught by anyone, and it was only after his letter arrived that efforts were made to correct it. The sentence on page 162 of *On Our Way* reads: "It is because I am willing to live myself, or to have my children and grand-children live, under an alien flag or an alien form of government, that I believe in the fundamental obligation of citizenship to don the uniform of our country. . . ."

President Roosevelt's secretary, Stephen Early, immediately tele-graphed the John Day Company of New York. The copy of *On Our Way* in the Roosevelt library at Hyde Park has the word "not" inserted in ink and initialled by the President. The error was corrected before publication in the Faber and Faber edition.

Pound's "Mr. Roosevelt at the Crossroads" appeared in *New Democracy* June 15, 1934.

He had also favored the President with a postcard, the front of which is described as a "shinplaster" by the director of the Franklin D. Roosevelt Library ("shinplaster, slang, a piece of poorly secured money; specifically, any one of the notes of small value issued by private bankers during the depression of 1837."—*Webster's Col-legiate Dictionary*). It was, in this case, the fifty-cent scrip issued by the Union Lumbering Company, of Chippewa Falls, described earlier. He wrote President Roosevelt about it:

"Lest you forget the nature of money/ i;e; that it is a ticket. For the govt. To issue it against any particular merchandise or metal, is merely to favour the owners of that metal and by just that much to betray the rest of the public. You can see that the bill here photod. has SERVED (I mean by the worn state of the note).

"Certificates of work done. That is what these notes were in fact/ before the bank swine got the monopoly.

"Thus was the wilderness conquered for the sake of pork-barrelers who followed [in the margin, a question mark]."

He signed himself, "cordiali saluti," but he hardly meant that.[8]

He conveniently overlooked the fact that Grandfather Pound's scrip was issued against Grandfather's commodities, and no other, and the only ones who got it for "work done" worked for the Union Lumbering Company in whose stores they were privileged to spend it, being unable to do so anywhere else. Family loyalty could not be carried farther; nor, with all due respect and reverence, fatuousness either. He was now signing his letters "E. Pound," with the "E" intertwined with the "P" in such a way that the whole resembled the profile portrait by Gaudier-Brzeska.

12.

New Democracy, for which Pound reviewed Roosevelt's book, was the organ of the New Economics Group, afterwards the American Social Credit Movement. It was edited by Gorham B. Munson, and Major Douglas was a contributor. Munson told me that Social Credit did not take root in the United States until 1931, when A. R. Orage, Pound's and Douglas's old friend, gave four lectures on the Douglas Plan in New York. The following year, when Orage was back in England, he started a new magazine of his own, the *New English Weekly,* with Munson as American representative. *New Democracy* was established in 1933.

"Pound wrote pieces for *New Democracy,*" Munson told me, "he filled the mails with advice to the New Economics Group of New York, he wrote to many individuals in the United States urging the Douglas point of view on them. William Carlos Williams became a Social Creditor, and it may be suspected that Pound first led him to the subject. Pound exerted a strong influence on James Laughlin IV, then a student at Harvard. When he came to see me, I gave him a poetry department in *New Democracy,* which I named 'New Directions,' the name, of course, Laughlin later took for his publishing house.

"Social Credit made rapid progress for a time. Senator Bronson Cutting was a sympathizer [he contributed an article to *New Democracy* entitled "Nationalizing Credit"]. Democratic Congressman T. Alan Goldsborough of Maryland introduced a Social Credit bill which was given a hearing before the House Committee on Banking.

Archibald MacLeish was the principal speaker at the first annual meeting of the New Economics Group of New York, and was instrumental in getting a full-scale exposition of Social Credit by Orage into *Fortune* [of which MacLeish was an editor]. Walter Hampden delivered an address on Social Credit at the Institute of Public Affairs, University of Virginia.

"As time went on, however, it became necessary to question the usefulness of Pound to American Social Credit. In three important respects he was a liability. Although Social Credit was inherently anti-fascist and anti-communist—it was an economic validation of political democracy—Pound was trying to combine social credit economic democracy with Fascist political totalitarianism. American Social Creditors did not like that.

"Second, although Pound rated Social Credit as the best economic scheme, he sometimes urged the dated money, stamp scrip scheme of Silvio Gesell as an alternate to Social Credit. Social Creditors considered the Gesell scheme unsound and authoritarian in nature.

"Third, Pound's anti-semitism was distasteful. When the American Social Credit Movement was organized in 1936, it officially banned anti-semites from membership. The same official ban was made by the Social Credit Party of Great Britain, headed by John Hargrave. Moreover, the point was often made in the *New Age* [Orage's defunct publication, now the organ of British Social Creditors] that anti-semitism was irrelevant—the financial system operated badly because of faults in the mechanism, not because of faults in the operators."

John Hargrave wrote Munson that Pound's propaganda for Social Credit was "worthless."

"It was like a series of explosions in a rock quarry."

It was a form of impatience. The impatience spilled over into literary criticism. In March of 1935, Zukofsky sent Pound a collection of manuscript poems, and Pound wrote back:

"The next anthology will be econ/conscious and L/Z won't be in it.

"People read books because the author tells em something. If his knowledge of life is less than their own the author is a BORE."

He also told Zukofsky that "every man gets more like his father as he gets older." In his own case it appears to have worked the other way. For a month later Homer Pound wrote Zukofsky:

"Ezra had me read your book of poems and I must confess that it seems to me you could spend your time and talents on a much more needed Message to the world. Put your book aside, take up Social Credit, get in touch with 'New Democracy 55–5th Ave. New York.' "

He enclosed Social Credit literature. His stationery bore this printed motto:

LEISURE SPARE TIME
FREE FROM ANXIETY

Now, still another young man came into Pound's orbit—John Slocum, introduced by Laughlin at Zell am See, July, 1935. Pound was on his way to Wörgl, in the Austrian Tyrol, where a kind of Gesellian scrip had circulated. Slocum was "faltbooting down the Salzach." Pound afterwards wrote: "At about the beginning of the second decade of the Fascist Era, the small Tyrolean town of Wörgl sent shivers down the backs of all the lice of Europe, Rothschildian and others, by issuing its own Gesellist money" ("Money Pamphlet, Number Four"; of which more later). Slocum lost his boat over a waterfall, "and boatless went to Venice with Laughlin, Pound and Olga Rudge."

13.

For a man whose chief faith was in the expert, and who thought of himself as one, Pound appears at this time to have been without humor and without judgment. From January 3, 1935, to April 2, 1936, he contributed "American Notes" to the *New English Weekly* —from Rapallo. This is one of them:

"The NEWS is that Huey Long has a 'magnificent education'; i.e., knowing the popular hatred of highbrows he is clever enough to conceal (etc.). Also the score is *reported* of 60,000 telegrams to 800 in favour of Coughlin against the Administration."

Long and Charles E. Coughlin were the chief American dema-

gogues of the Thirties, Long in Louisiana, of which he was governor,
Father Coughlin in New York. Coughlin's paper, *Social Justice,*
printed anti-semitic propaganda received from Germany, without
acknowledgment of the source, and he himself did not scruple to
give on the air, as his own, material supplied by the Nazi newsletter,
World Service, or written by Dr. Goebbels.[9] *Noscitur a sociis.* He
exhibited on the platform a well developed flair for the dramatic by
doffing his coat and Roman collar, rolling up his sleeves, and uttering
threats, which were loudly cheered. He was highly thought of in
Germany.[10] Long was assassinated, and Coughlin was finally silenced
by his superiors.

Pound was also interested in Representative George Holden Tinkham of Massachusetts, who sported a beard. He urged Laughlin to
meet "Uncle George," and sent a couplet summary of American
culture:

> "Oh land of Lydia Pinkham
> and of George Holden Tinkham."

His enormous correspondence continued with unabated vigor, although some of it, perforce, remained one-sided. A very strange letter
appeared in *Time and Tide* preceded by this note: "Sir—As the writer
of the enclosed letter—whom I have never seen or communicated
with in any way—would presumably like his views to have a wide
publicity, I send the enclosed to you for publication if you deem
it of any interest. It is addressed to me at the Bank of England (which
I have never entered) in 'Thread and needle street.' I am, etc., Norman Angell." The editors added parenthetically: "We do indeed
deem that the communication sent to us by Sir Norman Angell is of
considerable interest, literary and psychological, and we feel that
only facsimile reproduction can do it justice."

14.

In the thirteenth year of the Fascist era Pound published another
book, entitled *Jefferson and/or Mussolini.* It began: "The fundamental likenesses between these two men are probably greater than
their differences." In justice to Pound, it should be recalled that

there were many in the United States at that particular time who were ready to believe this, their admiration for Mussolini being unbounded, and their ignorance of Jefferson equal to it.

Pound as a flatterer is something else again: "The man least likely, I mean the man in all Europe or in all America least likely, to be surprised at my opening proposition is Benito Mussolini himself." But it surprised other people, particularly when Pound went on to say, "Jefferson was one genius and Mussolini is another." Even for a guest in another man's country, this was laying it on thick. But Pound laid it on even thicker: "I don't believe any estimate of Mussolini will be valid unless it *starts* from his passion for construction. Treat him as *artifex* [maker] and all the details fall into place. Take him as anything save the artist and you will get muddled with contradictions."

Nero was another "artist."

Pound also was getting muddled. Even his most fervent admirers saw a disintegration in his thought-process and style. Example: "The fascist revolution was FOR the preservation of certain liberties and FOR the maintenance of a certain level of culture, certain standards of living, it was NOT a refusal to come down to a level of riches or poverty, but a refusal to surrender certain immaterial prerogatives, a refusal to surrender a great slice of the cultural heritage." The final sentence in *Jefferson and/or Mussolini* is: "Towards which I assert again my own firm belief that the Duce will stand not with despots and lovers of power but with the lovers of ORDER."

His book appeared in the year of the Fascist invasion of Ethiopia and a year before the Fascist invasion of Spain.

I have already suggested that Pound's interest in the subject of economics stemmed from his concern for the welfare of his fellow man, and his notions about order were a part of that concern. "Monetary theory is worthy of study because it leads us to the contemplation of justice," he wrote in "Money Pamphlet, Number Four." It found expression in a series of poems, afterwards entitled "Verse of the Thirties, first printed in the *New English Weekly*," with prose commentaries by Orage. The sequence, added to *Personae* in 1949, consists of eighteen poems, with the signature "Alfred Venison, The Poet of Tichtfield Street," most of them built on very familiar, or schoolbook, stanza structures. This one is from "The Charge of the Bread Brigade":

> See 'em go slouching there,
> With cowed and crouching air
>   Dundering dullards!
> How the whole nation shook
> While Milord Beaverbrook
>   Fed 'em with hogwash!

From "Alf's Fifth Bit":

> The pomps of butchery, financial power,
> Told 'em to die in war, and then to save,
> Then cut their saving to the half or lower;
> When will this system lie down in its grave?

From "Alf's Eighth Bit":

> Vex not thou the banker's mind
>   (His *what?*) with a show of sense,
> Vex it not, Willie, his mind,
>   Or pierce its pretence. . . .

The collection appeared in 1935 as a pamphlet of thirty-two pages, published by S. Nott, of London, as No. 9 of "Pamphlets on the New Economics." It was titled *Alfred Venison's Poems: Social Credit Themes, by the Poet of Titchfield Street*—i.e., Pound. Throwing himself wholeheartedly into what he felt was a crusade, he achieved some measure of content. Such is the testimony of another visitor to Rapallo.

Phyllis Bottome, who had met Pound at May Sinclair's while still a young woman aspiring to become an author, came to Rapallo that year. Even before they resumed their acquaintance she heard tidings of him. She was shopping for a piano, and running into difficulties. An Italian said to her: "The Signor Pound is the person to go to for everything about artists." She went. She listened. His views about money made a deep impression on her. In her account of him written in 1935, and from which I have previously quoted, she said:

"Ezra Pound makes an interesting distinction between work, which is all men's heritage and should be their safe delight, and paid employment, which is only a necessity in given conditions, and does not imply either security or delight.

"At the present crisis he believes that the money problem should be the preoccupation of every intelligent person. To solve this problem, in his opinion, is the next step forward in the march of mankind.

"We have more or less cleared up the hypocrisy and sterility of our old-fashioned control of morals; now let us start clearing up the same hypocrisy and sterility and devitalize money.

"Control is necessary, but it should be a fair, reasoned, and publicly accepted control.

"Ezra Pound is pouring all his constructive ability, at the present moment, into the economic theories of C. H. Douglas, with whom he has a working accord.

"If there is a flaw in these theories, it is for men equally clear-minded and disinterested (should there be any such) in the financial world to point it out.

"The expert is necessary in every craft, but if his habits are decent there is no need for him to have to rely upon secrecy.

"Duplicity has no place in art; it has no place in morals; it has no place in science and it should have even less place in finance or in politics.

"This is the creed upon which Ezra Pound has based his life and his work, with no visible line drawn between the two."

Miss Bottome found him no longer nervous and vulnerable, but "with an unmistakable air of well-being," and she likened him to the "Happy Warrior."[11] In his rejuvenated mood he left a note for Louis Untermeyer at the latter's hotel:

"The fact that your taste in poetry is execrable shouldn't prevent us from having a vermouth together."

They had it. They sat in the public garden and talked about old times, old friends, chiefly Amy Lowell.[12]

15.

Pound's mind was operating on several levels, not all of them of equal perspicuity. Perspicuous or not, where did he find the time and the energy? A communication from Selwyn Jones, of Pontypridd, South Wales, led Pound to consult with two Italian writers—Aldo Camerino and Carlo Izzo—with the result that another movement was born. Camerino was the translator of Lope de Vega's *A mis soledades voy*, which Pound had praised for its "Spanish quality— the first time I had seen anything of the sort in Italy." Izzo had translated Pound's lyrical poems into Italian. Both lived in Venice; and from Venice, on September 29, 1935, there went forth a group of letters, over the signatures of Camerino and Izzo, which launched "a movement tending to establish a regular exchange of technical, mostly prosodic, information, suggestions etc., between literary people of different countries not limited to one time or language."

They quoted Pound's "main points" for, of course, it was his composition:

"a) Wish to liven up Italian verse.
"b) Wish to observe effects of what he calls injections on English verse.
"c) Dislike of monolingual culture.
"d) Possibility of examining multilingual stimuli."

The movement was to be "restricted to no more than ten persons —not for snobbishness but because larger number would make whole process of communication too clumsy."

There were rules: members were to "circulate works with either statement of prosodic intention or queries, notes, prosodic experiments, translations. Member *A* to send work etc. to *B*, *B* to *C* etc. Mr. Pound to be last recipient that he may be enabled to collate the notes and observations that preceding members are requested to write 'en marge.' " Of the regulations—numbering ten—seven and eight read:

"Ezra Pound's 'A.B.C. of Learning' [*ABC of Reading*, successor to *How To Read*] and Fenollosa's Chinese printed characters to be accepted not as gospel but at least as a basis of general reference and discussion till further notice.

"Persian and Welsh having been outside E.P.'s research means are an extension [i.e., presumably, of the above]."

The tenth: "Associates are on probation."

Copies of the letter went to Selwyn Jones, Louis Zukofsky, James Laughlin (now at Harvard), J. P. Angold of the *New English Weekly*, Pound, Camerino and Izzo; and to Basil Bunting, whose specialty was "Persian Studies." There is a reference to Rutherford:

"William Carlos Williams might be included if still interested in prosody and disposed to take action. His Spanish studies interesting."

Zukofsky, replying directly to Pound, said: "I propose that Bill Williams be asked to join as medical consultant."

Pound was not so engrossed in prosody as to neglect other subjects, and Zukofsky did his best to cope with a deteriorating situation. He wanted so much to please teacher; but the spit-gun of his mind fired away. He was not one of those impressed by Mussolini: "No one in the U.S.A. is interested in the Boss's reclamation of the marshes—& quite a number here are aware of the fact that Rome when it was caving in did something like it—sometime before 1935 A.D." He even suggested that Pound had not read Marx. Pound's reply began abruptly:

"Have you not even sense enough to USE A WORD with a meaning and let the meaning adhere to the word.

"A commodity is a material thing or substance/ it has a certain durability.

"If you don't dissociate ideas, and keep ONE LABEL for ONE thing or category, you will always be in a gormy mess.

"Labour may transmute material, it may put value into it, or make it serviceable.

"I suppose it comes of being a damn foreigner and not having bothered to learn english.

"Call me a liberal and I'll knock yr/ constipated block off."

In the same letter:

"I am fed up with half/gooks who don't know their private world has a relation to anything outside it. After all you LIVE in the — — country and daren't leave it.

"New Masses is quite right/ my poetry and my econ/ are NOT separate or opposed.

"Essential unity.

"You cant buy foreign books, cause you wd/ have to pay in MONEY and you are too hog lazy to think *what it* (money) *is.*

"And that condition will git more so/ until several people start thinking what M. is."

For a while the heavy artillery was silent; or the barrages were falling elsewhere. Zukofsky was, after all, devoted to him, he was a valuable source of information about the United States, and he answered letters. Pound's tone became conciliatory. He wrote Zukofsky in the summer of 1936:

"If it [is] any satisfaction to you, I had news yester p.m. from head of one of the small worker's parties in Eng/ that was sympathetic to Germany that they have dropped antisemitism. Three letters from yr/ aged friend in a week after some preliminary work.

"This is OFF the main line of argument. BUT yet it AINT *so* far off, as it indicates dropping of irrelevant fuss, for fundamentals."

But there is a penultimate blast:

"I shd/ have been better employed on Fenollosa, during the past 25 minutes or whatever. how many hours per day .. etc. are you worth. E. P."

Final blast, in longhand:

"You are merely becoming a bore from lack of mental intake & digestion."

Zukofsky asked:

"Has English been so natural to you that *you* no longer bother to weigh each word you handle, translate etc. The damn foreigner you say I am has more respect for English than you have.

"*Yr.* English! It's like your 'call me a liberal and I'll knock yr/ constipated block off,' like the line in a Fascist play we've heard about—'When I hear of culture, I cock my gun!' "

As for how much time he rated, Zukofsky generously wrote:

"Why ask me what I'm worth, how many hrs, of yr. day etc. when you can probably guess my answer. Not a minute of yr. time if you can produce anything to equal in value the first Canto or the opening of the XXXeth."

His letter concludes:

"Well, there's no use calling you a liberal—as you say. The next war will show your stand—will show whether *you've* been a liberal or not."

CHAPTER XVIII

POUND'S *CANTOS* AND
HIS ECONOMICS

Canto: division of a long poem.
Latin, *cantus:* a song.

1.

Its aesthetic achievement aside, Pound's *Cantos,* as readers of this book are already aware, is the most autobiographical poem in the English language, a record of the poet's life in letters—his forebears, teachers, reading—his beloved troubadours, Homer, Dante—his travels, even the restaurants he ate in—his views on economics—his friends, foes and *bêtes noires,* chiefly financiers—and what he experienced in the darkest part of his long, useful, strenuous and controversial career.

Aesthetically, it is now what he has claimed for it all along as the various sections appeared: an epic poem with a form that is original in concept and executed with energy and imagination, though often sagging from an overfreightage of materials, chiefly quoted ones, chiefly about economics. But wherever he writes out of himself—that is, when he is not quoting—he remains, what he has been from the beginning, a magician of metric, so much so that passages by the score make one fall in love again with the English tongue.

There are also scores of passages that are mere prose patchery, and

passages merely vulgar by reason of grubby anecdotes or even unadorned coprology, but perhaps necessary in a poem which has taken
all time and all conditions of men as its province. An example occurs
at the end of Canto XII which, when she read it, angered Miss
Heyman, who told a friend that the story had been current in Venice
in 1908; perhaps Pound told it then, for it is a college boy story.
I give the last eight lines:

> "But, father,
> "Don't, don't talk about me. I'm all right,
> "It's you, father."
>   "That's it, boy, you said it.
> "You called me your father, and I ain't.
> "I ain't your dad, no,
> "I am not your fader but your moder," quod he,
> "Your fader was a rich merchant in Stambouli."

There are other passages which are invidious or mendacious, not
qualities to be esteemed in a poet or historian. The following is from
Canto XLVI:

> Said Mr. RothSchild, hell knows which Roth-schild
> 1861, '64 or there sometime, "Very few people
> "will understand this. Those who do will be occupied
> "getting profits. The general public will probably not
> "see it's against their interest."

If a Rothschild said this, very well; but what if a Rothschild did not?
The words in quotation marks are from a letter received by the banking firm from one John Sherman, presumably the Senator from Ohio
who became Secretary of the Treasury.

Pound's preoccupation with the Rothschilds is extraordinary in
view of the fact that he never bothered to check anything. He wrote
as a teacher of youth in the *Little Magazine:*

"Your generation has got to BOTHER about economics, and even
politics, as mine bothered about philology, for the simple reason that
certain OBSTACLES are there in your path. The state of language in
1902 was the FIRST obstacle, that is the one immediately in front of

my generation. Before ANYTHING more could be done, the barnacles had to be scraped off the means of communication. BUT in 1934 the 'Liberator' saying that Bismark [*sic*] blamed the American Civil War on the Rothschilds is of vastly more use to your generation than a study of 'Calligrammes.'

"I haven't verified the 'Liberator's' statement. There is nothing improbable about it."

In it went:

> Bismarck
> blamed american civil war on the jews;
> particularly on the Rothschild
> one of whom remarked to Disraeli
> that nations were fools to pay rent for their credit
> (Canto XLVIII)

Bismarck was born to the anti-semitism of his class, but not only abandoned it but recommended intermarriage between the nobility and Jewesses.

As for Canto LII, I state without fear of contradiction that these two lines, also supplied by the *Liberator,* are a lie—

> Remarked Ben: better keep out the jews
> or yr/ grand children will curse you

—being a forgery of 1934, a decade significant for this sort of thing. Pound, already on the hate-mongers' mailing lists, used it as soon as received.[1]

On the same page on which these lines occur there are five black-barred suppressions by New Directions. Concerning them, Pound told a visitor in St. Elizabeths:

"It was 'No Directions' that suppressed that passage about the Rothschilds in *The Pisan Cantos*.[2] They wanted to leave the whole thing out without any indication of the omission, and I said, 'Black lines or nothing' and so in went the black lines, so all my readers could see the censorship. I guess they were afraid of losing the support of the New York banks, if they published the truth about international finance."[3]

Mr. Laughlin told me that he has no recollection of this, and questioned the accuracy of the quotation. The black-barred lines also occur in the Faber and Faber edition, which appeared first.

2.

What Pound set out to do, and has done very well, is to achieve a poetic synthesis of past and present times. Insofar as he has a model, it is Dante's *Commedia*. His theme is stated colloquially in Canto VII (as, presumably, first uttered to his friend, Fritz-René Vanderpyl, a Dutch writer living in Paris) :

> "Beer-bottle on the statue's pediment!
> "That, Fritz, is the era, to-day against the past,
> "Contemporary."

But he is no Miniver Cheevy, because active. Had he lived in the dawn of the Renaissance he would have been like that humanist he mentions in the third canto, Gian Francesco Poggio Bracciolini, remembered for his discoveries of lost Latin classics. Many, like Miniver, have dreamed of past eras in troubled or tawdry times; what Pound does in the *Cantos* is to reconstruct them out of his vast knowledge of persons, places and annals, both poetry and prose, so that we get, on his unfolding pages, as on a screen, visions and voices of the times that were. Nevertheless, he remains a man of his time. Dante was concerned with the morality of his age, Pound with human welfare in ours. In his own unreconstructed way he has expressed the Bolshevik ideal of "to each according to his need."

Nor has it been lost upon him that in the many vast upheavals of the twentieth century economics has played the dominant role, toppling kingdoms and states. The idea of order, so often discussed in London studios and restaurants, was a settled part of his thinking, and he felt, and felt strongly, that from the amelioration of poverty, which he and many of his friends had experienced, a new order would come into being. But no new order could come without monetary reform. Much of his zeal stems from that unfailing kindness, that concern for others, which had been bred in the bone. He really wished to help; he thought he could help most by doffing the poet's cloak and donning the economist's mantle. All over the United States, around the stove in winter or the cracker-barrel in summer, and between watches in the forecastles of ships, men like him have solved the problems of the universe, including money, which nevertheless, remained in short supply. Not all of them have been poets.

As for its form, the *Cantos* is to poetry, or to the development of poetry, what Joyce's *Ulysses* was to the novel. In both works there is the stream-of-consciousness technique—the evident stream, not merely the aesthetic unconscious which operates in the creation of all works of art. But Pound does not limit himself to Homer in modern metaphor, as Joyce did: he draws frequently on Homer, but he draws from other sources as well, and his eclecticism is universal, oriental and occidental.

Its range being wide, and its technique novel, its influence has been enormous. From *The Waste Land* on, no poem of any length has escaped the influence of the structure and flow of Pound's *Cantos*. It has its own laws, already adopted by other poets, and the poem itself, although susceptible to extended commentaries here and there, is sufficient text for the general reader, as is the case with other major poems in which systems, moral or political—here, historical and financial—have been incorporated. The impact of Pound's line, which has been felt by his fellow practitioners, will be the ultimate test of the poem's durability. That line is always handled with assurance, for Pound writes as though confident that even his obscurities will receive attention and exegesis, as indeed they have. Therefore his poem flows, for he is free to form it for structure and for sense, the over-all design being clear. But, as already suggested, there may be from time to time an apparent profusion, or proliferation, of quoted materials —statesmen's letters given verbatim, ministerial reports, the finances, and rise and fall, of dynasties, dukedoms and states. Still, as much of this material is unfamiliar to the general reader, criticism cannot but be muted, for the aim of reading is either pleasure or instruction, and the *Cantos* offers both. It can serve no purpose to question either Pound's intentions or design, for he is read best on his own terms. It may be useful to add that the *Cantos,* like other works of art, does not depend on initial reactions, whether of reader or critic. Time has sustained Pound's claims, first uttered long ago, when even Yeats and Eliot had doubts and did not hesitate to express them.

Pound did not follow Imagist rules in his work, or—the concept being original—any rules at all existing before; he depended, instead, on the source of all artistic rules, the artist's instinct. I do not mean any artist. The form is loose and impressionistic, and if there is a single, steady and pervading *modus operandi,* it is the stream-of-consciousness of a literary eclectic. His borrowings are impressive.

I have already quoted a number of references in the *Cantos* to particular persons or places. It remains to be added that almost every name thus far mentioned in this book occurs also in his poem. Almost everything he ever read is likewise to be found therein, so that the *Cantos* is, in effect, a vast storehouse of educational materials, embracing history, historical letters and other documents, archeology, art criticism, travel, and perhaps most important of all, an anthology of many literatures, quoted in the original, whether English or foreign, or translated by Pound with his incomparable skill. There is, of course, in addition, Pound's own poetry which, at its highest level, is unsurpassed in our time.

But as there are now a number of estimable works dealing with the *Cantos* in detail,[4] I shall confine myself to a statement of Pound's intentions, method and achievement, although I plan to return—briefly—to a section of this long poem, *The Pisan Cantos,* the contents of which were composed while the poet was a prisoner in a United States Army compound near Pisa.

3.

Although Pound does not consider the *Commedia* as an epic, but as "a great mystery play, or better, a cycle of mystery plays," it is nevertheless a poem which includes history. Steeped as he was in it—few men more so—this aspect of the poem cannot but have influenced him profoundly. Not only did Dante, in his circuit of Hell, usher in men and women famed of old, but fellow Florentines and other contemporaries, and he ushered them in with admiration or loathing, a device which Pound adopts. But Pound differs from Dante in essential respects; he is a modern man, without a sustaining faith, except the religion of art, which is quite different from that of a pre-Renaissance Catholic for whom the foundations of the world and the nether world were firm and fixed of old, and often more pagan than Christian, an incongruity with which Dante seems not to be concerned, nor his commentators either.

Thus, when the moment came to commence his poem, or the design of it, it was necessary for Pound to decide what kind of journey he would make. He chose the world that he knew, the world of men, whether living or dead, with occasional evocations of the classic past; but the Christian hell, which Tertullian prophesied with such unfatherly gloating and Dante depicted for the terror and triumph of the faithful, was left out. It was, after all, a literary device, and was already old when Dante used it. "There is nothing particularly new in describing the journey of a living man through Hell, or even of his translation into Paradise," Pound wrote in his chapter on Dante in *The Spirit of Romance*. "Arda Virap, in the Zoroastrian legend, was sent as ambassador, in the most accredited fashion; with full credentials he ascended into Paradise, and saw the pains of Hell shortly afterwards. The description of such journeys may be regarded as a confirmed habit of the race."

The form that he chose marks yet another difference from Dante's poem: though Pound uses the same name for the divisions of his poem, and aimed at the same number—one hundred—his cantos are written in irregular lines and are of irregular length, and are written in the modern mode which few are able to master or to use with perceptible effect. By and large, it suited Pound and his purpose.

The twin keys to the *Cantos* are Pound's life and reading, which has occupied so large a part of his life. The reading, perforce, included history and economics; and to the twin keys must be added a third —Pound's belief that the best government is the one which controls, as well as issues, money.

The poem being in effect an odyssey, it begins appositely with the wanderings of Odysseus and his descent to Hades where unburied Elpenor chides him and blind Tiresias prophesies safe, but solitary, return. This canto was not originally the first, but very early became so; and whatever the reasons for Pound's decision, not least, it may be thought, is Elpenor's suggested inscription for his own burial mound:

A man of no fortune, and with a name to come.

(Rouse's *Odyssey,* the best of the modern translations, which had the benefit of Pound's advice, has this rendering: "Burn me with all my arms, and pile up a barrow on the shore of the grey sea, that in days to come men may hear the story of an unhappy man.")

Pound's translation, however, is not from the Greek, but from the Renaissance Latin version which, it will be recalled, he had discovered on a Paris quai. He gives the source toward the end of the canto:

> Lie quiet Divus. I mean, that is Andreas Divus,
> In officina Wecheli, 1538, out of Homer.

"Lie quiet Divus" may appear enigmatic, but I prefer to think it is exultant: "Move over, Divus." He had come to the end, and he knew that he had done as well with Divus's Latin as Divus had done with Homer's Greek; and indeed it is throughout a miraculous translation, its rhythms recalling an earlier one—that of "The Seafarer," from the Anglo-Saxon—so spare, so pithy, so accented are its lines.

Divus's *Odyssey* also contains the *Hymni Deorum* of Homer in a rendering by Georgius Dartona Cretensis, and the canto ends with a reference to this translator and a snip or two of his Latin, from the opening of the second hymn to Aphrodite:

> Venerandam,
> In the Cretan's phrase, with the golden crown, Aphrodite,
> Cypri munimenta sortita est, mirthful, oricalchi, with golden
> Girdles and breast bands, thou with dark eyelids
> Bearing the golden bough of Argicida. So that:

"So that" and a colon opening on Canto II project Pound's method of historical synthesis:

> Hang it all, Robert Browning,
>   there can be but the one "Sordello."
> But Sordello, and my Sordello?
> Lo Sordels si fo di Mantovana.
> So-shu churned in the sea.

> Seal sports in the spray-whited circles of cliff-wash,
> Sleek head, daughter of Lir,
>   eyes of Picasso
> Under black fur-hood, lithe daughter of Ocean—

and so back to Homer, although the chief incident of the canto is from Ovid's *Metamorphoses,* the voyage of Dionysus to Naxos, when the god performed the miracle of the vines and leopards, the abducting sailors turned into dolphins, Acoetes alone being spared. (The incident is also in Homer's seventh hymn.) Sordello is the Italian troubadour who lived in Provence, is mentioned by Dante, and is the subject of Browning's obfuscating work. So-shu is the Japanese version of Li Po who, drunk, waded out to fetch the moon from the sea, and became part of the sea's churning, having drowned in moonlight. Lir is the Celtic sea god, Mamannan mac Lir, and Pound equates his daughter with the Homeric daughters of the sea, bestowing on her Picasso's dark, alive eyes which gave Cummings such a "feathery jolt or, so to speak, shock, of confrontation" when they met. Pound, apparently, also felt it, as have others.

The second canto ends with "And. . . ." The third begins:

> I sat on the Dogana's steps
> For the gondolas cost too much, that year

—i.e., the steps of the Dogana di Mare, the custom-house in Venice. Browning had also sat on a step in Venice, although his was "a ruined palace-step (*Sordello,* Book III); hence, Pound's advice to his father—and others—to become familiar with Browning in order to understand the *Cantos.* But *Sordello* is at best only an important segment of this literary jig-saw, and Homer Pound's query—"Ever read it?"—may not be thought irrelevant.

4.

Pound's stream of consciousness in Canto III would appear, as indicated, to operate by stages: through Browning, through Venice, and through the troubadour Sordello, which sets him to musing of the

antique past and of that "dream city" of Burgos, visited long ago;
for he now plunges into the story of El Cid—

> My Cid rode up to Burgos,
> Up to the studded gate between two towers,
> Beat with his lance butt, and the child came out,
> Una niña de nueve años . . . .

It had stayed in his mind not only because of the beauty of the
original "Poema del Cid," but quite probably because of the incident
of the pawnbrokers, not comprehending—one might think—that it
was beneath the dignity of a great Campeador to practice a fraud,
even if on Jews.

> And he came down from Bivar, Myo Cid,
> With no hawks left there on their perches,
> And no clothes there in the presses,
> And he left his trunk with Raquel and Vidas,
> That big box of sand, with the pawn-brokers,
> To get pay for his menie;
> Breaking his way to Valencia.

This is the first instance in the *Cantos* of Pound's preoccupation
with usury and usurers, which has remained constant in his thought,
conversation and work, marring the work, but at times raising it to
great beauty, as in Canto XLV:

> With usura hath no man a house of good stone
> each block cut smooth and well fitting
> that design might cover their face,
> with usura
> hath no man a painted paradise on his church wall
> *harpes et luthes*
> or where virgin receiveth message
> and halo projects from incision,
> with usura
> seeth no man Gonzaga his heirs and his concubines
> no picture is made to endure nor to live with
> but it is made to sell and sell quickly

with usura, sin against nature,
is thy bread ever more of stale rags
is thy bread dry as paper,
with no mountain wheat, no strong flour
with usura the line grows thick
with usura is no clear demarcation
and no man can find site for his dwelling.
Stone cutter is kept from his stone
weaver is kept from his loom
WITH USURA
wool comes not to market
sheep bringeth no gain with usura. . . .

Dante devotes fourteen cantos of the *Inferno*—XVII to XXX—
to types of fraud and their punishment, beginning with usurers, "who
are violent against Nature and Art" (Laurence Binyon's note).

5.

A man who dedicates himself to a profession in which no money is
to be made except by remaining mediocre or becoming middling good
is bound to spend some time pondering the shortage of it; and from
this, perhaps, to a consideration of the factors that make money
circulate. Pound differs from other poets by letting his thoughts become a preoccupation, and from a preoccupation an *idée fixe*. This, to
be sure, is an oversimplification; it now remains to annotate the propo-
sitions already set forth.

In *Make It New* Pound wrote:

"An epic is a poem including history. I don't see that anyone save
a sap-head can now think that he knows any history until he understands economics."

This is a Marxian interpretation, but Pound gives the credit to
someone else. In Number Five of his "Money Pamphlets," addressed
to Englishmen and dedicated "To the Green Shirts of England," he
wrote: "An epic is a poem including history. No one can understand
history without understanding economics. Gibbon's History of Rome
is a meaningless jumble till a man has read Douglas."

Clifford Hugh Douglas whom Pound met through Orage, as previously related, said during the unemployment demonstrations in England, 1930–1931, "I am not interested in the unemployed," adding: "If you want the solution, there it is—take it and apply it." The English did not take it, but two provinces in Canada—Alberta and British Columbia—did. It has not, to my knowledge, been adopted elsewhere. His solution, in the form of an economic formula, follows:

$$\text{Cost} : \text{Price} :: \text{Production} : \text{Consumption.}$$
$$\text{Price per ton} = \text{Cost per ton} \times \frac{\text{Cost value of Total Consumption}}{\text{Money value of Total Production.}}$$

Explanation: "the scientific price of any article to the consumer is the cost of production." It is based on the Social Credit doctrine that under the present financial system there must always be a shortage of consumer purchasing power. Douglas proposed a "consumer dividend" and application of the compensated price at the retail end. He appears in Canto XXII, as does Pound:

> And C. H. said to the renowned Mr. Bukos:
> "What is the cause of the H.C.L.?" and Mr. Bukos,
> The economist consulted of nations, said:
>   "Lack of labour."
> And there were two millions of men out of work.
> And C. H. shut up, he said
> He would save his breath to cool his own porridge,
> But I didn't, and I went on plaguing Mr. Bukos
> Who said finally: "I am an orthodox
> "Economist."
>   Jesu Christo!

It is thought by some that "Mr. Bukos" was John Maynard Keynes. (It is like the scene described by Mary Colum in Paris, when Lincoln Steffens gave his talk.) It is in this canto that the description of the service in the synagogue at Gibraltar occurs—Pound's subconscious at work linking economics and the Jews, although this recollection was a pleasant one.

Pound also has praise for Silvio Gesell, a German economist who evolved a theory of the velocity of money circulation, or Schwundgeld, "shrinking money," which not only was taxed if not used, but lost part of its value. It was, Pound wrote, "a paper-money system by which everyone was obliged, on the first of the month, to affix a stamp on every note he possessed equal to one per cent. of the note's face value. . . . From the humanitarian point of view, the advantage of this form of taxation over all others is that it can only fall on persons who have, at the moment the tax falls due, money in their pockets worth 100 times the tax itself. . . . As a remedy for inflation its advantages will be seen immediately. *Inflation* consists in a super-fluity of money. Under Gesell's system each issue of notes consumes itself in one hundred months—eight years and four months—thus bringing to the treasury a sum equal to the original issue."

He corresponded on the subject with Dr. Hugo Fack, who ex-pounded Gesell in the United States. Followers of Douglas did not, ordinarily, endorse other economic solutions or systems, and Pound's praise of Gesell was looked on askance by the orthodox. "Social Creditors considered the Gesell scheme unsound and authoritarian in nature," as Munson said.

Pound saw in Gesell's system an end to "the expense of numerous departments whose present function is to squeeze taxes out of the public" ("Money Pamphlet, Number Two"). Hence his encomium (in "Money Pamphlet, Number Five"): "Two men have ended the Marxist era. Douglas in conceiving the cultural heritage as the great and chief fountain of value. Gesell in seeing that 'Marx never ques-tioned money. He just took it for granted.' "

Whether Pound read Marx is problematical. Marx does not question money: he explains it. Stamps and scrip aside, all the ideas, and fragments of ideas, all the formulae and fragments of formulae, found in Douglas and Gesell—hence, in Pound—and even their particular manner of phrasing them, come from Marx's *Capital*.

6.

It is now a commonplace of criticism that Pound's prose writings provide parallel texts or, at the least, commentaries and footnotes to the *Cantos,* and have done so from the start. Whether a particular passage is about history, literature or economics, that passage will be found, sometimes more than once, in the prose; this includes his broadcasts from Rome, which will be taken up in a more appropriate place, and the little known "Money Pamphlets by £," composed between 1935 and 1944. The pamphlets were written in Rapallo, the first, second, fourth and sixth in Italian. Their titles are:

"An Introduction to the Economic Nature of the United States" ("Introduzione alla Natura Economica della S.U.A.")

"Gold and Work" ("Oro e Lavoro").

"What Is Money For?"

"A Visiting Card" ("Carta da Visita").

"Social Credit: An Impact."

"America, Roosevelt and the Causes of the Present War" (L'America, Roosevelt e le Cause della Guerra Presente").[5]

I shall quote from some of them, and return to them later. In the first he wrote:

"This is not a SHORT History of the Economy of the United States. For forty years I have schooled myself, not to write the Economic History of the U.S. or any other country, but to write an epic poem which begins 'In the Dark Forest,' crosses the Purgatory of human error, and ends in the light, 'fra i maestri di color che sanno.' For this reason I have had to understand the NATURE of error. But I don't think it necessary to refer to each particular case of error."

Again:

"The true history of the economy of the United States, as I see it, is to be found in the correspondence between Adams and Jefferson, in the writings of Van Buren, and in quotations from the intimate letters of the Fathers of the Republic. The elements remain the same: debts, altering the value of monetary units, and the attempts, and triumphs of usury, due to monoplies, or to a 'Corner.' "

All these matters are to be found in the *Cantos*. The prose texts are also loaded with autobiographical fragments, on which I have drawn. We learn from them that Pound was broadcasting from Rome long before World War II. In "Social Credit" he quotes two sentences from a broacast of January 11, 1935:

" 'Intellectuals' do not have any ideas, they get only the spare parts of ideas."

"The indifferent have never made history, they have never even understood any history."

The texts also serve as a running commentary on *Ezra Pound's ABC of Economics.* Chiefly, however, they constitute Pound's major effort to teach history and what is to him its underlying force, economics, to the ordinary man. In "What Is Money For?"—1939—he offers an "Introductory Text Book" of American history in four chapters:

CHAPTER I

All the perplexities, confusion, and distress in America arise, not from defects in their Constitution or confederation, not from want of honor or virtue, so much as from downright ignorance of the nature of coin, credit, and circulation.

John Adams

CHAPTER II

. . . and if the national bills issued be bottomed (as is indispensable) on pledges of specific taxes for their redemption within certain and moderate epochs, and be of proper denominations for circulation, no interest on them would be necessary or just, because they would answer to every one of the purposes of the metallic money withdrawn and replaced by them.

Thomas Jefferson (Letter to Crawford, 1816)

CHAPTER III

. . . and gave the people of this Republic the greatest blessing they ever had—their own paper to pay their own debts.

Abraham Lincoln

CHAPTER IV

The Congress shall have Power . . .

To coin Money, regulate the Value thereof, and of foreign Coin, and to fix the Standard of Weights and Measures.

*(Constitution of the United States, Article I
Legislative Department, Section 8, clause 5)*

done in Convention by the Unanimous Consent of the States present the Seventeenth Day of September in the Year of our

Lord one thousand seven hundred and Eighty-seven and of the
Independence of the United States of America the Twelfth.
In Witness whereof We have hereunto subscribed our Names.

George Washington—President
and Deputy from Virginia

In a "note" appended to this, he states:

"Douglas' proposals are a sub-head under the main idea in Lincoln's
sentence, Gesell's 'invention' is a special case under Jefferson's general
law."

The "Text Book" was repeated in "America, Roosevelt and the
Causes of the Present War"—first published in Venice in 1944—
with the following commentary:

"It should be noted that only the last of these statements [i.e.,
in the "Text Book"] is to be found in a publication easily accessible
to the great majority of the citizens of the great but denatured democracy [i.e., in the Constitution].

"Lincoln was assassinated after he made the statement given above.

"The theatrical gesture of the assassin does not explain how it
happened that he escaped from Washington, after the alarm had been
raised, by the *only* road that was not guarded; nor its synchronization
with the attempted assassination of Seward, the Secretary of State,
nor various other details of the affair. The fact remains that Lincoln
had assumed a position in clear opposition to the usurocracy."

Pound liked the "Text Book" so much that he had it printed
separately, which made it convenient for mailing.

7.

As with American, so with his interpretation of world history. Usury
is his point of departure, and the Rome to which all paths return.
No act of greatness, no deed of heroes, finds a place in Pound's teaching. All is swept aside that he may drive home the truth as he sees it,
unhampered by extraneous facts. There is no dialectic, and no effort
at persuasion. His view of the Reformation may appear surprising
in a Quaker:

"The Protestants did not wish to pay ecclesiastical taxes to Rome, and to the priests for their rites. The Bible was invented as a substitute-Priest. The Canonical prohibition against usury disappeared. Polite society did not consider usury as Dante did, that is, damned to the same circle of Hell as the sodomites, both acting against the potential abundance of nature."

He is fascinated by business transactions of olden times, when there was very little money in circulation.

"The state can LEND. The fleet that was victorious at Salamis was built with money lent to the shipbuilders by the Athenian state."

Even when he is hearing the music of a lost dynasty, economics provides the leit-motif.

"Until the seventh century after Christ, when an Emperor of the T'ang Dynasty issued state notes (*state* notes, not bank notes, mind you), the world was practically compelled to use as money a determined quantity of some commonly used commodity, such as salt or gold according to the degree of local sophistication. But since A.D. 654, at least, this metal has no longer been necessary for trading between civilized people. The state note of the T'ang Dynasty, of the year 856, which is still in existence, has an inscription almost identical with the one you read on your ten-lire notes."

In "Money Pamphlet, Number Four," he reproduces a state note of the T'ang Dynasty, while in Number Five he has a facsimile of the Union Lumbering Company's 50-cent note, which I have described earlier. Under it is the following:

"This money fulfills the primitive condition of honest money: the man who issued the money HAD the goods. My grandfather maintained the value of his money by himself watching the gang-saws, the planks of the Chippewa Company were an inch and a quarter thick *before* planing, a foot of lumber *after* planing was one foot square and an inch thick, no scamped planks were delivered.

"The public paid NO USURY for the use of this purchasing power."

Meanwhile, however, the money handed over to the Chippewa Company for goods received or delivered earned interest in Chippewa Falls banks.

He asks the reader of "What Is Money For?" to "note the paragraph from 'Mein Kampf' magnificently isolated by Wyndham Lewis in his 'Hitler'—'The struggle against international finance and loan capital has become the most important point in the National Socialist programme: the struggle of the German nation for its independence and freedom.' "

This was in 1939, when the most important point in the National Socialist programme might have appeared to be the conquest and enslavement of Europe. Pound deals with those who had the temerity to suggest such a thing:

"Some facts are now known above parties, some perceptions are the common heritage of all men of good will, and only the Jewspapers and worse than Jewspapers, try now to obscure them. Among the worse than Jewspapers we must list the hired professors who misteach new generations of young, who lie for hire and who continue to lie from sheer sloth and inertia and from dog-like contempt for the well-being of all mankind.

"At this point, and to prevent the dragging of red-herrings, I wish to distinguish between prejudice against the Jew as such and the suggestion that the Jew should face his own problem.

"DOES he in his individual case wish to observe the law of Moses?

"Does he propose to continue to rob other men by usury mechanism while wishing to be considered a 'neighbour'?

"This is the sort of double-standard which a befouled English delegation tried to enforce via the corrupt League of Nations (frontage and face wash for the worst international corruption at Basel.)

"USURY is the cancer of the world, which only the surgeon's knife of Fascism can cut out of the life of nations."

Some pruning had been practiced before:

> and on June 28th came men of Arezzo
> past the Porta Romana and went into the ghetto
> there to sack and burn hebrews
> part were burned with the liberty tree in the piazza
> and for the rest of that day and night
> 1799 anno domini
>
> (Canto XLIV)

But how many of these ghetto Jews were usurers? How many in the period under review? It is estimated that six million Jews—that is to say, men, women and children—were shot, gassed and burned simply because they were Jews, and perhaps to provide confirmation of a belief that the end product of Christianity is anti-semitism. I look once more at the official photograph of little boys and girls, not one over five years old, lying dead and slain in a heap, and I must confess I cannot, though I have looked hard and long, discover a single usurer among them. There are many bodies, and there may be one hidden from view.[6]

How they must have gloated in the twilight of Berlin to see the rich rewards of the free news service provided in six languages, including English, with which the nations the Nazis were planning to attack were divided internally before the first bombs fell.

8.

After the Hours Press limited edition of *A Draft of XXX Cantos*—there were, besides the two copies on vellum ten on Texas paper bound in orange vellum, and two hundred on Canson-Mongolfier paper with a canvas binding—the book of that title was published in a regular trade edition in the United States by Farrar and Rinehart, 1933, and in England by Faber and Faber, 1934. *Eleven New Cantos* appeared in 1934 and 1935—in the latter year as *A Draft of Cantos: XXXI-XLI*—under the imprint of those firms, which also published, in 1937, *The Fifth Decad of Cantos,* their number having reached fifty-one. Yeats, it will be recalled, had seen but twenty-seven when he was writing *A Packet for Ezra Pound;* when he wrote on the subject again, in September, 1936, he was presumably familiar with all but the last ten, and even these he might have seen in manuscript. The following is from the passage on Pound in his introduction to *The Oxford Book of Modern Verse:*

"When I consider his work as a whole, I find more style than form; at moments more style, more deliberate nobility and the means to convey it than in any contemporary poet known to me, but it is constantly interrupted, broken, twisted into nothing by its direct opposite, nervous obsession, nightmare, stammering confusion; he is an economist, poet, politician, raging at malignants with inexplicable characters and motives, grotesque figures out a child's book of beasts. This loss of self-control, common among uneducated revolutionists, is rare—Shelley had it in some degree—among men of Ezra Pound's culture and erudition."

Pound wrote Hubert Creekmore in 1939:

"God damn Yeats' bloody paragraph. Done more to prevent people reading Cantos for what is *on the page* than any other one smoke screen."

Eliot wrote in his account of Pound from which I have been quoting:

"If I am doubtful about some of *The Cantos,* it is not that I find any poetic decline in them. I am doubtful on somewhat the same ground as that on which I once complained to him about an article on the monetary theory of Gesell, which he had written at my suggestion for *The Criterion.* I said (as nearly as I can remember): 'I asked you to write an article which would explain this subject to people who had never heard of it; yet you write as if your readers knew about it already, but had failed to understand it.' In *The Cantos* there is an increasing defect of communication, not apparent when he is concerned with Sigismondo Malatesta, or with Chinese dynasties, but, for instance: whenever he mentions Martin Van Buren. Such passages are very opaque: they read as if the author was so irritated with his readers for not knowing all about anybody so important as Van Buren, that he refused to enlighten them."[7]

But in a postscript added in 1950, he wrote:

"On one point I should like to qualify my opinion. The foregoing was written shortly after the end of the War, when I had not yet had the opportunity to study *The Pisan Cantos;* and these *Cantos*—apart from their immense weight and solidity in themselves—do I find go far towards justifying the *longeurs* of earlier passages about mysteries of American history, in the first half of the last century, in which I, like most readers, am not adept."[8]

CHAPTER XIX

THE 1939 VISIT

1.

Carl Carmer, Hamilton '14, who told me he first heard Pound's name from Professor Shepard, wrote an entertaining account of the Loomis Gang in *Listen for a Lonesome Drum.* He was especially effective about the Loomis ladies. The year his book appeared—1936 —another alumnus, Professor Harold W. Thompson of Cornell, wrote about Pound in the *Hamilton Alumni Review.*[1] He referred, of course, to the Loomis Gang, which had operated only twenty miles from the sacred precincts of Hamilton: "Proud as he properly is of his grandfather's choice, I doubt whether the poet is aware of what an important gang the 'Lummises' were." And he referred to Carmer's book, "which will drop stars on New York State," a compliment to his most famous work, *Stars Fell on Alabama,* a title which a song writer stole and Pound used in the *Cantos,* though he got the state wrong.

Professor Thompson went on to write one of the most effective brief accounts of Pound's career and work in existence. He had an aim in view: "Harvard cackled a good deal over its importation of T. S. Eliot a couple of years ago. Would it be creditable to Hamilton to entertain the man whom Eliot calls Master? I am not speaking of honorary degrees—though we should certainly give him one if he will take it. He should visit us as friend and alumnus. He should read us his poems and let us enjoy a personality which has inspired some of the chief artists of our time. He should hear again, in a place which has the *dulcem memoriam* of youth, those American accents which his ear has almost lost." And he concluded:

"Would it not be a gracious deed if Hamilton's poet should be welcomed back to the hillside where he read the ballades of Villon and the plaint of the 'Wanderer' ["The Seafarer"]?"

Pound thanked Dr. Thompson for his article. In that unpublished letter he recalled his sojourn on College Hill.

"My favorite amusement 1903/'05 was lighting M. Woolsey Stryker's fuse for the fun of watching him explode," he wrote. "I still recall that purposeful gait of the Prexy as he exsurged toward the Commons on the question of the third breakfast biscuit."

Dr. Thompson told me "it was a mistake to think that Pound despised all professors," and quoted from the same letter: "At Hamilton in my time was Schnitz [H. C. G.] Brandt, who was pleased that I did NOT want to be bothered with German prose and skipeed me to the poetry courses, despite my ignorance of the choimun langwidg."

Praise of Professor Shepard followed:

"Bill shep gave me the Provençal. There was no provençal course, and I cd.n't have paid him. I mean GAVE."

He offered a piece of news for the *Hamilton Alumni Review:* "As Hamilton ITEM, might record that the CANTOS started in a talk with 'BIB' [Professor Joseph Darling Ibbotson, whom Thompson termed "a learned and charming man"], and Bib's remarks on Bentley's attempt to 'edit' Milton as he had edited, textually, Horace etc. I was in them days contemplatin a jejune trilogy on Merozia. Which Bib was naive enough to agree wd/ be a man's magnum opus if he pulled it off."

College Hill buzzed with it for a while, then Pound was once more forgotten. It was not until three years later, when he was planning a visit to the United States anyway, that Hamilton invited him, not to reside or to read, but to accept an honorary degree. He wrote to Hubert Creekmore before starting out:

"I don't have to *try* to be American. Merrymount, Braintree, Quincy, all I believe in or by, what had been 'a plantation named Weston's.'

"Vide also the host in Longfellow's 'Wayside Inn.' Wall ornament there mentioned still at my parents'. Am I American? Yes, and buggar the present state of the country, the utter betrayal of the American Constitution, the filth of the Universities, and the — — — system of publication whereby you can buy Lenin, Trotsky (the messiest mutt of the lot), Stalin for 10 cents and 25 cents, and it takes *seven* years to get a set of John Adams at about 30 dollars. Van Buren's autobiog not printed till 1920.

"An Ars Poetica might in time evolve from the *Ta Hio*. Note esp. my 'Mencius' in last summer's *Criterion*. And as to 'am I American': wait for Cantos 62/71 now here in rough typescript."

Meanwhile, an event of some importance, unmentioned in Pound's published correspondence, occurred in London. Yeats wrote Lady Dorothy Wellesley on October 8, 1938:

"Yesterday morning I had tragic news. Olivia Shakespear has died suddenly. For more than forty years she has been the centre of my life in London and during all that time we have never had a quarrel, sadness sometimes but never a difference. When I first met her she was in her late twenties, but in looks a lovely young girl. When she died she was a lovely old woman. You would have approved her. She came of a long line of soldiers and during the last war thought it her duty to stay in London through all the air raids."

Omar Pound was twelve when his grandmother died. He told me that Pound, whom he had not seen since infancy, and his mother did not come to the funeral, but that Pound arrived shortly after on family business. He did not see his father again until 1945.

2.

Pound sailed on the Italian liner *Rex* April 13, 1939, and arrived in New York April 21st. It was his first visit to his native land in almost three decades. Gorham B. Munson sent a wireless message advising, "give economic but not political views to the press when interviewed," and John Cournos sent a welcoming telegram when the liner docked. Munson also went to meet Pound but missed him. He told me: "The liner had already docked by the time I reached the pier, and Pound, travelling first-class in a luxury suite, cleared customs quickly and had left for Cummings's apartment." Before he left, he met the press.

Dressed in a doubled-breasted tweed jacket and powder-blue trousers, shirt as usual open at the neck, seated in a lounge chair with head thrown back and legs outstretched, he answered questions oracularly but, as it turned out, mistakenly. Asked by ship news reporters whether there would be a war he replied:

"Nothing but devilment can start a new war west of the Vistula. I'm not making any accusation against anyone. But the bankers and the munitions interests, whoever and wherever they may be, are more responsible for the present talk of war than are the intentions of Mussolini or anyone else."

Of Mussolini he said: "He has a mind with the quickest uptake of any man I know of except Picabia." Perhaps the reporters looked blank at this point; he added, "Picabia is the man who ties the knots in Picasso's tail."

On current literature: "I regard the literature of social significance as of no significance. It is pseudo pink blah. The men who are worth anything today are definitely down on money—writing about money, the problem of money, exchange, gold and silver. I have yet to find a Bolshevik who has written of it."

On Joyce:

"When Joyce was writing I ballyhooed him. Not since he retrogressed."

On Hemingway:

"Hemingway is a good guy, but I don't suppose we'd want to meet him personally. Spain."

On poets:

"I can name one poet writing today. I mean Cummings."

He went directly from the pier to Patchin Place. He stayed with John Slocum, then went to Washington. He hoped to see Roosevelt, although he had nothing but contempt for the New Deal (Canto XLVI).

His sojourn in the capital is not without some mystery, both as to its duration and persons seen. His letters might have helped to clear things up; unfortunately, they are not, for this period, where one would expect to find them—either in the published selection or in possession of the recipients. It was while he was in Washington, apparently, that he accepted the offer of an honorary degree from Hamilton College. The letters dealing with this were sold, together with other Pound letters, at the Parke-Bernet Galleries in 1958. Three of them are described as follows in the sale catalogue:

"Lot 331. POUND, EZRA. Three letters, all directed to the President of Hamilton College, as follows: Letter typed and signed by Pound. 1 p. 4to. Rapallo, March 10, 1939. A. L.s., in pencil. 1 p., 4to. Washington, /April/, 1939. A.L.s., 3 pp., 4to. Washington, /May/, 1939.

"In the first, Pound transmits a leaflet with four suggestions for the teaching of economics and history. In the second, he asks why he has not been told whether these matters are covered at Hamilton, and in the third discusses taking a doctorate at the College. The first two are filled with bitter remarks on American education and probably represent the poet's political thinking of the period."[2]

The abbreviations stand for "autograph letter signed" and "quarto," meaning the standard 8 ½ by 11 inch typewriter sheet. The leaflet enclosed in the first letter is the "Text Book" of four historical quotations, referred to in the previous chapter. He also displayed it at the Library of Congress. He afterwards wrote in "America, Roosevelt and the Causes of the Present War," a title which, it may be thought, is suggestive of a great deal of knowledge of the "inside" or "lowdown" variety on the part of the author:

"One day, thinking of the trouble it had cost me to unearth these four 'chapters,' I asked the head of the American history department of the Library of Congress if there existed a history of America, whether in one volume or in ten, that contained these four chapters, or the substance of them.

"After reflecting for a while he replied that so far as he knew I was the first to have brought together and in relation to each other the four great names of the greatest presidents of the Republic."

The remark does credit to the Library of Congress, and might even be worthy of the State Department.

3.

In 1939, President Roosevelt was too busy to see him. Pound saw Secretary of Agriculture (afterwards Vice President) Henry A. Wallace, to whom he was introduced by letter by Paul de Kruif, whose work he had reviewed in the *New English Weekly,* and with whom he had corresponded. Mr. de Kruif and Mr. Wallace were old friends; "it was because of Paul that Pound dropped in to see me," Mr. Wallace wrote in reply to my inquiry.

"Pound had some ideas as to proper economic organization but I have forgotten what they were. I have no doubt that de Kruif remembers. Pound seemed normal enough when he called on me but rather pessimistic as to the future of the U.S. I was much surprised to learn later that he had broadcast for Mussolini. I do not think that he intended to hurt the U.S.A. But I do think he operated in a different world from most of us."

Mr. de Kruif wrote me:

"A letter from Mr. Pound to me in 1933 had a profound influence on my book, *Why Keep Them Alive?*, published in 1936. Mr. Pound first told me that I knew little about the art of writing, still was kind enough to suggest that I look into what he believed to be an important cause of death, namely poverty. He was then interested in the economic work of Major C. H. Douglas. If you can get hold of *Why Keep Them Alive?* you will find how much I owe to Mr. Pound for his help on that book."

Mr. de Kruif wrote in that book:

"Pound pointed out that I apparently knew nothing of a man-made cause of dying that was more murderous than all the swarming subvisible billions of man-killing microbes put together.

"Pound said that cause was poverty."[3]

In addition to Mr. Wallace, Pound saw several members of Congress, including some Senators. He was received courteously as the grandson of a Congressman. In the affidavit in support of an application for bail for Pound in 1945, Pound's counsel stated that "he saw such statesmen as Bankhead, Borah, Bridges, Byrd, Downey, Lodge, MacLeish, Tinkham, Voorhis and Wallace, all in a vain effort to move the nation's policies toward paths which he thought were the paths to peace." (MacLeish was Librarian of Congress in 1939.)

Pound, at his first arraignment, told the presiding judge that he had made the journey in 1939 to "keep hell from breaking loose in the world."

This, too, was pure fancy.

In Canto LXXXIV, the last of *The Pisan Cantos,* Pound recollects some snippets of conversation with two of the Senators named above (Borah was the Senator from Idaho, Pound's native state):

"an' doan you think he chop and change all the time
stubborn az a mule, sah, stubborn as a MULE,
got the eastern idea about money"
                    Thus Senator Bankhead
"am sure I don't know what a man like you
        would find to *do* here"
                    said Senator Borah
Thus the solons, in Washington,
on the executive, and on the country, a.d. 1939

(In 1958, just after his release from St. Elizabeths, he told Representative Burdick of North Dakota that Senator Wheeler had told him Roosevelt "had packed the Supreme Court and now he can declare anything constitutional.")

Pound also attended a session of Congress.

William Carlos Williams and his wife, en route to Virginia, stopped off to see him at the home of Horace Holley, a writer who had been associated with the *Others* group, and Pound stayed overnight in the Williams house in Rutherford on his way back to New York. He did not meet MacLeish in Washington, but in Cambridge, Massachusetts.

4.

He was back in New York City early in May—according to Cummings, wearing an immense Borsalino. John Slocum put him up again. Slocum told me: "I recall that we went to Englewood, N. J., to pick up the daughter of an old friend one evening, but that we were refused admission to the Stork Club because of Pound's costume—tieless, in a shirt open at the throat with broad purple stripes—and that when I asked him why he had endorsed Il Duce so passionately and so idiotically for the *World Telegram,* he replied: 'They won't pay attention to me if I don't say something sensational,' which led me to believe that his trip had been underwritten by the Italian Line and/or the Ministry of Propaganda."

He stayed with other friends and acquaintances while in New York. He told Julien Cornell in 1945: "I spent only one night in a hotel all the time I was here, and I came unexpected. That one night was getting into New York late and wanting to be there in the a.m." It may have been after a visit to New Haven, where he saw James Angleton, of *Furioso,* in which Pound's "Introductory Text Book" appeared (Summer, 1939). There is also a reference to Greenwich in one of his letters. He was so busy shuttling back and forth between lodgings for a night that Mrs. Cummings recalls seeing him with a pair of rolled-up pajamas in an envelope under his arm.

He went often to the Museum of Modern Art, sometimes accompanied by Wyndham Lewis. He saw Iris Barry, now curator of the Museum's film library. He was critical of the Museum's collection; after all, Lewis was not represented, neither was Gaudier-Brzeska. The collection was good "of what was left after Europeans had got the best." Miss Barry was not so glad to see him. She told me that she had last heard from him in 1934 when, she said, "he hoped I might be able to start a magazine, or get millionaires to buy some Gaudier-Brzeska, or the American government to accept his own peculiar economic-political ideas—all three of which, as you may imagine, lay far beyond my powers. I had had no contact with him at all until that time since 1918, and when I say contact I mean not correspondence or any sort of communication: relations were severely severed and I hope we don't have to go into *that.*" She added: "I do not mean that I have in any way changed my gratitude to him for his help to me when young nor my admiration for his constant and splendid generosity and aid to so many. I just simply had reasons and some of them extremely personal for not wanting to see him."

He saw Tibor Serly in his West Fifty-eighth studio, where he consumed quantities of Hungarian pastries with his tea. He appeared to like sweets so much that Mrs. Serly baked a "real old-fashioned home-made strawberry shortcake" for him, which he enjoyed immensely. As Serly's studio was only five blocks from the Museum, Pound got into the habit of calling on the composer after visits there. Serly told me that Pound tried to adapt New York to Rapallo "conditions." He was "a great dropper-in," and brought a "crowd" with him, "mostly from the Museum of Modern Art." After years of mulling this over, Serly concluded that Pound did this "to be of help to me." But: "I was—I am—angry at Pound. He should have known better."

In Serly's studio he met Louis Zukofsky, whom he had not seen since 1933. Despite their strange correspondence, parts of which had so infuriated him, Pound had dedicated *Guide to Kulchur* (1938) to Zukofsky and Basil Bunting. Now, on the eve of the war which Zukofsky had predicted, and Pound did not believe was coming (like Senator Borah, who arrogantly told reporters in the summer of 1939 that he had better sources of information than the State Department) Pound was full of queries about the political situation—he had been listening hopefully to the radio. He got small comfort.

"When he asked me if it was possible to educate certain politicians, I retorted, 'Whatever you don't know, Ezra, you ought to know *voices.*' "

This, Zukofsky told me, was a reference to Father Coughlin. He also said: "I told him that I did not doubt his integrity had decided his political action, but I pointed to his head, indicating something had gone wrong."

Zukofsky, like Williams, never believed in the reality of Pound's anti-semitism. "It never bothered me," he says.

"I never felt the least trace of anti-semitism in his presence. Nothing he ever said to me made me feel the embarrassment I always have for the 'Goy' in whom a residue of antagonism to 'Jew' remains. If we had occasion to use the words 'Jew' and 'Goy' they were no more or less ethnological in their sense than 'Chinese' and 'Italian.' "

Pound saw Ford Madox Ford at 12 Fifth Avenue. Ford's widow, the painter Janice Biala, now the wife of *The New Yorker* cartoonist Alain, wrote me:

"I cannot remember anything special about Pound's visit in 1939 except that he seemed irritated at the thought that Ford might think he was in Mussolini's pay because he came over in the royal suite on an Italian boat. (I don't think Ford thought it.) He said he came primarily to interest politicians in the Douglas plan."

He saw Katherine Ruth Heyman at 26 Perry Street. He dined with Mencken at Robert's.

One night, he telephoned Marianne Moore, who lived in Brooklyn, to say he would come for supper. They had never met. She said there was a restaurant near the subway, and invited him there. He suggested cold cuts or eggs at home, but Miss Moore told him, "I haven't any cold cuts or eggs." They ate in the restaurant, then returned to her apartment, which Miss Moore shared with her mother. After fifteen minutes he realized that her mother was tired, and remarked, "Two short visits might be better than one long one," and left. Miss Moore walked to the subway with him. She told me that when she described Eliot's brother Henry (whom Pound did not know) as "more the artist than anyone I've ever met," he turned to her and said, "Now, now, be careful." Pound did not make a second visit to Brooklyn. They met again when Miss Moore called on him in St. Elizabeths Hospital.

5.

On the morning of May 12th Pound telephoned Gorham Munson from Ford's apartment. Munson, who lived at 66 Fifth Avenue, asked him to walk over and then lunch at the Players. Mrs. Munson, a dancer, was reluctant to meet Pound because of his views, but was soon charmed by the red-bearded poet in reddish-brown tweeds who talked vivaciously about her friend Katherine Ruth Heyman who, she told me, "played Scriabin like nobody else." The Munson studio was big enough for dance rehearsals for groups of fifteen, "and cocktail parties for seventy-five," Munson said, and Pound began to project "evenings" for the arts there—poetry, music, the dance.

The Players was next door to the National Arts Club on Gramercy Park, where Pound had attended a meeting of the Poetry Society of America almost three decades before. He and Munson were joined by Paul Hampden who, Munson told me, "might be called the economist of the American Social Credit Movement." Hampden was the son of the famous stage star. They sat in the corner of the high-ceilinged, raftered dining room which Stanford White had designed when he adapted Edwin Booth's house to a clubhouse. Pewter tankards hang from a shelf which runs around the room, and the walls are covered with old playbills and portraits. Pound took the corner seat, from which he could see and be seen. "Everyone looked at him," Munson said.

"He wore a flaring white sport shirt, no tie, a casual, baggy, tweedy suit, and rolled around in his chair," Munson told me. "He was rather pudgy, bearded, of course—and certainly striking. Whether members lunching there that day knew who the bearded casual character in the corner was, is not known, but certainly they stared at him—in a polite way," he added.

"Pound talked about his stay in Washington where he had been seeing Congressmen in the interest of money reform, and he talked reassuringly of the international situation. He was not explicit about his Washington interviews, and was chary of names. He did not think war was in the offing. He often used an indecent expletive"— *videlicet,* a four-letter word.

Hampden thought Pound had been away too long, and was "very much at sea."

From New York, Pound went to Cambridge, where he stayed with Professor Theodore Spencer and his wife. Their house was on Oxford Street, back of Memorial Hall. There were several parties in his honor, and the two poets played a great deal of tennis. James Laughlin told me: "Ted fancied himself a good tennis player, but Pound beat him." Mrs. Spencer's recollections of her famous guest have for their core the big new refrigerator in her kitchen, which appeared to fascinate Pound. Occasionally, when she went to open it to feed other guests, she found that she had been forestalled.

Pound had no desire to meet anyone in the Department of English at Harvard, only the head of the Economics Department; this, I have been told, Spencer arranged. But the Department of English wanted very much to have Pound appear at Harvard, and he was asked to give a reading. It took place in the semi-circular lecture room in Sever Hall, where Bliss Perry had lectured on Emerson. Spencer made the introduction. The steep rows of seats were occupied by undergraduates, with a sprinkling of faculty. It was warm, and Pound had on a light jacket on which the collar of his open shirt was rolled back. To John Holmes, who was present, he looked older than his pictures; his face was fuller, and with his small beard he reminded Holmes of old pictures of Ben Jonson. Holmes told me: "Pound seemed to read an extraordinarily long time on one breath, and then take a deep one, and go on again." He read from long sheets of paper typed in large blue type. "He read sitting down, held his breath for an incredible time before drawing another for the next few lines of poetry, and yet the voice was too soft to be heard, unless, as he did unexpectedly, he yelled."

There was another department at Harvard that was interested in Pound's presence in Cambridge—the Department of Speech. The chairman, Professor Frederick Packard, who was critical of Pound's reading in Sever Hall, nevertheless invited Pound to make a recording for his series of Harvard Vocarium readings. Pound agreed, but asked for a pair of kettle-drums to accompany himself while reading "The Seafarer." The drums were supplied. Holmes, who was assisting Professor Packard, thought it would have been magnificent with a rehearsal; as it was, Pound gave "a few reverberating strokes," then merely waved the sticks in the air, with only an occasional thump on one drum or the other, having become engrossed in his text. He also read Canto XVII and what he called the "Bloody Sestina"—"Sestina: Altaforte." When he heard the playback, he was startled at the strange voice, an experience common to all who have made recordings. He termed it "Irish brogue coming out as his reading style." He afterwards wrote Packard to destroy the record, that he did not want it heard; in Packard's recollection, "It is not to be played by anyone the hell ever." Laughlin said it was because Pound felt the "Bloody Sestina" was an invocation to war; World War I had followed the first reading.

The recording session took place on May 17th. Pound signed three books for Holmes on this occasion—*A Draft of Thirty Cantos, Eleven New Cantos,* and *the Fifth Decad of Cantos.* In his haste he signed the last one in the back. He also dated it, Fascist style.

Walking through Harvard Yard with Packard and Holmes he spoke of his stay in Washington. When he mentioned the session of Congress he had attended, he shook his head over what had been, for him, a stupid and boring spectacle.

One night, Pound came to dinner in the private home in Boston where Laughlin stayed during his last year at Harvard. The lady of the house said of Pound: "He talked too much, ate too much, and was extremely ill-at-ease." Laughlin also brought Pound to a house in the suburbs for Sunday lunch. After lunch he asked their hostess to take a picture of Pound, but when Pound saw the camera, she told me, he slumped down in his chair, closed his eyes and said he didn't want his picture taken. "To please Jay I made two exposures and then put the camera way." The resultant photo shows Pound resting his head, as in later years. Nestled in his lapel is an enormous rose.

Back in New York, he made preparations for his trip to Clinton. The commencement exercises were scheduled for Monday, June 12th, but he had been invited to come earlier.

"One Saturday night," Serly told me, "Pound came in a great rush

Pound in Paris: the studio courtyard, September, 1923

Pound as broadcaster:
Rome residence

Pound in custody:
Genoa, 1945

of confusion to my place—he was to go to Hamilton College the next day to receive an honorary degree and had no black shoes, just the big brown shoes he always wore. My feet were too small, but I think I finally found a pair to fit him."

6.

Pound stayed, in Clinton, at the home of Mr. and Mrs. Edward Root on College Hill. Root, one of the students with whom he had taken a course in Old French under Professor Shepard, as previously related, was now teaching a course in appreciation of art at Hamilton. The important Root collection of art is now a memorial to him. Mrs. Root told me:

"Pound came to our house after he had been in Washington where he had talked with senators about credit. He said Representative Tinkham was the only man to be President, and damned the Roosevelts.

"My husband and I discussed it that night. We were not isolationists, and we felt that if war came we should get into it. We decided to tell Pound the truth of what we felt. Edward was gentle but explicit—he took Ezra aside in the morning. From that time on there was not a word about isolation.

"Edward asked Pound if he thought Fascism would work here, and Pound replied, 'No, I don't think so.' "

He was interviewed Friday morning, June 9th, by a reporter and photographer from the Utica *Observer-Dispatch*. "If God loved the American people," he told them, "the Republican party would nominate for President George Holden Tinkham, the representative from Massachusetts, in 1940." He also talked "quite a little and fiercely about England." The interview took place on the verandah of the Root home. Pound was dressed in a blue blouse and dazzling white shorts. He said he was having "a very delightful time." There was an awkward moment. Asked what fraternity he had belonged to, he retorted: "None."

Mrs. Root told me he played tennis a great deal on the college courts, chiefly with Olivia Saunders, the daughter of Professor A. P. Saunders, onetime Dean of the College. Despite his athletic prowess, Mrs. Root said, Pound "was awkward, always bumping into things going out of a room."

Olivia Saunders (Mrs. Robert W. Wood, Jr.) wrote me:

"I have a vivid recollection of playing one or two doubles matches in Clinton with him because he was the most individualistic partner I ever played with. When we were receiving I was instructed to stand in the middle of the baseline and take any balls which might get by him. He placed himself in the middle of the court at net and was such an agile and fiery tennis player that few balls got back to me. When we served he did the same thing, served, got to net midcourt and returned almost every ball, I again standing on the baseline in the middle of the court."

She added: "We won easily."

Another guest in the Root house was Charles A. Miller, a Hoover appointee who had been asked to stay on by Roosevelt as head of the Reconstruction Finance Corporation. He was an expert on savings banks, and was himself head of the Utica Savings Bank. He was also a trustee of Hamilton. Pound, Mrs. Root said, talked to him at such length about the Douglas Plan that she finally had to interpose, saying: "Charles must have his rest."

Alexander Woollcott also turned up at the Root house. The Roots feared a clash between the two men, but Woollcott was on his best behavior, asked questions, listened, and "couldn't have been more humble-minded before another celebrity."

7.

The commencement exercises were held in the college chapel, completed in 1827, which Carmer terms the most beautiful example of Georgian Colonial in the state. The academic procession which preceded the exercises was led by seniors who formed ranks in the quadrangle. Just outside the chapel, under the stone gaze of Alexander Hamilton, the seniors formed an aisle through which the faculty and honored guests marched, Pound among them. Also present to be honored was H. V. Kaltenborn, the veteran news analyst.

Pound was awarded the honory degree of Doctor of Letters. He was presented to President William Harold Cowley by Dean F. H. Ristine. The citation, which took note of his political and economic activities as well as his literary ones, reads:

"*Ezra Pound:* Native of Idaho, graduate of Hamilton College in the Class of 1905, poet, critic, and prose writer of great distinction. Since completing your college career you have had a life full of significance in the arts. You have found that you could work more happily in Europe than in America and so have lived most of the past thirty years an expatriate making your home in England, France and Italy, but your writings are known wherever English is read. Your feet have trodden paths, however, where the great reading public could give you few followers—into Provençal and Italian poetry, into Anglo-Saxon and Chinese. From all these excursions you have brought back treasure. Your translations from the Chinese have, for example, led one of the most gifted of contemporary poets to call you the inventor of Chinese poetry for our time. Your Alma Mater, however, is an old lady who has not always understood where you have been going, but she has watched you with interest and pride if not always with understanding. The larger public has also been at times amazed at your political and economic as well as your artistic credo, and you have retaliated by making yourself—not unintentionally perhaps— their gadfly. Your range of interests is immense, and whether or not your theories of society survive, your name is permanently linked with the development of English poetry in the twentieth century. Your reputation is international, you have guided many poets into new paths, you have pointed new directions, and the historian of the future in tracing the development of your growing mind will inevitably, we are happy to think, be led to Hamilton and to the influence of your college teachers. You have ever been a generous champion of younger writers as well as of artists in other fields, and for this fine and rare human quality and for your own achievements in poetry and prose, we honor you."

At the conclusion of these words, President Cowley placed over Pound's head the buff and blue hood commemorating the colors of the Revolutionary uniform.

The exercises were followed by the traditional alumni luncheon in the Hall of Commons. One of the alumni present was Robert U. Hayes, president of the Hayes National Bank of Clinton, who had been a schoolmate of Pound's. On one side of Pound sat Professor Saunders, on the other the secretary of the College, Wallace B. Johnson. Mr. Kaltenborn, the principal speaker, declared: "It is written

in history that dictatorships shall die, but democracies shall live."
Democracies, he said, "are more expensive and less efficient in organizing for a single purpose, but they are not as wasteful of fundamental
human values." He had praise for England, whose monarchs were
guests of the United States, and referred to the "doubtful" alliance
between Italy and Germany.

At this point he was interrupted by Pound, who wanted to know
what he meant by "doubtful." Mr. Kaltenborn attempted to explain,
but found it difficult; Pound was regaling him and York State
Americans with praise of Mussolini and Fascism. Mr. Kaltenborn
said "praise God that in America people of varying points of view
can still speak out," but Pound was not content with this. As Mr.
Kaltenborn's succeeding remarks were not reported in the press, I
offer the account he gave me:

"I pointed out how wrong it was to preach such anti-democratic
doctrine within the confines of an American college. The audience
applauded my address with unusual vigor and many of those present
thanked me for this immediate reply to what they considered Ezra
Pound's unfortunate comments."

There was a great deal of anger on both sides. Olivia Saunders,
who was in the balcony, told me that her father, "who was always
very fond of him," tried to calm Pound, but "the situation almost got
out of hand as both men were thoroughly irritated with the other's
point of view." "It was a hot dispute," Mr. Hayes told me, "and the
President intervened and stopped the uproar." In a letter to President
Cowley Pound inferred that Kaltenborn had goaded him into making
his outburst. "I sat in the next chair to Mr. Pound at the occasion
and can assure you that it was Pound that displayed bad manners,"
Mr. Johnson wrote me.

Pound followed Kaltenborn as speaker. He told his audience:

"You can get the works of Marx and Trotsky in select editions for
ten or twenty-five cents. And yet, while I was abroad, I spent seven
years trying to get a copy of John Adams's writings. It is my conviction that you ought to be able to purchase the thoughts and writings
of America's founders as easily and cheaply as you can those of sub-
versive propagandists."

The Utica *Daily Press,* which quoted the above, said:

"In closing, he advocated as required reading his own 'Text Book,' a four-page leaflet attributing America's ills to its currency program."

Pound left Clinton in a disgruntled mood. A fellow alumnus offered to drive him to Albany, and on the way invited him to spend the night in Saratoga, where he had a summer home. He was a businessman, and was rather overwhelmed by Pound's monologue on economics. "Our visit was completely senseless and non-productive and I often wonder why I ever got into it." The next morning they drove to the station in Albany, where Pound took the train to New York.[4]

8.

He called on Virginia Rice, a literary agent who had placed four of his books, including the two collections of cantos published by Farrar and Rinehart, and *Jefferson and/or Mussolini*. She told me Pound was the only author she had ever handled whom she had read in college, and that he came to her through Kay Boyle. They had never met, and she had not handled his work since 1936. John Farrar had told her after Pound's letters began to arrive that he couldn't keep a secretary, and she herself, after reading some to her—she termed them "profane and arrogant"—and the *Jefferson and/or Mussolini*, expected not to like him. But when he appeared, "he was like a bombastic infant, pink-cheeked and rather appealing." He was also on the defensive.

"I don't want to roast little babies," he said. "I just happen to like the Fascist money system."

John Farrar told me that one of Pound's letters to him "was really so outrageous that I didn't care how great a poet he was, I didn't want to publish him, and said so to Stanley Rinehart."

He played host at Robert's, where he had dined well with Mencken. His guests were Cummings and his wife; Max Eastman, whom Pound wanted to meet, and Eastman's charming wife, the late Eliena Krylenko, a painter. With Pound was one of his young disciples, who never opened his mouth except to eat. (He's still mum, for he did not answer my letter.) Most of the conversation was between Pound and Eastman, both big and handsome in their different, effective ways. They clashed. I do not know what impressions Pound carried away of the man he had asked Cummings to introduce to him; Eastman told

me he had written down his impressions. "They were not very compli-
mentary."

He was indefatigable. He journeyed to Fordham University, in the
Bronx, to talk with the late Father Moorhouse Millar, S.J., professor
of political philosophy. He afterwards termed Father Millar "one of
the serious characters I saw in U.S." But he added, "he won't start
a Paideuma Europ. institution. Tho' he might push publication of
studies on Adams/ Jef/ etc. at any rate said he cd. steer student theses
toward 'em" (letter to Douglas Fox from Rapallo).[5]

On his last evening in New York, Pound's taxi stopped in front of
the Gotham Book Mart on West 47th Street. John Slocum, who was
accompanying Pound to the pier, got out to pick up a book—perhaps
one he wished to present to Pound, or one Pound had asked him to buy
for him. Slocum entered, asked for the book, and was told it was not
in stock. But just as he was getting into the taxi Miss Steloff's assistant
found it and hurried to the sidewalk with it. She returned to tell Miss
Steloff the astonishing news: Pound was in a taxi just outside her shop,
but had not entered. This, understandably, hurt Miss Steloff's feelings.
With the passage of years a story circulated that Pound had not gone
into her shop because she was Jewish. Miss Steloff told me she was
neither the source of that story, nor believed it to be true, and she was
very upset when it appeared in Samuel Putnam's book.[6] In 1948 she
wrote to Mrs. Pound, who replied from Washington:

"I think S. Putnam's statement that E. P. refused to enter your
shop because you are Jewish is an absolute falsehood. He was in N.Y.
for hours rather than days & entered no bookshops at all."

Pound contributed an essay on Eliot to Miss Steloff's 1940 catalogue, which marked the Gotham Book Mart's twentieth year.

9.

On August 7th he sent Douglas Fox seven pages of typescript headed
"European Paideuma," which he wanted Fox to translate into German
and place in a German publication "where it will get serious attention." The essay begins:

"To hell with Spengler. What we believe is EUROPEAN, & by no
means in a state of Untergang. In this essay I distinguish between 'in-

telligence' and 'intellect' using the latter term to indicate the mental scaffolding men erect to deal with what they don't understand. Belief is from intelligence.

"From the crying 'Ligo' in Lithuania, down to the Greek archipelago, certain things are believed. Book instruction obscures them. The people in Rapallo rushing down into the sea on Easter morning or bringing their gardens of Adonis to church on the Thursday before, have not learned it in school. Neither have the peasant women *read* anything telling them to bring silk-cocoons to church carefully concealed in their hands or under their aprons.

"The Xtian church was of very mixed elements. The valid elements European. The only vigorous feasts of the Church are grafted onto European roots, the sun, the grain, the harvest and Aphrodite."

He played the seer:

"The function of Germany, as I see it, in the next 40 years' art is indispensible. No where else is there enough force toward a purgation. The Italians are too easy going. Spain is African and Christian, and you can not trust Christianity for ten minutes."

He was once more contemplating a periodical. He wrote Fox again, who was now domiciled in New York:

"How do YOU get news IN America? Have you discovered ANY thought? or any tendency or desire to communicate and to bring ideas to precision, or test 'em on others?

"More and more editorials here in Italy are along my line. I don't mean because I said so first. BUT the U.S.Acans can't take any glory for shoving me into Italian, besides it means a loss of energy/ more friction in getting ideas out. May clarify ultimate expression BUT etc; etc;

"Meridiano has printed some strong E. P. BUT has to be inclusive and can't include all I have to put over IN a given time." He himself had brought "ideas to precision."

The *Meridiano di Roma* printed Pound's "The Jew, Disease Incarnate" ("l'ebreo malattia incarnata"), which pleased the Germans but few Italians. But if he wanted to reach Americans, why did he not stay in America? Or why did he not return? In fact, he was seriously thinking about returning. "If you keep on INSTRUCTIN Iris, *and* young Laughlin *and* Johannes the Slocum etc. you might mak a li'l nest fer ole Ez/ in N.Y." But perhaps he paused, and reflected, and recalling the opposition to his ideas, dropped the thought. Quite possibly *he* had met the wrong people. He asked Fox:

"Do *you* see any set of ten people (I don't mean a squad, but ten scattered, who wd. put up 3 or 10 dollars a year and/or one hour's work a month on organizing a paper. MINi(bloody) MUM of 12 pages monthly."

But he was prepared to return "if Crysler [*sic*] and the Gal/ Mod/ art [Museum of Modern Art] shd/ bid against each other" for his Gaudier-Brzeska drawings which, he said, were "worth 5000 bucks at least."

He was casting about for new worlds to conquer. This time it was the next one:

"Waaal you have lived in Europe long enough to know that THOUGHT can occur. Whether the F/Zeitung now wants yr/ translation of my remarks on European paideuma I don't know.

"I keep chewing on that. Wheat god. In fact now that I have about finished with economics mebbe some sucker will putt up something for a less COMprehensible subject, namely religion taken *sul serio*, not Mr. Eliot's pale Galilean rubbish."

10.

For several months, a request for biographical information had followed him half around the world, from the H. W. Wilson Company in New York, publishers of *Twentieth Century Authors*. He wrote from Sienna, where he was visiting Olga Rudge, that he would answer when he got back to a typewriter. This was in August. A month later he wrote from Rapallo:

"Arriving at U. of P. in 1901 I acknowledge debts to Profs. McDaniel and Child for latin and English, and to Ames for doing his best at a time when no profs of American History had got down to bedrock. Overholser had not made his admirable compendium of the real causes of the revolution and of the great and dastardly betrayal of the American people and the American system, by the trick clause, and the Bank Act of Feb. 25, 1863.

"When a writer merits mention in a work of reference his work is his autobiography, it is his first person record. If you can't print my one page 'Introductory Text Book' enclosed (and to appear here) [here, he circled in ink and put at the bottom of the page "Int. Txt. Bk."] then your profession of wanting an authentic record is mere bunk, and fit only to stand with the infamies that have raged in America since Johnson was kicked out of the White House, and in especial throughout the degration [*sic*] of the American state and system by Wilson and Roosevelt."

There is more of the same: "persistent double crossing of me by the Chicago clique," "the general futility of ALL American endowments," etc. Johnson was not kicked out of the White House. The editors used the statement and enclosure as sent, but added: "The foregoing 'autobiography' having been printed exactly as Mr. Pound requests, the factual details of his life remain to be related." This, the editors did, adding a bibliography of Pound's more important works.

11.

He wrote to Mrs. Lulu Cunningham, contemporary of his mother and father in Hailey, Idaho, who had requested some of his books for the Hailey library. In this letter to Mrs. Cunningham, who was then seventy-four years old, he listed what he considered his best work up to that time. Faber and Faber and New Directions had just published Cantos LII-LXXI (which includes the American cantos referred to in the letter to Creekmore).

"Dear Mrs. Cunningham

"It may be that I ought to donate the books but on the other hand a nation that does NOT feed its best writers is merely a barbarian horde. AND the American people have not yet learned to do this; and I take any opportunity to protest. They spend millions keeping up —— like Nic Butler, pseudo literature pseudo scholarship and endowing boards to pay secretaries and exclude every spark or jot of living energy.

"I suppose my best book is Cantos 52/71/ and probably the one before it, ('Kulch, or Ez) Guide to Kulchur' which the publishers blush to print with its real title, is the best prose. The best edtn/ of short poems is Liveright's 'Personae,' and by the time you have paid the duty on the eng/ edtn/ of 'Selected Poems' the latter will cost al-most as much.

"Possibly the 'Ta Hio' is better than 'Cathay,' nobody believes that YET.

"All depends on how much you have to spend. I believe the Cantos 52/71 are easier to understand than the earlier ones. And for a li-brary the short poems 'Personae' will probably find more readers, but the 52/71 ought to establish the fact that I am an AMERICAN writer, not a collection of bric a brac.

"I am sending a few items found on the premises, but doing it on the supposition that you are getting the core of the matter. The more important books.

"I wonder, in parenthesis, did the local edtr. print my open letter on Borah. I am very glad to have seen the Senator in Washington last spring and to have felt real affection for him. I used to rag him (by letter) about his having got to Idaho after I had. Whether he ever knew when I left, I don't know.

"If 'New Directions' or Faber want to let you have books at dis-count, they can waive my royalties.

"Another question arises, does anyone in Hailey or in the State University read Italian? or are there Italian groups in Hailey or Boise?

"As you may know, I have been pretty well excluded from the American press, and lately from the English press (with the death of the Morning Post etc.) at any rate I have been driven to write in Italian. If some student wants to translate the articles AND cd/ find local publisher, newspaper, or whatever, it might be of interest."

He signed himself "cordially yrs," then added:

"I shd/ say, to summarize that my best stuff is in *Cantos*. 1 to 71 (so far pubd) & complete as it stands. Tho' there's a final volume to be done. *Personae. Guide to Kulchur, Ta Hio, Make it New.* then in second category, *ABC of Economics, ABC of Reading,* oh yes, *Impact* (social credit pamphlet, price 6 pence)

"Not much saving on the Selectd Poems, as they omit the Proper-tius which is in the collected 'Personae.' "[7]

He was writing in Italian, for Italian readers. This compulsion to write anything, to publish anywhere, is one of the inexplicable traits in Pound's character and provides a remarkable contrast to the strict dedication of his friends—Yeats, Joyce, Eliot and Cummings. He wrote to Carlo Linati to ask whether he had enough influence with *Il Corriere* "to have them publish an article of mine *Why America Is Impossible.*" He explained: "It would take me a whole article to explain what commercial literature is, etc., and why a literature cannot exist in America." But as it does, I do not believe his view was shared by any cultured Italian, or by any cultured European of whatever nationality.

But Pound was not content to write merely on literature. He expressed, in column after column, page after page, wherever these were opened to him, extraordinary concerns and extraordinary hatreds, as in the article in *Meridiano di Roma.* This was the cultured man, the wishful founder of an institute of European Paideuma. His fulminations were to reach new heights in the wartime broadcasts on the Rome Radio, and then the United States shared with the Jews the fury of his blasts. Yet in *Guide to Kulchur,* which pleased him so much, and which he had dedicated to Zukofsky and Bunting, a Jew and a Quaker, he had written: "Race prejudice is red herring. The tool of the man defeated intellectually, and of the cheap politician."

The war started west of the Vistula, with the German bombardment of Danzig. Very little is known of Pound's activities from this time on, or until his broadcasts called attention to him. He occupied himself with some pretty queer stuff in English, too—"Rothschild Arrested," "Britain, Who Are Your Allies?" "The Just Price or Why Mosley?" Among the periodicals to which he contributed was Sir Oswald Mosley's *British Union Quarterly,* formerly the *Fascist Quarterly* (the original title did not sit too well with Britons at this juncture).

12.

The coming of war was like a gigantic confirmation of Pound's views. Here, I take up the thread of the "Money Pamphlets":

"Usurers provoke wars to impose monopolies in their own interests, so that they can get the world by the throat. Usurers provoke wars to create debts, so that they can extort the interest and rake in the profits resulting from changes in the values of monetary units."

"A NATION THAT WILL NOT GET ITSELF INTO DEBT DRIVES THE USURERS TO FURY."

"This war was no whim of Mussolini's, nor of Hitler's. This war is a chapter in the long and bloody tragedy which began with the foundation of the Bank of England in far-away 1694, with the openly declared intention of Paterson's now famous prospectus, which contains the words already quoted: 'the bank hath benefit of the interest on all moneys which it creates out of nothing.'

"To understand what this means it is necessary to understand what money *is*. Money is not a simple instrument like a spade. It is made up of two elements: one which measures the prices on the market, one which bestows the power to purchase the goods. It is this two fold aspect that the usurers have taken advantage of."

Over and over, the reiteration:

"Let us be quite clear.

MONEY IS A MEASURED TITLE OR CLAIM.

"That is its basic difference from unmeasured claims, such as a man's right to take all you've got, under war-time requisition or as an invader or thief just taking it all.

"Money is a measure which the taker hands over when he acquires the goods he takes. And no further formality need occur during the transfer, though sometimes a receipt is given.

"The idea of justice inheres in ideas of measure, and *money is a measure of price.*"

His definition leads naturally to the "just price" which, he says, "only the STATE can effectively fix."

"Douglas proposed to bring up the TOTAL purchasing power of the whole people by a *per capita* issue of tickets PROPORTIONAL to available goods. In England and U.S. today [1939] available and desired goods remain unbought because the total purchasing power (i.e. total sum of tickets) is inadequate.

"Mussolini and Hitler wasted very little time PROPOSING. They started and DO distribute BOTH tickets and actual goods on various graduated scales according to the virtues and activities of Italians and Germans."

"In the 1860's one of the Rothschilds was kind enough to admit that the banking system was contrary to public interest, and that was before the shadow of Hitler's jails had fallen ACROSS the family fortunes."

"The doctrine of Capital, in short, has shown itself as little else than the idea that unprincipled thieves and anti-social groups should be allowed to gnaw into the rights of ownership.

"This tendency 'to gnaw into' has been recognised and stigmatised from the time of the laws of Moses and he called it *neschek* [Hebrew, *neshek:* usury]."

Hitler's political testament, dictated in the Fuehrerbunker just before he shot himself, contains this statement: "It is untrue that I, or anybody else in Germany, wanted war in 1939. It was wanted and provoked exclusively by those international politicians who either came of Jewish stock, or worked for Jewish interests."[8]

13.

It is in Number Four—"A Visiting Card," published in Rome in 1942 and addressed to Italians—that Pound identifies himself with Fascism. Under the heading, "Autobiographical," he wrote:

"Having seen and experienced so-called reforms and revolutions which have not, in fact, taken place, the mystery of the Fascist and Nazi Revolutions interests me for reasons that would never occur to you, for you have lived through these revolutions instinctively and have experienced their results without worrying about the mystery.

"I insist on the identity of our American Revolution of 1776 with your Fascist Revolution. Two chapters in the same war against the usurers, the same who crushed Napoleon.

"Let them erect a commemorative urinal to Mond, whose brother said in the year of Sanctions:

> *"Napoleon wath a goodth man, it took uth*
> *20 yearth to crwuth him;*
> *it will not take uth 20 years to crwuth Mussolini"*

adding as an afterthought

> *"and the economic war has begun."*

"I know that drawing-room; that sofa where sat the brother of Imperial Chemicals. I know it. It is not something I read in some newspaper or other."

The words ascribed to Sir Alfred Mond's brother occur in Canto LXXVIII.

One other matter may be mentioned here. Pound was no longer a Douglasite. In a 1942 broadcast he said: "I am not a Social Creditor, I passed by that alley." And in this pamphlet: "I am not going back to Social Credit. The latter was the doorway through which I came to economic curiosity." He was critical of procedures in Alberta: "the prescribed stamp was impractically small and provided with a very unadhesive gum."

He wrote in "America, Roosevelt and the Causes of the Present War":

"The reason for the present publication, at this particular moment [it was 1944], is to indicate the incidence of the present war in the series of wars provoked by the same never-dying agency, namely the world *usurocracy,* or the congregation of High Finance: Roosevelt being in all this a kind of malignant tumour, not autonomous, not self-created, but an unclean exponent of something less circumscribed than his own evil personal existence; a magistrate with *legally* limited jurisdiction, a perjurer, not fully aware of what he does, why he does it, or where it leads to. His political life ought to be brought *sub judice.*"

He had already said worse things about the President on Rome Radio.

14.

Not all of the texts of the "Money Pamphlets" are concerned with politics or economics. "No man forgets his original trade: the rights of nations, and of kings, sink into questions of grammar, if grammarians discuss them." Thus Johnson on Milton, who had been a teacher. And thus Pound, addressing Italians in Number Four:

"I demand, and I shall never cease to demand a greater degree of communication. It is already too late for you to know eighty per cent. of the English and American books that I could have suggested to you in 1927, for translation or for reading in the original.

"Joyce is familiar to you, but not Wyndham Lewis or E. E. Cummings. You were introduced to Eliot without too serious a time-lag, but you do not know Ford Madox Ford, nor W. H. Hudson."

He thinks he is quoting Yeats, when he is really paraphrasing Housman:

"Yeats said: 'They don't like poetry; they like something else, but they like to think they like poetry.' "

Housman wrote: "I am convinced that most readers, when they think that they are admiring poetry, are deceived by inability to analyse their sensations, and that they are really admiring, not the poetry of the passage before them, but something else in it, which they like better than poetry" (from *The Name and Nature of Poetry,* reviewed by Pound in Eliot's *Criterion,* January, 1934).

He is critical of Eliot:

"In his *After Strange Gods* Eliot loses all the threads of Arachne. . . . Eliot, in this book, has not come through uncontaminated by the Jewish poison. . . . Until he succeeds in detaching the Jewish from the European elements of his peculiar variety of Christianity he will never find the right formula."

He discusses style, and has praise for Eliot and himself:

"For those without access to my criticism in English, I repeat: the art of poetry is divisible into *phanopoeia, melopoeia,* and *logopoeia.* Verbal composition, that is to say, is formed of words which evoke or define visual phenomena, of words which register or suggest auditory phenomena (i.e., which register the various conventional sounds of the alphabet and produce, or suggest, a raising or lowering of the tone which can sometimes be registered more accurately by musical notation), and thirdly, of a play or 'dance' among the concomitant meanings, customs, usages, and implied contexts of the words themselves.

"In this last category Eliot surpasses me; in the second I surpass him."

He offers to serve Italy:

"I believe that the most useful service that I could do for Italy would be to put before you, every year, a few lines of Confucius, so that they might sink into the brain."

He equates Rome with Love in a very neat palindrome:

```
"R O M A
 O     M
 M     O
 A M O R"
```

15.

In World War I, Yeats had elected silence; in World War II, Eliot, approached with a similar request to aid the war effort, wrote the following while London was under aerial bombardment:

DEFENSE OF THE ISLANDS

Let these memorials of built stone—music's
enduring instrument, of many centuries of
patient cultivation of the earth, of English
verse

be joined with the memory of this defense of
the islands

and the memory of those appointed to the grey
ships—battleship, merchantman, trawler—
contributing their share to the ages' pavement
of British bone on the sea floor

and of those who, in man's newest form of gamble
with death, fight the power of darkness in air
and fire

and of those who have followed their forebears
to Flanders and France, those undefeated in
defeat, unalterable in triumph, changing nothing
of their ancestors' ways but the weapons

and those again for whom the paths of glory are
the lanes and the streets of Britain:

to say, to the past and the future generations
of our kin and of our speech, that we took up
our positions, in obedience to instructions.[9]

It was, once more, a time for service or silence. What happened in
Pound's case is wrapped in mystery. Francesco Monotti wrote in
Il Mare:

"The American Government had notified American citizens scattered around the world, and the Pounds, like good citizens, were
ready to obey and return to the United States. But at the consulate
there must have been someone who thought of them as black sheep.
In those supreme moments between day and night in their lives, something of grave consequence must have happened at the consulate at
Rome. . . . He returned a completely changed man. . . . He decided
quickly, the tickets were returned to the airline, Ezra Pound decided
to remain in Italy."[10]

Monotti says Pound and his wife had arranged for a long absence,
settling the matter of their apartment in Rapallo, and distributing
prized works of art, furniture and books among their friends, one of
them being Admiral Ubaldo degli Uberti.

Richard Rovere states categorically:

"It is a matter of record that he tried in 1942 to get aboard the last
diplomatic train that took Americans from Rome to Lisbon. He was
refused permission to board it. He had no choice but to stay in
Rapallo."[11]

However, a Library of Congress report states:

"Several writers have suggested that Mr. Pound attempted to return
to the United States in 1941 and that he was denied permission to
return to this country. An examination of pertinent State Department
Passport Division files does not substantiate this claim. To the contrary, it appears that the State Department was officially eager to have
Mr. Pound return to the United States and in 1941 his passport was
extended for six months only, in order to compel his return. However,
the documents in the State Department files do not preclude the possibility of the development of a misunderstanding between Mr. Pound

and a consular official which might have unintentionally aborted Mr. Pound's 'attempt' to leave Italy."[12]

A State Department memorandum (Division of Foreign Activities) reads as follows:

"On July 12, 1941, this Department instructed the American embassy at Rome to limit Pound's passport for immediate return to United States. However, he refused to return home and to best of our knowledge is still residing in Italy."[13]

Another State Department memorandum in the Passport Office, dated October 11, 1941, referred to him as a "pseudo American."[14]

It sounds vindictive, and may have been written by the consular official with whom Pound quarreled, if quarrel there was.

16.

It is not difficult to understand how Pound came to broadcast on the Rome Radio before the United States was attacked. The air was another—and larger—classroom for his ideas. It is not so easy after Pearl Harbor. He told a reporter who came to see him in the District of Columbia jail in 1945:

"I see they call me Mussolini's boy. I only saw the bastard once. No German or Italian was ever in position to give me an order. So I took none. But a German near my home at Rapallo told me they were paying good money for broadcasts. That was a fatal mistake. I visited Rome shortly thereafter on four or five other matters, the importance of which skips me for the nonce but, coincidentally, I wound up making broadcasts on the American hour. Naturally, I couldn't talk about Fascism so I talked about international money power."[15]

I do not know who the German "near my home" was. It is a fact, however, that Pound's broadcasts on the Rome Radio, like Father Coughlin's earlier harangues in the United States, were replete with Nazi propaganda. Pound not only broadcast himself, but wrote scripts for others. He told a reporter in Genoa after his arrest that he received 350 lire for scripts that he wrote and broadcast, and 300 for scripts he wrote for other broadcasters. He was on the air twice weekly, sometimes three times, from January, 1941, ceased for a few weeks after Pearl Harbor, and resumed in January, 1942.

It was on January 29, 1942, that the announcer on the Rome Radio reintroduced him as follows:

"We now present a talk by Ezra Pound.

"The Italian radio, acting in accordance with the Fascist policy of intellectual freedom and free expression of opinion by those who are qualified to hold it, [and] following the tradition of Italian hospitality, has offered Dr. Ezra Pound the use of the microphone twice a week. It is understood that he will not be asked to say anything whatsoever that goes against his conscience or anything incompatible with his duties as a citizen of the United States of America."

Pound began:

"Ezra Pound speaking, speaking from Europe. Pearl Arbor Day, or Pearl Harbor Day, at 12 noon, I retired from the capital of the old Roman empire, that is, Rome to Rapallo, to seek wisdom from the ancients. I wanted to figure things out."

The United States had been cruelly and treacherously attacked by Japan while the imperial plenipotentiaries were smiling and bowing in Washington; and Italy and Germany had declared war on the side of their Axis partner. Having communed with the ancients, Pound said on the air that January day:

"The United States has been for months and illegally at war through what I consider to be the criminal acts of a President whose mental condition was not, so far as I could see, all that could or should be desired of a man in so responsible a position or office."

He also said:

"The United States has been misinformed. The United States has been led down the garden-path and maybe down under the daisies. All through shutting out the news."

He had "spent a month trying to figure things out."

I venture to suggest that the greatest wisdom of the ancients, which Pound says he sought, resided—on December 7, 1941—in a two-line poem in the Greek Anthology about Thermopylae:

> We lie here in obedience to your laws,
> O Sparta!

CHAPTER XX

"EZRA POUND SPEAKING"

1.

"The case is also of some human interest, for it illustrates the dangers of anti-semitism. Any negative belief, enthusiastically held, which is based on prejudice and not on evidence, is apt to be dangerous, and if in addition it is founded on hatred, it may well prove to have disastrous consequences on the judgment and outlook of those who hold it." (Solicitor-General, the Earl Jowitt, in "The Case of Tyler Kent.")[1]

2.

The teller at the bank asked Florence Williams if her husband knew someone in Italy named Ezra Pound. The teller had heard a person of that name on the radio the night before say "something about 'ol' Doc Williams of Rutherford, New Jersey, would understand.' Something like that." She told her husband, who was none too pleased.

"What the hell right has he to drag me into his dirty messes?" said William Carlos Williams to his wife.[2]

He was even less pleased when the F.B.I. sent an agent to his home.

It was in some such way—by word of mouth, that is—that Americans first began to hear about, and to listen to, the short-wave broadcasts to the "home folks" on the Rome Radio in World War II. Those who knew Pound's poetry were incredulous; those who knew Pound were skeptical. Between the views expressed, whether literary or political, and the voice—or voices—used in expressing them there was room for confusion and doubt. Was it really Pound? Or was Rome putting something over?

For, with his gift for mimicry, and reveling in his role of air-borne explainer and cracker-barrel philosopher, Pound gave many of his talks in stage-American sectional accents—if Yankee, more nasal than anything ever heard north of Boston, if western, more "folksey" and drawling than anything ever heard west of the Mississippi; which may be saying a great deal. But in flat Pennsylvania accents he was vituperative, with a degree of abusiveness that seemed incredible in a man of his background and education, except in the light of the feminine cast of his mind, of which I have spoken earlier. Another view: Professor G. Giovannini, of the Catholic University of America, wrote of Pound: "From the broadcasts it appears he thought of himself as the scourge of usury in the modern world, and the intensity of passion which governs his attacks is probably unmatched in the entire history of the subject."[3]

Pound also talked about culture and literature, as in the "Money Pamphlets." Often, however, he appeared to be talking about nothing in particular, for he rambled on, as though extemporaneously, one sentence like another, and all strung together like damp firecrackers. Italians wondered why he was permitted to speak at all; to many of them, he seemed merely an eccentric American. Camillo Pellizzi, a friend of Pound's for twenty years, wrote in *Il Tempo* that the Italian government "mistrusted the broadcasts, even suspecting that they hid a code language." This must have been before Pearl Harbor. After Pearl Harbor he took his stand with Italy; and all the apologetic articles about him, and all his own utterances since to the contrary, cannot gainsay what he actually did. But his compulsion to do it is probably a medical, not a political, matter; or so I believe.

The talks were, of course, monitored in Great Britain and the United States. In Washington, in the analysis division, Foreign Broadcast Intelligence Service of the F.C.C., transcripts of the talks began to be examined for "treasonable passages."[4]

Thus it came about that, thirty years after the events recorded by Harriet Monroe in her autobiography, the following editorial appeared in *Poetry* (April, 1942) under the heading "The End of Ezra Pound":

"The time has come to put a formal end to the countenancing of Ezra Pound. For a number of years, at the beginning of the magazine, he was associated with *Poetry,* and the association was valuable on both sides. Then he quarreled with us, as he has quarreled with everyone, yet continued to use the magazine as an outlet for the publication of his *Cantos* and other poems. Now, so far as we and the rest of the English-speaking world of letters are concerned, he has effectively written *finis* to his long career as inspired *enfant terrible.*

"*Poetry* has forgiven Ezra much throughout the latter years because of his great service to the art of poetry in English during his youth. . . . But now the situation has changed; now we are at war; now the broadcasts, which he continues to make, have become the deliberate attempts to undermine the country of his birth through enemy propaganda.

"That it should be one of the poets who is thus playing Lord Haw-Haw, no matter how ineffectually, seems to cast a slur on the whole craft. In the name of American poetry, and of all who practise the art, let us hope that this is the end of Ezra Pound."

And in the July, 1943, criminal term of the District Court of the United States for the District of Columbia, a Grand Jury returned a true bill indicting Pound for committing "each and every one of the overt acts herein described for the purpose of and with the intent to adhere to and give aid and comfort to the Kingdom of Italy, and its military allies, enemies of the United States, and the said defendant Ezra Pound committed each and every one of the said overt acts contrary to his duty of allegiance to the United States and to the form of the statute in such case made and provided and against the peace and dignity of the United States."

It was the classic definition of treason, but in republican phraseology.

3.

Pound afterwards told his counsel that he heard of the indictment via the B.B.C. He said he went to the United States Embassy in Rome, which was in charge of Swiss nationals, and left a written protest.

Back in Rapallo, he wrote a letter to Francis Biddle, United States Attorney General. This was on August 4, 1943.

"I understand that I am under indictment for treason. I have done my best to get an authentic report of your statement to this effect. And I wish to place the following facts before you.

"I do not believe that the simple fact of speaking over the radio, wherever placed, can in itself constitute treason. I think that must depend on what is said, and on the motives for speaking.

"I obtained the concession to speak over Rome radio with the following proviso. Namely that nothing should be asked of me contrary to my conscience or contrary to my duties as an American citizen. I obtained a declaration on their part of a belief in 'the free expression of opinion by those qualified to have an opinion.'

"The legal mind of the Attorney General will understand the interest inherent in this distinction, as from unqualified right of expression.

"This declaration was made several times in the announcement of my speeches; with the declaration 'He will not be asked to say anything contrary to his conscience, or contrary to his duties as an American citizen' (Citizen of the U.S.).

"These conditions have been adhered to. The only time I had an opinion as to what might be interesting as subject matter, I was asked whether I would speak of religion. This seemed to me hardly my subject, though I did transmit on one occasion some passages from Confucius, under the title 'The Organum of Confucius.'

"I have not spoken with regard to *this* war, but in protest against a system which creates one war after another, in series and in system. I have not spoken to the troops, and have not suggested that the troops should mutiny or revolt.

"The whole basis of democratic or majority government assumes that the citizen shall be informed of the facts. I have not claimed to know all the facts, but I have claimed to know some of the facts which are an essential part of the total that should be known to the people.

"I have for years believed that the American people should be better informed as to Europe, and informed by men who are not tied to a special interest or under definite control.

"The freedom of the press has become a farce, as everyone knows that the press is controlled, if not by its titular owners, at least by the advertisers.

"Free speech under modern conditions becomes a mockery if it do not include the right to free speech over the radio.

"And this point is worth establishing. The assumption of the right to punish and take vengeance regardless of the area of jurisdiction is dangerous. I do not mean in a small way; but for the nation.

"I returned to America before the war to protest against particular forces then engaged in trying to create war and to make sure that the U.S.A. should be dragged into it.

"Arthur Kitson's testimony before the Cunliffe and Macmillan commissions was insufficiently known. Brooks Adams brought to light several currents in history that should be better known. The course of events following the foundation of the Bank of England should be known, and considered in sequence: the suppression of colonial paper money, especially in Pennsylvania! [Biddle was a Philadelphian.] The similar curves following the Napoleonic wars, and our Civil War and Versailles need more attention.

"We have not the right to drift into another error similar to that of the Versailles Treaty.

"We have, I think, the right to a moderate expansion including defence of the Caribbean, the elimination of foreign powers from the American continent, but such expansion should not take place at the cost of deteriorating or ruining the internal structure of the U.S.A. The ruin of markets, the perversions of trade routes, in fact all the matters on which my talks have been based is of importance to the American citizen; [whom] neither you nor I should betray either in time of war *or* peace. I may say in passing that I took out a life membership in the American Academy of Social and Political Science in the hope of obtaining fuller discussion of some of these issues, but did not find them ready for full and frank expression of certain vital elements in the case, this may in part have been due to their incomprehension of the nature of the case.

"At any rate a man's duties increase with his knowledge. A war between the U.S. and Italy is monstrous and should not have occurred. And a peace without justice is no peace but merely a prelude to future wars. Someone must take count of these things. And having taken count must act on his knowledge; admitting that his knowledge is partial and his judgment subject to error."

He may not have remembered, at the time he wrote this, what he had said on the air. (When he arrived in the United States in 1945, he asked: "Does anyone really know what I said?")

4.

Pound stayed at the Albergo d'Italia, Via dei Giardini, while a broadcaster. I give here one complete broadcast, and excerpts from several others, some of whose dates correspond with those in the indictments handed up by the District of Columbia Grand Juries in 1943 and 1945.[5] All his talks were prefaced by the paragraph about Fascist hospitality and freedom of expression, previously given. He told his countrymen on February 3, 1942, in the darkest days of the war for the United States as well as Britain:

"You are at war for the duration of the Germans' pleasure. You are at war for the duration of Japan's pleasure. Nothing in the Western world, nothing in the whole of our occident can help you dodge that. Nothing can help you dodge it."

And on April 16, 1942:

"For the United States to be making war on Italy and on Europe is just plain damn nonsense, and every native-born American of American stock knows that it is plain downright damn nonsense. And for this state of things Franklin Roosevelt is more than any other one man responsible."

April 23, 1942:

"The drift of Mr. Archibald MacLeish's remarks towards the end of March seems fairly clear. [MacLeish was, at this time, an Under-Secretary of State.] He has been given a gangster's brief and he has been entrusted with the defense of a gang of criminals and he is a-doing his damnedest. I object and have objected to the crime, regardless of who may be related to the men who have committed it and I accept the conditions of the debate, namely that the Morgenthau-Lehman gang control 99 per cent of all means of communication inside the United States and that they can drown out and buy out nearly all opposition, on top of which Roosevelt has, characteristically, resorted to blackmail. Any man who does not accept the gigantic frauds perpetrated by the Morgenthau-Roosevelt treasury is to be held up as a traitor to the United States.

"The reply is that any man who submits to Roosevelt's treason to the public commits [a] breach of citizen's duty. There is no connection between submittin' to the Roosevelt-Morgenthau frauds and patriotism. There is no connection between such submission and winning this war—or any other. There is no patriotism in submittin' to the prolonged and multiple frauds of the Roosevelt administration and to try to make the present support of these frauds figure as loyalty to the American Union, to the American Constitution, to the American heritage is just so much dirt or bunkum. Doubtless the tactics of evasion will be used to the uttermost, blackmail will be used to the uttermost—but if the American people submit to either or both of these wheezes the American people will be mugs.

"There are several historic facts which the opulent of the Morgenthau-Lehman gang would do well to dig up. Our Mr. MacLeish has not gone out—all out—for the printing of the defects of American history in handy and available volumes, so there are several historic facts which the opulent of the Morgenthau swindle would be well advised to extract and use.

"Of course for you to go looking for my point—points of my bi-weekly talk in the maze of Jew-governed American radio transmissions—is like looking for one needle in a whole flock of haystacks. And your press is not very open. However, if some lone watcher or listener on Back Bay or on top of the Blue Ridge does hear me, I suggest he make notes and ask Advocate Archibald whether it does win anything to have the people pay two dollars for every dollar spent by the government. I ask whether the spirit of '76 is helped by a-floodin' the lower ranks of the navy with bridge-sweepin's; whether war is won by mercantilist ethics and, in any case, whether men like Knox and Stimson and Morgenthau can be expected to fill the heart of youth with martial ardor and spirit of sacrifice.

"I ask Archie to say openly why he handed out four billion dollars in excess profits on the gold [word or words missing] between 1932 and 1940, handing it to a dirty gang of kikes and hyper-kikes on the London gold exchange firms. Why is that expected to help Americanism? Or why should it be regarded as a model of devotion to the American spirit? Or why should any honest American vote for the continuance of that swindle or of keeping in office the men and kikes who were responsible for putting it over the people?

"And that of course is not the whole story of Roosevelt, Lehman, Baruch, Morgenthau, dipping into the country's resources. The break with our tradition exemplified by Donovan's intrigues in Yugoslavia is no Cornelia's jewel. In fact, all Roosevelt's talk about patriotism is nothing but the gilding on the outside of base metal. Keeping Roosevelt in the White House is not essential to winning the war. The two things can be considered quite apart one from the other.

"Had you had the sense to eliminate Roosevelt and his Jews or the Jews and their Roosevelt at the last election, you would not now be at war. That is one point. But to suppose that you will win the war by goin' on bein' mugs in any and every internal conflict, to suppose that you will strengthen the United States abroad by submittin' to continued internal bleedin' and swindlin' is just so much hokum or nonsense.

"The first step towards a bright new world, so far as the rising American generation is concerned, is to git on to Roosevelt and all his works and the second is to eliminate him and all his damned gang from public life in America. The alternative is annihilation for the youth of America and the end of everything decent the U.S. ever stood for. If you allow yourself to be dazzled, if you are persuaded to identify the Morgenthau-Baruch control of the U.S. by secret committees for the war birds with victory, then you are mugs. If you confuse these things and the promise of army contracts even with national defense, then you are plain downright suckers.

"I shall be highly interested to see whether Archibald takes up any of the points of this discourse. If he don't, some bright lad ought to help him. Someone ought to dig up a point here and there."

May 5, 1942:

"Europe callin'—Pound speakin'. . . .

"The kike, and the unmitigated evil that has been centered in London since the British government set on the Red Indians to murder the American frontier settlers, has herded the Slavs, the Mongols, the Tartar openly against Germany and Poland and Finland. And secretly against all that is decent in America, against the total American heritage.

"This is my war all right, I've been in it for twenty years—my granddad was in it before me.

"Ezra Pound speakin'."

May 10, 1942:

"The next peace will not be based on international lending. Get that for one. The next peace will not be based on international lending, and England certainly will have nothing whatever to say about what its terms are. Neither, I think, will simple-hearted Joe Stalin, not wholly trusted by the kikery which is his master."

May 26, 1942:

"Every hour that you go on with this war is an hour lost to you and your children. And every sane act you commit is committed in homage to Mussolini and Hitler. Every reform, every lurch toward the just price, toward the control of a market is an act of homage to Mussolini and Hitler. They are your leaders however much you think you are conducted by Roosevelt or told by Churchill. You follow Mussolini and Hitler in every constructive act of your government."

May 31, 1942:

"The melting pot in America may have been a noble experiment, though I very much doubt it. At any rate it is lost."

June 28, 1942:

"You are not going to win this war. None of our best minds ever thought you could win it. You have never had a chance in this war."

July 20, 1942:

"You ought not to be at war against Italy. You ought not to be giving or ever have given the slightest or most picayune aid to any man or nation engaged in waging war against Italy. You are doing it for the sake of a false accountancy system."

July 22, 1942:

"Europe calling . . . Ezra Pound speaking!

"I hear that my views are shared, most of them, by a large number of my compatriots, so it would seem, or maybe an increasing number of my compatriots. And there is a comforting thought on a warm day in a fine climate. I should hate to think that all America had gone haywire. I should like to feel that the American race in North America, in the North American continent, had some wish towards survival. That they wanted there to be a United States of tomorrow. . . .

"Well, you have been fed on lies, for twenty years you have been fed on lies, and I don't say maybe. And Mr. Squirmy and Mr. Slime are still feeding it to you right over the BBC radio, and every one of the Jew radios of Schenectady, New York, and Boston—and

Boston was once an American city; that was when it was about the size of Rapallo. . . .

"And how much liberty have you got, anyhow? And as to the arsenal—are you the arsenal of democracy or of judeocracy? And who rules your rulers? Where does public responsibility end and what races can mix in America without ruin of the American stock, the American brain? Who is organized? What say have you in the choice of your rulers? What control of their policy? And who does own most of your press and your radio? E. P. asking you. . . ."

On May 4, 1943, while the Americans, the British and the French were driving close to the Axis strongholds of Tunis and Bizerte, in North Africa, Pound asked America (and was heard by American troops):

"What are you doing in the war at all? What are you doing in Africa? Who amongst you have the nerve or the sense to do something that would conduce to getting you out of it before you are mortgaged up to the neck and over it? Every day of war is a dead day as well as a death day. More death, more future servitude, less and less of American liberty of any variety. . . ."

5.

Although he had taken his stand with the Kingdom of Italy and, by justifiable inference, the other Axis partner, when the Germans overran Italy he was unceremoniously "chased out" of Rapallo in the spring of 1944 (from a conversation with his counsel in the District of Columbia jail). The entire waterfront area was transformed with ferro-concrete anti-invasion obstacles and bunkers. Pound also told his counsel that he and his wife went to live in Sant' Ambrogio, in the hills outside Rapallo. There, in a country house, with an olive press on the first floor, he was at work on his translation of Mencius (Mêng-tzǔ, follower of Confucius) when the *partigiani* came to his front door with a Tommy gun. This was in the spring of 1945. He was taken to a United States command post at Lavagna, and from Lavagna to the counter-intelligence center at Genoa. (Olga Rudge, however, told Douglas Paige that Pound escaped from the *partigiani* and got to Genoa by himself, where he surrendered.) In Genoa, on May 5th, he said:

"If I ain't worth more alive than dead, that's that. If a man isn't willing to take some risk for his opinions, either his opinions are no good or he's no good."

On May 8th he was interviewed on the sixth floor of an office building overlooking the main square of Genoa. He appears to have thought that if he could speak to President Truman or Premier Stalin for five or ten minutes, the world's ills would vanish. (In the District of Columbia jail he actually asked for a Georgian dictionary, so he could learn how to converse with Stalin. I have been told that such a dictionary was furnished him.) He told the reporter in Genoa:

"There is no doubt which I preferred between Mussolini and Roosevelt. In my radio broadcasts I spoke in favor of the economic construction of Fascism. Mussolini was a very human, imperfect character who lost his head.

"Winston [Churchill] believes in the maximum of injustice enforced with the maximum of brutality.

"Stalin is the best brain in politics today. But that does not mean that I have become a Bolshevik.

"I do not believe that I will be shot for treason. I rely on the American sense of justice."

The reporter asked Pound "if he really believed either President Truman or Premier Stalin would be interested in seeing him." He replied:

" 'One might say that I am in an unfavorable position at the present time to be received at the White House. If I am not shot for treason, I think my chances of seeing Truman are good.' "

He told the reporter that "Hitler and Mussolini were successful insofar as they followed Confucius, and that they failed because they did not follow him more closely." He termed Hitler "a Jeanne d'Arc, a saint." "He was a martyr," Pound declared. "Like many martyrs, he held extreme views."[6]

He was under house arrest in Genoa for several weeks, and was interviewed by an agent from the Department of Justice. Then he was taken to a military prison compound near Pisa. This was the Disciplinary Training Center of the Mediterranean Theater of Operations (the word "Training" being a euphemism). I quote now from the notes made by Julien Cornell, Pound's counsel, in the District of Columbia jail November 20, 1945, at their first interview:

"At Pisa, Pound was confined in a cage made of air-strip, and in solitary confinement. Cage was in yard with little shelter from sun or rain. Bright lights on stockade shone at night. Two guards outside at all times. Slept on cement floor with 6 blankets. Can for toilet. Allowed no reading matter except Confucius he was working on. Incommunicado. Was told nobody knew where he was.

"After 3 weeks, Pound collapsed. Taken out of cage and put in tent. Partial amnesia. Claustrophobia. Not allowed to talk to other prisoners (told this was ordered by Washington).

"No communication with outside until Oct. 3 when saw wife. No letters in or out. No recreation. Little reading matter. Suffered hysteria and terror. Spoke only to Negro attendant who brought food.

"Visit from daughter Oct. 17 and wife Nov. 3."

6.

The Disciplinary Training Center in which Pound was confined occupied a field north of Pisa, on the road to Viareggio. In its barbed wire stockade were the brawlers, killers, rapists, malingerers, and other species of recalcitrant soldiery which the hard-fisted hand of the Armed Forces had snatched from line and service outfits and segregated for rehabilitation. Some of the "trainees" were destined for federal prisons in the United States, some were hanged at Aversa, and others were shot down in attempts to escape. Pound was the only civilian prisoner. The commandant during his incarceration was Lt. Col. John L. Steele, whose name occurs in *The Pisan Cantos,* as do the names of fellow prisoners. A medical section attendant has recalled seeing, one May night, the blue light of acetylene torches reinforcing the cage that was to hold Ezra Pound. It was on the extreme end of a row of such cages. The excuse for this, and for the cage itself, was the fear that Fascists might attempt to rescue him. No such attempt was ever made, and it was an incredible barbarity for Americans to conceive and execute. The next morning all DTC personnel were ordered to stay away from him and not to speak to him.

"He wore an Army fatigue uniform, unbuttoned at the neck. He walked back and forth on the concrete floor, making no effort to look outside. His trousers hung loose and his shoes were unlaced. (Belts and shoelaces were always taken away from men in the cages.) A special guard stood outside his cage which, at night, was brightly lighted."[7]

It became so cold at night that he was permitted to put up a pup tent inside the cage, in which he slept.

As in happier times and places he became a camp character. He was observed by the other inmates as he took his daily exercise. He boxed, fenced and played tennis with imaginary opponents, inside as well as outside his cage. Finally he got hold of an old broom handle which became, in turn, "a tennis racquet, a billiard cue, a rapier, a baseball bat to hit small stones and a stick to which he swung out smartly to match his long stride. His constitutionals wore a circular path in the compound grass."[8]

When his eyes became inflamed because of the dust and sun, he was transferred to a pyramidal tent in the medical compound. In it were a cot and a small wooden packing crate. A fellow prisoner secretly gave him a table, on which he worked on the Cantos and his translation of Confucius. A guard wrote: "Pound's volume of Confucius was by his side continually, and the prisoner read for hours, or simply sat and combed his ragged beard, watching the Pisa road where passersby and an occasional white ox were visible."[9]

In the heat, his usual dress was olive drab underwear, fatigue cap, G.I. shoes and socks. His meals were handed to him in an Army mess kit. He went on sick call after the other "trainees" and was usually treated in the evenings; his most frequent prescriptions were eye drops and foot baths. The medics made a good audience. He told them he would never be brought to trial because he "had too much on several people in Washington." But while he admitted that he had made broadcasts from Rome, he said they had not been treasonable and that he had "never supported the Fascists."[10]

He was interviewed by the camp psychiatrist. The word afterwards spread that he had "made a dummy of the psychiatrist." This, in turn, made him a hero to the "trainees."

The medics let him use the dispensary typewriter, and he sometimes typed letters home for G.I.'s. When he was creating, his typing was accompanied by "a high-pitched humming sound" and occa-

The poet freed: Pound outside United States District Court,
Washington, D.C., April 18, 1958

With his grandchildren, Patricia and Walter de Rachewiltz:
Schloss Brunnenburg, Merano (Tirolo), Italy, the residence
of his daughter, Princess Mary de Rachewiltz

sionally he "swore well and profusely over typing errors." In the late hours the only other person in the dispensary was the Charge of Quarters, to whom Pound would "rant and rave about the 'dunghill usurers' and 'usuring cutthroats.' "

"His green eyes snapped as he tapped his glasses on the desk and shouted that the American people had been swindled on monetary exchanges. He insisted that wars could be avoided if the true nature of money were understood. 'When,' he would ask, 'will the United States return to Constitutional government?' "[11]

On October 5th, two days after the first visit from his wife, he replied to Shakespear and Parkyn, his father-in-law's firm, which had advised him in a September letter to retain good counsel and stand mute. He was glad to observe from the firm's stationery that John Street has not been bombed out of existence, and happy over news of Omar. (Omar Pound told me: "I presume my father was referring to my volunteering for the U.S. Army." This he did while living in England. He took his basic training in France, and served in the Army of Occupation in Germany. He afterwards attended Hamilton College.)

7.

> If the hoar frost grip thy tent
> Thou wilt give thanks when night is spent.
> *(The Pisan Cantos)*

He could not understand why he was not flown to the United States, and began to despair of ever leaving the compound. Long and long he looked at the road—

> and there was a smell of mint under the tent flaps
> especially after the rain
>   and a white ox on the road toward Pisa
>   as if facing the tower

—and he heard, at night, the close-order punishment drills.

The past merged with the present. He remembered Scudder's Falls on the Schuylkill River in Pennsylvania, and his first arrival

in Clinton, and how he left America with eighty dollars. He wondered
if he would ever see Venice again. The names of teachers and friends
follow one another in the endless narrative of his life:

> nothing matters but the quality
> of the affection—
> in the end—that has carved the trace in the mind.

His moods alternated; one day he wrote,

> I have been hard as youth sixty years,

but on another,

> Oh let an old man rest.

And once,

> the loneliness of death came upon me
> (at 3 P.M. for an instant).

What was he doing there, what had he done?

> free speech without free radio speech is as zero—

but looking out from under the tent flaps he saw the machine-gun
towers and the barbed wire, and heard the news by grapevine:

> Till was hung yesterday
> for murder and rape with trimmings

—St. Louis Till they called him; and the speech of the turnkey,
Whiteside by name:

> "ah certainly dew lak dawgs,
> ah goin' tuh wash you"
> (no, not to the author, to the canine unwilling in question).

His gift for reporting speech was as good as ever.

All creatures sustained him—a lizard kept him from faltering, but when he tried to feed the birds by his tent he found that they would not eat the white bread of the Army. He peered hard at the green world,

> pervenche and a sort of dwarf morning-glory
> that knots in the grass, and a sort of buttercup,

observed the ant, "a centaur in his dragon world," and counseled with himself:

> Pull down thy vanity, it is not man
> Made courage, or made order, or made grace,
>   Pull down thy vanity, I say pull down.
> Learn of the green world what can be thy place
> Pull down thy vanity. . . .

> But to have done instead of not doing
>   this is not vanity
> To have, with decency, knocked
> That a Blunt should open
>   To have gathered from the air a live tradition
> or from a fine old eye the unconquered flame
> This is not vanity.
>   Here error is all in the not done,
> all in the diffidence that faltered.

And, of course, if there was a cat around, it would come to him—which it did:

> Prowling night-puss leave my hard squares alone
>   they are in no case cat food
>   if you had sense
> you wd/ come here at meal time
>   when meat is superabundant
> you can neither eat manuscript nor Confucius
>   nor even the hebrew scriptures

get out of that bacon box
contract W, 11 oh oh 9 oh
now used as a wardrobe. . . .

The days passed, and he marked their stages in his work—

sunset grand couturier

and the nights:

Under white clouds, cielo di Pisa
out of all this beauty something must come,

O moon my pin-up

and in the morning,

Old Ez folded his blankets
Neither Eos nor Hesperus has suffered wrong at my hands.

The old themes are also there, snips and snatches of economy and
history—

the state can lend money
and the fleet that went out to Salamis
was built by state loan to the builders
hence the attack on classical studies—

and the marching names: Joe Gould, Bunting, Cummings; Joyce
"at the haunt of Catullus," Yeats's old "da" on an elephant at Coney
Island, and Yeats himself—over and over; Jepson, "lover of jade,"
and Ford, his first mentor; with a mourning roster of all the companions, beginning

Lordly men are to earth o'ergiven.

He also mourned for Mussolini, hanged by the heels in Milan—

and as to poor old Benito
         one had a safety-pin
one had a bit of string, one had a button
     all of them so far beneath him
half-baked and amateur
     or mere scoundrels. . . .

Churchill's defeat at the polls pleased him:

     Oh to be in England now that Winston's out
     Now that there's room for doubt
         And the bank may be the nation's. . . .

He felt alarmed for Pétain, charged with treason:

     Pétain defended Verdun while Blum
                was defending a bidet. . . .

The ersatz themes are there,

         the goyim are undoubtedly in great numbers cattle
    whereas a jew will receive information
         he will gather up information,

and so forth. But often his verse soars with the stone of a shrine—

     till the shrine be again white with marble
     till the stone eyes look again seaward
                The wind is part of the process
                The rain is part of the process
    and the Pleiades set in her mirror

When he was not writing or resting he read the books and magazines circulated by the trainees: the Mediterranean edition of *Stars and Stripes,* overseas editions of *Time* and *Newsweek,* other magazines and novels. His sixtieth birthday came and went. A November issue of *Stars and Stripes* reported that seven Italian radio

technicians and announcers were being flown to Washington to testify
against Pound.

"His tone of conversation changed and occasionally he spoke of
himself in the past tense. Several times he said, 'If I go down, someone must carry on.' "[12]

He was sitting in the dispensary one evening reading Joseph E.
Davies' *Mission to Moscow,* and commenting from time to time
to the Charge of Quarters. Suddenly two young lieutenants entered
and told Pound he would be flown to Washington "in one hour" and
to get his things together. When they left, he handed the book to
the C.Q. and asked him to thank all the medics for him. At the door,
he turned, and half smiling, put both hands about his neck and
jerked up his chin.

He was taken to Rome in a jeep, riding all night, thence by plane
to London, and via the Azores and Bermuda to Washington. He
told Julien Cornell he was "well treated" by Army men on the trip.
Cornell told me that the government hoped to put on a big trial in
New York, but there was fog over the field, and the plane flew on
to Washington. The plane reached Washington the night of November 18th, and he was immediately lodged in the District of Columbia
jail. Weary and disheveled, he had on a soiled G.I. sweatshirt, a pair
of baggy trousers and coat, and oversized G.I. shoes. He said he had
only twenty-three dollars. He was arraigned before Judge Bolitha J.
Laws the next day and asked for permission to act as his own counsel,
but was told the charge was too serious for that. He also said he
wanted Wallace and MacLeish to testify for him; he had talked with
them in 1939, he explained, his purpose having been "to keep hell
from breaking loose in the world." Judge Laws set November 27th
for a formal arraignment, and Pound was taken back to the District
jail, where Cornell saw him the next day.

8.

With Pound's arrival in Washington, which followed by six days
the arrival of the radio technicians from Italy, a new true bill was
returned:

"The Grand Jurors for the United States of America duly impaneled and sworn in the District Court of the United States for the District of Columbia and inquiring for that District upon their oath present;

"1. Ezra Pound, the defendant herein, was born at Hailey, Idaho, October 30, 1885, and that he has been at all times herein mentioned and now is a citizen of the United States of America and a person owing allegiance to the United States of America.

"2. That the defendant, Ezra Pound, at Rome, Italy and other places within the Kingdom of Italy and outside the jurisdiction of any particular state or district, but within the jurisdiction of the United States and of this Court, the District of Columbia being the district in which he was found and into which was first brought, continuously, and at all times beginning on the 11th day of December 1941, and continuing thereafter to and including the 3rd day of May 1945, under the circumstances and conditions hereinafter set forth, then and there being a citizen of the United States, and a person owing allegiance to the United States, in violation of said duty of allegiance, knowingly, intentionally, wilfully, unlawfully, feloniously, traitorously and treasonably did adhere to the enemies of the United States, to-wit; the Kingdom of Italy and the military allies of the said Kingdom of Italy, with which the United States at all times since December 11, 1941, and during the times set forth in this indictment, have been at war, giving to the said enemies of the United States aid and comfort within the United States and elsewhere, that is to say:

"3. That the aforesaid adherence of the said defendant, Ezra Pound, to the Kingdom of Italy and its military allies and the giving of aid and comfort by the said defendant, Ezra Pound, to the aforesaid enemies of the United States during the time aforesaid consisted:

"(a) Of accepting employment from the Kingdom of Italy in the capacity of a radio propagandist and in the performance of the duties thereof which involved the composition of texts, speeches, talks and announcements and the recording thereof for subsequent broadcast over short-wave radio on wave lengths audible in the United States and elsewhere on ordinary commercial radio receiving sets having short-wave reception facilities; and

"(b) Of counselling and aiding the Kingdom of Italy and its military allies and proposing and advocating to the officials of the

Government of the Kingdom of Italy ideas and thoughts, as well as methods by which such ideas and thoughts could be disseminated, which the said defendant, Ezra Pound, believed suitable and useful to the Kingdom of Italy for propaganda purposes in the prosecution of said war;

"That the aforesaid activities of the said defendant, Ezra Pound, were intended to persuade citizens and residents of the United States to decline to support the United States in the conduct of the said war, to weaken or destroy confidence in the Government of the United States and in the integrity and loyalty of the Allies of the United States, and to further bind together and increase the morale of the subjects of the Kingdom of Italy in support of the prosecution of the said war by the Kingdom of Italy and its military allies.

"4. And the Grand Jurors aforesaid upon their oath aforesaid do further present that the said defendant, Ezra Pound, in the prosecution, performance and execution of said treason and of said unlawful, traitorous and treasonable adhering and giving aid and comfort to the enemies of the United States, at the several times hereinafter set forth in the specifications hereof (being times when the United States were at war with the Kingdom of Italy and its military allies), unlawfully, feloniously, wilfully, knowingly, traitorously and treasonably and with intent to adhere to and give aid and comfort to the said enemies, did do, perform, and commit certain overt and manifest acts."

There follow nineteen specifications, the first seven dated:

1. "The said defendant asserted, in substance, that the war is an economic war in which the United States and its allies are the aggressors."

2. "The purport of said messages, speeches and talks was to create racial prejudice in the United States."

3. "The said defendant . . . recorded and caused to be recorded certain messages, speeches and talks for subsequent broadcasts to the United States and its military allies."

4. "The purpose of said messages, speeches and talks was, among other things, to cause dissension and distrust between the United States and England and Russia."

5. "The said defendant asserted, among other things and in substance, that Italy is the natural ally of the United States; that the

true nature of the Axis regime has been misrepresented to the people in the United States and that England, Russia and the United States are aggressor nations."

6. "The purport of said messages, speeches and talks was to create racial prejudice and distrust of the Government of the United States."

7. "The said defendant praised Italy, urged the people in the United States to read European publications rather than the American press and to listen to European radio transmissions, and stated further that he spoke 'from Rome, in a regime where liberty is considered a duty.' "

Beginning with the eighth, the specifications are for "a day and date to these Grand Jurors unknown," but the defendant, "in the presence of Armando Giovagnoli and Giuseppe Bruni, spoke into a microphone in a radio station at Rome, Italy, controlled by the Italian Government and thereby recorded and caused to be recorded certain messages, speeches and talks for subsequent broadcast to the United States and its military allies."

The significance of the names lies in this: that in a case of treason the testimony of two witnesses is required. The names of the other witnesses from Italy appear in subsequent specifications. The new indictment ended:

"The defendant, Ezra Pound, committed each and every one of the overt acts herein described for the purpose of, and with the intent to adhere to and give aid and comfort to the Kingdom of Italy, and its military allies, enemies of the United States, and the said defendant, Ezra Pound, committed each and every one of the said overt acts contrary to his duty of allegiance to the United States and to the form of the statute and constitution in such case made and provided and against the peace and dignity of the United States. (Section 1, United States Criminal Code)."

This formidable document was signed by the foreman of the Grand Jury, and by the following: Edward M. Curran, United States Attorney in and for the District of Columbia; Isaiah Matlack, Special Assistant to the Attorney General; Samuel C. Ely, Special Assistant to the Attorney General; Donald B. Anderson, Special Assistant to the Attorney General, and Theron L. Caudle, Assistant Attorney General.

9.

Julien Cornell, a man of compact figure and attractive personality, was only thirty-five years old when he was retained as Pound's counsel. He was a graduate of Swarthmore College and Yale Law School, with offices in downtown New York. He had been asked to enter the case by his friend James Laughlin, Pound's American publisher, who also got the approval of Shakespear and Parkyn. After seeing Pound, Cornell wrote Laughlin:

"I found the poor devil in a rather desperate condition. He is very wobbly in his mind and while his talk is entirely rational, he flits from one idea to another and is unable to concentrate even to the extent of answering a single question without immediately wandering off the subject. We spent most of the time talking about Confucius, Jefferson and the economic and political implications of their ideas. I let him ramble on, even though I did not get much of the information which I wanted, as it seemed a shame to deprive him of the pleasure of talking, which has been almost entirely denied to him for a long while."

Cornell was convinced that the after-effects of Pound's breakdown in Pisa were still present:

"I would say that he is still under a considerable mental cloud," he wrote. "For instance, he kept talking about the possibility that powerful government officials with whom he had no acquaintance whatever, might interest themselves in his case if they could be persuaded of the soundness of his economic views. He said that whether or not he is convicted he could be of tremendous help to President Truman, because of his knowledge of conditions in Italy and Japan. He added, with a wry smile, that the greatest benefit which can come to a poet is to be hung."

They discussed "the possibility of pleading insanity as a defense." Pound, he said, had no objection. "He told me that the idea had already occurred to him."

"When I told Pound that there was some possibility of his being admitted to bail and I hoped that his wife's British funds could be used as security, he said that he would have no place to live, and his only funds are twenty-three dollars. I hope that his friends can arrange to help him, if by good fortune he should be released. I learned this morning from Charles Norman of *PM* that the paper is sending him $50 for poems used in Norman's article which is to appear this Sunday."

His letter concludes:

"Pound wants you to publish his translations of Confucius, which are ready, and also a new volume of Cantos, some of which I believe he sent out from prison in Italy. He seems to think the Confucius is world shaking in its import and should be published immediately."

At the arraignment on the 27th, Cornell told the Court:

"Mr. Pound is not sufficiently in possession of judgment and perhaps mentality to plead. I ask that he be allowed to stand mute."

He also said that he had asked Pound that morning about his plea, and that he received no answer. Cornell termed it a "grave mistake" to have brought Pound to this country when he was just beginning to recover from his mental breakdown in the DTC.

By order of the Court, Pound was transferred to Gallinger Municipal Hospital for psychiatric examination, and Cornell returned to New York, to learn what he could about Pound from friends of his, and to raise money for him, Mrs. Pound's funds being at this time blocked in England and she herself unable to reach the United States because of visa difficulties. Among those he saw was E. E. Cummings, who, having received that very day—November 30th—a check for one thousand dollars for one of his paintings, turned the check over to Cornell. Cornell told me: "I was, of course, much surprised and moved by this spontaneous generosity, and by the large amount of the gift. I told Cummings that the money would be used to secure psychiatric and medical treatment for Pound. Although this was an outright gift, with no thought of repayment, Mrs. Pound repaid it after she had succeeded in obtaining the release of her personal funds."

Cornell also received the following sums: from James Laughlin, two hundred dollars; from Lida June Drew (Mrs. William L. Drew of Eagle Lake, Florida; forwarded by Archibald MacLeish), fifty dollars; from Liveright Publishing Corporation (royalties to June 30, 1945), $311.63, which, together with the money contributed by Cummings, made it possible for him to retain Dr. Wendell Muncie, Associate Professor of Psychiatry at the Johns Hopkins Hospital in

Baltimore, and consulting psychiatrist in other hospitals, as an independent examiner. The report of the doctors—three for the government, Dr. Muncie for the defendant—was unanimous.

FEDERAL SECURITY AGENCY
Saint Elizabeths Hospital
Washington 20, D.C.

December 14, 1945

Honorable Bolitha J. Laws
Chief Justice, U.S. District Court
Washington, D.C.

Sir:

The undersigned hereby respectfully report the results of their mental examination of Ezra Pound, now detained in Gallinger Hospital by transfer for observation from the District Jail on a charge of treason. Three of us (Drs. Gilbert, King, and Overholser) were appointed by your Honor to make this examination. At our suggestion, and with your approval, Dr. Wendell Muncie, acting upon the request of counsel for the accused, made an examination with us and associates himself with us in this joint report. Dr. Muncie spent several hours with the defendant, both alone and with us, on December 13, 1945, and the others of us have examined the defendant each on several occasions, separately and together, in the period from his admission to Gallinger Hospital on December 4, 1945 to December 13, 1945. We have had available to us the reports of laboratory, psychological and special physical examinations of the defendant and considerable material in the line of his writings and biographical data.

The defendant, now 60 years of age and in generally good physical condition, was a precocious student, specializing in literature. He has been a voluntary expatriate for nearly 40 years, living in England and France, and for the past 21 years in Italy, making an uncertain living by writing poetry and criticism. His poetry and literary criticism have achieved considerable recognition, but of recent years his preoccupation with monetary theories and economics has apparently obstructed his literary productivity. He has long been recognized as eccentric, querulous, and egocentric.

At the present time he exhibits extremely poor judgment as to his situation, its seriousness and the manner in which the charges are to be met. He insists that his broadcasts were not treasonable, but that all of his radio activities have stemmed from his self appointed mission to "save the Constitution." He is abnormally grandiose, is expansive and exuberant in manner, exhibiting pressure of speech, discursiveness, and distractibility.

In our opinion, with advancing years his personality, for many years abnormal, has undergone further distortion to the extent that he is now suffering from a paranoid state which renders him mentally unfit to advise properly with counsel or to participate intelligently and reasonably in his own defense. He is, in other words, insane and mentally unfit for trial, and is in need of care in a mental hospital.

Respectfully submitted,

Joseph L. Gilbert, M.D.   Marion R. King, M.D.
Wendell Muncie, M.D.   Winfred Overholser, M.D.

Dr. Gilbert, chief psychiatrist of Gallinger Municipal Hospital, afterwards testified:

"When I have seen him he has complained that for at least four years he has felt unusually fatigued . . . and that when those symptoms of fatigue are more marked he describes his feelings at the time as being unable to get flat enough in bed . . . during long periods of interviews with him he remained reclining in bed, with the additional symptom of restlessness, rather rapid movements about the bed, and suddenly sitting or rising to the upright sitting position, or to move quickly about from the bed to a table nearby to get some paper, book or manuscript, and to as suddenly throw himself on the bed and again assume the reclining position. This fatigue and exhaustion, which he states was completely reducing him, as he said, to the level of an imbecile in his thinking capacity, was nothwithstanding the fact that he was undergoing no amount of physical activity.

"He spoke of his mental processes being in a fog, to use his own words, that he admits during these periods of severe fatigue that he was unable to undertake temporarily any mental activity, and also complained of pressure throughout various regions of the head, what he described as a feeling of hollowness, going through this gesture (indicating) with his fingers, describing the vortex of the skull, indicating that there was a feeling not only of pressure but of hollowness in that particular part of the cranium" (Transcript of Testimony, Wednesday, February 13, 1946, United States of America against Ezra Pound, Defendant).

10.

A motion for bail was heard and denied on December 21st, and Pound was transferred to St. Elizabeths Hospital of which Dr. Winfred Overholser was Superintendent. In the affidavit in support of the application for bail Cornell declared:

"In order to furnish the court with further information about the defendant, if desired, I have appended as Exhibit A, a copy of the only material concerning him which has been published currently, namely, an article which appeared in the newspaper *PM* (New York) for November 25, 1945."

He afterwards wrote me:

"My purpose in using your material was to supply the Court with biographical and literary data concerning the defendant which I believe helped the Court to reach a decision."

The material included contributions by other poets. The essay by Mr. Eliot from which I have been quoting was projected for the *PM* symposium, but afterwards appeared in *Poetry*.[13] William Carlos Williams replied as follows (several paragraphs from this communication were used earlier):

"I can't write about Ezra Pound with any sort of composure. When I think of the callousness of some of his letters during the last six or seven years, blithe comments touching 'fresh meat on the Russian steppes' or the war in Spain as being of 'no more importance than the draining of some mosquito swamp in deepest Africa,' 'Hitler the martyr' and all that—I want to forget that I ever knew him. His vicious anti-semitism and much else have lowered him in my mind further than I ever thought it possible to lower a man whom I had once admired. But that isn't the whole story.

"Somehow I am compelled to think of something I once heard about a poet during one of the former Mexican revolutions. This poor guy seeing the men with guns coming down the street shinnied up a telegraph pole—the only thing available to give him any elevation under the circumstances. The troops seeing him up there thought they might as well take a few pot-shots at him—anyhow it was in enemy territory. But at this the man up the pole started to yell, I'm a poet! I'm a poet! The soldiers at that invited him down, gave him a drink and told him to go ahead, poetize for them. Maybe they shot him later, I don't know.

"Ezra Pound is one of the most competent poets in our language, possessed of the most acute ear for metrical sequences, to the point of genius, that we have ever known. He is also, it must be confessed, the biggest damn fool and faker in the business. You can't allow yourself to be too serious about a person like that—and yet he is important. He knows all this and plays on it to perfection.

"One trait I always held against Ezra was that he'd never let you in on his personal affairs; close as we were for several years when we were kids I just never knew what he was up to. It didn't make really much difference but in a pal it was annoying. Never explain anything, was his motto. He carried it off well—and in his verse too, later. The purpose was to impress everyone about him with the profundity of his wit. I know the answer now and it isn't flattering. Generally speaking his head was fairly empty.

"But he always felt himself superior to anyone about him and could never brook a rival. We accepted it on terms he little suspected, for after all he was and remains, in his field, a genius. He just lived on a different plane from anyone else in the world, a higher plane! This gave him certain prerogatives. If he was your friend you just forgave it. We were friends.

"I think this trait or whatever it was bred from—if not plain emptiness—is the thing that finally ruined Ezra. He tried to make good and with better financial success in his field might have done so—but he was a lazy animal in many ways and couldn't be bothered. We had a chronic argument going on between us, he and I, over which was the proper objective for the writer, caviar or bread. I held out for bread, Ezra for caviar. This went on for years. Finally one day I got a letter from London saying: bread.

"But that was only a momentary aberration on the part of the grrrrrrreatest poet drawing breath in our day! And he meant it. That was no joke to Ezra. He really lived the poet as few of us had the nerve to live that exalted reality in our time. As always the details are best omitted, they were part of the aura.

"I say these things because I can't help saying them—they are part of the Ezra Pound I knew, the man now in jeopardy of his life as a traitor to his country. Ezra always insisted, in the loudest terms, on the brilliance and profundity of his mind. He doesn't have a great mind and never did but that doesn't make him any the less a good poet. His stupidities coupled with his overweening self esteem have brought him down—but to try to make a criminal of him because of that is to lay ourselves open to the accusation of being moved by an even greater stupidity than that which we are facing. There are plenty of others in his category with far less talent.

"Ezra Pound the consummate poet taken as any sort of menace to America when compared with some of the vicious minds at large among us in, say for instance the newspaper game, as well as other rackets which have the public ear, is sheer childishness. He just isn't dangerous, they are. I am not trying to minimize his crime, it was a crime and he committed it wilfully. But under the circumstances and knowing what goes on 'in committee' and elsewhere in our magnificently destined country—I don't think we should be too hard on him. I have thought, in spite of his infantile mental pattern, and still think—knowing what goes on about me every day as reported in the drivel of the press—that as a poet Ezra had some sort of right to speak his mind, such as it had become, as he did.

"I have to qualify the above paragraph, however, by saying that I never heard a word that Ezra Pound broadcast during the war from Italy. The only thing I know directly about his broadcasts is a single sentence, referring to myself, which one of the tellers in our bank told my wife one morning more than a year ago. From the quality of that I judge of the rest, dull stuff.

"When they lock the man up with Jim and John and Henry and Mary and Dolores and Grace—I hope they will give him access to books, with paper enough for him to go on making translations for us from the classics such as we have never seen except at his hands in our language.

"It would be the greatest miscarriage of justice, human justice, to shoot him."

Memorable was the statement by E. E. Cummings:

"Re Ezra Pound—poetry happens to be an art;and artists happen to be human beings.

"An artist doesn't live in some geographical abstraction,superimposed on a part of this beautiful earth by the nonimagination of unanimals and dedicated to the proposition that massacre is a social virtue because murder is an individual vice. Nor does an artist live in some soi-disant world,nor does he live in some socalled universe, nor does he live in any number of 'worlds' or in any number of 'universes.' As for a few trifling delusions like the 'past' and 'present' and 'future' of quote mankind unquote,they may be big enough for a couple of billion supermechanized submorons but they're much too small for one human being.

"Every artist's strictly illimitable country is himself.

"An artist who plays that country false has committed suicide;and even a good lawyer cannot kill the dead. But a human being who's true to himself—whoever himself may be—is immortal;and all the atomic bombs of all the anti-artists in spacetime will never civilize immortality."

Conrad Aiken wrote me:

"I am glad you are doing a piece on Pound. For his tragic predicament he has of course only himself to blame, and like anyone else in the same situation he must alone take the consequences. That he knew this he made quite apparent on his arrest, when he remarked that if a man values his beliefs he values them enough to die for them, and if they are worth having at all they are worth the speaking out. In my own opinion Pound is less traitor than fool: his political infatuations or obsessions led him by insensible degrees across international borders; the internationalism that always marked his poetry began increasingly to stamp his political thinking; and now he finds himself under charge of treason for having, according to his own queer lights, betrayed a particular society of men for man in the abstract.

"But whatever the United States government decides to be justice in his case as traitor, I think we must all see to it that justice should be done to him also as poet. He was a poet, perhaps a great one, long before he became a Fascist, he is still that poet, and one of the great creative influences of our time, and we must not permit these facts, nor his work, to be forgotten. It is for this reason that recently, when the editors of Random House refused to print Pound's poems in an anthology, or to be more exact in a new edition of that anthology, I was moved to protest. It seemed to me that a burning of the books was a kind of intellectual and moral suicide which we might more wisely leave to our enemies."

I agreed with Mr. Aiken. More; I felt that the issue of censorship, if true, transcended the case of Pound in importance. I therefore asked Bennett Cerf, president of Random House, for a statement. I was referred by him to the late Saxe Commins, editor, who told me:

"Random House is not going to publish any Fascist. As a matter of fact, we don't think that Ezra Pound is good enough, or important enough, to include. If we thought he was, we might have carried him anyway. We just don't think he is."

Mr. Commins said that in place of Pound's poems the book would carry a note explaining their omission. Two days later I received the following letter from him: "I am sending you herewith a copy of the note which will appear on Page 788 of our forthcoming Modern Library Giant volume, *An Anthology of Famous English and American Poetry*, edited by William Rose Benét and Conrad Aiken." This was the note:

"At this point Conrad Aiken included in the Modern Library edition of his anthology, on which the present text is based, the following poems by Ezra Pound: *Envoi* (1919), *The Tree, The Tomb at Akr Caar, Portrait d'une Femme, Apparuit, A Virginal, The Return, The River Merchant's Wife, The Flame, Dance Figure, Lament of the Frontier Guard,* and *Taking Leave of a Friend*. When the publishers insisted on omitting these poems from the present edition, he consented upon one condition: that it be clearly stated in print that his wishes were overruled by the publishers, who flatly refused at this time to include a single line by Ezra Pound. This is a statement that the publishers are not only willing but delighted to print."

I am glad that I had the opportunity afforded me by my article to bring this to public notice. It led the editors to rescind their decision respecting future editions of the Benét-Aiken book, although not before Mr. Cerf took his dilemma to readers of the *Saturday Review*.

On May 2, 1946, Mr. Cornell wrote his client:

"You are somewhat familiar with the rumpus which has been stirring in the public prints over the refusal of Random House to include your poems in the Modern Library anthology edited by Conrad Aiken. The gist of the matter is that Bennett Cerf, President of Random House, disliking your political opinions and activities, refused to print the poems selected by Mr. Aiken, and, upon the latter's insistence, published a foot-note in the anthology explaining the omission. Incidentally, Mr. Cerf has probably committed a technical libel against you, but I would not recommend suit, both because you would thereby degrade yourself to his level, and also because the chances for success in a jury trial would be very slim. Mr. Cerf has admitted publicly that he was wrong in omitting the poems for such a reason and now desires to include them in the next edition of the anthology. Twelve poems were selected for which Random House offers $25. each, which Jas. [Laughlin] and I think is a handsome price.

"Assuming that the price is agreeable to you, there remains the question of Mr. Cerf explaining to his readers the inclusion of the poems in view of their omission from the previous volume. I discussed this matter with him and told him that I felt sure that you would refuse to permit the poems to be printed if the publisher should insist upon repeating their derogatory statements about you.

"Mr. Cerf is apparently now anxious to withdraw from the political arena and to confine himself to editing and publishing. He does feel the necessity, however, of explaining his change of heart to his readers and proposes to print with the poems the following explanatory note:

" 'After the publishers of the Modern Library omitted the poems of Ezra Pound from the first edition of this volume, a veritable avalanche of praise and blame, equally divided, descended upon them.

"Nothing could have been farther from the intention of the publishers than to exercise arbitrary rights of censorship. We now have decided to include these poems of Ezra Pound in order to remove any possible hint of suppression, and because we concede that it may be wrong to confuse Pound the poet with Pound the man.' "

Pound replied, May 4th, with the following notation, scrawled large on the top of Cornell's first page: "All right."

CHAPTER XXI

THE TRIAL

1.

It was believed by many at the time that Pound was not brought to trial on his indictment because of some sinister "deal," which remained unspecified. The fact that he was not tried was particularly vexing to the Communist *New Masses,* which followed the publication of the *PM* symposium with one of its own, in which all the contributors declared that Pound should be executed forthwith, some favoring hanging, some shooting. But as he had not been tried and consequently was, by our laws, presumed innocent, the performance was pitiful.

The truth was otherwise. The government wanted very much to try Pound. It had not accepted the unanimous finding of the four psychiatrists as final. For now the Attorney General's office moved for trial on this question, in order to resolve formally and publicly the issue of Pound's mental condition. The trial took place on February 13, 1946, before Judge Laws. Isaiah Matlack and Donald Anderson appeared for the Department of Justice, and Julien Cornell for the defendant. Judge Laws said:

"Certain representations have been made to the Court that Mr. Pound is not in mental condition such as that he is able to participate with counsel in the trial of a criminal case, and he is not in position to understand the full nature of the charges against him. Based upon that showing which has been made to me by psychiatrists, I am going to impanel a jury to pass upon that question. In the event the jury finds that his mental state is as has been represented to me, then Mr. Pound will not be brought to trial because, under the law, it would not be proper to prosecute him if his mental condition is as has been stated to me."

The jury, having been sworn, the doctors who had examined Pound in Gallinger Municipal Hospital were called, and again testified to his paranoid state. I select a portion of the testimony given by Dr. Winfred Overholser, Superintendent of St. Elizabeths Hospital, both in direct and cross-examination.

Examined by Mr. Cornell on Pound's condition, Dr. Overholser said:

"He is thoroughly convinced that if he had been allowed to send his messages to the Axis, which he wished to send, prior to 1940, there would have been no Axis even. In other words, that if given a free hand by those who were engaged in stultifying him, he could have prevented the war.

"He lays a great deal of his difficulties at the door of British Secret Service, and other groups, which have opposed him.

"He assures me, too, that he served a very useful purpose to the United States by remaining at the Italian prison camp to complete his translation of Confucius, which he regards as the greatest contribution to literature.

"He is sure he should not have been brought to this country in the capacity of a prisoner, but in the capacity of someone who was to be of great benefit to the United States in its post-war activities.

"I might state that this constitutes a grandiosity of ideas and beliefs that goes far beyond the normal, even in a person who is as distraught in his mind as he is."

Dr. Overholser was cross-examined by Mr. Matlack.

Q. "Now, what part does his background history play in your opinion as to his present sanity?"

A. "It shows that we are dealing now with the end-product of an individual who throughout his lifetime has been highly antagonistic, highly eccentric, the whole world has revolved around him, he has been a querulous person, he has been less and less able to order his life. This has been a gradual evolution through his life, so that now we are dealing with the end-product, so to speak."

Q. "Do you think that because he is eccentric that makes him unable to consult counsel?"

A. "Oh, no."

Q. "That is true of many people?"

A. "Yes."

Q. "That does not make him unable to consult with counsel?"

A. "It might make him a nuisance."

Q. "Make him a nuisance but not insane?"

A. "Yes."

Q. "I think you said one of the characteristics was that he was very vituperative to one who opposed his will?"

A. "He has been."

Q. "Do you think that, in itself, displays a person who could not be able to consult with counsel?"

A. "Not in itself. I haven't said that any one of these things in itself would."

Q. "I am going to come to that. I have forgotten what other thing you did say. I did understand you to say that he is vituperative, and eccentric; I don't know whether you used the word 'sensitive' or not."

A. "No, but he is highly supersensitive."

Q. "Now, couldn't a man who was eccentric, and vituperative, and all the other attributes that you have given to him rolled into one, still be able to consult with counsel?"

A. "Even with all those three, and with nothing else, very likely, yes."

Q. "I understand that what we are concerned with in this inquiry is not the question of the difference between right and wrong, that is, as to being able to distinguish between right and wrong, but whether he is able to consult with counsel and conduct a defense."

A. "That is correct."

Q. "Did he give you in his general history anything about his belief in Fascism?"

A. "I did not discuss that with him particularly."

At this point the defendant, who was seated at the counsel table, jumped up, banged the table with his fist, and shouted at the top of his voice.

The Defendant: "I never did believe in Fascism, God damn it; I am opposed to Fascism."

Q. "I don't know whether you answered the question, or not."

The Court: "I think he answered it."

Q. "Did he ever discuss with you his advocacy of Mussolini and his politics?"

A. "In the most general terms. I didn't go into that in great detail, either. I looked upon that as a political matter."

Q. "Well, that is what I am beginning to get at. Did you read his book entitled Jefferson and Mussolini?"

A. "No."

Q. "Did you take into consideration the fact that living in Italy, where the political philosophy was Fascism, that he may have become imbued with that philosophy?"

Mr. Cornell: "Your Honor, I object to this line of questioning and characterization of Mr. Pound, which I think is very distressing to him."

The Court [to Mr. Matlack]: "I will give you a certain latitude, but try not to disturb him if you can help it."

Q. "What delusions do you say he suffers from?"

A. "Well, I think they are both delusions of grandeur and delusions of persecution, both of which are characteristic of what we call the paranoid condition."

Q. "You don't say that he suffers with paranoia though?"

A. "I will say it is a paranoid condition; the distinction between paranoia, schizophrenia and one thing and another run into each other, but it resembles paranoia, if you wish to put it that way."

Q. "Do you feel that he was so imbued with his economic theories, or whatever his message might have been, that even if he had realized the consequences of his treasonable act that he still would have broadcast?"

A. "I haven't an opinion on it."

Pound was not called. Mr. Cornell did not desire it, and Mr. Matlack asked the Court about it. Judge Laws said: "I don't think so. If we call him he will take two or three hours. I don't think it is necessary. The Court of Appeals says very plainly you cannot disregard an opinion of the psychiatrists."

Mr. Cornell: "I am afraid he might blow up. He has been pretty nervous." (The foregoing was spoken out of hearing of the jury.)

The Court: "You don't want to argue the case, do you?"

Mr. Cornell: "No."

Mr. Matlack: "No."

Mr. Cornell: "I intend to make a motion for a directed verdict."

The Court: "I will take the verdict, and so just for the record I will overrule it [the motion] and note an exception.

"Members of the Jury, there is a provision of our Code in the Laws of the District of Columbia to the effect that whenever a person is indicted for an offense, and before trial evidence is submitted to the judge that the accused is then insane the judge may cause a jury to be impanelled to inquire into the sanity or insanity of the accused, and if the jury shall find the accused to be then insane the Court may then bring about a commitment of the defendant to hospitalization, to remain in hospitalization until or unless there comes a time when it is found that he has recovered from his mental difficulties, and in that event he is certified back into the court for trial.

"The reason for that law, of course, is obvious to all of us I am sure. It is absolutely essential that any person accused of the commission of a crime must be in a position to cooperate with counsel who is to defend him. He must understand the nature of the charges and be familiar and able to understand the offense which was alleged in the charge against him, to be able to tell the names of witnesses, what they might be able to say, and be able to give his own version to these acts which are alleged against him.

"It is important, also, of course, that in the trial of the case that he be in position to cooperate with his counsel in his defense and, if he sees fit, if he chooses to take the stand, to testify understandingly and intelligently with regard to the facts in the case and to be cross-examined by the prosecution with regard to those facts and, of course, the law is humane to the extent that it does not want to bring about a person's breakdown at the trial of a criminal case if he is mentally ill and not able to stand the stress of a criminal trial.

"In this particular case the defendant is charged with a serious offense, the offense of treason which, under certain conditions might result, if he is found guilty, in his punishment by electrocution, and when he was arraigned in court there was some suggestion made to me as the presiding judge that he was having mental difficulty, and on the strength of the showing that was then made, and later made in the form of affidavits, I committed him to Gallinger Hospital for examination.

"It has been testified to before you correctly that we brought him to the point of having him examined by psychiatrists and physicians on mental diseases; we brought Dr. Overholser, who is the head of St. Elizabeths Hospital, one of the outstanding institutions of the United States, and run by the United States, and we brought to examine him also Dr. King who, as you have been told on the witness stand, holds a responsible position in the Public Health Service which attends to the mental as well as the physical conditions of persons in the penal institutions throughout the United States. We brought into consultation also Dr. Gilbert, who is the head of the Division of Psychiatry at Gallinger Hospital, with which I think you are doubtless familiar. Then there was permitted to examine him at the request of Mr. Cornell, who appeared for Mr. Pound, Dr. Muncie, who is a leading psychiatrist, and I think the head of the department at Johns Hopkins University. You heard his qualifications.

"These doctors, after consultation, filed a written certificate with the Court indicating their unanimous view that Mr. Pound under his then present state of mind was not in a position to stand a trial, to cooperate with his counsel, and go through with a serious charge of this nature.

"Government counsel have cooperated very readily in the investigation and were very fair in the entire situation and they, feeling that the code of law which I have explained to you should be complied with, filed in this court a motion that a jury be impanelled to pass upon this proposition. I agreed with the view of Government counsel that a jury be impanelled to look into it notwithstanding the unanimous opinion of these psychiatrists, and that is the reason why you have been impanelled today to hear the whole story, and those physicians have been questioned before you fully with regard to the situation.

"It therefore becomes your duty now to advise me whether in your judgment you find that Mr. Pound is in position to cooperate with his counsel, to stand trial without causing him to crack up or break down; whether he is able to testify, if he sees fit, at the trial, to stand cross-examination, and in that regard, of course, you have heard the testimony of all these physicians on the subject, and there is no testimony to the contrary and, of course, these are men who have given a large part of their professional careers to the study of matters of this sort, who have been brought here for your guidance.

"Under the state of the law you are not necessarily bound by what they say; you can disregard what they say and bring in a different verdict, but in a case of this type where the Government and the defense representatives have united in a clear and unequivocal view with regard to the situation, I presume you will have no difficulty in making up your mind."

The jury retired at 3:55 P.M. and was out three minutes.

The Clerk of the Court: "Mr. Foreman, has the jury agreed upon its verdict?"

The Foreman of the Jury: "It has."

The Clerk of the Court: "What say you as to the respondent Ezra Pound? Is he of sound or unsound mind?"

The Foreman of the Jury: "Unsound mind."

Pound was remanded to St. Elizabeths Hospital.

2.

On January 3, 1947, Mr. Cornell drew up a new motion for bail. The pertinent paragraphs follow:

"6. Defendant's attorney has been informed by Dr. Winfred Overholser, Superintendent of St. Elizabeths Hospital, based upon his examination and treatment of the defendant which covers a period of about one year beginning at about the time of his admission to Gallinger Hospital on December 4, 1945, that in his opinion (1) the defendant has been insane for many years and will never recover his sanity or become mentally fit to stand trial to the indictment (2) the defendant's mental condition is not benefited by his close confinement at St. Elizabeths Hospital where he is kept in a building with violent patients because of the necessity for keeping him under guard, and it would be desirable from the point of view of the health and welfare of the defendant if he could be removed to a private sanatorium and (3) the defendant is not violent, does not require close confinement and the public safety would not be impaired if he were allowed the degree of liberty which a private sanatorium permits for patients who are mildly insane.

"7. It therefore appears from Dr. Overholser's opinion, based upon a full year of observation and treatment, that the defendant can never be brought to trial on this indictment and will for the rest of his life be presumed innocent in law, although he may remain under the charge of treason. It appears also from the medical standpoint that the continuance of his present incarceration is not desirable and his transfer to a private sanatorium would benefit him.

"8. If on medical grounds the defendant should be released from custody, then to continue to hold him would be equivalent to a sentence of life imprisonment upon a man who is and always will be presumed innocent. He would be confined for the rest of his life because of an accusation which can never be proved. It is respectfully submitted that such confinement would be unlawful and unconstitutional."

The motion was denied. Some of the arguments were repeated in a petition for a writ of habeas corpus, also drawn up by Mr. Cornell and filed by Dorothy Pound in 1948. (Her visa finally cleared, for more than a decade she was a daily visitor, living first with Omar, then by herself, in a succession of small apartments in Congress Heights, near the hospital.) Dorothy Pound's petition was also dismissed, and the writ, against Dr. Winfred Overholser, as well as "aids and assistants and whoever has the custody of the body of Ezra Pound," was never issued. Mr. Cornell told me he knew he would not win in the lower courts, and that the issue would have to go to the Supreme Court where, he said, he was confident he could win. Pound, however, asked his wife to discontinue the proceedings. The legal question at issue is not without interest and, so far as is known, has never been resolved. They are best stated in Mrs. Pound's petition of 1948, the pertinent paragraphs being the following:

"11. My husband, Ezra Pound, is held in custody pursuant to the authority of Section 211 of Title 24 of the United States Code which provides as follows:

" 'If any person, charged with crime, be found, in the court before which he is so charged, to be an insane person, such court shall certify the same to the Federal Security Administrator, who may order such person to be confined in Saint Elizabeths Hospital, and, if he be not indigent, he and his estate shall be charged with expenses of his support in the hospital.'

"12. The release from custody of persons so confined is provided in Section 211b of Title 24 of the United States Code which is as follows:

" 'When any person confined in Saint Elizabeths Hospital charged with crime and subject to be tried therefor, or convicted of crime and undergoing sentence therefor, shall be restored to sanity, the superintendent of the hospital shall give notice thereof to the judge of the criminal court, and deliver him to the court in obedience to the proper precept.'

"13. There is no provision in the statutes for the release from custody of a person who is found to be permanently insane and consequently unable to be tried, yet whose mental condition does not require confinement in a hospital or asylum. The statute does not prohibit release of a person confined under such circumstances, but merely fails to make any provision to cover such an eventuality.

"14. I am informed by counsel that my husband has the legal and constitutional right to be released from custody, because there is no justification in law for his continued confinement. When a person has been accused of crime and found to be of unsound mind, he may be properly confined for the reason that (1) there is an indictment pending against him under which he may be brought to trial if and when he recovers his sanity, or (2) his mental condition is such that he requires hospitalization, or (3) it would be dangerous to the public safety for him to remain at liberty. In the first case, the state is exercising its police power under which it may apprehend and confine persons awaiting trial while in the other cases the state is acting as the guardian and *parens patriae* of persons who are unable to provide for their own welfare. But unless the state can properly bring to bear either its police power or its power of control over insane persons for the welfare of themselves and the general public, the state has no legal or constitutional right to hold in custody an insane person merely because he has been found to be insane. The Constitution still guarantees to him that his liberty shall not be taken away without due process of law, and if his own and the public welfare does not require it, he may not be deprived of his liberty by confinement in an institution. In the case of my husband, Ezra Pound, there is no reasonable possibility that he will recover his sanity, and, therefore, he can never be brought to trial under the indictment. It is also clear that his insanity is of a mild sort which does not require his continued hospitalization. Under these circumstances, if my husband is held indefinitely in confinement, he will in effect be confined for the rest of his life, solely because an indictment is pending against him which can never be resolved by trial.

"15. It is a fundamental principle of law that every person is presumed to be innocent until he has been found guilty, and also that no person may be imprisoned until his guilt has been determined by process of law. Under these principles, the indictment against my husband is no evidence of his guilt, and he must be presumed innocent of the charge against him, and such presumption will endure for the rest of his life, because he will never be in condition for trial. As a result, a presumably innocent man is being held in confinement and will be confined for life, merely because he has been charged with crime, and has not sufficient mental capacity to meet the charge. His confinement on such grounds is nowhere authorized by statute, or by any principle of law, and would deprive him of his liberty without due process of law in violation of the Fifth Amendment to the United States Constitution.

"Wherefore, your petitioner prays that a Writ of Habeas Corpus be issued by this court directed to Dr. Winfred Overholser, Superintendent of St. Elizabeths Hospital, to produce the body of Ezra Pound before this court, at a time and place to be specified therein, then and there to receive and do what this court shall order concerning the detention and restraint of Ezra Pound, and that he shall be ordered to be discharged from the custody of the respondent and released to the care of the petitioner, as the Committee of his person and estate.

"Dated: Washington, D.C.
 "February 11, 1948.
  "(signed) Dorothy Pound
              "Petitioner."

3.

It now appeared that Pound would remain a prisoner for the rest of his life. Actually, he was a prisoner for twelve years. Mr. Cornell wrote me in 1959: "Eventually the Government came around to the same way of thinking as I did, at least as a practical matter, if not a legal theory."

Pound himself appears to have been very little concerned over the question of his sanity. He was, understandably, touchy about the question of his alleged treason. He did not believe that he had committed any act "contrary to his allegiance" by broadcasting from Rome, an idea which was to grow and to take hold—of him, of his wife, of some of his friends, and all of his "disciples," that odd cluster of fringe-men and -women with whom he beguiled much of the tedium of his long confinement. The idea was also held in some quarters in Europe. Olga Rudge printed in Siena a pamphlet entitled *If This Be Treason* which contains five of Pound's broadcasts entitled "e.e. cummings/examined," "James Joyce: to his memory," "A french accent," "Canto 45," and "Blast." It is a way of looking. Another: "Pound, Ezra. For understanding this author's prose and poetry on American matters, study of 'The Constitution of the U.S.A.' is vital. We can supply new copies, 12mo, pp. 32 at 3s. 6d." (From a catalogue issued by Peter Russell, publisher of Pound's "Money Pamphlets.")

It took extreme forms in the other direction. The following admonition was sent to the *Saturday Review of Literature* by Mr. Cornell:

"In your issue of September 4, 1948, there is a review of Ezra Pound's Cantos, in which it is stated that Mr. Pound committed treason, that he espoused Fascism and that he was led into the camp of the enemy.

"I have been asked by Mr. Pound and his wife to protest these statements. The truth is that Mr. Pound was indicted on a charge of treason but was found mentally unfit to stand trial. Accordingly, he has not been convicted and is presumed before the law to be innocent.

"As your review correctly points out, Mr. Pound has in late years been obsessed with certain economic theories and these were the subject of his radio broadcasts on which the treason charge was based. If such actions were treasonable that could only be established by a trial which has not taken place. If there should be a trial, I am convinced that Mr. Pound would be acquitted on the ground that he was not responsible mentally for his actions.

"Upon reflection, I hope that you will agree that it is both untrue and unfair to assume that Ezra Pound is guilty of treason when this has merely been charged and not proven, and he has been found mentally irresponsible."

A carbon copy went to Mrs. Pound at 5211-10th Place S.E., Washington, and she showed it to her husband. His typed memorandum to Cornell follows:

"I don't weep over mere nastiness, but object to libel.

"Present dirt tries to overlook Guarantee from Ital. govt that I wd not be asked to (and never was asked to say anything vs/ conscience or duties as Am. Cit."

Beneath this, Mrs. Pound wrote:

"EP. is not interested in the question of his sanity—but in establishing that he did NOT commit treason—

"The treason was in the White House, not in Rapallo—& people are beginning to see that at last."

Pound, who was shown this passage in proof in 1960, commented in the margin: "She is quoting E. P."

The bolstering idea, that the Italian government had somehow sustained his Americanism, appears in two published statements by Pound—in the British *Who's Who* and in the biographical note prefixed to his *Selected Poems*. In the latter, he also called attention to the 1939 visit to the United States "in endeavour to stave off war." The final paragraph reads: "1940 after continued opposition obtained permission to use Rome radio for personal propaganda in support of U.S. Constitution, continuing after America's official entry into the war only on condition that he should never be asked to say anything contrary to his conscience or contrary to his duties as an American Citizen. Which promise was faithfully observed by the Italian Government."

Pound continued to object to the "libel." He typed and scribbled notes to his counsel and others; in some of them the spelling seems done by ear, as in his twenties. He attended to business, transferring *Personae* from the Liveright Publishing Corporation to James Laughlin, and authorizing Cornell to pay all moneys that come in to

his daughter, at that time a resident of Genoa. "I want her to get used to handling the business. She has more of sense of that kind than I have." He asked Cornell to "see that my deposit here is so fixed that small supply orders (for 20 cents worth of saltine biscuit etc.) don't get held up 3 weeks." He appealed for reading matter: "Anybody who wants to send me *novels,* not criticism or highbrow tosh can do so & welcome." He complained: "Young doctors absolutely useless—must have 15 minutes sane conversation daily." Some of the memoranda appear to be addressed to himself:

"enormous work to be done & no driving force & everyone's inexactitude very fatiguing."

> "mental torture
> constitution a religion
> a world lost
> grey mist barrier impasible
>   ignorance absolute
>   anonyme
> futility of 'might have been'
> coherent areas
>   constantly
>   invaded"

There were also letters. His new stationery bore the device, "J'Ayme Donc Je Suis." The letters flowed from St. Elizabeths in a steady stream to every part of the Union and to lands beyond the sea. Then they flowed back from their recipients to dealers and libraries in the United States. The letters are on every conceivable subject. A professor at Haverford College was thinking of starting a "Catullian Quarterly" —Pound names someone who will be interested. He plucked names from the remote and recent past: "Freud, Marx, Necker, that sow Mrs. de Stael . . . what a punktheon." "Titus, Antoninus/ Roman Arms, bitched by fraud and forgery." He wrote on Christianity: "The more Patrologia I read the WORSE the corruption labld Christianity appears/

← "Letterhead" portrait by Gaudier-Brzeska and (bottom) Pound's signature representation of it in recent years. Other signatures: 1909 and 1933. Reproductions actual size.

I don't know that even the kikes can be blamed for all of it." He wrote on the decline of culture: "Horrible decay of mental QUALITY can be measured from Plotinus to Augie of Hippo/ praps worse than the stink introduced between Dante and Milton." He received hate literature and commented: "Bright paper from Detroit with a lot that I have been saying and quoting for 20 and 30 years. labld 'Truth and the Constitution.' "

One day he occupied himself by drawing up a list of books "chosen by Ezra Pound, from the estate of the late Miss May Sinclair." There were 173 items, of which he named thirty-four by Miss Sinclair, seventeen by himself, two by Yeats, one by Joyce, one by Eliot, one by D. H. Lawrence, and nine by Ford Madox Ford, plus several Ford had done in collaboration with Conrad and Violet Hunt. He could not resist punning on one of his own titles, but gave it correctly in parenthesis: "I'm a Pauper Armair. (Quia Pauper Amavi)."

4.

Despite his surroundings, he was able to work. In 1947 New Directions published his *Confucius: The Unwobbling Pivot and The Great Digest,* a translation with notes and commentary on the text and ideograms, and the following year *The Pisan Cantos,* comprising LXXIV to LXXXIV (there are, at present, 109 cantos in print). In February, 1949, *The Pisan Cantos* was awarded the first Bollingen Prize for poetry, which carried with it an honorarium of one thousand dollars. The award was made by vote of the Fellows in American Letters of the Library of Congress, an honorary and advisory group appointed by the Librarian of Congress. The awarding judges were: Conrad Aiken, W. H. Auden, Louise Bogan, Katherine Garrison Chapin, T. S. Eliot, Paul Green, Robert Lowell, Katherine Anne Porter, Karl Shapiro, Allen Tate, Willard Thorp, Robert Penn Warren, Theodore Spencer, and Léonie Adams, the Library's Consultant in Poetry in English for that year, who took the news to Pound. In view of the protests which followed, on the floor of Congress and elsewhere, I offer the statement of the Fellows at the time they recommended the award:

"The Fellows are aware that objections may be made to awarding a prize to a man situated as is Mr. Pound. In their view, however, the possibility of such objection did not alter the responsibility assumed by the Jury of Selection. This was to make a choice for the award among the eligible books, provided any one merited such recognition, according to the stated terms of the Bollingen Prize. To permit other considerations than that of poetry achievement to sway the decision would destroy the significance of the award and would in principle deny the validity of that objective perception of value on which civilized society must rest."[1]

I am not sure that the wisdom of the Fellows was equal to their faith. Their act commemorates the first and last time that the United States government was involved in an award for poetry. The Bollingen Prize is now domiciled at Yale University. It has been upped to $2,500, which helps.

A new and enlarged *Personae* appeared under the imprint of New Directions, as did the volume entitled *Selected Poems.* In 1950 *The Letters of Ezra Pound* was published by Harcourt, Brace and by Faber and Faber a year later. There was a preface by Mark Van Doren. The editor was a young man named Douglas Duncan Paige.

Paige, like Pound, had attended the University of Pennsylvania and was teaching at Wellesley when Eliot came there to read. At the reception which followed he met Eliot and Theodore Spencer. Paige told me: "Somehow we got on the subject of Ezra, and Spencer said it was really a shame, nobody would see him and he had no contact with the outer world and so on, and this was 1947, and it was true at that time. I had just been reading the new cantos that had appeared in several magazines, and I wrote him a letter to cheer him up. I was very surprised to get an answer. Pound said he would like to receive letters."

In 1947, Paige was twenty-nine years old. He had long been an admirer of Pound's work—"I have it memorized, I've read it so often" —and he had planned to go abroad to meet him when the war started. He told me that the idea of a collection of Pound's letters had occurred to him as early as 1939, for he had read those in Margaret Anderson's book, and had been much struck by Eliot's praise—"his epistolary style is masterly" [The *Dial,* January, 1928]. "So in one of my letters to him, it was a fairly early one, I suggested that a book of his letters be published. I felt that if anything could help Ezra it would be the letters, because here would be documentation of everything he had done, for Joyce, for Eliot, and for hundreds of others. I suggested that James Laughlin do the editing, but Pound wrote back and said no, that I should do the letters, and I took that as a go-ahead and said all right, I'll be glad to do them. He thought it would be a help to me, too, in my career, but I have an awful lot of doubt as to how much help a book of that sort was. Even so late as 1953 you had to be careful to whom you told the fact that you had done this work on Pound. A lot of people considered that you were a traitor, too."

Pound gave him a list of people with whom he had corresponded, including some in Idaho who never replied, Paige said. Others raised objections, or said it was too much trouble to look up the letters. Some hadn't kept them—"Bunting, for example, kept nothing except income tax reports."

"I had reached a sort of impasse, when Ezra suddenly got the bright idea and said: 'Why in the world don't you go over to Rapallo, you can go in my archives, I've got letters there from about 1933 onward.' "

Paige told me that he and his wife saved up for the trip and in 1948 went to Rapallo. They were astonished when they got into the apartment and saw the files. "The quantity of correspondence was fantastic. You can't form any idea unless you see it. And when you see it you'll hardly believe it because it covered less than ten years. It would cover your wall here."

"What kind of a welcome did you get in that apartment?"

"Oh, a marvelous welcome. These were Italians, Italians who loved Ezra, and they said 'Ah, Signor, when is he coming back?' and so on, and everything opened up to me."

"How long did you work there?"

"About two years. It went like this. I picked up a volume of the correspondence, looked through it all and tried to get the earliest. Then, I would read through with these criteria in mind—development of modern poetry, criticism, Ezra's kindness to his fellow workers, explications of his own text, or otherwise of general interest to the reader—and I would put a marker in and then I would give them to Marie and she would type them out. She must have typed four thousand pages. We worked in there about twelve hours a day, I reading, and Marie typing.

"This was just collecting the raw material and of course, at the same time, I was writing around to other people trying to get letters, and I got letters from various people, and we typed those up as well. After the whole bulk of the manuscript was got together we arranged everything chronologically. And then we read from the beginning and whenever we got bored, why, we took out a letter. And, looking back on it, I can see probably it was the wisest way to do it because this meant, if it wasn't interesting to me, who was interested in everything about Ezra, including his laundry list, it wasn't going to interest the general reader.

"I didn't care how obscure the person was to whom the letter was addressed, if it expressed interesting ideas, it had to stay in. So a letter to Hemingway went out and a letter to John Peale Bishop went out—I don't know whether there were any others. Harcourt, Brace restored those two letters, at least, and took out two others instead. And, additionally, they went around chopping out sentences here and there. For example, there's one here to William Rose Benét. It looks like one of Ezra's suspensive points. Actually, it's an omission on the part of the publisher—the sentence goes on. This goes on for letter after letter. And it gives a totally erroneous idea. It's very clear where I speak about excisions in the front that I do not use suspensive points at any time to indicate such. So this appears to be Ezra's actual words and that that was the end of this thought, and it isn't. And, as a matter of fact when Ezra received a copy of this book which came out first, and, while he liked it, when the English edition came out, I sent it to Ezra, and he said, 'Damn me if I can figure it out. This one seems to have a hell of a lot more punch than the other one.' "

Paige, one of the earliest visitors to St. Elizabeths, returned to bring greetings from Pound's Italian friends. Other early callers were Bö Setterlind, the Swedish poet; Edith Hamilton, the Greek scholar; E. E. Cummings, H. L. Mencken, Allen Tate, T. S. Eliot, Theodore Spencer, Juan Ramón Jiménez and Stephen Spender.[2]

CHAPTER XXII

POUND IN ST. ELIZABETHS

1.

Pound was confined at first in a security building with other patients charged with criminal offenses. Cummings told me that, when he went to call, the clang of the door behind him, and which a guard then locked, shutting him in with those confined there, was the second worst experience of this sort he had ever had—the first, of course, being his own incarceration in France in 1917. Pound had placed a screen near a window in the waiting room, with chairs with their backs to the ward, while he himself sat facing it. But always present in the minds of those who sat opposite him were the men moving about behind them, or sitting by the walls and staring, staring at nothing. Pound gave Cummings and his wife a simultaneous bear-hug, crushing them to his ample chest, being overjoyed to see them. Then they listened. Pound was afterwards transferred to the Center Building, where he had a room of his own, really a cubicle without a door, and it was there that Eliot found him. (Perhaps it was on this visit to Washington that Mr. Eliot also saw Colonel F. Granville Munson who had attended the University of Pennsylvania with Pound, as related in Chapter 1.) Eliot wrote Cornell from Princeton, New Jersey, November 24, 1948:

"My dear Cornell,
"After my visit to St. Elizabeths Hospital I came away with one

very clear notion of something that should be done for Ezra Pound which his well-being seems to me to require.

"Mrs. Pound told me that Pound was only allowed out of doors at the times when the other inmates of his ward were allowed to go out, under the supervision of a warder. She told me that in consequence he was never out of doors during the winter. It seems to me that it ought to be permissible for him to go out alone in the grounds with his wife, and with her responsible for his returning in due time. This would, incidentally, give a relatively greater degree of privacy than is possible under the conditions in which he can be visited indoors. I am not in the least suggesting that he should be allowed to leave the grounds.

"Could you take this point up with Dr. Overholser? I saw him only before I had visited Pound, and before Mrs. Pound had told me of this restriction. Surely he is entitled to have some fresh air daily, upon this condition.

"I also think that it would be desirable to enquire whether there is not some other building on the grounds in which he could be confined, where he could have somewhat more normal conditions, and not be among patients of the types of insanity among which he is at present.

"I am writing in some haste, as I have still to pack for my departure from Princeton tomorrow."

Cornell forwarded a copy of this letter to Dr. Overholser, who replied as follows:

"I have your letter of November 29th enclosing the inquiry from Mr. T. S. Eliot about Mr. Ezra Pound. I had a brief talk with Mr. Eliot at the time of his visit to Washington, but unfortunately as he says in his letter, this was before he had seen Mr. Pound. I have some hesitation in accepting the suggestions made by Mr. Eliot. It remains a fact that Mr. Pound is under indictment for the most serious crime in the calendar and that he has at the present time far more privileges than any other prisoner in the Hospital. He is on a quiet ward, has a room by himself and is allowed a good deal of latitude in the way he occupies himself. His wife visits him very frequently. When I found that the walking parties had been suspended in the winter I saw to it that on days when the weather was good these were reinstituted, but I found that Mr. Pound refused to go on any but the first.

"He has supreme contempt for the patients on the ward regardless of the ward he might be on since he is inclined to be rather supercilious in his views of practically everyone with whom he comes in contact.

"I can assure you that we shall do everything within reason for the comfort of Mr. Pound, but in spite of his being a well known author, I question whether I should put myself in the position of giving unusual privileges to him over and above those which he already enjoys."

But with the passage of time, Pound's privileges grew. He even played tennis. Dr. Overholser wrote me, January 8, 1960:

"In going through Pound's record I find that it was not until August 1955 we formally gave him permission to have evening privileges, that is, the privilege of sitting out on the grounds until about 8:00 P.M. From the time, however, that he was transferred from Howard Hall to Chestnut Ward a good deal of latitude was given to him and he went out practically daily with his visitors. He always followed meticulously such liberal rules as were laid down and, so far as I am aware, until the day the Court ordered his discharge he never went out of sight of the Center Building. I may add that the tennis courts on which he played frequently are in sight of that building."

Dr. Overholser's personal relationship with Pound was, he said, "always most pleasant," and Pound's attitude toward him was "always friendly, in spite of the fact that at least technically I was his custodian." Pound has written to him several times since his return to Italy.

2.

It is a curious fact that, wherever Pound has dwelt, the world has come to him, and it came to him in St. Elizabeths—old friends and new, the age's renowned men and women, *les jeunes;* and others who saw in him, perhaps, an opportunity for the furtherance of their own pet schemes or ambitions. These last, who in other days might not have been suffered long, were now most welcome, for they held views which confirmed some of his own—notably that President Roosevelt had betrayed the Constitution, whereas he, Pound, had upheld it. They were a type of little mccarthy, whom fortune and the electorate had not encumbered with responsibilities, which, however, they assumed for themselves, being more patriotic than most. Some of them called themselves "Defenders of the American Constitution, Inc.," and had a publication all their own—"An American Publication for Loyal Americans," says the masthead—entitled *Task Force*. Its contributors included officers of the Armed Forces, retired, and some members of Congress, types perennially alarmed by legislation of a liberal cast, and by the Supreme Court. I cannot say that the noble language of the Founding Fathers has had any noticeable effect on their own prose styles. A general's article on Pound's confinement was headed "Retribution or Revenge," which is suggestive, to say the least, and a civilian's, endorsing Pound's release, "The Background of the Pound Case: Economics." On the whole, I have had to conclude that the Defenders' news sense does not suffer by comparison with their loxodromic prose. But perhaps they helped to sustain Pound during his long confinement.

He was sustained by other things. "Start paying attention to basic issues, at least to the extent of Sq. $ and EDGE contents," he wrote to correspondents, stuffing his envelopes with the literature of these two groups.

The "Square $ Series" was published in Washington by David Horton and John Kasper. Its list included work by Pound, and a volume entitled *Barbara Villiers, or a History of Monetary Crimes*, by Alexander Del Mar. The lady of this title is perhaps better known to history as Lady Castlemaine, Charles II's mistress-in-chief. I am in the dark about the rest of it, and likely to remain so.

Edge, a monthly published in Melbourne, Australia, was inspired by Pound's views. There were eight issues. A mimeographed handout which Pound stuffed into envelopes began: "E. P. can NOT be bothered to answer letters from people who do not support 'EDGE' which is, so far as he knows, the ONLY present means of communication between people with serious AGENDA." He termed it "a bloody disgrace there is nothing in the U.S. half as good" and I may yet get to it.

Marianne Moore came several times. When a member of the staff said, "Good of you to come to see him," she replied: "Good? You have no idea how helpful he has been to *me,* and many others. It is the least I can do." She saw Pound inside only once, when she arrived at four, two to four being the visiting hours. An official telephoned and found that Pound would see her; he accompanied her up a spiral iron stair and when the door had been unlocked left her with an attendant. She had brought, as she usually did, candy; also peanuts for the squirrels and blue jays on the lawn. The attendant confided that Pound had been "a great help with other patients." She told me Pound had "an intuition about them and made them tractable." (One day, when Cummings and his wife were sitting in the ward with Pound, they saw him waving to someone behind them, at the same time shouting, "No! No! No! No!" They turned, surprised, and saw a fellow inmate, who had approached quietly to proffer candy to Pound's guests. Cummings, as readers of the book about him know, was a believer in personal totems; his own was the elephant. One day, on the lawn of St. Elizabeths, he saw his friend feeding blue jays and realized, he told me afterwards, that that angry, screaming, crested bird was Pound's.)

Pound, Miss Moore said, talked brilliantly, his talk full of allusions she didn't catch immediately—"it was too allusive, too rapid for me to catch, and I didn't like to trouble him to explain." Like the other visitors, she merely listened.

Pound, however, had encouraged her translating of the La Fontaine fables.

"I was at an impasse," she told me, "then thought of him; have boasted of never asking help but sent him about six fables and said, 'The editor in charge suggests putting the thing away for a time (ten years, I think he said). I infer that my ear is not good. Could you take time to tell me if the rhythms grate on you?' "

He replied on stationery bearing the motto "J'Ayme Donc Je Suis":
"Yes m'dr Marianna

"the least taint of quality an/or merit upsets these blighters. Lez see the rest of 'em. I shd try Faber or at least someone in London."

He wrote again:
"let E.P. attempt having 'em printed in one of the few periodicals he reads."

More than a year later:
"E. wd/ be glad to help but cannot concentrate.

"(on back) KICK OUT this god damned french syntax, with relative clauses. WRITE the sense in plain english, PROSE, and then versify the SENSE of your prose."

He suggested variant readings, admonished her to remember subject, predicate and object, and recommended reading Yeats's early lyrics, George Herbert and Jane Austen.

"He was very severe with me," she said.

Olga Rudge came from Sienna. In New York she telephoned Yves Tinayre, but could not stop to see him. "I am rushing to Washington," she said. Pound's daughter came. Cornell took her to lunch at the Bankers Club in the Equitable Building to meet Arthur Garfield Hays, attorney for the American Civil Liberties Union, which was becoming interested in Pound's case.

3.

A twenty-minute taxi ride from the Library of Congress—he was now the resident Consultant in Poetry—brought William Carlos Williams to the hospital. He found Pound and his wife under the trees, in brand-new beach chairs, Mrs. Pound reading to her husband. Williams had not announced his coming. Pound leaped from his chair, grabbed his hand and embraced him. Mrs. Pound said: "Well, it's Bill Williams. Isn't it?" The visit lasted about an hour. Williams recalled: "He looked much as I had always found him, the same beard and restless twitching of the hands, shifting his shoulders about as he lay back in the chair studying me, the same bantering smile, screwing up his eyes, the half-coughing laugh and short, swift words, no sentence structure worth mentioning."

Williams says Pound was still critical of him; as for "the situation of letters in our world—not good." The transition from letters to economics was quickly made; in Williams's summary, "it is international finance that brings us all at always shorter and shorter intervals to our ruin . . . wars are made by the international gang . . . in the present instance F.D.R. was the prime criminal. All I could do was to listen."[1]

As he listened, the criminally mad who inhabited St. Elizabeths drifted effortlessly, and as though unseeing, across the lawn. It was a new experience for him, and it took several visits before he was able to disregard their presence, drifting like wraiths of men or stopping to stare at the group under the chestnut trees.

Conrad Aiken went to see him. He told me:

"In 1949, the year after Robert Lowell had been at the Library of Congress, Lowell, Allen Tate and I went to visit Pound in St. Elizabeths. Pound was detraqué; he would go off on some *idée fixe*—credit, usury, politics; however, since Lowell had been in Washington the year before, and had become used to humoring Pound, he would say, 'Tell us about such and such,' and then you could see the juke box slide along the records and choose the new record."

Thornton Wilder said after a visit: "Is he crazy? I don't know. You see, when one is as old as I am, most of one's friends and oneself—but you see what I mean."

Witter Bynner went to see him and found "the same great, booming boy, or so he seemed, who clutched me with a bear-hug and cried out, 'After forty years!' Time and the beard had made little change for me in his presence."

He also sent books, including Pound's *Provença* published by Small, Maynard in 1910 with Bynner's help. The box in which he sent them stayed under Pound's bed, a receptacle for food and sweets.

Louis Zukofsky went to see him. With him were his wife and son, Paul, ten years old, a violin prodigy. They were en route to North Carolina, where Paul was to play. But first he played on the lawn of St. Elizabeths, under the trees where the deck chairs were brought each fair day by Pound and his wife and where they received visitors. Paul played some Mozart and Bach, and the Italian composer Corelli, which made Pound exclaim with delight, and Canto LXXV, the musical canto.

Two other visitors were present—Sheri Martinelli, whom Pound called *La* Martinelli, a Greenwich Village painter, and David Horton, Kasper's partner in the Square Dollar series. Miss Martinelli's name for Pound was "Grandpa."

On the lawn of St. Elizabeths, Labor Day, 1952, when birds were twittering in the chestnut trees, Pound gave a reading of Provençal poetry, full of the onomatopoetic twittering of birds, and was recorded on equipment borrowed from a Washington radio station. In the distance, other inmates stared. The recording had been arranged by two recent Hunter College graduates, Marianne Mantell and Barbara Holdridge, publishers of Caedmon records. Pound had agreed to make the recording on their promise not to release the record while he was confined. "Bird in cage does not sing," he said.

In Rome, a number of Italian citizens called at the United States Embassy to plead for Pound's release "from what they generally called 'jail,' " Clare Boothe Luce, Ambassador during this period, wrote me, and there were others who spoke to her about the case outside the office, "on an informal basis."

"From early 1954 through the latter part of 1956," Mrs. Luce wrote, "there was also a considerable public campaign conducted to effect Mr. Pound's release. Intellectuals, personal friends and admirers of Pound, the Communists and the Vatican Radio all publicly pleaded for the U.S. Government to 'pardon' Pound.

"Upon the first inquiry made of me, in 1954, I undertook to obtain full information from Washington concerning Mr. Pound's incarceration. Thereafter, until 1957, a number of messages passed between me and the State Department, according to the Department files, and in all of them I drew attention to the feeling that seemed to exist in Italy on this score. Twice, on trips home, I personally took up the matter with officials in State, and once I discussed it with the Attorney General.

"The difficulty that the Pound case presented to the Embassy lay in the fact that few Italians seemed to understand the real situation. The campaign to free Pound was plainly based on the widely held view among Italians that Pound was innocent, as indicted, of treason to his country; that he was nevertheless sentenced and sent to prison where he was being kept long after his wartime crime (if indeed he ever committed one) had been forgotten and forgiven by most Americans. It was felt that Mr. Pound's situation cried before the world for mercy, i.e., 'pardon,' and that in refusing to show it, almost a decade after the war, the U.S. Government was being harsh and brutal.

"The Italian Government never made any official representations on the subject, no doubt because they knew the legal facts concerning Mr. Pound through their own Embassy in Washington."

4.

The young came.

"How's that old son-of-a-bitch Cornie!" Pound exclaimed to Ronald Goodman, a student at the University of Pennsylvania, who brought regards from Professor Cornelius Weygandt. Goodman told me: "Professor Weygandt was teaching the same goddam course he taught Pound fifty years ago. All he had done was change the title of the course from 'Celtic Renaissance' to 'Celtic Twilight.'"

Goodman was accompanied by his friend, Robert Mezey, of Kenyon College. Both wrote poetry, and they went to see Pound partly in homage, partly to learn. They saw him "eight or ten times" over a five-year period. Pound told them that his "Near Perigord" was "as far as you could go in free verse." To their great delight, he recited from memory the two beautiful love poems he had written in London long ago—"A Virginal," and the poem beginning "Be in me as the eternal moods," from *Ripostes*. Dorothy Pound was present.

In reply to a question about how the Cantos were progressing, Pound said:

"Well, you know, Grandpa can't do it all—he's gettin' old. Well, what I mean to say, Grandpa's burst his mainspring. Now it's up to your generation to raise the cultural status.

"All that quoting from different languages is just the easiest way to show that it's all been said before. If I don't translate as such, well, the same ideas in English are in the neighborhood.

"It takes a while till you get your bearings—like a detective story—and see how it's going to go. I hit my stride in the *Fifth Decad of Cantos*.

"You've got to get at least one person in your generation to listen to you. It often happens that a man fails when his friends fail him."

He praised Wallace Stevens: "I don't know of any one around that's new who's worth a damn except Stevens." He said languages were "what to get" while in college. "My Greek is still not as good as I want it." And he advised them to stay in America. "Jefferson couldn't imagine anyone leaving the States. After Grant, they couldn't imagine anyone staying. But stay in America—it's nearly all that's left."

He advised them to "write in a strict form, until you *know* that form." He said that when he was younger "I probably wrote one sonnet a day for about a year. I threw them all away, but I did learn about the quatrain from it."

Goodman told me that during one visit Pound kept using the words "major poet" in a way which seemed to exclude anyone who had not written an epic. "But don't you think Yeats is a major poet?" he asked.

Pound: "Is he a Homer, is he a Dante?"

Goodman: "That's a mighty high standard."

Pound (laughing): "I think Yeats is the greatest minor poet who ever lived!"

One New Year's Day, Goodman and Mezey found the screen and chairs where they usually sat with Pound gone. In their place was a television set, with patients watching the Rose Bowl game. They were pretty noisy about it. Pound came storming out of his room and exclaimed:

"They're trying to bring the intelligence of the people on the inside down to the level of the people on the outside."

Another young man, Michael Reck, called on him. He was just out of Harvard and attending some courses at the Institute of Contemporary Arts in Washington. Since Canto LXXXIX ends,

> I want Frémont looking at mountains
> or, if you like, Reck, at Lake Biwa,

I made inquiries. Reck wrote me: "I found him an astonishingly fine human being, and he didn't seem shocked by the fact that I ardently disagreed with some of his political views. In fact he showed more tolerance than some professional tolerators." This was in 1951. In 1954 on a trip to Japan, he went to the temple near Kyoto where Ernest Fenollosa is buried. He was accompanied by the Japanese poet Fujitomi Yasuo. "From the temple is an immense vista of Lake Biwa, a great blue surrounded by mountains. Beneath, an American army camp, but fortunately the mountain on which the temple was located was so steep you couldn't see the camp. I wrote Mr. Pound about my visit there, and that is what he reported in the last line of Canto 89."

A young and attractive teacher in a Washington junior college came. She discussed with Pound the idea of a "Junior Anthology." He responded eagerly; soon, his letters and circular letters went forth to poets all over the world. Her name was Marcella Spann.

Louis Zukofsky wrote. Innocently—as he supposed—he related that he had seen Eliot in England and had commiserated with him over Pound's bracketing of Eliot with Reinhold Niebuhr. It was a disastrous confidence. Pound replied: "If you are capable of encouraging

or consoling Possum for tolerating Niebuhr our correspondence had
better draw to a close. Vale. E. P." There was no salutation. But even
this was not the end of their association. Pound wrote Zukofsky from
Rapallo in 1959:

"Mass of literary criticism in Letters of L. Z. to E. P. wd/ make
one vol or 6 if well selected. came on some here, also poems possibly
inedit. Any practical use to L. Z.? E. P."

*

5.

On August 24, 1954, a young Princeton man who was writing a critical article about Cummings went to see Pound. After a brief and
brilliant career as a critic he dropped literature for diplomacy, and is
now with the State Department. His name is David Burns. He wrote
me the day of his visit:

"This afternoon I went to visit Ezra Pound. A fortyish woman was
also there to visit Pound, and the doctor had an attendant take our
names out to him. While the attendant was gone I asked the doctor
if Mr. Pound were well, and he assured me that he was and was capable of handling his own end of any conversation and that he had his
own ideas (very definite) about whom he wanted to see and when
and under what circumstances. The attendant came back and said that
Mr. Pound had a visitor from overseas and could only see us for half
an hour. He took our names and addresses, and told us that Pound,
Mrs. Pound and the visitor were seated on the broad front lawn in
deck chairs. As the woman and I went out she told me that she was a
writer. She started laughing as we approached the group.

" 'It's really ha-ha incredible,' said the woman writer.

"Pound was stretched way out in a beach chair, his shirt off and
showing the red and white hair on his chest and the effects of much
exposure to the sun—red and brown. The tripartite beard is scrag-
glier and white now. But he looks remarkably healthy and even happy.
He seems well-fed, rested, and full of zest. St. Elizabeths is a model
hospital, and in many ways everyone can be happy that he is here,
instead of the possibility he faced of jail or, at the least, a terrible trial.
Mrs. Pound and the visitor (who proved to be a young Englishman)
stood up, Pound made the introductions, we sat down on a proffered

bench 'so the old man won't have to crane his neck,' and waited. Pound turned to the woman and said: 'Is the Kumrad still up in the wilds of New Hampshire?' The woman looked blank, and I volunteered: 'You mean Kumrad Cummings? Yes, he'll be up there till the end of September.'[2]

"Then Pound began expounding on the virtues of our mutual friend, recalling how he had headed straight for Patchin Place when he landed here in 1939. I mentioned the *Six Nonlectures* and Pound seemed familiar with them, but made little comment. He did feel that Cummings was being funny or humorous about the subjects he had raised so much propaganda about from Rome, the idea being that this is all so important that Cummings should not pull his punches. I said that in my opinion, on the contrary, his later poems were dead serious—even embittered—as contrasted with the satires of the 20s or 30s. I mentioned that Harcourt, Brace were bringing out Cummings's complete poems and that this would coincide with C's 60th birthday. He asked me if Oxford University Press hadn't already done that, and I said I didn't think so—perhaps he meant *Xaipe: seventy-one poems*? I asked him if he would be willing to write something for C's 60th birthday. He said if something were being gathered together it should certainly begin with 'plato told,'[3] for he considered that—'and you may quote me'—the best of the Kumrad's work. He suggested also that I get hold of Edmondo Dodsworth's article on Cummings which had been printed in *Broletto* about 1937 and, he believed, had never been translated from the Italian. But would *he* write something?

" 'Well, you could have the Rome broadcast,' he said.

"I looked puzzled.

" 'The broadcast on Cummings.'

" 'That might be fine—but was it available?'

" 'Well, if you started your thing with 'plato told' and then the translation of Dodsworth's article,[4] I think'—here a gleam appeared in his eye—'I might just be able to scare up one of those broadcasts.' [This was probably a reference to the pamphlet printed by Olga Rudge.]

"Then, as though answering some question the Englishman had asked before we had come up, or continuing with some discussion they had been at before, he began explaining how he came to do the broadcasts from Rome, and the innumerable problems that came up with that; how H. L. Mencken was one of the first to visit him in the 'bughouse'; how Wyndham Lewis and 'my generation'—turning to me—had gone wrong; then inquired if, during my three years in the Air Force, they had given me benzedrine; told how dope was being bought in the high schools, and about the juvenile crimes one read about every day, and how he had warned about them and how they were the result of Amurrica being the way it was. All this and more: the conscript army, treason and the higher truth.

"He talked easily, with an astounding memory for people, places, names, literary allusions—'Abe Lard and his boys,' etc.—skipping from century to century, from cracker-barrel horse-sense and the truths of the Founding Fathers, to what could have been (but I'll never be sure) flights of fancy which, if not actually insane, were at least far removed from the commonplace world. His voice and accent were piercing, mimic, with an Idaho twang and a faint trace of Continental (semi-British) inflection intertwined. He was now excoriating people and causes I didn't know.

"And all the while we listened (I don't think the woman writer ever said a word) and listened, while Pound lay back in the comfortable chair on a comfortable afternoon in August. Dorothy Pound doodled on a small pad and asked an occasional question, the Englishman listened and asked more questions, and I listened and waited, while the far-staring and peaceably removed old men wandered around in groups, not talking, or just sitting, having, of course, nowhere to go, or nowhere they *could* go.

"There followed a short side trip into his problems with an 'asinine wop' who had sold sandpaper to Fiat, and how he had come to write fifteen questions to Old Muss, and what all this and censor trouble had to do with how he had come to broadcast on Cummings and Swinburne 'in the fust place'; I feeling, meanwhile, that Gertrude Stein was right and that the man was a wonderful, even miraculous Village Explainer, and wondering and marvelling at just how completely and unalterably *American* the man is, and how that had been, alas, his downfall.

"Then he looked at his watch, explained how 'this gentleman' (the Englishman) was in the country only for the next two days and how they must finish some business, offered us another chocolate from the

box someone had given him (he had stuffed us with them before),
and we all rose, shook hands several times, and prepared to leave.
I asked if I could write, having in mind the Cummings material
he had mentioned.

" 'Well,' he said, '*you* people can write in anything you want to,
but us in *here* must get our mail checked over to see if we are making
the *mistake* of telling the truth or sending Bess Truman a message
with the Facks of Life.'

"For me, meeting him and talking with him was a very exciting
and interesting experience. He is certainly not in step with our world.
And the fault is, I think, with the world, not with Mr. Pound. He
has in mind an ideal of independence, individualism, liberty, that is,
unfortunately, completely mixed up with wrong ideas on governments
and how they should be run and his own prejudices, of which he has
many and strong ones, and the so-called Fascist taint. And while I
disagree terribly with so much of what he says, I cannot help but
admire the man, and feel beaten and humiliated that 'our world' had
no place for him.

"I was sorry to go."

6.

"Grandpa's got to do it with suicide troops. Like Kasper" (Miss
Martinelli, as reported by David Rattray, *The Nation,* November
16, 1957).

As readers of newspapers and news magazines know, Pound had
another and constant visitor. This was his "disciple," John Kasper,
the New Jersey segregationist. Neither poetry nor pity was his concern. To judge by his writings—which seek to subvert the law of the
land—and the yahoo utterances which have brought grief to so
many, his knowledge of books is such as might have been gained from
dusting them in a book store; this, indeed, was his occupation for a
time. His views on economics are equally jejune. "We've got to eliminate all taxes except taxes on money itself," he has explained glibly,
never having had any.

Although Kasper can write "B.Sc." after his name, his schooling
has been irregular, if not odd: elementary and junior high school

in Camden, New Jersey, the Riverside Military Academy in Gaines-
ville, Georgia, Yankton College, Yankton, South Dakota, and finally
the School of General Studies, Columbia University. It was while
he was attending Columbia that he took a course in poetry under
Babette Deutsch, a much respected practitioner and teacher. On
reaching the work of Pound, Miss Deutsch told the class: "We should
reject his politics and respect his poetry."

Kasper, she afterwards told a reporter, "had seemed to her to be
a quiet, unobtrusive student. But this time he spoke up with considerable vigor, saying he didn't like Pound's poetry, but did like
his politics" (New York *Herald Tribune,* January 31, 1957). The
reaction of teacher and class to this declaration made an impression
on Kasper. He would make one on them. He wrote a retraction in
the form of a term paper. It began:

"Strange, but I always thought myself free from insidious falsehood. I was the one who childishly railed at superstition and malicious
teaching. And yet I fell into the pit like any other subnormal inhuman
beast of an uncivilized age. I thrilled at Nicolo Machiavelli, Fried-
rich Nietzsche and the political Ezra Pound. Hitler and Stalin are
clever men and Wilson a fool. The weak have no justification for
living except in service of the strong. What is a little cruelty to the
innocuous when it is expedient for the strong ones who have the
right to alter the laws of life and death before their natural limits?

"This was me, and I am yet a child ungrown to the fullest sense
of human dignity. But I have seen the seriousness of values as it
relates to the good and evil of Man."

If Kasper's mawkish composition reveals anything, it is an inability to think or to form sentences, which may be the same thing.
There is present, however, something almost always to be found in
the anti-social and unstable man—a tendency to self-pity. But the
retraction may have been sincere at the time Kasper made it. The
book shop which he afterwards ran on Bleecker Street, on borrowed
money, was less remarkable for its daytime sales than for its nightly
gatherings of young Jews and Christians, and Negroes of both sexes,
who danced and held discourse there. For this year's rabble-rouser
was last year's liberal, a transient bohemian such as Greenwich Village has always harbored in the meaner hovels of its meaner streets,
where the bull sessions of college days are pursued with a new

earnestness, and where "bottle parties" and "rent parties" hold out hopes for future survival as well as present joys. *Then,* to his Negro friends, he recommended membership in the National Association for the Advancement of Colored People, and to all—white as well as colored—he defended integration.

Greatly liked, young, attractive, surrounded by friends of many races and artistic pursuits, what more could he have desired?

Nothing is so conducive to the bolstering of a bohemian ego as the ability to brag, in impetiginous and quasi-intellectual circles, of association with men and women of genius. The association may be distant, or it may have been forced; no matter. To the shadowy dwellers in Bohemia it is a vision and a goal. The vision came to Kasper on a day, and he went to Washington to call on Pound. He was encouraged to call again, and to correspond. He did both. Soon, in the book shop, and in the apartments of his friends, the first intimations of the new Kasper appeared. At those youthful gatherings, once so carefree, once so harmonious, his talk was now about the iniquity of the Jews. Coming from a blood brother of a race which had slaughtered them only half a generation before—not in fair battle—this surely was grotesque. It was, of course, also shocking both to members of his circle who were Jewish and to some who were not. The circle began to break up. This was natural, for the man with a message or a mission is nearly always a destructor, to use Graham Greene's terrible, new word which epitomizes our time. In the event, Kasper followed the classical pattern. He disappeared.

His Sinai was Washington. There, he communed with Pound. And there, once more, he tried his fortunes with a book shop, with no better luck than before. But night after night, the lights burned.

As the tension over the Supreme Court's unanimous decision on integration mounted, he suddenly took the spotlight as the founder and executive secretary of the Seaboard White Citizens Council. In hand-lettered leaflets he introduced himself as "John Kasper, Segregation Chief," and gave his program to the world. The young idealist who had urged his Negro friends to join the N.A.A.C.P. now proffered other advice to their enemies (with an assist from Pound):

> "JAIL NAACP, alien, unclean, unchristian
> BLAST irreverent ungodly LEADERS

HANG 9 SUPREME COURT SWINE
(this year domine '56)
BANISH LIARS
Destroy REDS (ALL muscovite savages)
rooseveltian dupes
EXPOSE BERIA'S 'psycho-politics'
DEATH TO USURERS."

"Loud clamor is always more or less insane," wrote Carlyle.

Kasper's first effusions were addressed to neighboring Virginia; but the Old Dominion, serene in its greatness, thronged by the greatest ghosts of the Western world, spurned his vulgarity. He plunged deeper into the South.

In Louisville, Kentucky, the erstwhile companion of Negroes declared: "They might have a soul, they might have a right to pray. I know some men who claim that they have seen niggers with tails."

But Louisville was not far south enough for him to receive the response worthy of his message. It was in Clinton, Tennessee, that he achieved his heart's desire—he addressed his audience of "hillbillies and rednecks" affectionately as the "real" people of this country, and the "hillbillies and rednecks" responded. One day, integration of the schools was proceeding quietly, if with misgivings; the next, bayonets and tanks guarded the tumultuous town. The violence he had inspired was directed against school children. So much for the B.Sc. from the School of General Studies. Arrested on a Federal warrant charging interference with court-ordered integration at Clinton High School, he was sentenced to a year in prison, but was quickly released in ten thousand dollars bail raised by the White Citizens Councils.

From Tennessee, Kasper went to Florida. He had, for that southern vacation state, a novel explanation for its racial troubles. It was not the N.A.A.C.P. but the Jews. "He told a rally Saturday night in Inverness he would demand that the Florida legislature raise voting requirements to five years' residence in the state, four years in the county, and three years in the precinct. The object, he said, is to 'deal with those Jews in Dade County (Miami) who keep moving back and forth and yet control the state machinery'" (New York *Post*, March 11, 1957). His blast made mischief, but the fallout almost smothered him. Subpoenaed by the Florida legislature, he was closely questioned about his past associations with Negroes in Greenwich Village. Cautioned that he was under oath, he told the truth, and several leaders of the White Citizens Council repudiated him publicly.

Back in Tennessee, among the "real" people, he triumphed once more as "Segregation Chief," and once more was arrested and charged with criminal contempt of the Federal district court "on grounds he violated a permanent injunction against interference with peaceful integration of Clinton High School" (New York *Times,* March 24, 1957). Released in bail of $7,500, he asked for a jury trial. At the time of this writing he had served two prison terms and faced a third.

It is not Pound's fault, of course, that Kasper became what he did. The embracers of causes are mere weather vanes; some are opportunists. Kasper would have reached his goal, by other brutish paths, without Pound's prejudices to ramrod his instability. But we have come a long way from poets as "the unacknowledged legislators of the world."

Hemingway, interviewed by the *Paris Review* (Spring, 1958) said: "I believe Ezra should be released and allowed to write poetry in Italy on an undertaking by him to abstain from any politics. I would be happy to see Kasper jailed as soon as possible."

There were now many voices for Pound's release. One of them was heard in the august halls of Congress, where Representative Usher L. Burdick, of North Dakota, introduced a bill calling for review of the Pound case.

Robert Frost went to see the Attorney General. He told Ralph Nading Hill in Ripton, Vermont: "I went down to the Attorney General's office and said 'I'm here to get Ezra Pound out.' They saw I was going to sit there until they did something about it—and they did."

Attorney General William P. Rogers afterwards said: "Is there any point in keeping him there if he never can be tried?"

The Hailey (Idaho) *Times* got into the act with this headline: "EZRA POUND MUST BE OFF, OR WHY DID HE LEAVE WOOD RIVER VALLEY?"[5]

7.

On April 14, 1958, a motion was filed in the United States District
Court for the District of Columbia for dismissal of the thirteen-year-
old indictment. It was supported by an affidavit from Dr. Overholser,
and by a statement by Frost, with which a number of prominent
writers and poets associated themselves, many of them with declara-
tions of their own. The motion was filed by Thurman Arnold, who
had attended Wabash College and had been Julien Cornell's law
professor at Yale, and was heard by Chief Judge Bolitha J. Laws,
who had presided at Pound's arraignment and trial. This was the
statement by Frost, which was read in court:

"I am here to register my admiration for a government that can
rouse in conscience to a case like this. Relief seems to be in sight
for many of us besides the Ezra Pound in question and his faithful
wife. He has countless admirers the world over who will rejoice in
the news that he has hopes of freedom. I append a page or so of
what they have been saying lately about him and his predicament. I
myself speak as much in the general interest as in his. And I feel
authorized to speak very specially for my friends, Archibald Mac-
Leish, Ernest Hemingway and T. S. Eliot. None of us can bear the
disgrace of our letting Ezra Pound come to his end where he is. It
would leave too woeful a story in American literature. He went very
wrongheaded in his egotism, but he insists it was from patriotism—
love of America. He has never admitted that he went over to the
enemy any more than the writers at home who have despaired of the
Republic. I hate such nonsense and can only listen to it as an evidence
of mental disorder. But mental disorder is what we are considering.
I rest the case on Dr. Overholser's pronouncement that Ezra Pound
is not too dangerous to go free in his wife's care, and too insane ever
to be tried—a very nice discrimination."

On April 18th, with the consent of the government, the indictment
against Pound was dismissed by Judge Laws. Mr. Arnold said he
represented not only Mrs. Pound but also "the world community of
poets and writers." United States Attorney Oliver Gasch said the
motion was "in the interest of justice and should be granted," it being
virtually impossible to produce evidence of Pound's sanity during

the war years. Pound was in the courtroom, as were his wife and son. He sat on a rear bench. He had on an old blue jacket, a tan sport shirt which he had not bothered to tuck in, and blue slacks. As the order from the bench was issued Mrs. Pound, who had been sitting with Mr. Arnold at the counsel table, walked to the rear of the courtroom and gave her husband a kiss. That afternoon Pound went to downtown Washington unattended.

8.

On April 29th, Pound called on Representative Burdick at the latter's home. He had on an open-necked cotton shirt with short sleeves, green cotton trousers and brown shoes only partly laced. Around his neck was a string from which hung a small canvas bag; in it were his two pairs of glasses. He shook Burdick's hand, exclaiming, "This is a historic occasion." Photographers, who were present, thought so, too, and went into action. Pound sat down in an easy chair.

"I can't hold my head up for long," he said.

A seventy-five-minute monologue followed.

He talked about Venice and his great-aunt, when there was no bother with passports and frontiers "and all that malarkey." He mentioned his grandfather, the representative from Wisconsin. "T. C. was asking for the same things I am asking for in very much the same way." He himself wanted "some of the sanity of the Green-back Party" restored [it stood for currency expansion, or fiat money].

"I thought when Herbert Hoover came into the White House the prejudices against expatriates might diminish a little. I don't know how you feel about Herbert Hoover. Any man may make errors in his youth."

(Mr. Hoover had lived much abroad, at one time in Kensington when Pound lived there; but they never met.)[6]

"You know, Ike invited me to dinner once. Yes, when he was President of Columbia. I was a member of the Academy of Social and Political Sciences. He didn't know what he was signing. I was in the hell-hole [St. Elizabeths] at the time. The American Institute of Arts and Letters never had the guts to throw me out or send me notices."

"I am not anti-semitic. I have been making jokes about Jews all my life. Fifty years ago we had jokes about the Scotch and the Irish and the Jews, and the best stories you got were from the Jews."

"I would trust Mr. Cournos a damned sight more than Winston Churchill."

He turned suddenly to Burdick and said:

"I'm talking too much. I don't have to tell it all in one day. I can come back. But you've had a chance to talk as much as you like. It is what you're paid for. I've had the plug in for twelve years. When I was in the gorilla cage, the guard said: 'We've got a man here either for two hours or two months, but any man who talks to him gets the box' [meaning the sweat-box]. Few men of letters have these opportunities."

"I thought I was being flown home to give information to the State Department. I could see why a lot of this stuff shouldn't go to the public, but why not give it to the State Department? I could have been of considerable use. In a conquered country, the essential thing is to separate the honest men."

"I never told the troops not to fight. What I am interested in is the American Constitution."

Outside, he told reporters he wouldn't have been released "if they didn't think I would go back to Italy." One of them mentioned Frost's efforts in his behalf. Pound said dryly:

"He ain't been in much of a hurry."[7]

On June 12th and 13th Pound accompanied James Laughlin to a Washington studio, where he recorded his poems. He went again, alone, on the 26th. In the spring of 1960 Caedmon released the first selection, consisting of Cantos I, IV, XXXVI and LXXXIV, and "Hugh Selwyn Mauberley," "Cantico del Sole" and "Moeurs Contemporaines." It is a masterly compilation, being in effect a summary of his poetic achievement, both early and late. The reading is impressive for its vigor, warmth and clarity, and places Pound in the foremost rank of the readers of poetry in our time.

9.

The suburbs knew him, and the adjacent states. By car and train, surrounded by well-wishers and reporters, he dashed back and forth talking all the time. Or he talked and walked, striding with giant strides through the bright, unending streets and large air of freedom. In truth, he never talked better, if too much. "I don't have a one-track mind," he said. He put his head back. "I cannot hold my head up for long; I have to rest it on something. I offered to be tried *in camera,* lying on a couch, but their reverences thought not. No wonder my head hurts, all of Europe fell on it. When I talk it is like an explosion in an art museum, you have to hunt around for the pieces."[8]

On his next to the last weekend in the United States, Pound and his wife went to a country house near Hopewell, New Jersey. With them were Marcella Spann, Pound's collaborator on the Junior Anthology; Eugene C. Pomeroy, vice president of the Defenders of the American Constitution, and David Horton, erst of Kasper and Horton, now sole publisher of the Square Dollar series, and Mrs. Horton. Their hosts were Alan C. Collins, president of Curtis Brown, Ltd., a literary agency whose London branch had handled Pound's work years before, and Mrs. Collins, who is Mr. Pomeroy's daughter. The group arrived Saturday in time for lunch. Mr. Collins, who had not met Pound before, told me:

"Saturday evening was spent with Pound talking and the others listening. I must admit I failed to comprehend much that he was driving at but I came to the conclusion that the man, although he felt fanatically about everything he touched on, was far from being insane or even mentally deranged."

Sunday, there was the inevitable tennis game. Pound and Collins teamed up against two neighbors, men in their mid-thirties. They played two sets, losing the first and winning the second. "As we were warming up to start," Collins told me, "Pound said, 'Come on, let's go, I am not getting any younger.' For a man his age, Pound was an energetically good court coverer and topnotch at the net. His service wasn't much good." After tennis, Pound swam in the pool next to the court. "He was an extremely active and eager swimmer and spent practically the rest of the day in the sun at the pool, being in and out of the water continuously."

With his wife and son, and still accompanied by Miss Spann, Pound left Washington at last. He returned to Wyncote, to the house where he had grown up, to which he had brought Bill Williams and other schoolfellows, and a succession of girls, and finally Hilda Doolittle. There, where the Elmwood road makes a sharp turn at the top of the hill, it still stands above its retaining wall covered with ivy, a white shingle house of three stories, with green trim around the windows. Rhododendron grows by the front porch, and there are two big trees, a Spanish oak and maple; and in the back a crooked apple tree. He had asked, and received, permission to make the visit.

From Wyncote the party drove to Rutherford, where Pound and his wife stayed overnight at the Williams home. The next day they boarded the *Cristoforo Colombo*. They had a small, air-conditioned stateroom, with two beds and several lounge chairs. Dressed in shorts, and with shirt open at the front, Pound received friends who had come to see him off, among them the Italian cultural attaché in New York. Michael Reck, of Canto LXXXIX, brought a potted ivy plant—"so he wouldn't lose touch with the earth"—and someone else brought champagne, which was passed around. On the sun deck of the liner in the harbor of Naples Pound gave the Fascist salute and told Italian reporters "all America is an insane asylum."

CHAPTER XXIII

THE RETURN

1.

To the crowd on the pier at Genoa the first glimpse of him was of a white-bearded man at the top of the gangplank grasping two bags. He had on a shapeless gray felt hat and a red shirt open at the chest. (One Italian reporter thought he resembled Buffalo Bill.) Dorothy Pound, dressed in black—her hair was white now, too— tried to hold him back, but Pound, descending, was already talking.

"Are you glad to be back in Italy?" a reporter asked.

"Ha—I ought to kiss the sacred ground, but here I see only cement. Give me a meadow, give me some fresh grass."

In reply to another question—

"How did it go in the madhouse? Rather badly. But what other place could one live in America? Ah-ha."

A young priest appeared out of the crowd, embraced him, and whispered in his ear. Young Italians distributed yellow-leaved booklets containing two cantos; some of those who took them came up for autographs. A photographer said, "Don't look into the machine," and Pound replied: "I shouldn't look into the machine? And why not? Do you believe the machine is afraid of old Ez? Who am I? I am famous, I. My name is in all the dictionaries: Pound, English measure; see 'libbra.' Ah-ha, ah-ha."

To the reporters: "Yes, friends, write what you want. The only way not to get it printed in all the newspapers of the world is to write the truth."

Surrounded by a milling throng, Pound entered the customs office. The customs officer, astonished, asked: "Who is this person?" The crowd answered, "a poet," "the poet Ezra Pound." The customs officer looked at the bags, chalked them, and said, "Away! Away!"

Pound went out, followed by the crowd. He said:

"Here we are outside, in the open, no fingerprints, no question-naires—Italy—free country!"

An unknown man appeared and took Pound by the arm and led him to an automobile.

Hours later, in a garden in Genoa, on a reclining chair, he held court. He said:

"I have a great wish to make a leap to Rapallo, 'the navel of the world'. Who knows what has happened to my house in Via Marsala, to how many friends at Rapallo! Many have written to me in these years, and used to send flowers. They used to say that my song was lively. They have never forgotten Old Ez. What's the matter, Dorothy, why are you laughing?"

"I was thinking," she said, "about the evening when you went out half naked from the house and I ran after you—you had dis-covered in I know not what book the word 'lattizzo' and you wanted to shout it in all the streets."

He laughed; but his thoughts were already elsewhere.

"Do you know why they freed me?" he asked. "Because I promised them that I would leave America. Otherwise I would still be there, inside, in the midst of those furious madmen. I know that band of traitors."

A monologue followed, about his mysterious, implacable perse-cutors, and it was not clear to the reporter whether they were men or demons, the "usurai" whom he had excoriated in his *Cantos*. Then, in a lighter vein he asked:

"Do you know that the inmates of St. Elizabeths are congenial people, no more mad than you or I? I knew one who was indeed wise (giudizioso). There was just one thing the matter, he had killed his wife and four sons. Dorothy wasn't very fond of him. Ah-ha."

He had survived all perils, and triumphed over enemies, who, how-ever, were still pursuing him.

"They freed me," he began again, "in order that I should go away —international Machiavellism is always the same. They made me pass for a madman, in order that young people should not listen to me any more."

His monologue continued, about plots, betrayals, conspiracies. He seemed to think that he had gone to Downing Street, date unspecified, as earlier he thought he had gone to the United States to stop the war.

"At that time I went to see Eden and Churchill, but I understood that their minds were made up, they had decided to have their war. Thereupon I was seized with disgust, and I returned to old Muss."

He spoke of Eden, Churchill, Léon Blum, Truman, Hitler and Mussolini as though speaking of people he had known intimately. Then he turned to his wife.

"Do you remember, Dorothy, the first time that we met Hem, in Paris? As a boxer, Hem was courageous, and even at writing he could give an account of himself. But there was another fellow, Bob McAlmon, who was much more courageous; who knows what happened to him? Hem, I know what happened to him—he also sold himself to the god dollar." (Pound denied making this remark.)

Giorgio Bocca, the reporter from whose account I have been quoting, commented here: "Thus Uncle Ez spoke of Hemingway, who wanted to renounce the Nobel Prize in his favor. And of Eliot, who never abandoned him, he said, 'He is worthy of the toothless Megera [Megaera sdentata], of which he became a citizen.' [Megaera: one of the three Furies.] But who could suppose that he is ungrateful? Is he not the greatest of all poets, is he not 'il miglior fabbro'?"

Signor Bocca, in his account of the return, asked another question, this time directed to Pound. It was:

"How is it that you who merited fame as a seer did not see?"[1]

2.

Pound's destination was Schloss Brunnenburg, a castle near Merano, in the Italian Alps, where his daughter Mary lived with her husband, Prince Boris de Rachewiltz, and their two children. The castle, dating from the twelfth century, has a commanding view of one of the most romantic regions of Europe. It is full of art treasures, chiefly Egyptian, Prince de Rachewiltz being a noted Egyptologist. (He recently translated the *Book of the Dead,* from the papyrus in the Egyptian Museum

in Turin, the first such translation into Italian.) There is also a room
full of Gaudier-Brzeska sculptures. On the walls hang paintings
and drawings by Picasso and Brancusi; Japanese tragic masks and
carnival masks from the Tyrol. Ranged on shelves are the early
volumes, signed for Pound, of Joyce, Yeats, Aldington, H. D., Eliot
and Marianne Moore, and others, and Pound's own books in their
original editions. Outside, on a garden terrace, stands the hieratic
head.

Mary de Rachewiltz went to meet Pound and his wife at Verona,
and they returned together to Merano, followed by reporters. There
was a happy meeting with his handsome grandchildren. At a reception in the castle he read Canto LXXXI, the canto dealing with
vanity. In good weather he read and wrote in a reclining chair in the
castle garden. He took his grandchildren to town to the horse races
at the Hippodrome, where he bet, making a pool with friends; whenever he won, he burst into loud laughter and sent the children to buy
enormous ice creams.

Thus the summer passed. On his seventy-third birthday, October
30th, there was an exhibition of his books and other memorabilia,
including his clavichord, in Merano. Dressed in blue, with a Quaker-
ish black hat, and tieless (his tie was in his pocket, in case it was
called for), he spoke briefly in Italian to those present, and in German over the Innsbruck radio, being interviewed on the spot. He said
that after the fogs of London and Paris he had found in Rapallo
sunshine the possibility of renewing himself; it had been a good
place for his poetry, it was, in fact, the place where most of the Cantos
were written. Now he hoped that Merano would revive him after
his long sojourn in St. Elizabeths, and that here he could bring to
an end his magnum opus. The exhibition had been organized with
the help of Vanni Scheiwiller, his Italian publisher.

One of those who heard Pound interviewed was Dr. George Steiner,
a Fulbright grant professor at Franz Leopold Universität in Innsbruck. He wrote asking if he could call. Steiner, formerly on the
faculty of the Princeton Institute of Advanced Research and one-time
editor of the "American Survey" for *The Economist,* had long admired Pound and was now lecturing on his work in a course entitled
"American Literature Comes of Age." He told his class that Canto
LXXXI was "the greatest piece of modesty and humility since the

Book of Job." Pound, however, replied with a questionnaire on economics, which Dr. Steiner did his best to complete, but apparently flunked; instead of an invitation to Schloss Brunnenburg he received an abusive post card.[2]

Pound was more agreeable on the subject of music. A letter came from Thomas Putsché, of the Hartford Conservatory of Music, offering to give him a performance of his opera about Villon. He replied: "Might take an interest if you or anyone showed an interest in providing board and lodging." He wrote to Carl Dolmetsch, the son of his old friend:

"I have at last got back to my clavicord [*sic*], after interruptions of a more or less drastic nature. In fact the Plus Fai Douceur que Violence, and the frame of the instrument was included with some eclat at my semi-centennial show in Merano BUT the strings have been almost entirely liberated by the enemies of gawd, man, civilization, Mihaelovitch etc.

"Not sure that the local zither fixer can deal with the whole problem. I suppose he cd/ tune it IF he can get the strings.

"I think your father used to import 'em from Germany, in which case it would probably, seeing that Ooozefeld and W. C. have pretty well buggered the amenities, dogane etc. probably simpler for me to get 'em direct from over the alps and not under Eden's jo-house as way station, IF the lords temporal haven't bombed the factory. (Of course the Farben weren't bombed, but I never heard they carried the arts as a side line.)

"I shd/ be glad of any helpful suggests you can send me. My grandson seems to get noise pleasantly out of various sonorous bodies from decrepit lutes to mouth organ and he might use the instrument better than I have, if it can [be] got back into order.

"Best regards to survivors of Haslemere civil life."

Carl Dolmetsch was on a concert tour when the letter reached Haslemere, and his secretary replied: "You do not mention whether your clavichord is single or double strung, but a set of single strings would cost £6. 10. 0. and the set of double strings would cost £13. 0. 0." Pound wrote back:

"A. Dolmetsch hammered it into MY head that the principle of the claivicord [*sic*] WAS that there are two strings for every note, slightly out of tune with each other.

"At any rate mine had 'em until the war 'liberated' 'em. It was the small size, black 'plus fai douceur etc,' about a metre long, say 42 inches. Not the big six footer. Mrs. Dolmetsch will probably remember it, as it was A. D.'s own but he couldn't be bothered to make a duplicate at the moment I wanted it."

The strings came, and Pound wrote Carl Dolmetsch:

"Yr. father's clavicord [*sic*] now in order, & with a little playing will get back tone—despite 15 years stillness.

"But as I can't live @ this altitude, nor can deprive my grandson of it—what can you make me another for? Of those dimensions?"[8]

A price list was sent him.

3.

The town that was in his heart and in his thoughts—whose name he had once set down in St. Elizabeths, then saw his mistake and added, "Would that it were!"—drew him irresistibly across the Italian peninsula to the Ligurian coast and Rapallo. The apartment on the Via Marsala was in other hands; Dorothy Pound had held it until she could hold it no longer, and its furnishings had been transported to Brunnenburg. This time they stayed at the Albergo Grande Italia and Lido, "direttamente al mare," as its stationery proudly proclaims, that stationery which was to cascade, by land and sea and air, all over the world in Pound's new and prodigious correspondence.

Part of the spring and summer were spent in Rapallo, Pound, to judge by his correspondence and work, chiefly at his typewriter; in the fall, he and his wife returned to Merano. There were reports that he was not well; he was having trouble holding his head up, and much of the time he reclined. The correspondence subsided; now there were reports that he was seriously ill. But there were occasional letters, sprightly, or maledictory—he favored me with both kinds —like the Pound of old. His ire was still directed against universities and foundations. "When one considers what I have had out of american floundations [*sic*] in 50 years," he wrote me, "average about $62.50 per year, with the Univs. of Calif. Oxon etc. subsidizing parasites on my work, you have a topic that might be fruitful for biographic study."

There were also occasional bursts of activity. His *Women of Trachis,* completed in St. Elizabeths, had had a triumphal production in Berlin, and was about to be performed in Darmstadt. The mayor of Darmstadt invited him to be a guest of honor of the city. He went, accompanied by his daughter. On the day of the premiere he donned what he termed his "fancy suit," the velvet jacket he used to wear at concerts in Rapallo. Eva Hesse, the German translator of Pound, Eliot and Cummings, accompanied him and his daughter to the theater.

The Darmstadt theater is in the wing of a baroque castle, and does not have private boxes. Pound, apparently, was disappointed at this and seemed about to leave. Miss Hesse said, "This is hardly what Mr. Eliot would do under the circumstances," and Pound took his place in the audience. But just before the end of the performance he suddenly jumped up and disappeared. Everyone thought he had left the theater; but there, on the stage, taking the applause with the cast, was the author. The applause turned into an ovation, and he was called back five or six times.

"He cut a very fine figure standing out there," Miss Hesse wrote James Laughlin.

Christmas, 1959, saw completion of the 111th canto. He told a visitor he hoped "to make it 120." He worked in a tower room reached by a winding stair.

Soon, however, the old patterns of his life began to repeat themselves, and he divided his time between Merano and Rome, then between Rapallo and Venice. He settled at last, with his wife, in Sant' Ambrogio, the little town in the hills where he had once sought sanctuary. Occasionally, in letters to Laughlin and others, there were intimations of nostalgia. He told an American reporter: "After a number of years abroad, foreigners begin to appear as unreal. Then you suddenly feel a hunger to go home again."[4]

In recent years his public appearances have been rare. He was seen twice at Gian Carlo Menotti's Festival of Two Worlds at Spoleto— once as poet, the other time as a composer, when his opera was performed. He attended the memorial service for T. S. Eliot in Westminster Abbey, and followed it with a surprise visit to Mrs. William Butler Yeats in Dublin.

He spent his eightieth birthday, October 30, 1965, in Paris, a white-haired, silent figure from the past. "I did not enter into silence," he was reported to have said. "Silence captured me." A friend told newsmen he was "in a state of profound remorse."

Such was Ezra Pound, endowed at birth with extraordinary ability, and great goodness of heart; a man who befriended all whom he ever met, never hesitating to share what he had, even when he had little, whether of money or clothes, shelter or books, and by putting their work before his own, helping many to deserved renown; with a sure judgment of art in all its forms, yet without judgment about himself, or the issues which have perplexed mankind, and at length undone by a mixture of vanity, flattery, cocksureness and too-long involvement with ideas which were clear neither when he adopted them nor after he began to expound them, and so falling into abusiveness because mankind refused to listen, and listened to in the end only by obscure sycophants full of flattery for one who had been the friend of Yeats, Joyce, Eliot and Cummings. But what was noble in his nature will not be forgotten, and what is truly great in his work will surely endure.

NOTES AND
ACKNOWLEDGMENTS

NOTES

I.

1. William Carlos Williams, *Selected Letters*, New York: McDowell, Obolensky, 1957. 2. Williams, *I Wanted to Write a Poem*, Boston: Beacon Press, 1958. 3. Professor Harold W. Thompson of Cornell; see also notes to XIII. 4. Interview with Mary Dixon Thayer, Philadelphia *Evening Bulletin*, Feb. 20, 1928. 5. John Cournos, *Autobiography*, New York: G. P. Putnam's Sons, 1935. 6. Pound, *The Spirit of Romance* (a reissue), Norfolk, Conn.: New Directions, 1952. 7. Pound, *Patria Mia*, Chicago: Ralph Fletcher Seymour, 1950. 8. *Ibid.* 9. In praise of an attack on Pound's poetry by Hyatt Howe Waggoner. 10. To Prof. John H. Edwards, University of California; Mr. Bynner also supplied the present author with a copy. 11. Pound, *Indiscretions*, Paris: Three Mountains Press, 1923; also in *Pavannes and Divagations*, New Directions, 1958. 12. *Cf.*, "Andreas Divus" in *The Egoist*, V. 7 (August, 1918); also *The Literary Essays of Ezra Pound*, edited by T. S. Eliot, New Directions and London: Faber and Faber, 1954. 13. Ford Madox Ford, *It Was the Nightingale*, Philadelphia and London: J. B. Lippincott Co., 1933. 14. It fetched $150 in the U.S. in 1948, while an inscribed copy brought £75 in London in 1957. 15. Philadelphia *Evening Bulletin*, Feb. 20, 1928. 16. The original manuscript is in the Yale University Library.

II.

1. Philadelphia *Evening Bulletin*, Feb. 20, 1928. 2. Edgar Jepson, *Memories of an Edwardian and Neo-Georgian*, London: Grant Richards, 1937. 3. *The Literary Essays of Ezra Pound*. 4. Philadelphia *Evening Bulletin*, Feb. 20, 1928. 5. *The Letters of Ezra Pound 1907–1941*, edited by D. D. Paige, with an Introduction by Mark Van Doren, New York: Harcourt,

EZRA POUND

Brace and Co., 1950; London: Faber and Faber, 1951. 6. S. Foster Damon terms it "Undoubtedly the most vigorous sestina in English" (*Amy Lowell*, Boston and New York: Houghton Mifflin Co., 1935). 7. The quoted passages from Hulme are from *Speculations*, edited by Herbert Read, London: Routledge & Kegan Paul, Ltd., 1958. 8. David Garnett, *The Golden Echo*, London: Chatto & Windus, 1953. 9. Douglas Goldring, *South Lodge*, London: Constable & Co., Ltd., 1943. 10. *D. H. Lawrence: A Composite Biography*, gathered, arranged and edited by Edward Nehls, Madison: University of Wisconsin Press, 1957–1959. 11. Garnett, *op. cit.* 12. Eliot met Lady Mond below, instead; the story is that when he read the stanza with her husband's name, she flounced out of the drawing room. 13. Violet Hunt, *I Have This To Say*, New York: Boni and Liveright, 1926. 14. Ford Madox Ford, *Return to Yesterday*, New York: Horace Liveright, Inc., 1932. 15. Garnett, *op. cit.* 16. Ernest Rhys, *Everyman Remembers*, London: J. M. Dent and Sons, Ltd., 1931. 17. Harriet Monroe, *A Poet's Life*, New York: The Macmillan Company, 1938.

III.

1. Williams, *Autobiography*, New York: Random House, 1951. 2. *The Dial*, November, 1928. 3. Pound, *Patria Mia*. 4. J. B. Yeats, *Letters to His Son W. B. Yeats and Others 1869–1922*, edited with a Memoir by Joseph Hone and a Preface by Oliver Elton, London: Faber and Faber, 1946. 5. Pound, *op. cit.* 6. Jessie B. Rittenhouse, *My House of Life*, Boston and New York: Houghton Mifflin Co., 1934. 7. Letter to Amy Lowell from Richard Aldington, Nov. 20, 1917; original in Harvard University Library. 8. Wyndham Lewis, "Ezra: The Portrait of a Personality," *Quarterly Review of Literature*, December, 1949. Also in [*An Examination of*] *Ezra Pound, A Collection of Essays edited by Peter Russell to be Presented to Ezra Pound on his sixty-fifth Birthday*, London: Peter Russell, Norfolk, Conn.: New Directions, 1950. 9. Pound, *op. cit.* 10. *Ibid*.

IV.

1. Richard Aldington, *Life for Life's Sake*, New York: The Viking Press, 1941. 2. Pound, *The Spirit of Romance*. 3. "As to *The Spirit of Romance*, it's too late for you to be recommending it to me; I've been recommending it to you for years. I read it in the Twenties" (Willard R. Trask to the author). 4. London: Stephen Swift and Co., Ltd., Boston, Small, Maynard and Co., 1912. 5. Horace Gregory and Marya Zaturenska, *A History of American Poetry 1900–1940*, New York: Harcourt, Brace and Co., 1946. 6. Hugh Kenner, *The Poetry of Ezra Pound*, New Directions and Faber and Faber, 1951. The sentence (p. 337) is not strictly accurate, since

Canzoni was bound with *Ripostes*, hence reissued, in 1913. "Au Salon" also appears in the later *Personae*. 7. Pound, *Patria Mia*. 8. Willard Huntington Wright. 9. Charles Norman, *The Magic-Maker: E. E. Cummings*, New York: The Macmillan Company, 1958. 10. This was told me by Louis Zukofsky. 11. Edward Marsh, *A Number of People*, London: W. Heinemann, Ltd.-H. Hamilton, Ltd., 1939. 12. Christopher Hassall, *A Biography of Edward Marsh*, New York: Harcourt, Brace and Co., 1959.

V.

1. Harriet Monroe, *op. cit.* 2. Aldington, *op. cit.* 3. See III, note 7. 4. Aldington, *op. cit.* 5. *Ibid.* 6. *Ibid.* 7. *Ibid.* 8. Harriet Monroe, *op. cit.*; footnote by Pound. 9. Wasilly Kandinsky, *Ueber das Geistige in der Kunst*, Munich: R. Piper and Co., 1912. 10. *Gaudier-Brzeska: A Memoir* by Ezra Pound, London: John Lane-The Bodley Head, 1916; New Directions, 1960. 11. *The Translations of Ezra Pound*, with an Introduction by Hugh Kenner, New Directions and Faber and Faber, 1953.

VI.

1. Harriet Monroe, *op. cit.* 2. John Gould Fletcher, *Life Is My Song*, New York: Farrar and Rinehart, Inc., 1937. 3. *Ibid.* 4. *Ibid.* 5. *Ibid.* 6. Damon, *op. cit.* 7. Hassall, *op. cit.* 8. Alfred Kreymborg, *Troubadour: An Autobiography*, New York: Liveright, Inc., 1925. 9. *Ibid.* 10. Cournos, *op. cit.* 11. *Ibid.* 12. *Ibid.* 13. Original in Harvard University Library. 14. Interview with the author.

VII.

1. Fletcher, *op. cit.* 2. Gregory and Zaturenska, *op. cit.* 3. Fletcher, *op. cit.* 4. Gorham B. Munson, *Robert Frost: A Study in Sensibility and Good Taste*, New York: George H. Doran Co., 1927. 5. From a manuscript journal by John Holmes. 6. Ralph Fletcher Seymour, *Some Went This Way*, Chicago: R. F. Seymour, 1945. 7. Fletcher, *op. cit.* 8. Cournos, *op. cit.* In *Babel*, a novel, published in 1922, and thus closer to the event than his *Autobiography*, Cournos gives a more fanciful form of the letter. His hero, Gombarov, says to Bagg [Pound]: "Worthy of Whistler!" Cournos's text continues: "He was in his way a child, playful and malicious, and he took as great pleasure in a prank as in writing a poem. If Gombarov's supposition that he had modelled his career on Whistler's was correct, to say that he had done something 'worthy of Whistler' was to give him the moon itself." 9. Joseph Hone, *W. B. Yeats 1865–1939*,

New York: The Macmillan Company, 1943. 11. Presumably William Stanley Braithwaite, reviewer and anthologist.

VIII.

1. *D. H. Lawrence: A Composite Biography*, Vol. II. A note on p. 509 states: "Mrs. Idella Purnell Stone's adaptation (August, 1956) of a series of letters she had written to Witter Bynner, and published as such in Bynner [*Journey with Genius*], pp. 194-195." Bynner reminded Lawrence in New Mexico of his own part in launching Pound's career. 2. J. B. Yeats, *Letters to His Son*. 3. Pound, *Gaudier-Brzeska*. 4. Cournos, *Autobiography*. 5. Pound, *op. cit.* 6. *Ibid.* 7. *Ibid.* 8. Edith Finch, *Wilfrid Scawen Blunt, 1840–1922*, London: Jonathan Cape, p. 138. 9. *Ibid.* 10. *The Translations of Ezra Pound*. 11. Quoted by Michael Roberts in *T. E. Hulme*, London: Faber and Faber, 1938. 12. J. B. Yeats, *op. cit.* 13. Philadelphia *Evening Bulletin*, March 26, 1914. 14. Philadelphia *Inquirer*, April 18, 1914. 15. From a certified copy of the marriage entry, sent the author by Stanley Eley, Reverend Prebendary and Vicar of St. Mary Abbot's, Kensington.

IX.

1. Goldring, *op. cit.*, 2. Pound, *Guide to Kulchur* (pp. 64 and 266), New Directions and Faber and Faber, 1938. 3. F. O. Matthiessen, *The James Family*, New York: Alfred A. Knopf, 1948. 4. Damon, *op. cit.* 5. *Ibid.* 6. I know of only one other observation like this one. In one of the war-time letters which landed him and E. E. Cummings in prison, William Slater Brown wrote to a friend: "I had forgotten all about her until the other night when I talked to a drunken French soldier who had eyes exactly like hers. So much like hers that it gave me a terrific start and I could not remember for some time whose eyes they resembled" (*The Magic-Maker: E. E. Cummings*). 7. Jacob Epstein, *Let There Be Sculpture*, New York: E. P. Dutton, 1940. 8. *Ibid.* 9. Cournos, *Autobiography*.

X.

1. Harriet Monroe, *op. cit.* 2. T. S. Eliot, "Ezra Pound," *Poetry*, September, 1946. 3. *Ibid.* 4. *Ibid.* 5. Lewis, *op. cit.* 6. Not £100. (*Cf.*, Herbert Gorman, *James Joyce*, New York: Rinehart & Co., Inc., 1948, p. 233; Richard Ellmann, *James Joyce*, New York: Oxford University Press, 1959, p. 419; Hone, *op. cit.*, p. 312; and Allan Wade, *The Letters of W. B. Yeats*, New York: The Macmillan Company, 1955, p. 600.) 7. Ellmann, *op. cit.* 8.

Lewis, *op. cit.* 9. Phyllis Bottome, *This Week,* Dec. 1, 1935; expanded in *From the Life,* London: Faber and Faber, 1944. 10. Aldington, *op. cit.* 11. *Cf.,* Geoffrey Wagner, *Wyndham Lewis: A Portrait of the Artist as Enemy,* New Haven: Yale University Press, 1957. 12. Eliot, *After Strange Gods.* 13. C. H. Douglas, *The Control and Distribution of Production,* London: Cecil Palmer, 1922. 14. Sir William Rothenstein, *Since Fifty,* London: Faber and Faber, 1939. 15. *The Literary Essays of Ezra Pound.* 16. Eliot, *op. cit.*

XI.

1. *The Bookman* (U.S.A.), October, 1931. 2. Margaret Anderson, *My Thirty Years' War,* New York: Covici, Friede, 1930. 3. Josephine Horton, of the Washington Square Book Shop, told me: "Margaret Anderson and Jane Heap were in the country—but came back quickly to assume full responsibility in the case."

XII.

1. *Ezra Pound: Selected Poems.* Edited with an Introduction by T. S. Eliot. London: Faber and Faber, 1928. 2. Aldington, *op. cit.* 3. *Criterion,* July, 1932. 4. Aldington, *op. cit.* 5. Sir Osbert Sitwell, *Laughter in the Next Room,* London: Macmillan & Co., 1949. 6. Hugh Kenner, *The Poetry of Ezra Pound*; John J. Espey, *Ezra Pound's Mauberley: a Study in Composition,* Berkeley and Los Angeles: University of California Press, 1955; René Taupin, *L'Influence du symbolisme français sur la poésie américaine, de 1910 à 1920,* Paris: Champion, 1930; R. P. Blackmur, *Form and Value in Modern Poetry,* New York: Doubleday Anchor Books, 1957. 7. Eliot, Introduction, *Ezra Pound: Selected Poems* (see above). 8. Ford Madox Ford, *It Was the Nightingale.* 9. Kenner, *op. cit.* 10. An account of *The Dial* appears in Norman, *The Magic-Maker: E. E. Cummings,* pp. 149-170. 11. From an uncollected letter, first printed in *Nine,* No. 4 (summer, 1950). 12. *New Republic,* Feb. 27, 1956.

XIII.

1. Pound apparently got hold of the records letter. In a June, 1959, letter to the New York State Historical Association, Cooperstown, N.Y., he said: "I spose I ought to keep old Loomis Court docket in the family, tho no one likely to read it in Brunnenburg." 2. *Cf.,* Carl Carmer, *Listen for a Lonesome Drum,* New York: Farrar and Rinehart, 1936, and Harold W. Thompson, *Body, Boots and Britches,* Philadelphia: Lippincott, 1940. 3. "Money Pamphlets," No. 1. 4. *Ibid.* 5. Variously related in *Patria Mia,*

Indiscretions, and "Money Pamphlets," No. 1. 6. "Money Pamphlets," No. 1. 7. *Ibid.* 8. *Indiscretions.* 9. *Ibid.* 10. Pound, *Pavannes and Divagations,* New Directions, 1958; frontispiece, framed portrait of "Hermione." The resemblance to her son is striking.

XIV.

1. Sylvia Beach, *Shakespeare and Company,* New York: Harcourt, Brace and Co., 1959. But Richard Ellmann (*op. cit.*) says it was Mme. Bloch-Savitsky who brought Joyce and his wife to the Spires that day. 2. Sylvia Beach, *op. cit.* 3. Kreymborg, *op. cit.* 4. Harold Loeb, *The Way It Was,* New York: Criterion Books, 1959. 5. *Poetry,* September, 1946. 6. Malcolm Cowley, *Exile's Return,* New York: The Viking Press, 1934. 7. Lewis, *op. cit.* 8. Aldington, *op. cit.* 9. George Antheil, *Bad Boy of Music,* New York: Doubleday, Doran & Co., Inc., 1945. 10. Harriet Monroe, *op. cit.* 11. Margaret Anderson, *op. cit.* 12. Ford, *It Was the Nightingale.* 13. *Ibid.* 14. Williams, *Autobiography.* 15. "Homage to Ezra," *This Quarter,* Vol. I, No. 1 (spring, 1925). 16. Professor Vernon Loggins, then of New York University, later of Columbia. 17. Mary Colum, *Life and the Dream,* New York: Doubleday and Co., 1947. 18. *Ibid.* 19. *PM,* Aug. 15, 1943. 20. *This Quarter,* Vol. I, No. 1; also in *The Critical Writings of James Joyce,* edited by Ellsworth Mason and Richard Ellmann, London: Faber and Faber, 1959. 21. Sylvia Beach, *op. cit.* 22. *This Quarter,* Vol. I, No. 1. 23. *The Letters of Lincoln Steffens,* edited with Introductory Notes by Ella Winter and Granville Hicks with a Memorandum by Carl Sandburg, New York: Harcourt, Brace and Co., 1938. 24. Rattray, *op. cit.* 25. From an unpublished letter. 26. Ditto.

XV.

1. Uncollected letter. 2. Antheil, *op. cit.* 3. *Ibid.*

XVI.

1. Sitwell, *op. cit.* 2. Aldington, *op. cit.* 3. *Ibid.* 4. Antheil, *op. cit.* 5. *Ibid.* 6. Now Mrs. Robert Johnston.

XVII.

1. The correspondence between Pound and Zukofsky appears here for the first time. 2. Williams, *Autobiography.* 3. Williams, *I Wanted to Write a*

Poem. 4. Robert Fitzgerald, "Gloom and Gold in Ezra Pound," *Encounter* (London), July, 1956. 5. Preface to *The King of the Great Clock Tower.* 6. Letter to Julien Cornell, Dec. 11, 1945. 7. Papers of President Franklin D. Roosevelt, P.P.F. 98, Franklin D. Roosevelt Library, Hyde Park, N.Y. 8. *Ibid.,* Alphabetical File. 9. *The Black Book: The Nazi Crime Against the Jewish People,* New York: The Jewish Black Book Committee, 1946, pp. 64-66. 10. "The German hero in America for the moment is the Rev. Charles E. Coughlin, because of his radio speech representing National Socialism as the defensive front against Bolshevism" (The New York *Times,* Nov. 27, 1938; quoted in *The Black Book,* p. 66). 11. Phyllis Bottome, *op. cit.* 12. Louis Untermeyer, *From Another World,* New York: Harcourt, Brace and Co., 1939.

XVIII.

1. *Cf.,* Carl Van Doren, *Benjamin Franklin,* New York: The Viking Press, 1938, p. 745: "His important speeches have been more accurately preserved than those of any other delegate. (Of course he did not make the speech against the Jews which was impudently forged and maliciously ascribed to him in 1934.)" See, also, his note on p. 806: "The forged speech, called *Franklin's Prophecy,* seems to have appeared first in *Liberator* (Asheville) February 3, 1934; often reprinted." 2. Canto LII is earlier than *The Pisan Cantos.* 3. Rattray, *op. cit.* 4. The most useful is *Annotated Index to the Cantos of Ezra Pound* (Cantos I-LXXXIV) by John Hamilton Edwards and William W. Vasse, Berkeley and Los Angeles: University of California Press, 1959. 5. Published in England by Peter Russell, 1950, 1951 and 1952. 6. Official photo from the U.S. Office of War Information; reproduced in *The Black Book* (see above) facing p. 50. 7. *Poetry,* September, 1946. 8. Russell, ed., *Ezra Pound.*

XIX.

1. Vol. I, No. 3 (March, 1936). Prof. Thompson also wrote about the Loomis Gang in his book, *Body, Boots and Britches;* see XIII and Notes. 2. Sale No. 1825, April 29-30, 1958. Lot sold for $40. 3. Paul de Kruif, *Why Keep Them Alive?* New York: Harcourt, Brace and Co., 1936. 4. From a letter to the author from Harry D. Yates, Feb. 28, 1959. 5. Extracts from letters to Douglas C. Fox appear here for the first time. 6. Uncollected. 7. Samuel Putnam, *Paris Was Our Mistress,* New York: The Viking Press, 1947. 8. H. R. Trevor-Roper, *The Last Days of Hitler,* New York: The Macmillan Company, 1947. 9. Mr. Eliot wrote me, May 1, 1957: "I was indeed very glad to receive from you a copy of the lines I wrote in 1940 as I did not possess a copy until then. I should explain

that it never occurred to me at the time of writing that my lines would be spoken of later as a 'poem'. They were written for an exhibition of war photographs to be shown in New York and each separate section was to be shown in large letters over the particular part of the exhibition to which it referred. It did not occur to me that these lines would have any permanence or any interest apart from that exhibition of photographs which was arranged, I think, by our Ministry of Information, at the behest of which my words were written. I still think of the piece rather as a collection of captions than as a poem." 10. *Il Mare*, Oct. 31, 1954; translation by G. Giovannini. 11. Richard Rovere, "The Question of Ezra Pound," *Esquire*, September, 1957. 12. "The Medical, Legal, Literary and Political Status of Ezra Weston (Loomis) Pound (1885-   )—Selected Facts and Comments—Part I" by H. A. Sieber, Research Assistant, Senior Specialists Division, the Library of Congress Legislative Reference Service, March 31, 1958, Revised April 14, 1958. *Congressional Record—Appendix*, April 29, 1958, pp. A3895–A3901. 13. *Congressional Record—Appendix*, April 30, 1958, p. A3944. 14. *Ibid.* 15. Philadelphia *Record*, Nov. 29, 1945.

XX.

1. The Earl Jowitt, *Some Were Spies*, London: Hodder and Stoughton, 1954. 2. Williams, *Autobiography*. 3. G. Giovannini, "The Strange Case of Ezra Pound," *New Times* (Melbourne), Aug. 26, 1955. 4. Mrs. Marquis James, who was employed there, to the writer. 5. I am indebted to the British Information Services, an agency of the British Government, New York City, for most of the transcripts used here, and for an opportunity to hear the recordings afforded me in 1945. A more or less complete transcript of all the broadcasts may be obtained on microfilm from the Library of Congress. 6. Interview by Edd Johnson, Philadelphia *Record*-Chicago *Sun*, May 9, 1945. 7. Robert L. Allen, "The Cage," *Esquire*, February, 1958. 8. *Ibid.* 9. David Park Williams, "The Background of The Pisan Cantos," *Poetry*, January, 1949. 10. *Ibid.* 11. Allen, *op. cit.* 12. *Ibid.* 13. Norman, "The Case of Ezra Pound," *PM*, Nov. 25, 1945; also New York: The Bodley Press, 1948. The statement by Cummings also appears in his *i: Six Nonlectures*, Cambridge: Harvard University Press, 1953.

XXI.

1. Library of Congress Press Release No. 542, Feb. 20, 1949. 2. From a list given the author by Dr. Winfred Overholser.

XXII.

1. Williams, *Autobiography*. 2. From Cummings's use of this word in his poetry, and/or *Eimi*, his book on Russia. 3. A poem in *1 x 1*. 4. See Introduction to *The Magic-Maker: E. E. Cummings*. 5. Nov. 28, 1957. 6. Letter to the author. 7. Mary McGrory, "Ezra Pound Still Sees Mad World Out of Step," Washington *Star*, April 30, 1958. 8. James Jackson Kilpatrick, "A Conversation with Ezra Pound," *National Review*, May 24, 1958.

XXIII.

1. Giorgio Bocca, "Bentornato Zio Ez," *L'Europeo*, July 20, 1958; translated by Francesco M. Bianco. 2. From a communication by Richard P. Critchfield, Oakton, Va. 3. Dolmetsch correspondence uncollected. 4. *Newsweek*, March 21, 1960.

ACKNOWLEDGMENTS

It must be apparent to anyone who has read this book that I could not have written it without the cooperation of a great many persons here and abroad. In general, if the name of a living person occurs in the text I have had the cooperation of that person. To name each one here would be pleasant; but they—and now the reader—know my debt. I thank them all collectively, from Conrad Aiken to Louis Zukofsky. Nevertheless, some individual acts of kindness ought not to go unspecified, not least Mr. Pound's.

This is not an authorized biography. Mr. Pound offered advice, made useful suggestions, and wished me luck; but he declined to answer specific questions, and he has not read the text prior to publication. Here, I wish to thank him for his generosity in permitting me to use unpublished material, including letters to writers and others. I also wish to thank Mrs. Pound.

I am grateful to Pound's college classmates and schoolmates who replied to my queries, and thank Charles A. Springstead for his thoughtfulness in also sending me the photograph of Pound at Hamilton which appears in this book. I thank Mrs. Grace Root, of New York City and Clinton, for her recollections of Pound as student and distinguished guest. And I particularly thank T. Mark Hodges, reference librarian at Hamilton, for his many acts of kindness in sending me material.

I am also indebted to the libraries—and librarians—of the University of Pennsylvania, Harvard University, Yale University, New York University, the University of Buffalo; the New York Public Library, the Utica Public Library, and the Franklin D. Roosevelt Library; the Library of Congress, the National Archives and Records Service of the United States, the New York State Historical Association, the State Historical Society of Wisconsin, the Museum of Modern Art, the Poetry Society of America, the British

Information Services, New York City, the British Broadcasting Corporation, and The Polytechnic Institute of London.

I also wish to thank Nancy Wilson Ross who directed me to Mrs. Lulu Cunningham of Hailey, Idaho, Pound's birthplace, with excellent results; Mrs. Cunningham herself, ninety-three when she first replied to my inquiries, and her fellow townswoman, Dorothy L. Povey, Blaine County Treasurer and Public Administrator; Dr. Norman Holmes Pearson of Yale who served as liaison for H. D. concerning Pound's Philadelphia period and engagement to her; Professor Harold W. Thompson of Cornell, a Hamilton alumnus, who filled in some of the gaps in Pound's Hamilton College background; Julien Cornell, Pound's counsel, who placed his enormous file and personal knowledge at my disposal, and was also kind enough to read over the many pages dealing with the legal aspects of the Pound case; and Professor G. Giovannini, of the Catholic University of America, Washington, D.C., for advice and material on the aftermath.

I thank Mrs. Clare Boothe Luce, former United States Ambassador to Italy, for her account of Embassy activities in connection with Pound; Morrill Cody, of the United States Embassy in Paris, and David Burns of the State Department. And I thank Dr. Winfred Overholser, Superintendent of St. Elizabeths Hospital.

I thank Mr. Eliot for his kindness in letting me use the uncollected poem on page 382, which he thinks of "rather as a collection of captions than as a poem" (see Notes, Ch. XIX), but which I have always regarded as a supreme utterance of wartime. I thank Mr. Cummings for his contributions, and Mrs. Cummings for many useful suggestions. I particularly thank Dr. James Sibley Watson for permission to use the announcement of the *Dial* Award to Pound, which he wrote. I also wish to thank Alyse Gregory, a former managing editor of *The Dial,* and Addison M. Metcalf's Collection of Gertrude Steiniana, for Scofield Thayer's account of Pound and Miss Stein. And I thank Marianne Moore for her encouragement and labors in my behalf.

I thank the Countess Jowitt for her gracious permission to use the paragraph from the late Earl Jowitt's book, *Some Were Spies,* with which Chapter XX opens; Mrs. Douglas Goldring, for permission to quote from *South Lodge;* and Margaret Anderson, for permission to use material in both *My Thirty Years' War* and *The Little Review Anthology.*

I am grateful to Richard Aldington for permission to quote from his book, *Life for Life's Sake,* and from two unpublished letters to Amy Lowell. I wish also to thank Phyllis Bottome for her kindness in letting me quote from her portrait of Pound in *From the Life.* And I thank Janice Biala for permission to quote from Ford Madox Ford's *It Was the Nightingale* and *Return to Yesterday.* I also wish to thank Edith Heal, Elizabeth Shaw, Willard R. Trask, Robert Fitzgerald, John Holmes, Geoffrey Wagner and Eric Bentley.

I thank James Laughlin, Pound's American publisher, for his sympathetic help; Arthur Pell, of the Liveright Publishing Corporation, who placed the old Liveright files at my service; and Margaret Marshall, of Harcourt, Brace and Co., for her kindness in letting me see an early version of a chapter in Sylvia Beach's book, *Shakespeare and Company*.

I am particularly grateful to Mr. Rupert Hart-Davis, as well as The Macmillan Company, for permission to quote from *The Letters of W. B. Yeats;* and to Laurence Gomme, for permitting me to quote the poem by Pound and a stanza by Clement Wood from *The Newark Anniversary Poems*. Other acknowledgments will be found on the copyright page, in the text, and in the Notes. Every effort has been made to clear permissions for the use of quoted materials, and any errors or omissions will be corrected in a subsequent printing.

I owe a special debt of gratitude to Mary Bowen, who helped me in my research, and to Karen Termohlen, who took shorthand notes at my more lengthy interviews; to Henry Christman, for letting me use his extensive library of poetry and Americana; to Frances McClernan, Faubion Bowers and Howard W. Lipman, for the loan of first editions; to J. Q. Bennett, of Scribner's Rare Book Store, for tracking down some elusive correspondence for me; and to John Cournos and Omar Shakespear Pound, for the loan of early photographs of Olivia Shakespear and Dorothy Pound, respectively.

I also wish to thank William B. Dickinson of the Philadelphia *Evening Bulletin,* and B. M. McKelway of the Washington *Star*; and M. J. Wing and Charles A. Grumich of The Associated Press.

Much of the book was written at The MacDowell Colony, Peterborough, New Hampshire.

INDEX OF FIRST LINES

GENERAL INDEX